Publications of the Committee on
Taxation, Resources and Economic Development

7

*Proceedings of a Symposium Sponsored by the
Committee on Taxation, Resources and
Economic Development (TRED)
At the University of Wisconsin–Madison, 1972*

Other TRED Publications

Property Taxation and the Finance of Education

Edited by Richard W. Lindholm

*Published for the Committee on
Taxation, Resources and
Economic Development by*
THE UNIVERSITY OF WISCONSIN PRESS

Published 1974
The University of Wisconsin Press
Box 1379, Madison, Wisconsin 53701

The University of Wisconsin Press, Ltd.
70 Great Russell Street, London

First printing

Printed in the United States of America

For LC CIP information see the colophon
ISBN 0-299-06440-9

Contributors

Morris Beck
Professor of Economics, Rutgers University

Peter J. G. Bohm
Associate Professor of Economics, University of Stockholm

Anthony M. Cresswell
Assistant Professor of Educational Administration, Northwestern University

Terrie Jean Gale
Social Science Analyst, Congressional Research Service, Library of Congress

James L. Green
Professor of Economics, University of Georgia

Ronald E. Grieson
Assistant Professor of Economics, Queens College

Noel M. Edelson
Assistant Professor of Economics, University of Pennsylvania

Richard W. Lindholm
Professor of Finance, University of Oregon

Arthur D. Lynn
Professor of Economics and Public Administration, The Ohio State University

Harold J. Noah
Professor of Economics and Education, Teachers College, Columbia University

William H. Oakland
Professor of Economics, The Ohio State University

George M. Raymond
Professor of Regional Planning, Pratt Institute

John Riew
Professor of Economics, Pennsylvania State University

Daniel L. Rubinfeld
Assistant Professor of Economics, University of Michigan

Seymour Sacks
Professor of Economics, Syracuse University

Robert N. Schoeplein
Associate Professor of Economics, University of Illinois

W. Craig Stubblebine
Associate Professor of Economics, Claremont Men's College

Ronald K. Teeples
Assistant Professor of Economics, Claremont Men's College

Douglas Y. Thorson
Professor of Economics, Bradley University

Charles Waldauer
Professor of Economics, Widener College

CONFERENCE HOUR

Arthur P. Becker
Professor of Economics, University of Wisconsin–Milwaukee

Harvey E. Brazer
Professor of Economics, University of Michigan

Joseph S. De Salvo
Professor of Economics, University of Wisconsin–Milwaukee

Paul B. Downing
Associate Professor of Economics, University of California–Riverside

Karl Falk
First Federal Savings & Loan Association, Fresno, California

Daniel R. Fusfeld
Professor of Economics, University of Michigan

William S. Vickrey
Professor of Economics, Columbia University

M. Mason Gaffney

Director, British Columbia Institute for Economic Policy Analysis, University of Victoria

Carl W. McGuire

Professor of Economics, University of Colorado

Richard Rossmiller

Professor of Education, University of Wisconsin–Madison

Jonathan A. Rowe

Tax Reform Research Group, Washington, D.C.

Ferdinand P. Schoettle

Professor of Law, University of Minnesota

John Shannon

Assistant Director, Advisory Commission on Intergovernmental Relations, Washington, D.C.

Conference Hour Moderator, Daniel M. Holland

Professor of Finance, Massachusetts Institute of Technology

Conference Hour Editor, Eli Schwartz

Professor of Economics, Lehigh University

Contents

x   Contents

Preface

The costs of education provided for the young people of America has skyrocketed because of the greater numbers in the basic education age bracket and the rapidly rising costs of instruction. One result of this situation has been a greater increase of property tax collections than was generally considered possible twenty years ago. Rising costs have caused local property tax collections to increase more rapidly than personal income.

For many years the data have clearly demonstrated a close association in many sections of the nation between property tax rates and school financing requirements, and the lack of a close association between the value of taxable property and school revenue needs. State education foundation programs and related state revenue allocation schemes have been adopted to reduce the obvious inequitableness of the situation. It is very generally realized these programs have failed to do the equalization of the economic burden of public education that is required under the general understanding of equal treatment clauses of many state constitutions. As a result, court decisions, citizen protests, and the findings of numerous studies have examined new approaches to the finance of education. It has become one of America's major areas for social-political-economic examination aimed at change.

This book presents the papers and discussions of a conference titled *Property Taxation and the Finance of Education,* that was held on the campus of the University of Wisconsin, Madison, Wisconsin, during the period October 20-22, 1972. The conference's purpose was to examine what has been learned in this general area through special studies, legal considerations, and theoretical economic analyses.

Twenty of the participants presented papers that carefully considered important aspects of the finance of education. Although the emphasis is on finance and American procedures, consideration is given to expenditure effectiveness and foreign experience.

The four groupings of papers and discussions have been made to assist the

xiii

reader in deciding where to place his original emphasis. Understanding of the problem requires the interaction and combination of many types of information. Therefore, compartmentalization and a given organization can only be offered as one approach to understanding.

The first grouping used is titled "Theoretical and General Considerations." The papers and discussions of Part I give perspective to the problem through provision of background materials of a historical, international, theoretical, and political character. The Conference Review Hour tackles the question of the relationship between financing and the purpose of education.

Part II, titled "Statewide Approaches," examines the general character of the property tax as a source of education financing funds. Attention is concentrated on the use of uniform statewide taxes. Although some emphasis is given to statewide taxes other than a property tax, it is the property tax, and particularly site value taxation, i.e., taxation of land, that receives the major attention. The Conference Review Hour is largely concerned with the location of the economic burden of the property tax.

Part III, "Legal Adjustments and Restrictions," considers the legal adjustments that court decisions are requiring and the restrictions that may be placed on taxation procedures used to finance education. The experts and the states have been chosen to assure consideration of a variety of legal and legislative situations. The Conference Review Hour examines the relation of local control to statewide financing.

Part IV centers on school finance developments in metropolitan areas and is titled "Metropolitan Area and City Fiscal Environment." Again, revenue sources other than a property tax are considered, but this time the desirability of alternatives is related to local conditions. Consideration is given to spending decisions for education arising from the local election process. The Conference Review Hour considers a variety of topics, including the taxable base of the income tax and the local government needs of older people.

The moderator of the Conference Review Hour was Professor Daniel M. Holland, editor of the *National Tax Journal.* Professor Eli Schwartz of Lehigh University has edited the materials presented at the Conference Review Hours. The editor wishes to thank all of the participants for their wonderful cooperation and to ask forgiveness for all inconveniences his efforts caused.

The Conference and this book owe much to the stimulus and support of the Committee on Taxation Resources and Economic Development (TRED) and the John C. Lincoln and the Robert Schalkenbach Foundations.

Richard W. Lindholm

Eugene, Oregon
November 1, 1973

Richard W. Lindholm

Introduction

These introductory remarks will briefly consider three quite different topics. They are only tangentially related to the real work of this Conference, and each pretty largely stands by itself.

First, I will consider the efficiency with which local school district property tax collections have been spent. Secondly, I will identify the product being provided by local school districts. Finally, I want to point up the somewhat disturbing fact that none of the nations of the Third World make substantial use of property taxes to finance their educational efforts.

Each of these topics is certain to be a portion of the unexpressed thoughts of the participants in this consideration of *Property Taxation and the Finance of Education.* My justification, therefore, for this detour at the very start, is to make certain that the reader of the proceedings is aware of these three important aspects of our topic which were not considered in detail at the Conference.

EDUCATION EFFICIENCY

As education becomes a very major element in our lives, rather than a relatively minor activity largely aimed at handing down a few skills and social graces to the young, the appropriate financial arrangements also change. Attitudes accepted and developed toward financing education during the early portion of the century are in need of refurbishing.[1]

It remains too true that a school administrator opposing school district financial independence is in deep political trouble. At the same time, in only 23 states are the school districts so established that each district contains

1. Richard W. Lindholm, "Primary and Secondary Education, Area 21," *Project to Develop a Description and Analysis of Oregon's Fiscal System* (Salem, Oregon: Dept. of Revenue, January 1971).

enough financial resources and enough students to provide a good education program. In the past, voters, nearly without exception, voted for symbols of local control rather than education equality.[2] The result is widespread dissatisfaction with school financing as well as what is being done in the schools.

The old assumption that local control was needed for a "good" education program also assumed that local control was dependent on local financing. Neither assumption is acceptable in today's world. In the recent past it has been the federal and state education agencies that have induced local school districts to innovate, and the inducement has frequently included provision of financial resources.

A state system of education finance is frequently envisaged as a monolithic, unmanageable bureaucracy which would impede rather than advance the quality of education. Examples of this actually happening are not available to me. To the extent that such a bureaucracy does exist, its habitat is the large city districts and not state education departments. On the other hand, the underfinanced and ineffective local school district can be found in most regions of every state. State financing by allocating funds through the budgetary process of paying for what needs to be done can avoid both the big city bureaucracy problem and the misallocation of education costs existing under existing financing procedures. With this approach, big city bureaucracies are undermined by local control groups who now have the funds needed to do the education job. Underfinanced districts have funds to improve their programs without initiating unrealistic tax burdens.

It was back in 1968 that James B. Conant argued that local school boards, citizens and administrators could make much better educational decisions if the pressures of meeting financing from locally collected taxes were eliminated.[3] Through the years evidence has also been accumulating that show local school boards plus present conditions of finance have fostered the development of an inefficient education "industry." The pressures of local financing have not caused efficiency but instead have fostered local real estate developers, contractors and construction workers, plus organized and unorganized traditionalists to control spending allocations. These spending determiners have dominated decisions and it is largely accidental if they correspond to the education needs of student groups.

Impartial observers of locally financed education systems charge gross waste and inefficiency. School buildings are in use barely 1,000 hours a year compared with 2,000 hours or more for other types of facilities or for schools in many other countries with a centralized financing system.[4] Space allowances

2. Committee for Economic Development, *Paying for Better Public Schools* (New York: Committee for Economic Development, 1959), p. 71.

3. *Nation's Schools,* 83 (January 1969), 70-71.

4. Roger A. Freeman, "Do We Need More Dollars for Education or More Education for Our Dollars?" *Congressional Record,* 86th Cong., 1st sess., March 26, 1959, pp. 5355-58.

per student have doubled despite lack of any evidence that more learning takes place if space per student is increased. Schools are built at the outskirts of population centers encouraging use of buses and the development of inefficient urban complexes. Emphasis on fundamental skills and knowledge has declined while the number and variety of courses has proliferated.[5] American students at sixteen years of age are reported to be two years behind their European counterparts attending schools financed with centrally raised revenues.

The case for the old canard that locally raised funds are more carefully and efficiently spent is weak in the area of school spending when the comparison is limited to management and resource costs. The inefficiency appears to expand when educational goals become the measurement base for judgment.

Education spending under the existing local-state aided system fails to spend the amount required to overcome education deficiencies caused by mental, physical, social or economic handicaps. The schools have forgotten under the existing state-local finance system that their claim to public support arises basically from the need of educated citizens to continue our democracy. All other claims for school services possess a considerable element of private gain, or are based on a belief that local demands for a particular type of vocational training in the schools increase well-being more than if its provision is limited to privately financed offerings or programs established under national and state priorities.

EDUCATION GOALS

If education spending is investment that has a very important impact on the economic growth of the nation, then, according to one school of thought, central government payment of full costs of capable student education through university plus refresher courses makes good economic sense.[6] However, if resources devoted to education are resources wisely invested because of their effect on economic productivity, then private funds should be available to finance what is required to make the marginal productivity of investment dollars in education equal to those invested in other areas. If the latter situation is the true one, then government spending either replaces private education spending that would otherwise take place, or investment in education is pushed so high that the addition to productivity would be greater if the resources were used in other areas.

There is also the point of view that much education spending is consumption in nature. Consumption can take place with private resources as well as

5. Daniel Seligman, "The Low Productivity of the Education Industry," *Fortune,* October 1958.

6. Edward F. Denison, *The Sources of Economic Growth in the United States and the Alternatives before Us,* Supplementary Paper no. 13 (New York: Committee for Economic Development, 1962).

public. However, consumption spending in public education, financed with local taxes used locally, finds favor, particularly in middle and upper class communities. Part of the attractiveness arises because the payment as a general tax is deductible from income subject to the federal income tax. This deduction is not currently available for expenditures for athletic equipment, art supplies, musical instruments, and the like, purchased directly with family funds. A portion of the current push toward making school tuition payments deductible is aimed at removing the existing tax advantage possessed by locally raised and locally spent property taxes to finance expenditures for education consumption and investment in people.

Education spending finds justification from three conceptual sources: It is investment in human capital, the basic source of our expanding productivity. It is aimed at making "good" consumption opportunities available to participants and observers. Finally, it is an activity required to develop the basic skills and understandings needed for the continuance of the concept of a nation and a people developed through the years in thousands of legislative acts and through thousands more resolutions of private groupings.

EDUCATION FINANCE IN LDC's

The use of the property tax to finance as complex and varied an activity as local education is uniquely an American approach, with a spillover into Canada. Education at the local level is generally financed at the national level with here and there some examples of revenue input at the provincial or state level. None of the national, or in some cases partially provincial, local education finance systems utilize a special tax on property to raise the revenues needed.

In many areas of government the Less Developed Countries (LDC's) of the world have been "blessed" with a multitude of American advisers and consultants who have generally recommended and stimulated through financial assistance the development of the "American Way." An outstanding exception to this generalization is in the use of the property tax to finance local education. Apparently there is not a single LDC, including those where American aid was important as well as unimportant, that uses the property tax as a major source of education finance.

The reason for this situation existing is undoubtedly related to America's very nearly unique use of the property tax to finance much of the cost of education. In addition, the property tax did not benefit from a generally favorable American tax expert's attitude. The old Seligman animosity toward the property tax colored much of their research and advising.[7] So a situation existed where the property tax to finance education was largely an American

7. Edwin R. A. Seligman, "The General Property Tax," *Essays in Taxation*, 9th ed. (New York: Macmillan, 1921).

phenomenon, but it was not viewed with favor by the education and tax advisers from America. With this the prevailing environment, the case for the use of the property tax to finance the desperate education needs of LDC's has not been strong enough to overcome the opposition of entrenched large land ownership groups.[8] Basically, land taxes and general property taxes are not an important LDC tax source.[9] Whether or not greater use should be made of land and general property taxes by LDC's is not a subject under consideration here. However, the general topic of property taxation and the finance of local education of LDC's cannot be dropped without mention of a current development that may be a harbinger of change.

The government of Colombia is on the point of initiating a nationwide property tax. The base of the tax would be largely land, and the collections would be used to finance much of the cost of education. The rate, except for some rather unimportant exceptions, will be uniform nationwide.

The very interesting Colombian legislative proposal limits the financing from the national property tax to the first six years of schooling. The law exempts the first 50,000 pesos (about $2,000) of property of a property owner. The law does not go so far as to distribute collections on the basis of education costs. Rather, the collections will be returned to the municipality from which they were raised.[10] This promising legislation has been postponed until after the 1974 elections. The proposed legislation has been modified to increase the rate on large urban properties and to reduce the rate on large rural properties.

One doesn't have to go back very far in American education finance history to note that uniform statewide property taxes to finance education were in use. For example, in 1920, as a result of declining state support of education, Oregon adopted legislation levying a .002 property tax on each dollar of taxable property in the state. The funds were used to finance elementary schools.[11] It is quite possible that the LDC's of the world will start to seriously consider using property taxes, and particularly a national tax on land, as the best source of revenue to finance elementary education where economic development goals and administrative problems, as well as ability-to-pay requirements, are taken into account, and the influence of American and other advisers from the developed nations has decreased.

8. *1966 International Seminar on Land Taxation, Land Tenure, and Land Reform in Developing Countries* (West Hartford, Conn.: University of Hartford, 1966).

9. Raja J. Chelliah, "Trends in Taxation in Developing Countries," *International Monetary Fund Staff Papers*, 18, no. 2 (July 1971), 286.

10. *El Espectator* (Bogotá, Colombia), August 4, 1972.

11. Thomas Rigby, *History of School Finance in Oregon*, 7, no. 5, Oregon School Study Council, School of Education, University of Oregon (Eugene, November 1963).

Part I
Theoretical and General Considerations

1 Arthur D. Lynn, Jr.

Financing Education in the United States: Selected Historical Perspectives

Established patterns of financing education, particularly as they rely upon ad valorem property taxation, are currently under urgent review. Policymakers and taxpayers alike have intensified their perennial search for effective, equitable, acceptable, administrable, and legal means of financing the educational process. The long-term American love affair with education taking place under a local school board financed from revenues raised from taxing the local property base is coming to an end. Accordingly, consideration, among other alternatives, of a state-administered property tax, or a state-administered land value tax in place of or in addition to the present local property tax, for the finance of education is timely.

This introductory paper provides but a brief review of some of the evolutionary developments that provide the historical foundation for current concern and controversy. What follows is an amalgam of two elements. One, a dash of the historical record and, two, a certain amount of that peculiar sort of historical anthropology not infrequently voiced by economists ever since the days of our venerable forefathers Adam Smith and David Ricardo.

The father of our discipline, Adam Smith, like any seasoned economist, was not without positive attitudes about the proper organization and financing of education.[1] Apparently Smith thought highly of the common schools of Scotland and most critically of faculty and administrative behavior at the universities of Oxford and Cambridge. His analytical mind searched for an explanation of perceived differences in pedagogical output and found one, not too unexpectedly perhaps, in different input arrangements. Teachers, motivated by self-interest and compensated in whole or in a substantial part upon a respectable professional fee basis, were alert, dedicated, effective, and productive. *Per contra,* in Smith's view, tenured academics with endowment-derived salaries performed otherwise—writing for more or less learned journals,

1. Adam Smith, *An Inquiry Into the Nature and Causes of the Wealth of Nations* (New York: Modern Library, 1937), pp. 716-40, esp. 737.

missing class to attend pleasant conferences, and even when actually present in the classroom reading ancient books to their students rather than delivering keen, contemporary, analytical presentations. Thus, the *laissez-faire* philosopher suggested that an appropriate policy included private financing of much of the educational process except for an elementary school minimum. Even in that case, he suggested that user charges (fees) should contribute to total expense. (See chap. 3 for a modern presentation of this position.)

At the time Smith wrote, education had been a responsibility of the individual, the family, and the church for centuries. Acceptance of education as a function properly in the public sector was slow to flower. Despite his endorsement of common schools, Smith did little to foster public education, and, as another indication of the contemporary policy views of that day, the Constitution of the United States can hardly be said to state a national educational policy with clarity, precision, and emphasis.

Nonetheless, as the American colonists came with their Bibles and later with Smith and Blackstone in their sea chests and saddle bags, they apparently valued education as a significant ingredient of the society they were in the process of creating. If their rhetoric outran their performance at times, they were our ancestors: the Boston Latin School was founded in 1663 and local voluntarily established public schools existed in New England before 1647. In that year, the Massachusetts General Assembly passed what came to be known, quaintly, as the "Old Deluder Satan Act," which legislation required every town with fifty (50) householders to provide a teacher and a school building where children would be taught to read and write, and towns with 100 families and upwards were to establish grammar schools adequate to fit youth for college entrance.[2] The resulting prototypical beginnings were financed, in part at least, by rudimentary property taxation. So even before the American Revolution, a loose alliance between precollegiate education and the property tax was formed and consummated.

While the middle colonies placed greater emphasis than New England upon parochial education and while the southern colonies, at least initially, tended to follow English precedent and rely upon private institutions, the New England model spread west with the keelboats and the wagons. While the Constitution was silent on educational policies, the great ordinances of the 1780's spoke to the subject. The Land Ordinance of 1785 laid the foundations for the public land system and, among many other things, "reserved the lot No. 16, of every township, for the maintenance of public schools within the

2. *Records of the Governor and Company of the Massachusetts Bay in New England,* 2: 203, given in Henry Steele Commager, ed., *Documents in American History,* 5th ed. (New York, Appleton-Century-Crofts, Inc. 1949), p. 29; see also Ellwood P. Cubberly, *The History of Education* (Boston: Houghton-Mifflin, 1920), p. 365.

said township . . . ."[3] Two years later a group of land speculators, members of the Ohio Company of Associates and the Society of the Cincinnati led by Rev. Manasseh Cutler, Samuel Parsons, and General Rufus Putnam, succeeded in lobbying the Northwest Ordinance of 1787 through Congress.[4] Article 4 provided an educational policy statement as follows:

"Religion, morality, and knowledge, being necessary to good government and the happiness of mankind, schools and the means of education shall forever be encouraged."

Parenthetically the next sentence pronounced: "The utmost good faith shall always be observed toward the Indians: their lands and property shall never be taken from them without their consent; and, in their property, rights, and liberty, they shall never be invaded or disturbed, unless in just and lawful wars authorized by Congress . . . ."[5]

In any event, these two policies and the prior New England experience established a pattern of local, largely locally financed schools which gradually came to be typical of the nineteenth-century United States as the little red school house supported by property taxation became a standard arrangement as the nation spread westward. While state constitutions voiced general platitudes about education and while state legislatures occasionally recalled their basic responsibility for the design and oversight of local institutions,[6] state systems developed slowly, and local control and local finance gradually became established norms. The United States did not develop a national school system. While the Constitution of every state makes it a duty of the legislature to maintain a system of free public schools, and for almost a century Congress has required such a constitutional provision as a requirement for admission to statehood, our schools have been in the main operated by independent local school districts within a state established local framework.

STAGES IN PUBLIC SCHOOL FINANCE: NON-TAX SUPPORT

A review of the successive stages in public school finance serves to remind us of past experience. Our early schools were essentially private, and *except* as to the so-called common schools, education was considered essential only for

3. J. C. Fitzpatrick, ed., *Journals of the Continental Congress,* 28: 375 ff., given in Commager, ed., *Documents,* pp. 123–24.
4. The Northwest Ordinance, July 13, 1787: F. N. Thorpe, ed., *Federal and State Constitutions,* 2: 957 ff., given in Commager, ed., *Documents,* p. 131.
5. Ibid.
6. See, e.g., Massachusetts High School Law adopted 1827, first enforced 1837, substantially implemented 1860: *Laws of Massachusetts,* January session, 1827, ch. 113, given in Commager, ed., *Documents,* p. 247.

those who could pay for it.[7] Given this pattern, prior to 1825 even public schools often derived much of their revenue from non-tax sources. These included land endowments, lotteries, gifts, rate bills (tuition charges), and services in lieu of rate bills or taxes.[8] One characteristic of this period of non-tax support was the idea, prevalent in the closing decades of the eighteenth century and in the early nineteenth century, that public elementary schools could be supported largely by the income from permanent endowments much as Adam Smith had earlier suggested. A permanent common school fund was established by Connecticut in 1795 and was emulated by a number of eastern states. Elsewhere to the west, permanent funds were encouraged by federal land grants of some 77.5 million acres for schools. With some notable exceptions, fund income did not correlate well with enrollment trends, and the story of the land grants, again with some exceptions, is a dismal record of shortsighted mismanagement.

DEVELOPMENT OF PROPERTY TAX SUPPORT

In one sense the real contribution of the state permanent school funds was to engage the states in the development of educational policy and to generate a policy of at least some state responsibility for education. The funds were for a time a relatively stable source of school revenues—at least they were a source.

Earlier many statewide permissive school property tax laws had been enacted authorizing local units to adopt a school property tax levy if approved by a majority or, in some instances, the levy was applicable only to consenting adults. After experience with state school funds and this early form of state aid to local elementary schools, property taxes in support of schools were made mandatory in jurisdiction after jurisdiction. Only in New England and in New York was the school tax mandatory before 1820.[9] Later came Ohio (1825), Massachusetts (1827), and Wisconsin (1848).

The real issue in all this was the question whether schools should be a function of government to be supported by nonconsenting, nonusing taxpayers. After the period of nontax support and the experiment with taxation of consenting residents, localities were given general taxing power and, in due course, were required to use it to finance a mandatory public school system. As Coons, Clune, and Sugarman have so well said:

> What is instructive in this process is the unwillingness of the state government to assume the function of education . . . . This vigorous buck-passing was in substantial degree ideological at root. Education

7. John E. Corbally, Jr., *School Finance* (Boston: Allyn & Bacon, 1962), p. 43.
8. This section relies in considerable part on Arvid J. Burke, *Financing Public Schools in the United States,* rev. ed. (New York: Harper & Bros. 1957), pp. 237 ff.
9. Ibid., p. 244.

was thought to be the sphere of the individual and every related act of government a potential intrusion. Pressed to take on the function of education but strongly opposed by powerful citizens espousing an individualistic philosophy, the legislatures sought and found the smallest workable unit for the task . . . . Given the relative uniformity of wealth and population distribution, the system was tolerable. Economic revolution swiftly turned the compromise into a monster. What the individual had surrendered to government was lost; what the egalitarian had gained from government was to be eliminated. What remained was accidental and haphazard privilege.[10]

But Coons, Clune, and Sugarman get us ahead of our story and almost out of bounds for an introduction. So back to the archives.

PROPERTY TAX TENDENCIES: REALIZED DIRECTIONS AND ABORTED POTENTIALS

Property tax history is such a well travelled path that only a precis is here required.[11] While at the beginning of the nineteenth century some observers regarded investment income from the proceeds of land grant sales as a primary revenue source, state program expansion including internal improvements as well as education in the 1820's and 1830's made increased taxation necessary.[12] State property taxation for local school purposes and almost universal organization of local school districts characterized this era.[13] This was the period (1796 to the Civil War) during which the property tax gradually became the dominant source of both state and local revenue. As Professor Ely of Wisconsin put it in a much quoted statement, this period "witnessed the complete establishment of the American system of state and local taxation. The distinguishing feature of the system may be described in a single sentence. It is the taxation of all

10. John E. Coons, William H. Clune III, Stephen D. Sugarman, *Private Wealth and Public Education* (Cambridge: Harvard University Press, 1970), pp. 48-49.

11. See, *inter alia,* Jens P. Jensen, *Property Taxation in the United States* (Chicago: University of Chicago Press, 1931); Dick Netzer, *Economics of the Property Tax* (Washington, D.C.: Brookings Institution, 1966); Summer Benson, "A History of the General Property Tax," in George C. S. Benson, ed., *The American Property Tax* (Claremont, Calif.: Claremont College Press, 1965); Richard W. Lindholm, "Financing Public Education and the Property Tax," *American Journal of Economics and Sociology,* 29 (January 1970), 33 ff.; Arthur D. Lynn, Jr. "Property Tax Developments: Selected Historical Perspectives," in Richard W. Lindholm, ed., *Property Taxation– U.S.A.* (Madison: University of Wisconsin Press, 1967), pp. 7-19. The literature is legion.

12. See, e.g., Catherine Ruggles Gerrish, "Public Finance and Fiscal Policy, 1789-1865," in Harold F. Williamson, ed., *The Growth of the American Economy* (New York: Prentice Hall, 1951), pp. 306-7, 631-45; and see Paul Studenski and Herman E. Kroos, *Financial History of the United States,* 2nd ed. (New York: McGraw-Hill, 1963), pp. 128-36, 192-200.

13. See Burke, *Financing Public Schools,* pp. 248 ff.

property, movable and immovable, visible and invisible, or real or personal, as we say in America, at one uniform rate."[14]

From the Civil War to World War I, the general property tax was a major source of state revenue and virtually the only significant source of local tax revenue. However, the taxation of all property proved to be inadequate for fiscal requirements and property tax administration often proved ineffective. The period saw various attempts to improve property tax administration by means of stricter legislation, the development of county then state boards of equalization and ultimately state tax commissions. Special study and other commissions proliferated, competitive underassessment in particular and uneven and often extralegal assessment in general were often noted. State assessment of complex property was adopted in an attempt to cure some trouble spots. Exemption of or classification of some types of property was utilized as an occasional remedy. Despite the seeds of discontent that sparked these several modifications, the property tax still provided 52 per cent of state revenues in 1902. By that time, however, grants-in-aid and state collected, locally shared taxes had emerged as significant fiscal arrangements, and many of the fiscal experts of that day were proposing separation of revenue sources as a device to improve the property tax, prevent competitive underassessment, and meet local fiscal requirements.[15]

Having now arrived in our story at the threshold of the twentieth century, wisdom would dictate prompt movement toward present concerns. However, Professor Lindholm's writings suggest a brief digression on a chapter in the Ohio story[16] given our conference topic.

As earlier reported,[17] the story runs as follows:

> From 1803 to 1825, Ohio derived the main part of its revenue from a land tax. Realty was not taxed *ad valorem* but was listed for tax purposes in one of three classes by local assessors, and a specific rate per acre was applied to each class. It is not particularly surprising to be informed by the fiscal historian of the period, E. L. Bogart, that gradually more and more property found its way into the lowest class. This system of land classification and specific rates caused much dissatisfaction, and numerous suggestions for adoption of an *ad valorem* system were made prior to 1825. In that year, the General Assembly

14. Richard T. Ely, *Taxation in American States and Cities* (New York: Thomas Crowell & Co., 1888), p. 131.

15. See, e.g., Mabel Newcomer, *Separation of State and Local Revenues in the United States,* 76, no. 2, Studies in History, Economics, and Public Law (New York: Columbia University, 1917).

16. Lindholm, "Financing Public Education and the Property Tax," p. 33.

17. Arthur D. Lynn, Jr., "Property Tax Developments: Selected Historical Perspectives," in Lindholm, *Property Taxation–U.S.A.,* pp. 13-15.

adopted "An Act establishing an equitable mode of levying the taxes of this state" which abolished the old system of land classification and provided for valuation of real property at its true value in money. The market-value standard has been a component of Ohio property-tax law since that time. Of possible interest to those concerned with land-value taxation is Section 15 of the 1825 Act, which provided that land should be valued "without taking into consideration the value of actual improvements made thereon." Apparently no formal economic analysis was devoted to the possible results of this pragmatic policy decision; it did not, in any event, long survive the trend to the general property tax.

The period 1825–1846 in Ohio property-tax history may be described as one in which legal property-tax base was extended to include more and more categories of property. This process culminated in the adoption of the Kelley Act in 1846, which applied the uniform rule of taxation according to value to all property not specifically exempted. An evident desire to remove it from the area of potential legislative caprice led to the inclusion of the uniform rule as Section 2, Article XII of the Ohio Constitution of 1851. The uniform rule remained applicable to realty and personalty alike until the adoption in 1929 of the classification amendment of Article XII, which became effective in 1931. Thereafter, both tangible and intangible personalty were classified for *ad valorem* tax purposes, leaving the uniform rule applicable only the land and the improvements thereon. [The question of land classification remains on the agenda but is not very high on the list.] This abbreviated version of the Ohio story is reasonably representative of developments in many other places.

Thus, there is midwestern historical precedent for state property tax administration and for the classification of land for property tax purposes. However, the nineteenth-century trend toward uniformity and universality in property taxation led tax development down another path, leaving these matters open for contemporary policy analysis. States developed alternative revenue sources. The property tax became essentially a local revenue and the relative lack of success of the states in providing an altogether effective legal and administrative framework for the property tax is a continuing and all too familiar chapter in fiscal history. It need not be detailed again here. School finance became a matter of combining local property tax revenues with expanded state aid in the form of grants, shared taxes, and/or foundation programs. While shared taxes were a vogue from 1920 to 1933, they declined in importance thereafter.

Accordingly, more recent history, which can only be briefly sketched here, involves the emergent concepts about how to aid local school districts and the actual implementation of that process.

STATE AID TO LOCAL SCHOOLS[18]

Long ago states recognized that some school districts lacked the taxable capacity to provide minimally acceptable educational programs and that per capita distributions failed to correct local fiscal inequalities. Initially crude equalization attempts gradually evolved into contemporary equalization programs combining state aid and local taxation. By 1905 over a fourth of the states had made crude equalization beginnings, when onto the stage stepped a forceful academic, Ellwood P. Cubberly of Columbia and later of Stanford, arguing, apparently persuasively, that the form of aid as well as its amount was critically important. He described the role of state in 1905 as follows:

> Theoretically all the children of the state are equally important and are entitled to have the same advantages; practically this can never be quite true. The duty of the state is to secure for all as high a minimum of good instruction as is possible, *but not to reduce* all *to this minimum;* to equalize the advantages to all as nearly as can be done with the resources at hand; to place a premium on those local efforts which will enable communities to rise above the legal minimum as far as possible; and to encourage communities to extend their educational energies to new and desirable undertakings.[19]

Cubberly suggested that the excessive burdens of local communities be covered by a state school tax. Later Henry C. Morrison, another specialist in school finance, suggested state assumption of school finance after concluding that all equalization attempts were functional failures.[20] Aside from Hawaii, this proposal was not well received. Policy tended to follow and then build upon a model suggested by George D. Strayer and Robert Murray Haig in 1923[21]

18. This section is largely based upon Burke, *Financing Public Schools in the United States;* Charles S. Benson, *The Economics of Public Education* (Boston: Houghton Mifflin Co., 1961); Charles S. Benson, ed., *Perspectives on the Economics of Education* (Boston: Houghton Mifflin Co., 1963); Stephen D. Sugarman, "The Selling of Serrano," *Proceedings of the National Tax Association* (Columbus, Ohio: 1972), pp. 243-46.

19. *School Funds and Their Apportionment* (New York: Teachers College Press, 1905), p. 17.

20. *School Revenue* (Chicago: University of Chicago Press, 1940).

21. The Strayer-Haig model is described in Roe L. Johns and Edgar L. Morphet, *The Economics and Financing of Education: A Systems Approach,* 2nd ed. (Englewood Cliffs, N.J.: Prentice Hall, 1969), p. 244, as follows:

   1. Compute the cost of a satisfactory minimum educational offering in each district of the state.

   2. Compute the yield in the district of a uniform state mandated local tax levy on the equalized valuation of property and

   3. Provide the difference between the cost of the minimum program and the yield of the required minimum program and the yield of the required minimum tax levy from state funds.

In effect they suggested a statewide uniform mandated levy which cover all costs in

which provided the conceptual background for many later developments in state school financial policy. Time, energy, and propriety preclude detailed coverage of subsequent developments which have been well covered by the work of Charles S. Benson as well as that of Johns and Morphet.[22] Coons, Clune, and Sugarman suggest that the theory of state aid to education has become more egalitarian but that "there has been an equally consistent history of successful emasculation of these theories" and that "probably nothing more can be expected in the absence of judicial intervention."[23]

The matter of *Serrano* v. *Priest*[24] and its aftermath are the subject of other papers at this conference (particularly chaps. 4 and 12). The matter of state assumption versus local control has been effectively considered by, among others, Charles S. Benson and Harvey Brazer at the 1971 Conference of the National Tax Association.[25] Current concerns will be further explored here.[26] Happily, an introductory historical piece is not required to suggest final solutions to complex allocational and policy problems. Given this particular conflict between equity and efficiency, subsidiarity and equality, one assumes that there will be a continuing role for property taxation which, as Lady Hicks suggests, has a certain inevitability[27] as one of our ancient but continuing political games.[28]

Even so, in this context, state levy and state administration merit reexamination. Finally, as Coons, Clune, and Sugarman have so well said:

"Lawyers, lobbyists, journalists, and school economists need a reasonably simple set of analytical and descriptive tools; (since) the degree and character, if not the fact, of inequity are somewhat esoteric."[29] One hopes this conference will contribute to that end and suggest appropriate compromises between input equality, output quality, and whatever degree of autonomous local choice proves to be an acceptable policy residual. The difference between inequality

---

the richest school district of the state with deficiencies in other districts being covered by state subventions.

22. Benson, *Perspectives on the Economics of Education;* Johns and Morphet, *Economics and Financing of Education.*

23. Coons, Clune, and Sugarman, *Private Wealth and Public Education,* p. 197.

24. *Serrano* v. *Priest,* 5 Cal. 3d 584, 487 P. 2d 1241 (1971).

25. Charles S. Benson, "State Assumption of Educational Costs," *Proceedings of the National Tax Association* (Columbus, Ohio: 1971), p. 750; Harvey E. Brazer, "The Case for Local Control and Financing of Elementary and Secondary Education," ibid., p. 763.

26. *San Antonio Independent School District* v. *Rodriguez,* 337 F. Supp. 280 (1972), U.S. Sup. Ct. No. 71-1332 (1973).

27. John R. Hicks, Ursula K. Hicks, and C. E. V. Leser, "The Inevitability of Rates," in Benson, ed., *Perspectives on the Economics of Education,* p. 242.

28. Glenn W. Fisher and Robert P. Fairbanks, "The Politics of Property Taxation," *Administrative Science Quarterly,* 12, no. 1 (June 1967), p. 48.

29. Coons, Clune, and Sugarman, *Private Wealth and Public Education,* p. 97.

and inequity is by no means *de minimis* and mechanical uniformity is not necessarily just or consistent with the traditional presuppositions of federalism. Accordingly, this review of the past leaves much work to be done by the contemporary analyst and policy maker.

2 Harold J. Noah

Financing Elementary and Secondary Schools in the Soviet Union

The focus of this paper is the financing of the network of "general education schools" (*shkoly obshchego obrazovaniia*) that forms the backbone of the Soviet system of formal education. At the age of seven over 95 percent of children in the Soviet Union enter these schools, where they pass through an eight or ten year course of study. Curricula and syllabi for each grade are standardized throughout the country, with only minor modifications to take care of national and linguistic variations, and urban and rural locations. No other country (not even the United States) is furnished on the immense Soviet scale with a comparable network of common schools attended by the overwhelming majority of children, almost without differentiation of any kind.

In 1970-71, there were in the Soviet Union 190,000 general education schools of all types (day and evening), employing 2,626,000 teachers, and enrolling 49,373,000 students, all at a cost to the State budget of the U.S.S.R. of nearly 7 billion rubles (for fiscal 1970). Table 2.1 provides data on the size of the general education school system for 1970-71 and for selected earlier years since 1940/41.[1]

1. Until January 1, 1961, the official exchange rate was set at 1 ruble = 25 cents U.S. On that date, the Soviet government instituted a monetary reform that cut the face value of the currency and all internal prices by a factor of ten. At the same time, the new ruble was set at a new parity of 1 ruble = $1.11 U.S. The ruble figures quoted in the present study are all expressed in terms of the new (post-1960) ruble. It is always very difficult to say what a foreign currency is really worth; with the ruble, this is especially difficult. According to rates prevailing on the black market, the official rate grossly overvalues the ruble: the ruble is currently bought and sold at a rate of three or four to the dollar. On the other hand, according to Soviet official calculations, the official rate actually *undervalues* the purchasing power of the ruble (vis-à-vis the dollar) by about 11 percent. Somewhere within these wide margins a reasonable rate must lie. If the reader converts ruble figures given in this paper at the rate of 3 to the dollar, he will probably not be too far out.

Table 2.1 – General Education Schools in the U.S.S.R., 1940-41 to 1970-71, Selected Years

	1940-41	1950-51	1960-61	1965-66	1969-70	1970-71
1. Number of general education schools of all types (thousands)	199	222	224	214	197	190
2. Number of teachers (thousands)	1,238	1,475	2,043	2,497	2,608	2,626
3. Number of students enrolled (thousands)	35,552	34,752	36,187	48,255	49,426	49,373
4. Grades 1-3 (elementary)	16,126	14,030	14,152	15,343	15,842	15,334
5. Grades 4-8 (incomplete secondary)	18,135	19,814	19,438	24,926	26,027	26,243
6. Grades 9-10(11) (complete secondary)	1,291	908	2,597	7,986	7,557	7,796
7. Expenditures on general education schools from the State budget of the U.S.S.R. (millions of rubles)	860	2,039	3,313	5,778	6,746	6,953

Data are for the beginning of each school year cited, except for expenditures (which relate to the calendar years 1940, 1950, etc.).
Source: Tsentral'noe statisticheskoe upravlenie pri Sovete Ministrov SSSR, Narodnoe khoziaistvo SSSR v 1970 g.: statisticheskii ezhegodnik (Moscow: Izdatel'stvo "Statistika," 1971), pp. 628, 733; henceforth cited as Narkhoz 1970.

As a result of these continued efforts, the 1970 census figures showed a literacy rate of 99.7 percent among the population aged 9-49. Among the entire population aged 10 years and older, 24 percent had an incomplete secondary education (i.e., less than 8 years), 12 percent had completed a general secondary education (10 or 11 years), 7 percent had specialized secondary education, 1 percent had incomplete higher education, and 4 percent had completed higher education. This left just over a half of the over-9-year-old population with an elementary (3 to 4 years) education only, or less.[2]

Of particular interest for our present purpose are the figures given on line 7 of Table 2.1. They show that since 1950-51 government expenditures on general education have risen nearly 3½ times, while total enrollments in general education schools have increased by less than one-half. Expenditures per student (see Table 2.2) have thus risen substantially over the 20 year period 1950-70 not just in money terms, but in real terms, too, for prices of education inputs have remained fairly stable over the period.[3]

Table 2.2—Per Student Outlays on General Education Schools of the U.S.S.R., 1950-51 to 1970-71, Selected Years

Year	Rubles	Index
1950-51	59	100
1960-61	91	154
1965-66	120	203
1969-70	136	231
1970-71	141	239

Source: Table 2.1.

It is worthwhile setting these per student expenditure increases in general education schools in the context of what has been happening to costs in the other major sectors of the Soviet educational system: kindergartens and nursery schools (enrolling 8,100,000 children in 1970-71); secondary specialized schools, called *tekhnikums* and offering 2-3 year courses of study at the senior secondary level (enrolling 4,223,000); and the universities and higher technical schools (enrolling 4,581,000 in 1970-71). It is noteworthy that none

2. Tsentral'noe statisticheskoe upravlenie pri Sovete Ministrov SSSR, *Narodnoe khoziaistvo SSSR v 1970 g.: statisticheskii sbornik* (Moscow: Izdatel'stvo "Statistika," 1971), p. 23. This statistical source will henceforth be cited as *Narkhoz 1970*.

3. The official general price index has remained virtually constant over the decade 1960-70. Compared with 1950, prices in the last decade were *down* about one-quarter. However, teachers' salaries were raised by about 25 percent in 1964 (they rose again on September 1, 1972), so we should expect an education price index to be not quite as stable as the general price index has been.

of these sectors has experienced as great an increase in per student expenditures as has the Soviet general elementary and secondary school. Indeed, the higher education sector now spends less per student per year than it did in 1950, kindergartens only 13 percent more, while cost increases in the secondary specialized schools alone approach the rise of the general education schools expenditures. Table 2.3 provides details on these matters.

Table 2.3—Expenditures per Student from the State Budget of the U.S.S.R., by Educational Sector, 1950-51 to 1970-71, Selected Years

Year	Kindergartens and nursery schools		Secondary specialized schools (*tekhnikums*)		Universities and higher technical institutes	
	Amount (rubles)	Index	Amount (rubles)	Index	Amount (rubles)	Index
1950-51	284	100	128	100	556	100
1960-61	212	75	155	121	450	81
1965-66	273	96	217	170	384	69
1969-70	318	112	277	216	455	82
1970-71	321	113	289	226	480	86

Source: *Narkhoz 1970,* pp. 628, 635, 733.

The important conclusion to be drawn from these summary figures contradicts, of course, the generally held view that the Soviet educational authorities are preoccupied primarily with the training of specialized workers at the expense of general education. If we can assume that the government puts its money where its priorities are (and one must note that the Soviet government keeps a very tight rein on spending for education, a tighter rein than most other central governments), then it has apparently given its top educational priority to raising the quality of general education schools, second priority to secondary specialized schools, third to kindergartens, and a poor fourth place to raising the quality of higher education.[4]

SOVIET ADMINISTRATION AND BUDGETS FOR EDUCATION

There are three main channels of funds for the support of elementary and secondary education in the Soviet Union. In sharply descending order of

4. For a detailed analysis of educational costs during the period 1950-61, showing that there was a major rise in State budget expenditure per pupil in general education, continuing steadily throughout the decade, and apparently quite unaffected by either the decline in total enrollments down to 1955, or by their subsequent recovery, see Harold J. Noah, *Financing Soviet Schools* (New York: Teachers College Press, 1966), pp. 87 ff.

importance, they are: the State budget of the U.S.S.R., nongovernmental institutions (collective farms, enterprises, artels, and trade unions), and private sources.

The system of public budgets in the Soviet Union reflects the formal political-administrative structure and can be understood only within the context of that structure. The U.S.S.R. is a federal union of 15 Union Republics, the largest of which is the Russian S.F.S.R., containing 56 percent of the Soviet Union's population and 76 percent of the land area. The policies and practices of the R.S.F.S.R. set the pattern for the other Union Republics, especially in educational and financial matters. Each Union Republic is subdivided into a number of "provinces" (*oblasti* or *kraia*). These in turn are subdivided into towns (*goroda*) and rural areas (*raiony*), while further subdivisions provide for local administration of workers' settlements, villages, and small towns under *raion* jurisdiction.[5] At each of these levels there are organs dealing with education. At the Union and Republic levels they are full-fledged ministries of education; at the provincial, town, and rural area level, there are departments of education, under the republic ministry. In all, as of January 1, 1971, the Soviet Union contained over 50,000 political-administrative units, each with its own apparatus for the administration of general education within its territory:

U.S.S.R.	1	Ministry of education
Union Republics	15	" " "
Autonomous Republics	20	" " "
Autonomous Provinces	8	Departments of education
Provinces	120	" " "
National districts	10	" " "
Rural areas (*raiony*)	3,030	" " "
Village soviets	40,866	" " "
Towns	1,943	" " "
Settlements	3,576	" " "
Raiony-in-towns	447	" " "
Total	50,036	

Each of these 50,036 units, moreover, has an official budget, part of which is devoted to the provision of education.

The State budget of the U.S.S.R. (*Gosudarstvennyi biudzhet SSSR*) standing at the apex of a pyramid of subordinate budgets is an aggregate of this myriad of governmental budgets from the budget of the Union government (*Soiuznyi biudzhet*) at the top to the budgets of the village soviets at the base. Immediately below the Union budget are the State budgets of the 15 Union

5. In addition, some republics contain Autonomous Republics (of which there are 20 in all). Although the Autonomous Republics have ministries of education, their powers are in fact no more than that of provincial departments of education.

Republics (*Gosudarstvennye biudzhety Soiuznykh respublik*). The inclusion of the term "State" in the title indicates that, like the State budget of the U.S.S.R., the State budgets of Union Republics are aggregates. Each comprises the budget of the central administration of the given republic (*Respublikanskii biudzhet soiuznoi respubliki*) *and* the budgets of all the subordinate government organs of the republic, from Autonomous Republics down to *raiony*-in-towns, in the listing given above.

The section of government budgets under which education is included also deals with the financing of cultural activities (theaters, sports facilities, publishing, press, clubs, libraries). Taken together, education and culture are denoted by the term: *prosveshchenie*, literally "enlightenment." (Education is denoted by the Russian word *obrazovanie*, a literal translation of the French *formation*.) The section of the State budget of the U.S.S.R. devoted to *prosveshchenie*, therefore, aggregates expenditures on education and culture in the Union budget and in over 50,000 other budgets of the subordinate organs of Soviet government.

Table 2.4 identifies these various budgetary divisions and aggregates for 1950, 1960, and 1965. The share of "education and culture" in total State budget expenditures (line 1) decreased between 1950 and 1965 from 12.5 percent to 7.7 percent; it had recovered to 8.5 percent in the figures for 1970 (not shown in Table 2.4). Most of these funds are spent through the State budgets of the Union republics, and the lion's share of these through the local budgets, in particular.

The Union budget provides for the needs of institutions serving the entire U.S.S.R.: national libraries, museums, theater-academies, national broadcasting, and the like. The republic budgets of the Union Republics are responsible for financing republicwide cultural institutions, plus provisions for the training of labor reserves, professional and technical institutes, institutions of higher education, and *tekhnikums*. Local budgets carry the principal burden of financing the mass of schools. Indeed, not only kindergartens and schools, but also local libraries, houses and palaces of culture, clubs, local press, theaters, art galleries, and broadcasting facilities derive most of the funds necessary for their support through the local budgets. Moreover, provision for these purposes appears to be the largest single category of expenditure in local budgets, larger even than the sums devoted to financing local aspects of the national economy.

The allocation of financial responsibility among the various types of local budgets follows the same principle of territorial-administrative assignment that governs the Union and Union Republic budgets. Provincial budgets are responsible for the cultural and educational institutions serving the entire province. These are usually *tekhnikums*, kindergartens attached to enterprises under provincial jurisdiction, laboratory schools attached to pedagogical institutes, and provincial libraries, museums, theaters, art galleries, and so forth.

Table 2.4—Expenditure on Education, Culture, and Scientific Research (*Prosveshchenie*) by Types of Budget, U.S.S.R., 1950, 1960, and 1965 (in billions of rubles)

Type of budget	Total budget expenditure			Expenditure on education and culture (*prosveshchenie*)		
	1950	1960	1965	1950	1960	1965
1. State budget of the U.S.S.R.	41.3	73.1	102.3	5.2	8.0	13.2
2. Union budget	31.7	30.1	43.2[a]	1.5	.3	1.0
3. State budgets of the Union Republics (15 budgets)	9.6	43.0	58.4[a]	3.7	7.5	12.3
4. Republic budgets of the Union Republics (15 budgets)	3.0	28.6	37.3	.6	2.4	3.8
5. Local budgets (50,000+ budgets)	6.6	14.4	21.1	3.1	5.1	8.5

[a]These two items do not add exactly to the corresponding total in Line 1, because the figure of 43.2 billion rubles excludes grants from the Union budget to three Union Republics.

Sources: G. F. Dundukov, ed., *Gosudarstvennyi biudzhet SSSR i biudzhety Soiuznykh respublik* (Moscow: Gosfinizdat, 1962), p. 5; and Ministerstvo finansov SSSR, *Gosudarstvennyi biudzhet SSSR i biudzhety Soiuznykh respublik* (Moscow: Izdatel'stvo "Finansy," 1966), pp. 23, 53, 96, and 99.

Table 2.5—Distribution of Expenditures from Local Budgets, U.S.S.R., 1950, 1960, and 1965

Expenditure category	1950	1960	1965
1. The national economy	15.0%	31.6%	27.0%
2. Social-cultural provisions	75.6	63.9	69.7
a) Education and culture	47.1	35.6	40.2
b) Health and physical culture	27.1	26.6	27.5
c) Social insurance	1.4	1.7	1.9
d) Family allowances	–	–	0.1
3. Administration	8.7	3.2	2.6
4. Other	0.7	1.3	0.7
	100	100	100

Source: *Gos. biudzhet SSSR* (1966), p. 97.

Town budgets finance town kindergartens, general education schools (and any boarding facilities they may have), boarding schools proper, continuation schools for young workers, and town cultural facilities. *Raion* budgets similarly take care of the expenses of the corresponding *raion* establishments. At the lowest level of Soviet administration, village soviet budgets provide for preschool, elementary and eight-year schools (except for the payment of teachers' salaries, which is a *raion* budget charge), village libraries, clubs, and other cultural facilities.

The current trend in Soviet government finance is to move more of the budget responsibility for educational expenditures to the lower levels of administration. This is in line with recent decisions to have local authorities "coordinate within their competence the activities of enterprises situated on their territories, no matter what the ministerial affiliation of the enterprise."[6] Along with greater provincial, town, and rural area responsibilities for the policies and practices of productive enterprises, the local authorities have been granted somewhat wider powers for the financing and administration of school affairs.

NONGOVERNMENTAL SUPPORT FOR EDUCATION

Collective farms are the most active of the nongovernment enterprises in the education field, although many instances of aid to the schools offered by industrial and commercial enterprises are also recorded. Permanent links between farms and schools are encouraged. Indeed, *shefy* (donor firms and farms) are made much of in the press, and *shefstvo* (patronage) is acclaimed as an important supplement to direct State financing of schools. In 1970, for example, education[7] drew 15.6 billion rubles from State funds and an estimated 4.3 billion from "other sources," representing mainly donations in cash and kind from collective farms and State enterprises.[8] Most of this "voluntary" assistance arises out of participation in the expenses of school construction, repair, and equipment. Indeed, in the early postwar period (1946-50), collective farms built more school places than the official authorities (1.3 as compared to 1.2 million respectively). In 1970, the State paid for 1.8 million new places, collective farms for 424,000.[9] Farms also provide

6. N. Glushenko, "Ukrepliat' material'no-finansovuiu bazu raionykh i gorodskikh Sovetov" (To strengthen the material-financial basis of *raion* and town Soviets). *Finansy SSSR 1971*, 6 (June 1971), 17.
7. Including kindergartens, secondary professional schools, higher education and vocational training, as well as the general education schools.
8. *Narkhoz 1970*, pp. 732-33. This sum is apart from the share of local authorities in local enterprize profits, in the form of revenues from the profits tax.
9. *Narkhoz 1970*, p. 551.

foodstuffs for school meals, and enterprises donate space, materials, machine time, and labor for the factory training of classes from neighboring schools. Factory training was a very important feature of the Soviet general education schools from 1958, but since the fall of Khrushchev from power in 1964, the labor-training of young people in school has been severely curtailed.

The Soviet government welcomes and encourages *shefstvo*, but only in so far as it can be harnessed to move the schools in the direction indicated by the State. Patronage which would allow a school to strike out along a path of its own is simply forbidden. Resources provided by school patrons may not be used at will to support school purposes desired by the patron or the school. "Voluntary" funds must be shown under a special heading in school budgets and they are subject to the same controls and audit provided for regular budget funds. This means that the freedom for a collective farm to spend money (and/ or labor and materials) on schools is a freedom to be exercised only within the framework of school regulations laid down by the State. It is this above all that distinguishes the Soviet educational system so sharply from its Western counterparts: the complete absence in the Soviet Union of the type of school so common in the West—schools which draw substantial financial support from other than State sources and which exist to serve other than direct State interests and aims.

There is no evidence that *shefstvo* is conducted on a scale or with the regularity that might permit favored schools to raise their quality clearly above the general level. The benefactions of donor farms and enterprises to schools rarely do more than raise the level of school provision to a tolerable level where it would otherwise be especially backward, particularly in rural areas.

PRIVATE RESOURCES

Private sources of support for Soviet general education must be mentioned, but need not detain us long, for they are small relative to the large sums spent from the State budget and by "patrons." There are two main categories.

First, there are the fees paid by parents for the maintenance of their children in State-provided institutions: children's homes, crèches, kindergartens, and dormitories attached to schools and boarding schools are the main types. No total of the amount paid is available, but in any case it is doubtful if fees should be included in strictly "educational" expenditure, because they are charged to defray the costs of housing, feeding, and clothing the children, and not to cover costs of schooling.[10]

10. If these fees were counted, it becomes logically necessary to include an estimated sum for the costs of maintenance at home of the majority of Soviet children who attend day schools. But this is undesirable in a study of education costs.

Second, there are the fees paid by parents for the private tuition of their children. Long-standing respect for culture and a realistic appraisal of social-economic interest foster demand for private tuition in music, foreign languages, mathematics, and other school subjects. Parents are drawn to make such private investments in their children's education in the Soviet Union, as elsewhere. There are, of course, no private schools to which the Soviet parent can send his children, but graduation from State schools with good grades pays off well in terms of entry into the better institutions of higher education, higher future income, and a more privileged social position. We can hazard only a rough guess at how important funds for private tuition fees are, alongside the sums expended by the authorities. In 1970 there were about 50,000,000 children enrolled in general education. Assume that one child in ten had some private paid tuition during the year, amounting on average to thirty hours a year. This implies some 150 million hours a year. In 1970 in Moscow, I am told, the going rate was about 3 rubles an hour; in the provinces, it is probably less. Assuming an average rate of 2 rubles 50 kopeks an hour, the total annual bill would be 375 million rubles. This sum equals 5 percent of the expenditures in 1970 out of the State budget for general education, and is therefore of only modest importance—if one has any faith in the values I have used in the calculation. It might be as well to remember that the final amount could easily be half the size stated, or twice as much, or more. We just have no way of knowing.

TAX REVENUES FOR THE SCHOOLS

The major taxes and their yields in 1970 for the U.S.S.R. as a whole were:[11]

	Billion rubles	Percentage
Turnover tax	49.4	31.5
Profits taxes	54.2	34.6
Income taxes on cooperatives, collective farms, and enterprises owned by social organizations	1.2	0.8
Receipts from State loans	0.5	0.3
Personal taxes	12.7	8.1
Social security receipts	8.3	5.3
Unspecified and omitted[12]	30.4	19.4
	156.7	100.0

11. *Narkhoz 1970*, pp. 730-31.

12. The published figures simply give a figure for total State budget receipts in 1970 (156.7 billion rubles) and the receipts under each of the named headings listed. These do not add up to 156.7 billion rubles, but leave an unexplained gap of 30.4 billions. However, there is a further item supplied; "Total revenues received from State and cooperative enterprises and organizations: 142.9 billion rubles," which is 29.8 billion rubles *more*

Most of the resources placed at the disposal of local authorities (and, hence, school authorities) are merely assignments (*otchisleniia*) from revenues raised in the respective territories of each local unit by all-Union and all-republic taxes.

Local authorities in the Soviet Union exercise virtually no control over how much revenue they receive; they themselves neither establish tax liability, nor set the rates. Table 2.6 shows that 69 percent of the revenue of local authority budgets in 1965 was derived from assignments from State taxes. Revenue sharing is alive and well in the U.S.S.R.!

Assignments of revenue from the income tax on collective farms are 100 percent in most cases, but in recent years these taxes have been lowered as a part of the general policy of encouraging agricultural production. Their place has been taken by an enlargement of the first category of receipts listed in Table 2.6: "receipts from enterprises, etc.," in the form of greatly increased assignments from the profits tax. These revenues are now paid directly to town and *raion* authorities, and not to provincial governments, as before. In the Ukrainian S.S.R., for example, up to half the total profits tax revenue may be assigned to local budgets, and the profits tax receipts of local budgets may constitute up to one-quarter of all their revenue. In most instances, local budgets approach these maxima. Nevertheless, it remains true that assignments from the turnover tax remains the most important single source of revenue for the support of local authorities and, hence, of the schools.

The principle of "democratic centralism" is applied to determine the size of assignments from the highest to the lowest levels of local authority. Just as the Union Republic determines the assignments to be allocated from State taxes to provinces, so the Soviets of Workers' Deputies of the provinces allocate shares of these assignments to the subordinate Soviets of rural areas and towns. These, in turn, allocate further shares of the receipts to the village and settlement budgets subordinate to them. "Democratic centralism" thus asserts the absolute control of the budgets of subordinate levels of administration by the financial authorities of the superior levels. This is often claimed as a particular advantage of Soviet fiscal arrangements over Western budgetary systems.[13]

---

than non-personal tax revenues and State loan receipts. Thus, an amount of about 30 billion rubles a year paid by Soviet State enterprises finds its way into the central budget grand total, but does not appear in the published analyses!

13. For example: "The absence of unity, the lack of articulation of budgets, is a characteristic of the capitalist budgetary system, and it finds expression in the fact that the central budget, the budgets of the members of the federal union, and the local budgets are not unified in a single budget, as is the case in socialist countries. Only under socialism is it possible to have the unification of the budgetary system . . . and development of the budgetary system of the socialist state according to the ever-wider development of the principle of democratic centralism." A. M. Aleksandrov, ed., *Gosudarstvennyi biudzhet SSSR* (Moscow: Gosfinizdat, 1961), p. 24.

Table 2.6–Sources of Budget Revenues of Autonomous S.S.R.'s and Other Local
Authorities, U.S.S.R., 1965

Source		Billion rubles
1. Receipts from enterprises, organizations and property under the jurisdiction of the Councils of Ministers of A.S.S.R.'s and executive committees of local Soviets		3.94
2. Local taxes and charges, income taxes on cooperatives, etc.		1.10
3. Assignments to local budgets from State taxes and nontax receipts, including assignments from		13.40
a) Turnover tax	8.74	
b) Agricultural tax	.36	
c) State loan	.01	
d) Income taxes on collective farms	.87	
e) Personal income tax	2.51	
4. Residual budget funds applied to meet expenses		.46
5. Other		.59
Total		19.47

Source: *Gos. biudzhet SSSR* (1966), p. 95.

Local school authorities appear to possess no significant financial discretion. The tax revenue that comes to them, to be spent through the local budgets on schools and other purposes, comes in amounts and from sources that are largely beyond their control. In fact, they receive the amounts to which they can lay claim on the basis of very closely drawn "norms" of expenditure.[14] These are for the most part legislated centrally, and they signify more than the statutory minima or permitted maxima common in United States' school regulation, for they are instead required standards of provision, to which local school authorities are expected to adhere.

Educational policy, in so far as it is reflected in budget allocations, is made at the top, between the officials of the Union Ministry of Education and the officials of the State Planning Office (Gosplan). It is at this level that the representatives of education make their demands upon resources and the Gosplan people state their requirements from education in terms of numbers of graduates of various types and desirable norms of resource-consumption per student. After negotiation, compromise and agreement, and armed with Gosplan authorizations, the Ministries of Education of the 15 republics can then command resources from their Ministries of Finance. It is then the responsibility of the Ministries of Finance to make sure that the revenues are

14. For example, number of students per class, number of teachers per class, size of classrooms, number of rooms per hundred students, heating, lighting and cleaning expenditures, and so on.

available for the school authorities to do their job, and to check that all the regulations concerning levels of staffing and equipment, payment of teachers, and so forth are being observed. One byproduct of this system is continual tension between officials of the two ministries at all levels of government. Finance suspects education of padding enrollment totals, miscalculating requirements of teachers and classroom space, not taking enough trouble to fill classes to capacity (40 students in grades 1-8; 35 in grades 9 and 10) before opening additional ones, and footdragging in the push to eliminate the costly very small schools, among other sins.[15] In turn, education accuses finance of over-zealousness and petty tyranny in its attempt to control the allocation and disbursement of every last kopek.

In one view it may appear unimportant whether tax revenues to be spent on schools are raised to a greater or lesser degree by local initiative, with local approval, and under local auspices. A tax is a tax, it might be argued. It is no more a tax where, as in the Soviet Union, the various Union, Republic, and local budgets merely represent conveniently demarcated, but not organically differentiated, sections of one fundamentally integrated purse. It is no less a tax where, as in the United States, the articulation of budgets is by no means as complete.

Economists, of course, will rightly insist that the matter can never be dismissed so cavalierly, even in a Soviet-type economy, where the financing of all expenditure (public and private, local and nonlocal) can be readily conceived as coming out of one, essentially social, purse. There are important questions not only of the effect on incentives of different tax structures, but also of the effect on the citizens' willingness to pay (and, hence, the subjectively perceived burden) of local taxes levied to support local needs versus centrally imposed taxes to support the needs of other areas of the country.

But there is an even more important point to be made in evaluating the particular fiscal structure the Soviet Union has developed for the schools: it ensures that control over the pace and form of school development is kept firmly in the hands of the top levels of government. The system admirably complements the direct political and administrative control from the center that has been the hallmark of Soviet (no less than Czarist) public administration, and it facilitates recasting of budgets to fit changes in central educational policy.

15. See, for example, P. Batyshchev, "Bol'she vnimaniia sotsial'no-kul'turnym uchrezhdeniiam" (More attention to socio-cultural establishments), *Finansy SSSR 1970,* 8 (August 1970), pp. 19-21. Also, by the same author, "Effektivnee ispol'zovat' sredtsva na soderzhanie sotsial'no-kul'turnykh uchrezhdenii" (To utilize more effectively funds for maintaining socio-cultural establishments), *Finansy SSSR 1971,* 11 (November 1971), pp. 14-20.

3 Peter Bohm

Financing Methods and Demand for Education

That different financing methods may affect observable demand for education from consumers-voters in general, i.e., observable in referenda or similar democratic political processes, has been mentioned in the economic literature.[1] It may be observed (a) that methods of finance may differ in their excess burden on the economy, i.e., in their effect on real national income, and hence in their income effect on real demand for education; and (b) that different methods of finance may affect the relation between real demand and observable ("revealed") demand in specific political decision processes. Problems of the following type are discussed here: if (residential) property taxes were replaced by tuition or (higher) personal income taxes to finance compulsory education, what would happen to overall efficiency in the economy (real national income) and hence, to real demand for education, and what can be expected to happen to the voters' willingness to reveal their actual preferences for education in a given political process? It should be emphasized that changes of this kind that are neutral with respect to income distribution will be discussed here.

In the first two sections we deal with the effects of different methods of financing *compulsory* education and *voluntary* education, respectively. In the third section we discuss the demand estimation problem for education as a public good.

COMPULSORY EDUCATION DEMAND

The concept of public goods means that one person's consumption of such a good does not diminish others' consumption of the same good. Education in the ordinary sense is obviously not covered by this definition; educational

1. See R. Barlow, "Efficiency Aspects of Local School Finance," *Journal of Political Economy,* 78 (September 1970), and references therein. Barlow discusses the specific question of whether the particular level of school spending associated with the property tax is allocatively efficient.

capacity is limited and, practically speaking, an additional student will bar another from access to education. However, as is well known from the theory of public sector economics, there are many goods and services which, although they do not obey the rules of a pure public good, present similar problems as pure public goods and hence can be treated as such a good in certain contexts. This is certainly true for *compulsory* education. The main question here is not that one consumer bars another from access to the good—by definition, all shall be served. Instead, the main problem is that of estimating individual demand (provided one likes to base supply decisions on information about consumers' preferences, wholly or partly): how much are the beneficiaries of compulsory education willing to pay for different amounts of educational services? This estimation problem runs into the same difficulties encountered when estimating demand for pure public goods. Attempts to find out about individual willingness to pay would be impeded—as goes the standard argument—by the "free-rider" incentive or other distortions of people's willingness to reveal their true preferences.

Before proceeding, let me note that identifying compulsory education as a public good, *from the view-point of demand estimation,* should not be confused with the fact that, from another view-point as well, educational services may be considered a public good. For example, whereas my own education— or that of my children—appears as a private good to me, the education of others' appears as a pure public good, i.e., as something I benefit from (or may benefit from) regardless of its benefits to other persons. This latter public good aspect, while included in our concept of demand for compulsory education, does not, however, have to be observed *separately* until we deal with the case of voluntary education.

Estimates of direct and indirect demand for compulsory education are relevant in two important ways. First, given a basic principle of consumer sovereignty, an optimal volume (quality and/or length) of compulsory education would ideally be based on an estimate of individual demand; but the relevance of such an estimate remains, of course, even when the government wants to deviate from the position of individual demand as the sole determinant of output in this field. Second, individual demand for compulsory education will influence individual willingness to be taxed for these purposes or at least affect the governments' and politicians' prospects of getting support for their ideas of optimal systems of education.

Thus, given that politicians would like to know the maximum willingness to pay for education among various subgroups of the population, we assume here that there are, in fact, feasible arrangements for making such inquiries (perhaps on a sample basis). Since this assumption, as it stands, is incompatible with present-day institutional conventions, it should be observed that real-world inquiries, in the form of referenda, polls, observation of pressure groups, etc., all can be assumed to have some of the ingredients of a willingness-to-pay inquiry. In other words, systematic differences among financing methods with respect to misrepresentation of preferences can be assumed to be present in other forms of inquiries as well.

COMPULSORY EDUCATION FINANCE

In many countries, compulsory education is financed through the national or local budget in such a way that general taxes can be regarded as used to withdraw resources from the market economy for the purpose of producing educational services. The case of general tax financing is discussed here as if compulsory education were in fact financed by personal income taxes. This case is characterized by two incentive effects crucial to our investigation:

1. Income taxes—or an increase in income taxes for the purpose of producing compulsory education—introduces (augments) a substitution effect which distorts incentives to work.

2. Attempts to reveal the population's demand (willingness to pay) for compulsory education—or political approximations to this approach—given that education is financed by income taxes in general, run into the problem of revealing preferences for public goods, as indicated above. To be specific, if a person's true willingness to pay falls short of what he expects the tax system will imply for his real disposable income (including the excess burden of the tax),[2] ordinary public good theory tells us that he is likely to *understate* his willingness to pay in order to do what he can to keep expenditure for compulsory education at a low level. Conversely, if his true willingness to pay exceeds what he expects the tax system to have in store for him and, in particular, if he regards the tax effect on him as practically negligible (essentially others pay), there is an incentive to *overstate* his willingness to pay according to standard public good theory.[3] For the time being, let us disregard the question of the probable net effect of these two opposing tendencies on observable demand in relation to true demand.

Let us now compare the income tax case to the case of compulsory education financed by a special "school tax." The (residential) property tax in the U.S. can be regarded as such a tax, given that the overwhelming part of increases in this tax has gone to financing education.

Let us assume for the moment that a tax on property (somehow defined) could be substituted for an income tax without affecting the income distribution. We may then observe the following effects from a hypothetical transformation from income tax financing to property tax financing (or vice versa):

2. Cf. D. Johnson and M. Pauly, "Excess Burden and the Voluntary Theory of Public Finance," *Economica,* 36, no. 143 (August 1969), 269-76.

3. Cf. e.g., R. Dorfman, "General Equilibrium with Public Goods," in *Public Economics,* ed. J. Margolis and H. Guitton (New York: St. Martin's Press, 1969).

1. As compared to the income tax, the incentive distortion between leisure and work is replaced by one concerning the use of income, i.e., between buying (taxable) property and other expenditure.[4]

2. Demand for compulsory education, on the other hand, would *ceteris paribus* develop as shown for the case of income tax financing.

Now, the *ceteris paribus* assumption cannot be taken for granted: first and foremost, the incentive effects on work and leisure vs. those on property and nonproperty expenditure can be expected to produce systematic differences in the excess burden of taxation and hence, in the real income level. Although there is little to be said a priori about the relative demand and supply elasticities which determine the sign of these effects,[5] it seems possible to argue, on the basis of the low price elasticity of labor supply (essentially for institutional reasons), that the excess burden at least cannot be smaller in the property tax case.

Second, given the assumption that property tax financing is at least not more efficient than income tax financing and hence, that a shift from property taxes to (higher) income taxes would imply a positive change in real income (if any), there is the question of whether there are practicable means for compensating those who might lose in the transition to income tax financing. In other words, we may question whether or not the income distribution can be kept "unchanged" in this process. Now, if it is true that the property tax is in fact regressive with respect to income, as is often pointed out, and if it can be assumed that the income tax progression can be changed in conjunction with the transition, this would cease to be a major problem. (See chap. 9.)

Thus, to sum up the argument so far, a distribution-neutral transition from property tax financing to income tax financing of compulsory education would a priori seem to involve (a) no effects on the level of demand revealed and (b) at least not a larger excess burden of taxation.

Let us now compare the two preceding methods of financing to a system of tuition extensive enough to cover costs of compulsory education (for the sake of the argument). It may be observed first that no distortive effects of the above-mentioned type will arise at all. The reason is, of course, that education being compulsory, all have to abide by the system and pay accordingly (the possible effects on the willingness to raise children being disregarded). What definitely becomes problematic now, however, is the prospect of keeping the real income distribution the same as in the preceding two cases. Let us deal with this issue before going into the probable effects on demand for compulsory education.

4. For a discussion of the effects of a general property tax, see P. Miezkowski, "The Property Tax: An Excise Tax or a Profits Tax?" *Journal of Public Economics,* 1, no. 1 (April 1972).

5. Cf., e.g., L. Johansen, *Public Economics* (Chicago: Rand McNally, 1965), chap. 7.6.

A system of uniform tuition would obviously tend to affect income distribution unless existing tax schemes could be revised to compensate families with schoolchildren. A compensation to this effect might, of course, produce a distortive effect. In fact, starting from a position of income tax financing of compulsory education and assuming as an extreme case that income taxes for parent families are reduced by exactly the amount of tuition for their schoolchildren, we would certainly expect the distortive effects to be the same after the transition to a system of tuition.[6]

Then, given that a distribution-neutral policy mix involving tuition would have no net efficiency benefits, we may discuss the demand for compulsory education from the point of view of a given real income level. Other things being equal, this would imply the same willingness to pay for such education as in the case of pure income tax financing. Again, other things will probably not be equal in at least one important respect. Recalling the public good aspect of the demand estimation problem for compulsory education, people's true willingness to pay will be confronted with tuition as the "price" for compulsory education (in spite of the fact that the true price has been regarded here as a combination of measures—tuition and tax scheme changes). With tuition viewed as such a "price" there will be systematic differences in demand—according to a standard public good theory—as compared to the case of income tax financing. Families with schoolchildren can be assumed to *regard* themselves (after some time, at least) as being confronted with a significantly higher cost for compulsory education with tuition than in the case where everybody is regarded as sharing the financial burden of these educational services. Hence, more families of this type would find that their true willingness to pay for changes in the volume (length) of compulsory education falls short of the amount of tuition. On the other hand, families without schoolchildren—assuming the existence of and recognition of external effects from education as well as a possible general belief in the value of education for the society they live in—would have the opposite relation between their (zero) price and their true willingness to pay. Given the presumption of the theory of public goods, as mentioned earlier, one would expect a relative decrease in stated demand for the first group and a relative increase for the second group. However, without any specific hypothesis about the relative size of these changes, it is impossible to forecast the effect (if any) on total stated demand for compulsory education.

The argument so far may be summarized as follows: while the choice between income taxes and property taxes in our context depends on their relative excess burdens, the choice between income taxes and tuition would seem to depend on the extent to which people would misrepresent their

6. For low-income families this may call for a negative income tax.

preferences for compulsory education. And on this latter point, standard public good theory fails to come up with an answer.

Before proceeding to the case of voluntary education, it should be noted that financing methods may differ in their ability to make people aware of education costs. And in this respect, tuition seems to be superior to taxes. In fact, tuition would seem to make the cost of education per student as clear to anyone as it could possibly be. Given then, that a value for political decision-making is assigned to this clarification in itself, that is, given that a more explicit awareness of the real per capita costs of education would facilitate a more cost-conscious expression of demand, the argument appears to favor tuition financing.

There is, however, an additional aspect of "financial illusion" that may be more important in terms of realistic policy making in this field. Even if actual effects on consumers can be shown to be the same in the two cases, income tax and tuition financing, people might (be taken to) prefer fees to taxes. Thus, given a political "constraint" on the tax volume, it would work in favor of tuition financing.

VOLUNTARY EDUCATION FINANCE

In the case of voluntary education, a distinction needs to be made between direct demand (student demand) and indirect demand (public good demand). These two aspects of demand are treated in turn.

The natural point of departure for discussing demand for a private good is to assume a system of prices. As an educational system involves a sizeable amount of overhead costs in terms of organization, research, textbooks, etc., it seems reasonable to regard it as a decreasing cost industry. Hence two different pricing principles may be observed here, tuition according to average and marginal costs, respectively. With tuition set according to the average cost pricing rule, education will, of course, be financed by tuition alone. Given the student demand for voluntary education under this scheme, we may study the effects of a transition to a system of marginal cost pricing. Marginal costs being smaller than average costs, tuition now will be reduced as compared to the previous case. This, in itself, would tend to increase demand for voluntary education. The fact that education now will be financed partly by increased taxes cannot be expected to bring forth any sufficiently strong countereffect. Even if the additional tax funds required could be raised from those who actually consumed the educational services, there would be a net tendency to increase demand for education (see Figure 3.1).

Voluntary education may in fact also be valued by others than those who directly consume the educational services. Under a system of marginal (or average) cost tuition, this demand component is simply not allowed to affect the volume of voluntary education. For education to be determined by *total* demand, students must be subsidized below marginal costs. Pure tuition financ-

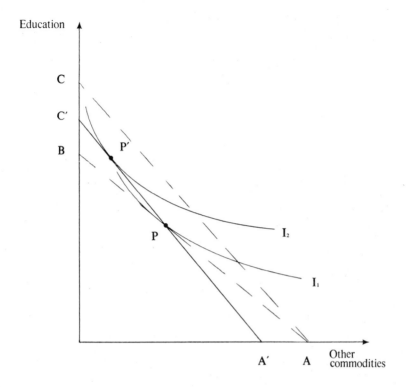

Figure 3.1. The case of average cost tuition is shown by the budget line *AB* and the optimum point *P*. At the lower marginal cost tuition level, the budget line shifts to *AC*. To cover total costs, the consumer is subjected to a general tax (preferably, a shift of a lump-sum character) which will move the budget line towards the origin to *A'C'*, which passes through *P*. In this situation, however, the consumer will prefer point *P'*. The cost of the change from *P* to *P'* is covered, of course, in the case of marginal cost pricing.

ing, in other words, while compatible with compulsory education, must be ruled out as a financial solution in the case of voluntary education (see Figure 3.2). In fact, both marginal cost pricing principles and the existence of external benefits of education contribute to this conclusion.

The government may disagree with the level of demand for voluntary education as discussed so far. Taking student demand first, the government may assume that potential students (and/or their parents) do not realize their own interest because of imperfect foresight; hence, the government would regard student demand as actually higher than is revealed by their behavior. This deviation may be further reinforced by the fact that social returns to education in terms of future production are generally regarded as higher than private

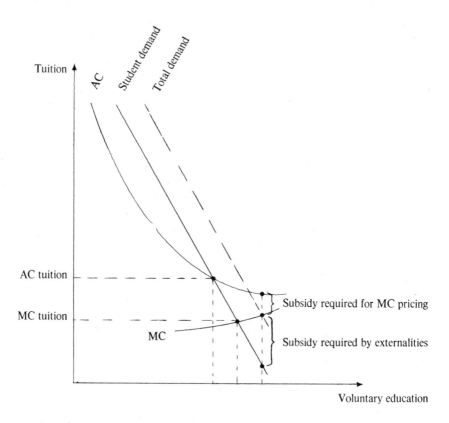

Figure 3.2. *AC* and *MC* denote average and marginal costs, respectively. Total demand equals student demand and public good demand for voluntary education.

returns in terms of future income. Moreover, the government may consider the external benefits of education to be more valuable to society than is in fact revealed by the indirect (public good) demand mentioned in the preceding paragraph. As a result, the total demand as conceived by the government will exceed the level of aggregate individual demand for voluntary education.

The "merit want" aspect just mentioned adds to the public good demand for voluntary education in making total demand exceed student demand. Whenever the difference between total demand and student demand becomes large, the possibility arises that an optimal volume of education cannot be achieved at any positive level of tuition. In fact, it may even be necessary to introduce a "negative tuition," i.e., scholarships to all students, for education actually to reach the optimum level (see the scholarship level *S* in Figure 3.3). In this case, tuition would be completely ruled out as a financial source in an optimal system of voluntary education.

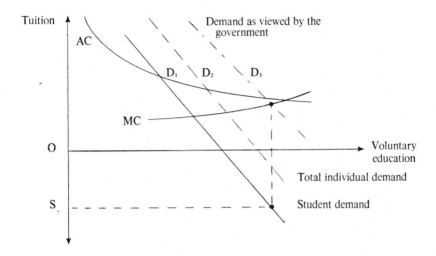

Figure 3.3.

Increasing the volume of education above the level of demand given by marginal cost tuition will make it impossible to prevent changes in income distribution. The amount of taxes required for such increases obviously exceeds the students' willingness to pay. Hence, the choice of financing method for voluntary education, in contrast to compulsory education, has to be made with distribution as well as efficiency aspects taken into account. Given this premise, we may, however, continue to discuss how the direction of the choice would be affected by efficiency aspects, i.e., as if distribution aspects did not exist.

Given, then, that a large amount of government finance is required from the point of view of reaching an optimum volume of voluntary education in the presence of a significant indirect demand and/or a significant merit want demand, the choice between special taxes such as property taxes (if at all relevant for voluntary education) and general taxes once again becomes an issue. It is difficult under these conditions to come up with an efficiency argument in favor of special taxes. However, there is still the problem of whether different methods of financing voluntary education—and, in particular, tuition versus general taxes—will differ in their effect on people's willingness to reveal the size of public good demand correctly. It should be kept in mind that a correct estimate of such demand is desirable even when a merit want aspect on education is present. In principle, the government will find it difficult to form an opinion of total demand and, in particular, whether and, if so, to what extent their demand deviates from demand as expressed by the citizens (see D_2 in Figure 3.3) without an estimate of the public good component of demand.

In the case of compulsory as well as voluntary education, the relation between observable (revealed) and true public good demand under alternative
financing methods would influence the choice of an optimal financing system.
If there were *no* risk or misrepresentation of public good demand, conclusions
from the above analyses would amount to the following unorthodox solution
concerning the optimum system of education finance: *tuition* financing of
compulsory education and essentially *general tax* financing of *voluntary* education.

PUBLIC GOOD THEORY

The conventional public good theory tells us that the revelation of individual preferences, in polls or referenda, by contacts between politicians and their
constituents or in more elaborate attempts to measure individual willingness to
pay for education, would be biased one way or another. Moreover, the theory
leads us to expect methods of finance to differ with respect to their effect on
the size of misrepresentation of individual preferences. New arguments have
recently been advanced on these points and it seems worthwhile in this context
to call attention to their content and implications.

One line of thought with respect to the problem of estimating demand for
public goods departs from the observation that knowledge or a dominant
preconception about the direction of changes in the volume of the public good
(whether it will increase or decrease) and hence about the direction of the
costs to the individual would lead to a bias in reported demand, whereas uncertainty about this direction would not. This is perhaps most easily explained
by the use of two diagrams.

In Figure 3.4, commodity E is the public good (say, the education volume
of society) and C represents other commodities. The individual consumer is
initially at point P on his indifference curve I_1, and he is asked about his maximum willingness to pay for a specified increase in E by ΔE. Obviously, his true
reply would be ΔC (in terms of other commodities), as this would not make
him worse off should the increase in E actually be made and should he be
called upon to pay his stated maximum amount. Now, he observes that by
understating his willingness to pay, say, by stating only $\overline{\Delta C}$ (as if his indifference curve actually looked like I_1), he would be better off, should E be
increased (he would actually reach I_2) and no worse off, should it not. Thus,
he will find that this kind of misrepresentation is more favorable for him than
correct reporting of preferences.

Now, if we instead succeeded in finding a volume $\overline{E}$ which did not create
any definite expectations as to its relation to a final choice of E and asked the
individual to state his maximum willingness to pay for an increase by ΔE,
which would also be taken as his minimum compensation amount required for a

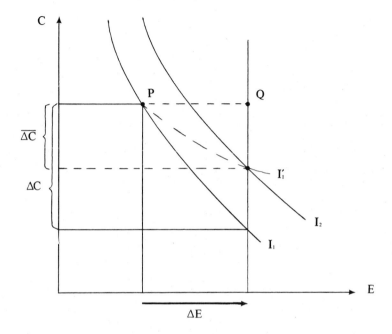

Fig. 3.4.

decrease by ΔE, he would be in an altogether different position (see Figure 3.5). Understating his willingness to pay by $\overline{\Delta C}$ would mean that he would end up in a worse situation than P', should the outcome of the inquiry be a *reduction* of E by ΔE, as indicated by I_0 in Figure 3.5. If he applied a minimax strategy, he would choose to reveal his true marginal willingness to pay (marginal compensation requirement) by which he could under no circumstances become worse off than in his initial position, as goes this argument.[7]

Another way out of the impasse of misrepresented preferences for public goods is to create a different kind of uncertainty as to the consequences for the individual. This is particularly valid for the common case where the consumer for practical purposes, if nothing else, is confronted with a specific

7. Cf., e.g., Jacques H. Drèze and Dominique de-la-Vallée Poussin, "A tâtonnement process for guiding and financing an efficient production of public goods," Paper presented at the Econometric Society Meeting, Brussels, 1969; abstract in *Econometrica*, 38, no. 4 (July 1970), 35.

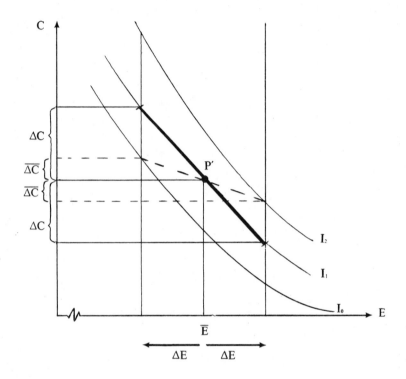

Fig. 3.5.

proposal such as having ΔE in Figure 3.4 or abstaining from it. A relevant example might be a proposal as to whether or not compulsory education be expanded
by one year. Given the inadequacy of the preceding solution here, we may
instead confront the consumers with a question about their maximum willingness to pay for ΔE, given an uncertainty about *what it would cost them* if actually carried out. The payment alternatives here are explicitly stated to include,
at least, equal payment (via taxes or otherwise) for all, payment in relation to
a stated willingness to pay and no payment at all for certain (yet unknown)
consumer groups. This uncertainty about actual payments could be made
credible to the voters due to the fact that it can be explained to them that
aspects of distribution and efficient payment systems have to be taken into
account and hence, that the optimal payment system can be determined only
after the willingness to pay has been established for various individuals or
groups. Thus, whenever there is an uncertainty of this kind, this approach

would in fact place the individual in a position where he cannot know whether he will get $\triangle E$ for nothing or for a price. (If the subcase where he should get it for nothing or for a price below his true willingness to pay is evaluated separately, he might be willing to overstate his willingness to pay—as has been observed in polls, for example, where people are asked to express their opinion without any obligations as to payment for, say, more police protection. In this way the individual would do what he can to bolster the increase in demand for $\triangle E$ in which case he would end up at point Q of Figure 3.4. In the reverse subcase, taken separately, he would have the incentive to understate his preferences as discussed above.) Then, given this situation of uncertainty as to the outcome, i.e., as to which subcase would materialize, the consumer might reveal his true preferences, since *simple* strategies of cheating by under- or overstating are ruled out.[8]

Obviously, a priori arguments cannot validate or refute the hypothesis just presented. In an attempt to test this approach along with other methods of making inquiries of this kind, including those which would give rise to simple cheating strategies according to standard theory, a rather surprising result was obtained. In an experimental situation which allowed actual collective decision making and real payments when relevant, no significant differences in the stated willingness to pay were registered for five different approaches, including the one just discussed.[9] More striking, perhaps, the outcome of an approach which on a priori grounds would provide incentives for understatements (payment equal to stated willingness to pay) did not deviate from the outcome of an approach with the opposite incentives (no payment at all). Without unduly exaggerating the implications of these results, they support the view that the risks for serious misrepresentations of preferences may have been overemphasized in standard theory and that, in fact, many approaches, also very simple ones, would give reliable responses from consumers.

In fact, once observed, there are arguments to support these tentative results: people do act in a responsible way in similar cases. For example, people turn up at the ballot boxes in general elections in spite of the fact that an individual vote cannot be expected to have a decisive influence on the

8. This approach is discussed in detail in Peter Bohm, "An Approach to Estimating Demand for Public Goods," *Swedish Journal of Economics,* 73 (March 1971), 55-66.

9. In short, the experiment involved asking representative samples about their willingness to pay for watching a new show of well-known "quality" on closed-circuit TV, given that the program would actually be shown only if the total maximum willingness to pay exceeded costs of showing (rental of video tape machines, payment of operators, etc.) and given that people then had to pay according to the rules of the inquiry (for one sample: nothing, another: a given price, another: their stated maximum willingness to pay, etc.). The experiment as well as its possible implications are discussed in detail in P. Bohm, "Estimating Demand for Public Goods: An Experiment," *European Economic Review,* 3, no. 3 (Sept. 1972).

outcome and that getting to the ballot box involves costs for the individual in many respects. Given the conclusions of standard public good theory, the individual would abstain from going to the ballot box under these circumstances.

CONCLUSION

In sum, there is preliminary empirical evidence which questions the conclusions of standard theory that there would be serious misrepresentations of preferences in elaborate attempts to estimate public good demand. Although additional social experiments are required before firm conclusions can be drawn, this observation would also seem to concern the problem of estimating public good demand for education. Of particular relevance here is the implication of these results, namely, that shifts between different methods of financing education would seem to have only moderate effects on the public good demand for education.

The decisive factors, then, would be the aspects of distribution and of overall efficiency in the economy. Given the existence of public good demand and of merit wants for higher education, efficiency aspects alone would require a considerable contribution from government financial sources (preferably, it seems, raised by income taxes), perhaps even to the extent of tuition-free higher education and general provision of scholarships. As far as compulsory education is concerned, however, efficiency arguments do not disfavor tuition financing. In fact, given a political prejudice that government funds to optimal education be kept at a minimum level, we would arrive at an argument in favor of tuition financed compulsory education and tax financed voluntary education.

4 Anthony M. Cresswell

Pitfalls and Policy Analysis in School Finance Reform

We are in the midst of what has come to be called a school finance reform movement. More than likely what we see as currents of school finance reform are a portion of a larger stream of reform throughout education. These reforms have as their general objectives the elimination of inequities in the financing of public schools and the overall improvement of the delivery of educational services. The school finance portion of the general education finance reform is aimed particularly at eliminating the available resource disparities which now exist. In the process of doing so, the property tax as a source of school revenues has been identified time and again as the culprit responsible for inequalities in educational opportunity. A number of major court decisions and commission studies have provided both an empirical basis and a legal justification for this point of view.[1] As a result of this movement, proposals for changes in property taxation and reorganization of school finance in general are now being considered which would have been unthinkable, or at least considered foolhardy, several years ago. Although well intended, some of these proposals have inherent in them serious flaws which may in fact interfere with the reduction of the inequities and frustrate attempts to improve educational systems. These flaws result, largely, from ignoring pitfalls along the path to reform. This paper will discuss some of these pitfalls and the steps which can be taken to avoid them.

SCHOOL FINANCE POLICY DECISIONS

To extend the metaphor a little further, the most foolproof and straightforward way to avoid a pitfall is to know precisely where it is. But mapping all the pitfalls in a conceptual jungle as dense as public finance and school reform is too large a task to attempt here. What can be done, however, is to

1. A summary of the characteristics of these cases is given at the end of this chapter.

outline an approach. The analysis of policy and research in education finance described here can help to identify and avoid serious blunders which may interfere with achieving the goals of reform. With a careful design for policy analysis we can hopefully avoid a narrow and shortsighted perspective on the study of school financing.

The core of this design for policy analysis is a focus on the impacts of school finance reform. Through attention to policy impacts, we can structure and interpret research to guide action. The research must be what Cronbach and Suppes have described as "decision-oriented," as opposed to "conclusion-oriented."[2] The latter is intended to contribute to knowledge and theory building in some area. But decision-oriented research is intended to be a guide to action. Coleman has pointed out that "there is no body of methods, no comprehensive methodology, for the study of the impact of public policy. When we ask why there is not, two points rise above the rest: first, it is a very recent development in the practice of governments to seriously ask questions about the impact of policy, and to expect or even hope to get a scientific answer."[3] This is certainly true of the study of school finance. This paper is intended to be a contribution in the direction of designing a methodology for the study of public policy impacts in school finance.

Policy analysis as described here rests on the normative foundation implicit in the notion of reform.[4] The objectives of reform are themselves expressions of value judgments. The purpose of policy analysis is to (1) translate the statements of global objectives into terms related to manipulation of policy variables, (2) discover to what extent current policies achieve the objectives, and (3) determine how to manipulate policy variables to better achieve the objectives. By viewing policy analysis in these terms we can easily identify where research based on positive methodology can be employed to guide reform. In the case of policy analysis for school finance, therefore, we can first look to the sources that will assist in specifying objectives for school finance systems. We can then examine research which demonstrates how to achieve policy objectives, and particularly studies which explore the relationship between policy variables and policy impacts.

This last point is the critical one. If reform means manipulating policy variables, then successful reform requires knowing the right policy variables to manipulate, and in what way. That knowledge can only come from research and the application of theories that have acquired firm empirical foundations.

2. Lee J. Cronbach and Patrick Suppes, eds., *Research for Tomorrow's Schools* (New York: Macmillan, 1969).

3. James S. Coleman, "Problems of Conceptualization and Measurement in Studying Policy Impacts," Paper presented at the Conference on the Impacts of Public Policies, 1971.

4. Anthony M. Cresswell, "Reforming School Finance: Proposals and Pitfalls," *Teachers College Record*, 73 (May 1972), contains a more detailed discussion of these points.

Translated into these terms then, a pitfall is a manipulation of policy variables which results in a move away from rather than toward an objective. Mapping pitfalls is thus a process of determining (1) what objectives are involved, (2) what policy variables are to be manipulated, and (3) analyzing or performing the research which shows what effects those changes will have.

The approach can be illustrated by applying it to the two major objectives of school finance reform: increased equity and improvements in efficiency. First, objectives must be translated into terms linked to policy variables. With regard to equity, the links with policy variables have been described by the courts, legal scholars, and finance researchers. For example, the opinion in *Rodriguez* v. *San Antonio* employs what might be called a neutral equity criterion. In discussing the selection of a means for financing public education the court says, "The selection may be made from a wide variety of financing plans so long as the program adopted does not make the quality of public education a function of wealth other than the wealth of the state as a whole."[5] In this opinion, the first of a number of school finance cases to be reviewed by the U.S. Supreme Court, the link of finance variables to equity is expressed in terms of what a school finance system *may not be.* Cases decided at other levels have dealt with positive proposals for new finance systems. But these approaches have generally been rejected, as was the proposal distribution according to need reviewed by a three-judge federal court in *McInnis* v. *Oglivie.*[6] Thus, the only definitive answer on an equity criterion derived directly from court decisions is that an equitable finance system may not be dependent on the wealth of a child's parents or the school district in which he resides.

EDUCATION OPPORTUNITY PITFALLS

Legal scholars have provided us with a number of definitions of equity in educational opportunity which go far beyond this neutral principle. It is here that the pitfalls begin to occur. The notion of equal revenues for equal effort proposed by Coons et al. is a good example.[7] This approach leaves the decision on the level of school spending to a family or school district. The finance system would be structured in such a way that equal tax effort produces equal revenues. As an equity criterion this is flawed on three grounds. First, there is both theoretical and empirical reason to expect local spending decisions to result in suboptimal expenditures on education due to ignoring spillovers and external-

5. *San Antonio Independent School District* v. *Rodriguez,* 337 F. Supp. 280 (1972), U.S. Sup. Ct. no. 71-1332 (1973).

6. *McInnis* v. *Oglivie,* 394 U.S. 322 (1969).

7. John B. Coons, William Clune III, and Stephen D. Sugarman, *Private Wealth and Public Education* (Cambridge: Harvard University Press, 1970).

ities.[8] Second, if the quality of a child's education should not be dependent on the *wealth* of parents, or neighbors, there is little justification for quality to be dependent on their *tastes* either. The third and most important flaw lies in the concept of linking a school subsidy program to local tax effort. This ignores the empirical problems of measuring municipal overburden and variations in local taste, and the theoretical problems of measuring effort. Thurow concludes "there is no way to distribute conditional or unconditional grants in accordance with some predetermined effort index. Effort . . . is already included in the system and has an effect on all the unknowns . . . The objective is not to reward effort but to achieve an optimum income distribution and undertake the correct mode of investment."[9] Thus to link a school finance reform to an effort mechanism can lead to undesired results.

School finance researchers have shown us what variations in local wealth produce disparities in educational resources. This suggests an equity criterion based on eliminating local wealth as the source of most educational revenues. But imputing too much of the villainy of the present finance system to property taxation can lead to some serious errors. First of all, the problem of wealth disparities among school districts results in differences in the ability to pay for schools (or other government services). But differences in property tax base are not the only source of variation in ability to pay. Sacks found that "variations in large city taxes are primarily accounted for by variations in noneducational expenditures. This is reversed in the suburban areas."[10] Thus there are higher overall levels of expenditures and taxes in cities. The result, as Sacks points out, is that "recent increases in the large city educational fiscal requirements, accompanied by the failure of the large city to keep up with national economic growth, have placed unparalleled burden on the cities which cannot be seen without taking the noneducational sphere into account."[11] The concept of ability to pay should, therefore, take into account the problem of *overall* tax burdens and noneducational financing as well as simple variations in real property value.

Tax capitalization effects of changes in the property tax structure can also interfere with achieving more equitable financing. Oates' study of changes in school property taxation suggests that about two-thirds of our increases (or

8. See, e.g., J. Ronnie Davis, "The Social and Economic Externalities of Education," in Roe L. Johns et al., *Economic Factors Affecting the Financing of Education* (Gainesville, Florida: National Educational Finance Project, 1970); and Burton Weisbrod, "Spillover Effects of Expenditures on Public Goods," *Journal of Political Economy,* 71 (November 1964).

9. Lester C. Thurow, "A Theory of Grants in Aid," 19, *National Tax Journal* (December 1966), 371.

10. Seymour Sacks, *City Schools, Suburban Schools: A History of Fiscal Conflict* (Syracuse: Syracuse University Press, 1972), p. 111.

11. Ibid., p. 113.

decreases) in rates would be capitalized in terms of depressed (increased) property values.[12] But increases (or decreases) in educational expenditure tend to enhance (depress) property values as well. So property tax relief and/or increases in educational expenditures can be expected to benefit property owners. Whether or not the resulting distribution of burden and services represents an increase in equity would then depend on the incidence of the tax instrument employed to replace property tax revenues and/or increase expenditures. Changes in property tax structures per se may or may not contribute to increased equity.

But even assuming equity in distribution of resources and tax burdens among school districts, equality in educational opportunity may yet elude us. Differences in resources among school buildings within districts, particularly in large ones, may exceed those among districts. In several Maryland county districts, for example, the range in the average teacher salaries per building within the county was greater than the range among the counties.[13] In short, an equity criterion must deal with more than the wealth-related disparities and should include attention to the administrative components of reform.

An equity criterion should also go beyond resource availability as a measure of equity. Educational opportunity involves achievement as well. And to date there is little evidence that greater resources alone will reduce disparities in achievement levels. The most recent and exhaustive review of the literature, done for the President's Commission on School Finance concluded that *"research has found nothing that consistently and unambiguously makes a difference in student outcomes"* (emphasis in the original).[14] This is consistent with the findings of Coleman and the reanalysis of his results in the Harvard Seminar.[15] To improve equity in outcomes, therefore, will require reforms that go beyond redistribution of resources and include incentives for improved performance. Reforms which rely on less than this are empty promises. One set of reforms which does offer some hope in this regard relates to the question of efficiency in school operation.

12. Wallace E. Oates, "The Effects of Property Taxes and Local Public Spending on Property Values: An Empirical Study of Tax Capitalization and the Tiebout Hypothesis," *Journal of Political Economy,* 77 (July/August 1969), 967.

13. Anthony M. Cresswell, *Equality and Educational Opportunity in Maryland's Public Schools,* A Report to the Citizens Commission on Maryland Government (Pittsburgh: School of Urban and Public Affairs, Carnegie-Mellon University, 1972), p. 63.

14. Harvey A. Averch et al., *How Effective Is Schooling? A Critical Review and Synthesis of Research Findings,* A Report to the President's Commission on School Finance (Santa Monica, Calif.: Rand, 1972).

15. James S. Coleman, "The Concept of Equality of Educational Opportunity," *Harvard Educational Review,* 38 (Winter 1968); and also Fredrick Mosteller and Daniel P. Moynihan, eds., *On Equality of Educational Opportunity* (New York: Random House, 1972).

EFFICIENCY AND FINANCE REFORM

The question of relationships between resources and performance is the central concern of reforms aimed at improvements in efficiency. To raise the efficiency of resource allocation within education one must know what makes a difference, i.e., we need to know about educational production functions. The present state of the art does not allow much to be said with confidence about educational production relationships.[16] Differences in physical resources seem to be the least important of the educational policy variables. Teacher characteristics, especially verbal ability, appear to be the variables with the most consistent relationship to student performance.[17] But while this may be heartening to teachers, it is of limited value as a policy variable since there will always be, presumably, variation in verbal ability among any collection of teachers. Therefore, any teacher assignment policy will result in poorer teacher quality for some and lower efficiency in some part of the program. It may be that teacher verbal ability is less important for some kinds of programs than others, so that some efficiency improvements may result from adjusting teacher assignments. But information on which to base these actions is presently unavailable. Neither are there reliable analysis of the relative effectiveness of alternative educational programs. In the absence of this information, reforms aimed at increases in efficiency are likely to be simply cost-cutting exercises with potentially damaging results.

Concern for efficiency includes more than allocations within educational systems. An efficient finance system includes attention to the size of the educational unit and the overall level of funding for educational programs. With respect to the size of the educational unit, there is reason to believe that many current finance policies which encourage school consolidation may be encouraging inefficiency as well. In studying economies of scale, the most important problem is the choice of objectives against which performance is judged. Riew examined the extent of curricular offerings in relation to school size by regression analysis, but did not examine achievement test data.[18] He found an optimal size for maximizing offerings in the 1700 pupil range. Roughly comparable results were reported by Cohn using a different objective: an achievement test

16. For some of the most interesting work in this area, see Samuel S. Bowles, *A Linear Programming Model in Planning Educational Systems for Economic Growth* (Cambridge, Mass.: Harvard University Press, 1969), pp. 156-214.

17. James S. Coleman et al., *Equality of Educational Opportunity, Summary* (Washington, D.C.: Government Printing Office, 1966); and Henry M. Levin, "New Model of School Effectiveness," in *Do Teachers Make a Difference?* (Washington, D.C.: Bureau of Education Professions Development, U.S. Office of Education, 1970).

18. John Riew, "Economics of Scale in High School Operation," *Review of Economics and Statistics,* 48 (August 1966).

measure.[19] But neither of these studies took into account the differences in student characteristics and are, therefore, of questionable value. Studies by Burkehead et al., Keisling, and Alkin did control for student characteristics and found, in general, a *negative* relationship between size and performance.[20] In the Keisling study the negative relationship held for a range of enrollment from less than 200 to greater than 400 pupils. In another regression study, Osburn found the net effect of increases from 200 to 2400 pupils of only $47 per pupil.[21] An amount that small does little to support arguments for significant scale economies.

In general, then, the evidence for economies of scale in school operation, particularly at the secondary level, is rather weak; whereas the evidence of diseconomies appears more persuasive, especially when student characteristics are taken into account. Problems in interpreting this kind of conclusion are many. To begin with, some of the studies deal with the school district as the unit of analysis, other with the secondary school building. A school district and a school building are clearly different kinds of organizational entities. What would be expected to produce economies of scale in one cannot be said to apply to the other.

The important reform question is whether the available evidence suggests conclusions about criteria of efficiency related to size. The answer for the present must be that it does not. Any efficiency criteria based on studies of economies due to scale must include comprehensive attention to objectives. That is, the efficiencies must be studied for a wide selection of educational outcomes. Only then can conclusions be drawn with respect to optimal size criteria for school buildings or districts. It is not clear whether certain kinds of objectives are more efficiently achieved in a large organization while others belong in a small one. One might find, for example, that reading instruction is more efficient in small organizational units but vocational education is best designed as a large-scale regional program. In the absence of this kind of evidence, one must conclude that school finance programs should not include incentives or criteria which encourage consolidation or other means of enlarging school districts. The conventional wisdom that small schools are inefficient is not supported by research and, therefore, should not become part of school finance policy.

19. Elchanan Cohn, "Economics of Scale in Iowa High School Operations," *Journal of Human Resources,* 3 (Fall 1968).

20. Jesse Burkehead, *Input and Output in Large-City High Schools* (Syracuse: Syracuse University Press, 1967); Herbert Keisling, "Measuring a Local Government Service: A Study of School Districts in New York State," *Review of Economics and Statistics,* 49 (August 1967); and Marvin C. Alkin, "Religious Factors in the Determination of Educational Expenditures," *Educational Administration Quarterly,* 2 (Spring 1966).

21. Donald D. Osburn, "Economics of Size Associated with Public High Schools," *Review of Economics and Statistics,* 52 (February 1970).

The structure of current finance systems and reforms may also lead to inefficiencies. A theoretical analysis by Barlow suggests that the frequent assumption of regressivity of property tax incidence would result in a general underprovision of resources for education.[22] Studies of rates of return to investment in education also indicate underinvestment. Optimal levels of investment in schooling would be indicated by rates of return comparable to alternative investment opportunities—perhaps 10-15 percent. Estimates of return to elementary schooling range as high as 100 percent and are consistently higher than returns to secondary and higher education.[23] Yet finance systems support secondary education at a higher level than elementary, encouraging higher expenditures in the upper grades. Of course, these rates of return studies must be interpreted with caution. Where the contribution of schooling to income has been compared to actual ability, ability has washed out the effects of schooling.[24] Also, rates of return to elementary education are probably overestimated as a result of ignoring the opportunity costs to parents of their contribution to elementary schooling. But even when these caveats are taken into account, the implication is strong that underinvestment and misallocation are characteristic of the current system and should be avoided in reform proposals.

CONCLUSION

The focus on policy impacts which characterizes this paper raises some critical points about the relationship between policy reform and research. Predicting and controlling policy outcomes depend first and foremost on understanding the relationships between policy variables and output variables. For most of the critical questions in school finance reform, the research on which this understanding must rest is either missing or largely incomplete.

Thus we can show that local wealth disparities are the source of inequities, when education finance is based on local revenues, but we cannot predict what effects changes in the character of the property tax will have on these inequities. Neither is it possible to foretell accurately what effects property tax reform will have on the functioning of noneducational government services. Property tax systems are the foundation of local government and locally controlled schools.

22. Robin Barlow, "Efficiency Aspects of Local School Finance," *Journal of Political Economy,* 78 (September/October 1970).

23. Detailed discussions of the returns on investment in schooling can be found in Theodore Schultz, "Human Capital: Policy Issues and Research Opportunities," A Paper prepared for the NBER Colloquium on Human Capital (1971); and Irving J. Goffman et al., *The Concept of Education as an Investment,* A Report to the President's Commission on School Finance (Gainesville, Fla.: University of Florida, 1971).

24. W. Lee Hansen et al., "Schooling and Earnings of Low Achievers," *American Economic Review,* 60 (June 1970).

But because externalities and geographical spillovers are characteristic of education, there is reason to believe that local decisionmaking for expenditures will result in underinvestment. Until more detailed studies of spillovers and external costs and benefits of education are available, these questions must remain unanswered. (See chap. 19.)

Most importantly, there is no firm empirical reason to expect that any changes in resource allocation will result in improvements in educational achievement. This is perhaps the most troublesome point of all. It is troublesome particularly because the results of available research are ambiguous. It is not true that nothing makes a difference. Some programs are clearly effective; others are not. The problem arises from the fact that we have yet to establish the links between success and the characteristics of the program content and resources.

Until this is done, and in the absence of other justification, there should be no differences in the level of resources available to pupils in the schools. This equalization can be accomplished through statewide budgeting and careful attention to tax burden impacts and income redistribution effects of finance reform. Where finance research is necessary to identify those impacts, it should receive prompt attention. But the first priority should be to the examination of education production relationships and the still-unknown links between educational resources, learning outcomes, good citizenship, and innovative, productive lives.

Appendix

Intrastate School Finance Court Cases

In August 1971, the California Supreme Court issued its watershed decision in *Serrano* v. *Priest*. For the first time a major judicial body held a state system of school finance unconstitutional when tested against the equal protection guarantees of both the Fourteenth Amendment and the California Constitution. A number of legal progeny have followed. Most have adopted *Serrano's* major premise: the quality of a child's education in the public schools of a state may not be a function of wealth other than the wealth of the state as a whole. These cases have mandated that state legislatures adhere to the concept of "fiscal neutrality" in developing alternative means of financing a state's school system. That is, while other factors may be considered, per pupil expenditures may not vary with the relative wealth of local districts.

Intrastate school finance litigation has become a fertile ground for judicial activism.[25] Despite the adverse decision of the U.S. Supreme Court in the case of *San Antonio Independent School District* v. *Rodriguez* on March 21, 1973, state courts will remain free to issue *Serrano*-type decisions based upon state constitutional grounds. Thus, there is little reason to believe that these cases will not leave their impact on American education.[26]

25. As can be quickly deduced from the chart in U.S., Congress, Senate, Select Committee on Equal Educational Opportunity, *Issues in School Finance*, 92d Cong., 2d sess., September 1972 (Washington, D.C., Government Printing Office, 1972), pp. 166-90. The progress of these cases in state courts is monitored by the Lawyers' Committee for Civil Rights Under Law, 733 15th Street, N.W., Room 520, Washington, D.C. 200005.

26. On March 21, 1973, the U.S. Supreme Court handed down its decision in the case of *San Antonio Independent School District* v. *Rodriguez*, 337 F. Supp. 280 (1972), U.S. Sup. Ct. No. 71-1332 (1973). The central finding in that opinion is that the school financing arrangements in Texas do not violate the Equal Protection Clause of the 14th Amendment to the U.S. Constitution. This decision applies to most other states, because of their similarities to Texas. That finding effectively eliminates the prospect of nationwide school finance reform through a Supreme Court ruling, but leaves open the possibility of state-level litigation based on state statutes and constitutions.

SUMMARY OF CURRENT SITUATION

31 States
52 Cases

Major Case Factors	Number of Cases
Plaintiffs	
Schoolchild	40
Taxpayer	39
Other	22
Court of Origin	
State Court	25
Federal Court	27
Constitutional Grounds for Plaintiffs' Action	
State Grounds Only	
Education Provisions	2
Federal Grounds Only	
Equal Protection	16
Both Federal and State Grounds	34
State Equal Protection	29
14th Amendment Equal Protection	34
State Education Provisions	16
Other	
Cases in Which Decisions Were Reached	12
Issued After Full Hearing	4
Decided on Motion for Summary Judgment	2
Decided on Demurrer or Motion to Dismiss	6
Serrano Rationale Adopted	6

5 James L. Green

Less Developed Nation
Education Need

Nearly 100 years ago (1879) Henry George published his land-tax thesis in *Progress and Poverty*. George was appalled at the economic extremes between rich and poor. The thrust of George's argument aims at monopolistic concentration of land and resource ownership and hence, control of the people who work and live on the land. He states:

> That rent *must* reduce wages, is as clear as that the greater sub-tractor the less the remainder. That rent *does* reduce wages, any one, wherever situated, can see by merely looking around him.

and

> That as land is necessary to the exertion of labor in the production of wealth, to command the land which is necessary to labor, is to command all the fruits of labor save enough to enable labor to exist.[1]

A still lingering characteristic of developing countries is mass poverty and a severe lack of domestic savings for investment in capital formation. Income distribution patterns, like land ownership patterns, are highly concentrated in the hands of a few. The degree of land ownership concentration in Latin America is startling. In Peru, some one hundred families own or control 90 percent of natural wealth.[2]

Land use patterns in Latin America range from too small subsistence plots from which, truly, only subsistence levels of existence are forthcoming to large haciendas owned frequently by absentee landlords. Lodge reports that only about 30 percent of arable land in Latin America is cultivated in any form unless some export (money income creating) crop is feasible. Incongruously, in regions of incomparable natural fertility, mass movements of people

1. Henry George, *Progress and Poverty* (New York: Robert Schalkenback Foundation, 1955), chap. 2; bk. 5.
2. George C. Lodge, *Engines of Change* (New York: Alfred A. Knopf, 1970), chaps. 2 and 5 in particular.

53

to urban centers occur "because they cannot get enough to eat in the country." Somehow the ongoing economic system provides a level of nutrition in the urban ghetto superior to that of subsistence farming. One result is an importation of foodstuffs from abroad, depleting already sparce foreign exchange holdings, which the developing nation can, and should, be producing.

Given an adequate revenue base, governments can innovate and lead the way in building the infrastructure on which the private sector then organizes for production and service in selected markets. In advanced nations this responsibility is assumed without question: governments provide streets, highways, airports, rapid transit; governments provide for an adequacy of electric power, natural gas, and communication media through telephones, radio, television, and the like; governments provide for progressive school systems including vocational and ancillary training facilities and programs; governments provide industrial and neighborhood water and sewer systems, recreation centers, garbage collections, and disposal; governments provide amenities with tree-lined streets, hospitals, public health programs, and progressive community leadership and identification.

In the lesser developed nations, the assumption above is untenable. However, change is in the offing. A new set of rules will tend, slowly or more probably quite rapidly, to change the economic games being played, broaden participation and encourage regional economic integration which will cross national boundaries. In substantiation of this trend the Committee for Economic Development (CED) states: "Central America has one of the most advanced movements toward economic integration among sovereign nations to be found anywhere in the less developed world."[3]

THE ECONOMIC DEVELOPMENT PROCESS

Orthodox economic theory follows the macro-economic path set forth by a range of simplistic to highly complicated variations of the Harrod-Damar model. Growth and expansion of production result from a synthesis of the propensity to save, the effective interest rate, the marginal efficiency of capital, and assumes a fairly stable capital output ratio.[4] Orthodox theory with its emphasis on fixed capital investment flows and changes in business inventories as the process that sparks economic development is incomplete and insufficient. Recent appraisals of development programs indicate that increases in the stock of physical capital and labor force in reality account for only a fraction of the growth in total output. Rather, improved resource allocation and utilization, technological innovation, investment in human capital, and the increase in

3. Committee for Economic Development, *Economic Development of Central America* (New York: Committee for Economic Development, November 1964).
4. Robert M. Solow, *Growth Theory: An Exposition* (Oxford: Clarendon Press, 1970).

knowledge and its application account for half to three-quarters of total growth in real output of goods and services.

In this regard, Simon Kuznets states:

> While the results would clearly vary among individual countries, the inescapable conclusion is that the direct contribution of man-hours and capital accumulation would hardly account for more than a tenth of the rate of growth in per capita output—and probably less. The large remainder must be assigned to an increase in efficiency in the productive resources—a rise in output per unit of input, due either to the improved quality of the resources, or to the effects of changing arrangements, or to the impact of the technological change, or to all three.[5]

It is accepted in this analysis that the environmental organization for economic activity is primarily a public function, and the flow of public investment funds must necessarily precede the flow of private investment funds.

The public sector (governments) can functionally play an innovative role in preparing the way for enterprising market-oriented economic development. In the context used here, "preparing the way" presupposes something less than "direct doing by governments" in activities normally considered as legitimate private enterprising activities.

Governments fulfill a primary responsibility through organizing their respective natural and regional socio-political environments for economic activity. Organization or system is best defined and described as the "rules governing play of the economic game." Military dictatorship provides one set of rules; communism provides another. An enterprising free market organization (system) prescribes a different set of rules, and the modified bureaucracy encountered in most developing nations illustrates still another set of rules. In each environmental or systemic setting a different economic ball game is played. Clearly, if the rules governing behavior of the players in the economic game are changed or revised sufficiently, an entirely new type of economic game emerges. The rules governing play of the game establish motivating and equity forces which in essence distinguish one socio-economic system from another. Forecasting the impact of socio-economic change comprises the most critical task in development. Here is where a change in the rules directly changes human behavior, relationships, relative income, and well-being.

Education as a potent force in human transformations of all kinds does, indeed, have its work cut out. There is, however, a considerable mix of skepticism and faith that "schooling" as distinct from the broader context of education is up to the task of facilitating a smooth human adjustment to cultural,

5. Simon Kuznets, *Modern Economic Growth* (New Haven: Yale University Press, 1966), pp. 80-81.

socio-economic, and political transformations which presage institutional and cultural change.

> Blaug, for example, specifically attributes the present employment crisis in Nigeria to the provision of a particular form of academic elementary education that has generated unrealistic employment expectations for clerical work, caused a flight from rural areas, and fostered a disdain for manual occupations.
>
> If this diagnosis of the problem were correct, the solution would be simple: change the curricula to provide instruction based on agriculture and technical subjects, and the aspirations of young people will, in consequence, be directed towards agricultural activities; the flight from the land will be checked and the volume of "frictional" unemployment will correspondingly diminish.
>
> This reasoning is largely fallacious. It has already been pointed out by others that the idea that children's vocational aspirations can be altered by massive changes in curriculum is no more than a piece of folklore with little empirical justification.[6]

Another widely held assumption is that vocational–trade–training has the highest economic payoff in lesser developed countries. Blaug reports again:

> ... many graduates of the Basel Mission school who received agricultural and industrial training entered clerical employment. Here the most saleable component of their education was literacy, not trade training, and the former was thus utilized in the job market. Wastage of skills must always be considered in assessing programs of vocational training.[7]

PUBLIC ECONOMY

This total social structure also determines the tax structure (as a process of change in the various stages of a region's development). Charles Mansfield pinpoints the tax structure at a particular time and place as depending on:

1. The set of available tax bases, with availability defined in terms of administrative feasibility.

2. The level of development reached, as indicated by such factors as the degree of monetization and per capita income.

3. All the range of factors that we might label social and political, including the cultural style of the taxing government, the degree of urbanization, and prevailing political interest groups and philosophies.[8]

Mansfield questions whether or not developing countries need necessarily

6. M. Blaug, ed., *Economics of Education* (Baltimore: Penguin Books, 1968), p. 245.
7. Ibid., p. 402.
8. Charles Mansfield, "Tax Structure in Developing Countries: An Introduction," *Finance and Development,* 8, no. 1 (March 1971), 39.

follow the historical path of developed countries in evolving their tax structures. He says that "current ideas of equity and the development of the technology of revenue collection may have an influence on tax structure in present-day, low income countries."[9]

A comparison of the ratio of tax revenue to G.N.P. between selected developed and underdeveloped countries can provide a better understanding for formulating a positive public sector action program.

Table 5.1 – Ratio of Tax Revenue to G.N.P. in Selected Developed and Undeveloped Countries

Developed countries	Ratio of total taxes including Social Security contribution to G.N.P.	Underdeveloped countries	Ratio of total taxes including Social Security contribution to G.N.P.
United States	28.8	India	11.6
Canada	29.9	Korea	11.8
Japan	18.8	Brazil	24.6
Belgium	32.3	Jamaica	16.9
Denmark	32.8	Guyana	20.6
France	36.8	Ecuador	15.8
Germany	34.9	Costa Rica	14.7
Netherlands	36.8	Indonesia	7.5
Sweden	40.7	Peru	15.3
United Kingdom	32.6	Colombia	11.5
Average for all countries reported	31.9	Average for all countries reported	14.8

Source: Raja J. Chelliah, "Trends in Taxation in Developing Countries," *International Monetary Fund Staff Papers,* 18, no. 2 (July 1971), 321, 324.

The tax bases in developing countries determine, essentially, the tax structure.[10] Lotz and Morss focus on data from which two significant conclusions have been drawn:

1. Revenue collected from the corporate income tax depends on the openness of the economy and is particularly related to the importance of oil and mineral industries as a proportion of total exports. These industries offer a concentrated source for taxation, are politically easier to tax because such tax rates are usually paid by foreigners and are frequently very profitable.

2. Sales taxes, stamp duties, and social security taxes are closely related to

9. Ibid.
10. Henry H. Henrichs, *A General Theory of Tax Structure Change During Economic Development* (Cambridge: Harvard Law School, 1966).

the degree of monetization of an economy, as distinct from its level of per capita income. These taxes are not self-assessed and so do not require literacy. They have been found to be important new taxes in developing countries.

These data indicate ample flexibility in tax policies enabling greater revenues to flow to the public sector as economic development advances and accelerates. This in turn depends upon how well developing countries can learn, adapt to, and adopt those policies which assure that resources are developed and utilized efficiently. That is, in a world where knowledge is highly mobile and available, "Can developing countries plow as well as they know how to plow?" Can tax policies encourage and guide economic development and assure a broadening of the economic base so that all involved in economic endeavor can share in the fruits of economic growth?

Once the goals, design, and style of economic growth are programmed by a developing country the methodology of doing the job becomes important. How does a nation guide all economically usable resources into the economic game being played so that the general welfare may be advanced?

1. The oligarchy that controls the capital wealth and land of the nation must be convinced that growth and advance in the general welfare is in their own best interest also.

2. The trod-upon masses, largely illiterate, unskilled, and unmotivated must be convinced that they can participate in the economic gain.

3. The shift to a more productive, industrialized, urbanized, and monetized economy leads to greater exercise of individual freedom of action, a more flexible system of allocating and utilizing resources in their most effective use, and a means of measuring the effectiveness of resource allocation.

THE PROPERTY TAX

The premise established here pinpoints the public sector's responsibility to organize the environment for economic endeavor. This is, in its essence, spelling out the rules of the economic game to be played. The second function in the established premise relates to public investment flows into capital base and human resource development that is the infrastructure. It is upon this economic base (infrastructure) that the private sector innovates and builds viable market oriented endeavors. The particular production mix—of land, labor, and capital and the subsequent assorted mix of diverse goods and services produced—is largely a function of the distribution of income among various segments of the population, the degree of monetization, the efficiency of markets and cultural political decisions.

A tax on land as a tax on property is a tax on wealth. Wealth in concentrated holdings is economic and political power which at first glance, would oppose

taxes on land. However, resource value in a market economy relates directly
to its use in the economic process and capitalization of the new return earned.
The productivity of land, depending upon the intensity of its use, relates to
how effectively the resource is engaged in productive economic activity. This,
in turn, reflects how accessible the land is to market production and distribution centers and how efficient the market functions in the developing economy.
Accessibility is no longer a matter of miles as much as it is a matter of time and
ease of access. The more accessible, the more involved in economic endeavor,
the more productive land becomes.

It seems completely safe to speculate that the increase in value of land will
tend to far outpace the costs incurred in bringing land resources into the economic game by improving accessibility. Taxes on land to finance a network of
roads giving access to markets promise to be an investment with a significant
return to land owner interests. Concomitantly, land taxes that contribute toward watershed conservation developments which tend to upgrade land areas,
irrigation projects, airport development—all of which improve accessibility and
productivity—offer payoff potentials which equal or exceed the development
costs incurred.

A land tax as a tax on wealth may also contribute to the motivation of
large land owners to make economic use of land. Land in its raw state grants
status and prestige to its owner. Such land, however, creates no money income.
A tax on the privilege of holding land, if sufficiently significant, will tend (1)
to encourage land owners to put their land to work in economic production
efforts, or (2) to force the dissolution of huge land holdings into smaller holdings and into the hands of enterprising men who will engage the land in economic endeavor. Such a land tax can effectively terminate long-term speculative holding of idle land holdings on the general assumption that some time in
the future the value will rise.

A tax on land imposed to either (1) force the resource into economic
production processes, or (2) force the dissolution of large holdings into smaller
units and encourage ownership by enterprising men who are economically
involved in market processes will almost assuredly be opposed by the landed
oligarchy. On the other hand, in the great transformation ongoing around us
in every corner and facet of life on an increasingly smaller planet, the masses
of the people who are hungry, deprived, and without human honor or dignity
are gaining a voice and a special claim on resources that can be used to improve
their standards of work and life styles. Their claims are being articulated and
heard. The transistor radio has initiated a broad awakening among a heretofore
sleeping and quiescent farm population. An articulation of those measures that
will remedy privation and absence of human dignity fills both the airways and
the written media. "The property tax classification . . . includes urban and
rural real estate taxes, land taxes, property transfer taxes, and all taxes on

motor vehicles." In the sentence that follows the importance of the property tax seems diminished: "Taxes on property are here combined with poll and personal taxes and all taxes that are not classified."

However, Bahl's final sentence in the paragraph clearly lays the problem of administering a property tax on the line. *"Because there seems no preferable, measurable alternative, total income is assumed to be the base of taxes on property"* (emphasis added).[11]

Bahl's conclusion aids analysis. Capital, a nebulous concept, need not be defined here as a precise measureable tax base. Instead we can procede from a tax on land as a means of facilitating its more efficient use as an economic, productive resource to a broader context of a tax on property, combining land and capital.

Without documenting the Ricardian land rent formula, it is clear that John Stuart Mill, who became President of the English Land Tenure Reform Association, preempted Henry George and provides the basis for the case presented here.

> Now this is actually the case with rent. The ordinary process of a society which increases in wealth, is at all times tending to augment the income of landlords; to give them both a greater amount and a greater proportion of the wealth of the community, independently of any trouble or outlay incurred by themselves. They grow richer, as it were, in their sleep, without working, risking, or economizing.[12]

The Land-Tenure Reform Association resolved:

> To claim for the benefit of the State, the Interception by Taxation of the Future Unearned Increase of the Rent of Land (so far as same can be ascertained), or a great part of that increase, which is continually taking place without any effort or outlay by the proprietors, merely through the growth of population and wealth; reserving to owners the option of relinquishing their property to the State, at the market value which it may have acquired at the time when this proposal may be adopted by the Legislature.[13]

Henry George thoroughly understood Ricardian doctrine and Mill's treatise. He argued for nationalization, not of land, but of the rent accruing to the land. Schumpeter legitimatizes the George thesis: "The proposal itself . . . though vitiated by association with the untenable theory that the phenomenon of poverty is entirely due to the absorption of all surpluses by the rent of land, is not *economically* unsound, except that it involves an unwarranted optimism

11. Roy W. Bahl, "A Representative Tax System Approach to Measuring Tax Effort in Developing Countries," *International Monetary Fund Staff Papers,* 19 (March 1972), 99.

12. Frances A. Walker, *Political Economy* (New York: Henry Holt and Company, 1888), p. 409.

13. Ibid., p. 414.

concerning the yield of such a tax. In any case, it should not be put down as nonsense."[14]

Henry George was not blinded by any misunderstanding or do-gooder prejudice. His competence as an economist is demonstrated by his care to enunciate policies designed to protect the efficiency of markets and the private enterprising system. Creativity, innovation, and entrepreneurial motivation are dampened not at all—the enterpriser who produces, who advances the general welfare, gains. There would be no inequitable deprivations through delimiting the benefits of ownership. The tax imposed on property, instead, would tax the increase of wealth, created by circumstances of social change, to the use and benefit of society rather than letting unearned gains accrue to the added income and wealth of existing owners of land and capital resources.

CONCLUSION

The only logical conclusion from this analysis is that sound tax policies on property can contribute to the dynamism and viability of economic development. Similarly, formal academic education, vocational training, literacy training, and measures, for example, that add variety and meaning to peoples' life and work styles all contribute toward improved motivation, improved productivity, and greater real income as production is enhanced.

Economic goals and education goals are interacting processes in a market-oriented economy. A self-sufficing growth process evolves from the interaction. As new knowledges and technologies are acquired and applied men tend to use their skills "to plow as well as they know how," and property taxation can both assist in making available the land to plow and the education required to plow better and to utilize the product to further the general welfare.

14. Joseph Schumpeter, *History of Economic Analysis* (New York: Oxford University Press, 1954), p. 865.

Conference Review Hour

Charles Waldauer: One of the problems apparent from our discussions is that we need some idea of the purposes or objectives of education.

We are discussing the financing of education, but until we know what the objectives are, we can't say much about the most proper ways of financing. If we think of education as a method for redistributing income or wealth, must the financing of it in and of itself be appropriate to that objective? This relates to the issue of inputs and outputs in education.

Would you take some measure of student achievement as some sort of norm to shoot at and increase your financing to cope with those districts with very low student achievement? Would you ignore the per capita tax base as a measure of financing needs? (Of course, the tax base and student achievement are probably quite highly related.)

If the purpose is to transfer income and wealth, perhaps there are far more efficient ways to do this than through the educational system. It does seem to me that objectives of education are never spelled out very well; until we do this, we run into problems talking about the financing of it.

Morris Beck: Just to start a little controversy, I disagree strongly. I do not think this conference ought to spend an undue proportion of its time on the objectives of education or the measurement of educational output or achievement. This is a proper field for the specialists and experts in the field of education. I think our task is to consider alternative ways of financing public schools, to consider the effects of using the local property tax versus some combination of local and state financing.

The point is often made that most state school aid formulas provide for minimum aid to the wealthy districts. I suspect that practically every state formula does contain such a provision. In New Jersey, I think the minimum is about $110 per pupil plus an additional $25 that was thrown into the pot last year, which gives the wealthy district, such as Teterboro with $75,000,000 of taxable base per pupil, about half as much in state aid as the city of Newark,

63

which has perhaps a few thousand dollars of property tax base per pupil.

I fail to see how this practice accomplishes an efficient allocation of resources. To me minimum aid is the result of pure politics. The affluent districts in New Jersay get $110 simply because the legislature is unwilling to leave them out of the distribution.

Charles Waldauer: Teterboro is a special example (see chap. 13). Of course there are many instances where comparatively rich districts pick up a sizeable amount of aid under this program. Nevertheless there is a good economic justification for some minimum amount of aid flowing down from either federal or state to local levels to take into account the existence of spillovers in educational costs and benefits.

If you leave school financing on a strictly local basis, spillover benefits may be ignored. The minimum amounts involved may be far in excess of what could be justified by any empirical evidence of the spillovers; however, conceptually, as long as one accepts their existence and one wishes an efficient allocation of resources, you can justify some federal and state aid down to local levels.

William Vickrey: If you are going to take spillovers into account, you should take them into account in a manner which will induce a proper response. A flat grant which is not dependent upon any extra effort by the locality is merely a fiscal transfer to the locality and has no effect in increasing efficiency. It doesn't reduce the price of a marginal increment of education to the community as it would if there were some sort of a matching element in it. However, fundamentally, while I find the concept of spillover is very attractive, it is very difficult to live with. If you look at the case of Delaware or the case of California from the federal view, the spillover element in Delaware is relatively very much greater than it is in California.

How can you develop a federal formula that will appropriately induce Delaware to increase its educational effort because of its spillouts, and not overstimulate California in terms of its spillouts? Comparably, if you turn to a state formula, how can you do this for Levittown on the one hand, and New York City on the other? It is a very intangible theory on which to base a grant system.

Noel Edelson: I thought Bill Vickrey, and perhaps Craig Stubblebine, would have said that the problem of regional spillovers is a complete red herring. I would have thought the spillover effects of $2,000 per pupil per year are very close to zero. (See chap. 16.)

I do not mean that if we didn't have an education system, no one could read or write. However, there are still externalities or spillover effects even at our current rate of expenditure. The idea of relative migration rates having any kind of significance leaves me completely cold.

Eli Schwartz: I should like to return for a moment to a more technical aspect of Morris Beck's problem. A flat per capita grant can have some effect towards equalization. Of course not so much so as a differential grant. It all depends on the tax base used.

Assume that you had a highly progressive state income tax, which fell across all districts rich and poor, and that you gave back to each district a flat amount—all of them, rich or poor—you would still get some net redistribution. You would have given the rich district less than you collected in taxes per capita, and you have given the poor district more. Therefore it is not true that a flat grant has no redistributive effects. It is simply not as effective, perhaps, as one that has a greater equalization formula built into it.

Seymour Sacks: I was going to suggest that this whole problem is associated not with the types of spillover, but with the political process.

The major reason for giving flat grants is to get the rich districts to participate in the changing of the pot by giving them back something in return. It may fall short on equity grounds. Any analysis of practically any state will show that the Teterboros would do much better without any aid program at all.

The interesting thing, of course, is not the Teterboro type situation; it certainly is the Scarsdale situation. What is fascinating about Scarsdale is that Scarsdale leads the parade to Albany to increase state aid. Without really going through the logic, they are the principle contributors to the increased state aid, they would do much better in not sharing it at all. However, the way the political process adjusts is by giving them a little of the additional money.

Daniel Fusfeld: I would like to get back to Morris Beck's first issue. He said we shouldn't concern ourselves with the outputs, but rather with the types of inputs that are available. That is the question of whether we finance a given amount of education in one way or another. However, it does seem to me that, as economists, we do have a responsibility to the people who are spending the money to tell them whether they are going to get anything for what they spend or not.

If the money we spend on education is wasted, then it seems to me the educators ought to be told by the economists that that is the case. Let me give you a couple of examples (for which I will probably be attacked), but I have put a couple of graduate students to work on studying the benefits from education. One bit of research is on pupil achievement levels related to the amount spent. Apparently there is no relation.

The least important factor in determining student achievement in school is the amount spent on education. This is also the finding of the Coleman report. Almost all of the serious studies of the effects of expenditures on education show that amount spent is, of all the factors, the least important.

In another area, I have someone at work on a doctoral dissertation on the question of the relationship between the amount of education and subsequent income earned. Surprisingly, there is only one occupational level in which amount of education is the most important determinant of income, and that is for our level: managerial, professional, and technical. Go down the occupational scale, and it's a lot more important if a man is a member of the teamsters union or building trades union. Further down the line, we ought to educate people not to be born black or Chicano. There are a wide variety of other factors that dominate the income earning capabilities down at the bottom of the occupational levels; the best thing you can say is that the amount of education is randomly distributed with respect to income. Perhaps as economists we should look at the value of the output that we produce with education, and whether we ought to be putting any resources into it at all.

Daniel Holland: However, when we do look at the value of educational output, we ought to look at all the output and all the values, including the intangible ones. We sometimes talk as if the ability to read a good book is not an output worth creating. I haven't heard it mentioned this morning. People who have some education are more likely to enjoy a good book than people who haven't; that may be worth investing in from some para-parental point of view, which is, of course, currently unfashionable. However, we know that at the age of 40 we will enjoy being able to read, even though at the age of 6 the child is not certain he even wants to do it.

Daniel Fusfeld: It still seems to me that we really ought to make some studies of what we get for the money we spend.

Paul Downing: I would like to put an addendum to a comment by Bill Vickrey. I have been disturbed by the lack of general consensus on what the economics of education is. I perceive it, perhaps, as being three things. One is the private benefit. One is a spillout when somebody who has benefited by a community financed education moves out, and the other falls under the general term of externality.[1]

Bill Vickrey suggests that we need to worry about spillouts and that we should make our financing redistribution scheme such that it will affect marginal decisions and equate spillout benefits. I would suggest that even if nobody ever moved out of the district, there is still a financing issue and an allocative efficiency issue, and these relate to the financing scheme we employ.

Using financing to develop allocative efficiency, I would suggest a user charge for those who benefit directly (parents and children) and a general tax placed on the rest of the local community who reap the externalities; that is, the local community and also the rest of the country.

Ferdinand Schoettle: I want to speak to the flat grant at the state level from a lawyer's point of view as it falls under the Equal Protection clause of the 14th

1. Editor's note: The terms "spillout," "spillover," and "externality" refer to benefits or disutilities to persons and resources not directly participating in the activity.

Amendment. I cannot believe that as long as the state has created a situation where there are disparities of opportunity because of the fiscal base in financing equal school systems, that the flat grant serves a rational purpose.

No one here has argued that it serves a rational educational purpose. They have centered on its political expediency. My own guess is if the Supreme Court does anything, it is going to strike down the flat grant. I don't think an argument which goes: "Well, yes, it is unfair to give Scarsdale money while there are children in real deprivation in New York City, but we needed to do it to get Scarsdale to go along politically," is likely to be accepted by the justices of the Supreme Court.

William Oakland: I want to speak on the flat grant issue. It has been pointed out that it does have a redistributive impact, if nothing else—and that is desirable. I want to raise the question as to whether or not we really want to redistribute income among regions, or whether we want to redistribute income among people. Educational grants are a fairly inefficient way of redistributing income, because there are rich people in virtually every district.

Also, I just don't understand the concepts of spillouts occurring when a man leaves an education district. When he was being educated the benefits are supported by the child's parents and accrue to the child. When he moves out, they go with him. I suppose one might argue, "Well, now he is a better citizen somewhere else"; however, at the margin, this kind of spillout must be zero from any practical standpoint.

Finally, I want to question the studies that show that the level of educational expenditure has no impact on performance. I might agree that expenditures are a necessary, but not a sufficient condition in educating a person. Certainly, however, you wouldn't want to go as far as someone suggested: abolishing the financing of education because it's useless from an economic point of view. It seems to me we have to put resources into education. Over the range of variation in which we observe educational expenditures, it may be that other factors are more important. It does not say that expenditure levels are not important. I fail to be convinced by studies which seem to indicate this.

William Vickrey: The issue of geographic spillout may be presented in its most extreme form. Suppose you have a community, for example, such as existed in the early days of Levittown, where you have a large number of children and tremendous school expenditure and no immediate tax-paying ability. Conceptually, at any rate, you have a community that is in the business of raising and educating children, and then these children when educated go elsewhere and become earners elsewhere, and the tax base that they produce becomes unavailable to the original community.

It has been argued that the South generally used to be in this position. They spent a large sum of money educating their children who eventually came North and paid the taxes which resulted from their increased earning power to a jurisdiction which had made no investment in their education. The South thereby lost the taxes that would have been paid by them as adults and which would have contributed eventually to the repayment of their education.

The trouble is that we don't really have an effective way of enabling people to borrow against their future prospects in order to pay for the investment in their education.

Morris Beck: Let me reply briefly to Dan Fusfeld on the importance of studying the economic effects of education and the benefits from educational expenditures. This is an extremely important topic, but the basic theme of this conference is the finance of education. I think some other time we can discuss other topics.

The matter of flat grants is extremely important. I think that Mr. Schoettle put his finger on the Constitutional issue. Namely, flat grants at a time when there are numerous school districts that cannot provide a minimum standard of education, are unwise and unconstitutional.

The New Jersey court decision clearly points to the flat grant as the culprit— the offending item in the present system of school aid. I suspect this is true elsewhere; the California decision makes the provision of a flat grant, a minimum aid to wealthy districts, the main offending item.

The idea of making flat grants for the purpose of smoothing the political processes—satisfying Scarsdale, Great Neck, and other affluent districts so that they, too, are getting some of the pot, some of the funds—is, it seems to me, no longer valid.

Eli Schwartz: I should like to go back again to the straight grant. Perhaps I am only taking the devil's advocate position here. However, to argue that a flat grant is absolutely unconstitutional is to argue that rich people are not entitled to any public goods at all. It is to argue that even if there is an overall broad based tax, rich people are not entitled to get anything back for their taxes; presumably they could and should pay for all services themselves. I might admit that the flat grant is not the most effective way of getting redistribution. However, suppose you started out without a property tax base and used a state sales tax or an income tax to finance education. If you redistributed the funds to the underlying areas on a flat basis, you would certainly have redistribution. You would certainly be getting more revenue from the richer areas than you gave back to them per capita. I don't see that this is particularly unconstitutional or anything of the sort.

Something else might be said about the property tax and its functions. The property tax might be classified as essentially a benefit-received tax. Since the property tax is generally spent on local goods and service, it improves the value of local properties. Possibly the homeowner completely recoups the property tax in services provided by the local area.

The question of the use of the property tax for educational purposes is a

little more sticky. Here the externalities may be very broad, and our desires to
have this particular public good distributed very evenly may be very strong.
This makes the property tax not quite the best base for the support of education. Certainly for fire protection, for police protection, and for any number
of other items the tax may be perfectly justified as a quid pro quo tax.

Charles Waldauer: I want to respond to the comments that spillovers may
not be important. As Bill Vickrey pointed out much more eloquently than I
could, there is substantial importance in geographic spillovers. There are both
benefits and costs involved. There are economic costs if poorly educated
people migrate in bringing with them many social problems—crime, etc. Every
large city can show an example of this.

Part of the problem arises out of the poor school system we have had in
the South in the past. One aggregate of costs flowed out, but also some benefits did because some of the better educated people moved out. If the financing was local, the area lost the expected economic benefits when well-educated
people moved out.

Other areas may also pick up the economic and other costs entailed by
poor levels of education if migrants come from these regions. There is no way
to prevent people from migrating. Spillovers may go both ways, but I can't
argue that the net is large enough to justify large amounts of grants.

Robert Schoeplein: I should like to respond to Daniel Fusfeld and Paul
Downing on the general discussion whether some energy should be devoted to
the study of spillouts.

I want to respond somewhat negatively, although I have no objections to
the assignment of the topic as a doctoral dissertation. My feeling is that spillouts, as a theoretical economic concept, have a market transaction orientation.
However, even if wealth were distributed optimally, consumers still would not
acknowledge or compute spillout effects. Consequently, we would not have an
optimum allocation of resources. Therefore, through public action, we affect
relative prices to reflect spillouts. However, it seems to me that the spillout
problem is the cart and that the horse is the prefacing phrase: "If wealth were
distributed optimally." Indeed in the *Serrano* decision, the court's opinion
held that in fact it is not on the education side of the fence that the argument
rests, but rather on the wealth or financing side. From my own point of view,
this conference should continue to discuss the wealth redistribution aspect of
school finance, rather than to explore considerations of spillouts.

Noel Edelson: Just a brief response to Charles Waldauer's comment. It
seems to me the spillout problem has a distorting effect on current expenditures for education. There may be a justifiable problem, but only if there is a
persistent drain in one direction. If it is simply a case of losing some current
people but gaining others, it does not appear to me that there is a persistent
bias.

I hope to try to bring out tomorrow that there is a good, sound, theoretical reason to argue that if you have a proper tax, there will be no bias whatsoever in voting procedures for financing education even with people leaving districts.

On the other hand some claim that there is a bias in the other direction: if by voting for bond issues (and assuming the future taxes to pay off the bond issue are not currently capitalized by a reduction in property values), there can be some shift of costs to future generations, there may be an incentive, a bias, towards current overspending.

Now I have a question which I would like to direct to our resident lawyer, Professor Schoettle. Some of the arguments you made on constitutional grounds suggest that perhaps a voucher scheme would be found unconstitutional.

If you distributed, by taxation, a voucher of equal value per child to all parents but allowed parents to supplement it privately if they so chose, could that not run afoul of the equal protection clause?

Ferdinand Schoettle: One other speaker has mentioned that. However, I think that it is only when one views the flat grant in connection with the existing scheme of funding education that one runs into difficulty. From the court's point of view, any system wherein the state gives an equal benefit to everybody in the state would be fine. However, the difficulty lies in the property tax system for funding education. Here is a system where the state allocates the tax base according to state laws in quite different arbitrary amounts to different school districts.

There isn't really, in my mind, a strong rational basis for that allocation, for saying that because some private decision-maker has decided to erect a structure where pupil A is defined to live, the state allows the tax money for A's education and not for B's.

If you add a flat grant on top of the existing state created inequality, of course you run into objections. However, I think this is an objection which would not be shared by a newly started program.

However, I have my own problem—economists have been using the terms spillover and spillout. From the context, I take it, you mean by spillout somebody who physically moves out of the area or jurisdiction which has made the decision to provide the goods, and by spillover you mean the benefit that flows to nonconsumers of the public good.

From this point of view, I was impressed with the essay on Russia and the historical study of Arthur Lynn. Apparently education is a good that has always been collectively provided, and almost every civilized society has decided there are benefits to nonusers.

I would suggest in the United States today, that if we in this room could absolutely allocate incomes evenly and, therefore, had no redistributional reason for education and if you took a vote among us, we probably would still decide for some reason that public education is a good idea. We are after all in a society which has opted for universal education since the Northwest Ordinance and Thomas Jefferson. It would seem that the world culture at the moment has resolved this issue in favor of the collective good.

W. Craig Stubblebine: The only question which we are raising here is the problem of the failure to distinguish between total value of spillouts and the spillouts at the margin. What is the evidence that at the margins the spillouts are so significant that they ought to be collectivized without changing prices at the margin?

The *Serrano* v. *Priest* decision in no sense discussed anything that might be called the optimal distribution of wealth. It made the mere observation that the tax base was distributed among the districts in such a way as to create unequal opportunities for access.

We have gotten all wrapped up in this flat grant; I am not certain what the court's view on it might be, but it is clear that a flat grant system redistributes from the rich to the poor, period. The flat grant doesn't affect opportunity at the margin, which is what the courts have been looking at.

Paul Downing: A redistribution of wealth may not affect marginal equivalents in the allocative efficiency sense. You can have something like an "optimal distribution" and still not have it lead to optimal allocative efficiency.

John Shannon: One of the perennial problems in school finance is that we are attempting to reconcile competing values. We have a widely held political value that the local school district should be allowed a substantial element of fiscal control, both horizontal and vertical, with respect to resources.

Then we have a kind of equity goal, a fairness goal, that might be best put in a negative way. We don't want children to be badly shortchanged on the resource side, nor do we want communities to be forced to carry extraordinary tax burdens in order to meet minimal requirements.

Increasingly we also have an accountability or efficiency goal. We want to be reassured that the dollars of expenditure make some difference. It is the juggling and the balancing of these political, these equity, and these efficiency objectives, keeping them in some kind of tolerable alignment, that creates problems for policy-makers.

Seymour Sacks: The question I should like to pose is this. Suppose New York City has a tax rate of 16 mills. Scarsdale has a 26 mill tax rate. Scarsdale receives a flat grant from the state. How do the courts come along and tell Scarsdale that it is supposed to lose its flat grant when practically every other school district in the state has a lower tax rate than it? For the sake of argument, assume that Scarsdale has the highest tax rate in the state—how do you take away its flat grant when it has, in effect, made the strongest tax effort?

Ferdinand Schoettle: I shall try to explain the Equal Protection clause. It says, in effect, that when the government discriminates among people (which it has to do all the time) and one who has been discriminated against comes into court, that that person is entitled to a rational explanation.

There are some rational reasons such as race that are not accepted. The government can't reply: "We have discriminated against you because of your race." A typical school finance case arises from a plaintiff in a poor school district who states that the state is distributing funds for education two ways. It is assigning the real property tax base in an arbitrary manner by drawing lines on the map, and it also has been distributing a pot of money at the state level. That plaintiff says: "The state has allocated a very low real property tax base to me, and on top of that it has allocated the state's pot of money all around the state in flat grants."

The plaintiff states: "There is no rational basis for allocating that money on flat grant to rich people while I, the plaintiff, am in this quite poor district."

The court is likely to listen to that argument, and it will require an explanation. Of course, if the money at the state level were allocated on an efficiency model, the state could say: "We give the smartest people the most money because we think that is the way to increase the skills in society. It is an accidental effect that this results in the wealthy families consuming most of the educational dollars." I am not saying that could not be a rational model.

Seymour Sacks: I think you are taking Baldwin Park in California as an example of a district which has a distinctly high tax rate but is poor. However, if you had another place, which was rich but had a high tax rate, shouldn't the question arise of equalizing the tax rates before you take away the grant? Does the court absolutely assume that a place with a very low tax rate has the right and option to a low tax rate without taking that into account?

Have the courts simply ignored the differences in tax rates as though they were absolutely irrelevant?

Ferdinand Schoettle: No. Not at all.

Seymour Sacks: Well then, give me a case.

Ferdinand Schoettle: What you are saying is that because the rich district has a higher rate, it is entitled to as much money from the state as a poor district that has a lower one. Why?

Seymour Sacks: Because until the point where the rates are equal, you can't say there is a discrimination against the poor district.

Ferdinand Schoettle: What I am saying is that what counts is the test of the state's purpose for inducing people to adopt a higher tax rate. The court could say it is rational for the state formula to be "for each 10 mills of effort, we will give you x hundred dollars." That would be rational because it would be tied to taxes. The current system isn't tied to the rational purpose of inducing people to tax themselves at a high rate.

Daniel Holland: Thank you. If we end on a note of rationality in this exchange, we should be pleased.

Harvey Brazer: A few minutes ago it was suggested that we would agree that elementary and secondary education is a collective good. I think that the Northwest Ordinance, Thomas Jefferson, the lawyers who sit on the supreme courts in the various states, and Ferdinand Schoettle notwithstanding, the economist has an impossible time defining elementary and secondary education as a collective or social good.

The one thing that education does not do is to conform with any economist's definition, that I am acquainted with, of a collective or social or public good.

A few years ago, economists would have called it a merit good or, better still, a good satisfying a merit want. In more recent, more sensible analysis, they have backed down quite considerably.

Daniel Holland: Is there a dialogue on this point? What does the economist call it? Does he exclude education from the public good category because exclusion is possible?

Harvey Brazer: I don't know that he calls it anything other than, perhaps, what I might call it. It seems to me that that is what we have been calling it in every discussion, and that is a mechanism through which we can achieve some redistribution of income by means of transfers in kind of the good that we call education.[2]

Richard Rossmiller: I have a couple of comments: one on the matter of expenditure versus achievement. I think most of the research, if not all of it, that has been done in this area has been exceedingly simplistic.

Before you can look at the relationship between expenditures and any rough measure of achievement of any kind, it seems to me you would have to look at the structure of the expenditures. For what and how were they arranged? What did they buy? How was the program put together?

Just another comment. In most of the educational literature, at least of any state that has a strong system of local school districts, people have the conception, real or not, that local control is inseparable from a substantial local tax. I would like to hear some comments at some point about whether there should be a local tax. Should education be financed to any extent by local expenditures?

Is it possible to separate certain kinds of decisions that have to do with education from the level of government that provides the financing?

Robert Schoeplein: With a room full of people who represent varying interests, we are bound to have some problems with terminology, and Professor

2. Editor's note: Not every economist would agree that there are no externalities (i.e., collective benefits) arising from a program of universal education.

Schoettle (as a lawyer), I am pleased that you are with us. The California Supreme Court did indeed use the term "wealth" in its decision; however, it used wealth, as I read it, as a synonym for real property resources.

The court, as I see it, says that there is a maldistribution of financial resources if school districts are forced to rely on local real property resources as a principal source of school finance.

William Oakland: Perhaps there are two issues that we should distinguish, and, perhaps, we would not argue so much about them.

One is that currently there exists an inequity because of an unequal distribution of industrial and commercial wealth across states. People are assigned different shares of that wealth to finance their education. It was suggested earlier that state-wide taxation or maybe national taxation only of business property would be a preferred basis for distributing those proceeds.

Second is the somewhat weaker proposition that an inequity exists because there is an unequal distribution of residential wealth. Residential property is rather highly correlated with income: this means essentially that there is inequity because there is an unequal distribution of income.

To argue that people can't use their greater wealth to spend it in many different ways, including improving the education of their children as they would like, seems to me to tackle the redistributive problem at the educational end; that is to tackle the wrong end. That has also been recognized. Let's agree that industrial wealth should not be in the local tax base; then we can decide whether or not inequities would still remain in the system.

Part II
Statewide Approaches

6 John Riew

Finance of Education with a Statewide Land Tax

The property tax has been on the defense for some time as the primary source of local revenue and especially as the financier of education. The sentiment against the tax in recent years has been reflected in numerous voter rejections in school construction bond issues and increases in substitute revenue sources.[1] Support for recent court rulings on school finance among large segments of the population can be attributed in part to the general resentment of the property tax per se or its rising levies apart from the public awareness of the basic problem of inequalities in educational opportunity.

In spite of the general belief that the property tax is overworked and of the hope that new revenue sources can be found for school finance, it appears that we are far from being able to relinquish the property tax as a major supporter of public education. According to an estimate of the National Education Association, the total expenditures for public schools in 1971-72 amounted to $46.8 billion. Of this amount, $19.0 billion represented state aids and $3.3 billion federal grants in aid. Localities provided $24.3 billion of which $23.0 billion came from property taxes.[2]

The author is greatly indebted to Mason Gaffney for his valuable suggestions. He wishes also to acknowledge helpful comments from John Shannon, Paul Downing, Elchanan Cohn, and Archie Buckmiller. The work was facilitated by an excellent cooperation from the research staff of Department of Revenue of the State of Wisconsin.

1. According to a recent report, about half of the requests for school tax increase were rejected in 1970. In that year, roughly half of all school bond issues were also turned down, whereas more than 70 percent were approved during the 1958-66 period. See Charles L. Schultze, Edward R. Fried, Alice M. Rivlin, and Nancy H. Teeters, *Settling National Priorities: The 1973 Budget* (Washington, D.C.: Brookings Institution, 1972), p. 324.

2. See National Education Association, *Estimates of School Statistics, 1971-72,* Research Report 1971-R13 (Washington, D.C.: National Education Association, 1971), p. 5. The property tax portion of the local contribution was derived from an unpublished ACIR staff compilation.

Considering the magnitude of property tax contributions, a complete release of the tax from school finance responsibilities, favored in some quarters, would seem hardly feasible. The present level of aid commitments to localities[3] by state governments will not be easily expanded. With mounting pressure for additional funds for various unmet domestic needs, in welfare, housing, urban renewal, mass transits, environmental control, etc., the ability of the federal government to expand its commitment is also limited. Even with a new revenue source, such as a federal value added tax from which the administration reportedly seeks $12 billion to $13 billion, the current school levies on property are too large to replace, especially when we consider other competing claims for federal funds. Add to this situation the need for improving educational standards. The report of the President's Commission on School Finance shows that the costs of raising per pupil expenditures within each state up to approximately the 90th percentile (derived by arraying all pupils in the state by per pupil expenditure levels) for all states would have amounted to about $9 billion in the 1969-70 academic year.[4] This sum has probably grown to between $10 billion and $11 billion in 1972. Various aspects considered, it is most likely that the property tax will continue to bear a major part of the cost of public education for some time to come.

LAND TAX AND SCHOOL FINANCE

If we accept the proposition that the property tax is here to stay as a major source of support of public schools, the implied mandate is an obvious one which calls for improvement of the tax. Fulfilling this objective, it seems, would require institutional changes and operational improvements in property taxa-

3. State payments to local governments in the United States amounted to $32.6 billion in fiscal 1971. This sum was $15.8 billion above, or more than double, the 1966 total. The 1971 state payments to local governments in the aggregate constituted 33 percent of the states' general expenditures. See U.S. Bureau of Census, *State Government Finances in 1966,* pp. 28, 29, and *State Government Finances in 1971,* pp. 7, 38 (Washington, D.C.: Government Printing Office).

4. See President's Commission on School Finance, *Review of Existing State School Finance Programs,* Vol. 2, in *Documentation of Disparities in the Financing of Public Elementary and Secondary School Systems—by State,* a Commission Staff Report submitted to the President's Commission on School Finance (Washington, D.C.: Government Printing Office, 1972), p. 15. Actually the table presented in the report shows the amount of $8.8 billion as the cost of equalizing expenditures to the 95th percentile. But it was noted in the text that the top and bottom 5 percent were eliminated as atypical and that the 95th percentile is related to the remaining 90 percent of the total pupil enrollment. Thus, what was listed in the table as the "95th percentile" should be considered more accurately as approximately the 90th percentile for the entire pupil population.

tion. In the context of school finance, an institutional change which involves a partial shift in the hands, from local to state, that oversee the property tax would be extremely desirable. Such a change could be an important first step toward reducing great inequalities in educational opportunity between rich and poor areas.

The total shift of property tax to the state is unwarranted, however. For most cities in the United States, the property tax is still the primary revenue source and it will be reasonable to expect that the tax will remain as a major, if not the primary, source of local revenue even with tax reforms involving introduction of local income or sales taxes. If the state shares with the local government in the yield of the property tax, the question arises as to what specific parts of the tax the state and the local governments respectively should claim. The state, for instance, could seek a certain portion of the total tax dollar or a specific component of the tax base such as land apart from improvements as the domain over which it would claim its share.

With regard to school financing, a plausible case can be made for a state use of land tax. There are elements of externalities in both the benefits of public education and the value of land. As it was true in the time of Henry George it is still true that increment to land value accrues from social forces, ranging from highly visible ones, such as highways and expressways, parks, dams, and resource conservation projects, to less salient factors, such as zoning, tax system (the progressive income tax combined with the deductibility of mortgage payment, for instance), farm subsidies, increase in population, rising income, aggregate demand, etc. Wisconsin data covering much of the decade of the sixties show a high level of bouyancy of the land value in the rural as well as in the urban areas and reveal an interesting pattern of the land value behavior that can be related to differential social influences. The unique nature of land values enables us to see more easily the link between a tax on land and the support of education than the linkage between a tax on all-inclusive properties and education.

Here the argument is not put forward that a solution to the problem of financing schools should be found solely in improvement of property tax nor is it suggested that the externalities of public education can be most meaningfully related to the externalities affecting land value. It is simply pointed out that under the present circumstance where the property tax must continue its major role in education finance, a state levy of the tax is an important first step and that defining the state's domain primarily on land rests on a very plausible rationale.

A state-levied land tax, superimposed on the local property tax subject to the rule of uniform levy on land and improvements, would effectively lead to a situation where the aggregate tax rate on land is higher than on improvements.[5] One may suspect that local government, in deference to the added tax burden on land, might tend to assess land more generously than improvements. This in fact has reportedly been the case where the local government itself levied a higher rate on land, as in Pittsburgh. But a state levy, which is independent of local decisions and has no bearing on local revenues, is unlikely to affect the locality's traditional assessment practices.

Today's school finance controversy centers on the problem of financial difficulties as well as the question of inequalities. The scheme of a state land tax, along with other measures, is expected to help solve both of these problems. It will add to the resources channelled into schools and further the equality of educational opportunity. Few important questions remain, however. How would such a scheme of taxation score under the test of equity? Specifically, there is a long-held contention that a differentially heavy tax on land is inequitable because the land/improvement ratios vary among taxpayers. One also could question the revenue potential of a tax on land. The land, it has been argued, typically constitutes a relatively small part of the total value of real estate. The issues of equity and productivity both weigh heavily in our canons of taxation. The present paper addresses itself primarily to these two issues.

INTRAURBAN EQUITY

For a closer look at the problem, we propose to concentrate on a specific area, the Urban Area of Milwaukee, Wisconsin. In 1970 the ratio of the total value of land to the total value of improvements (values of taxable land and improvements as equalized by the state) for the city of Milwaukee was 38.3 percent while the average equivalent ratio for the 28 suburban municipalities was 39.8 percent.[6] Dividing the suburbs by function and income class, we find a pattern of the ratio variation concealed in the average.[7] As shown in Table

5. Use of a uniform, statewide land value tax for school purposes was envisaged earlier by Lindholm. Such a tax, it was suggested, is an appropriate source of revenue for public education and serves as an instrument promoting greater equality in educational opportunity. See Richard W. Lindholm, "Financing Public Education and the Property Taxes," *American Journal of Economics and Sociology,* 29, no. 1 (January 1970), pp. 44-45.

6. The Milwaukee Urban Area as defined by the Census Bureau in 1960 includes all 19 municipalities of Milwaukee County and 10 incorporated municipalities of the adjacent counties of Waukesha and Ozaukee.

7. The 29 municipalities are divided into the central city of Milwaukee, 5 balanced municipalities, 2 industrial municipalities, and 21 residential municipalities—the last being further divided into 6 high-income, 7 medium-income, and 8 low-income units. Classification by function is based on the ratio of business property to total property within each municipality. Thus, industrial municipalities are those in which total equalized value of business real properties constituted more than 60 percent of total real property in 1966, while balanced municipalities are those in which this ratio was between

6.1, the high-income suburbs carry the highest land/improvement (*L/I* here-after) ratio of 48 percent which compares with 41 percent for the medium-income suburbs and the lower ratios of 38 and 37 respectively of the central city and the low-income suburbs.[8] The industrial enclaves understandably have the lowest ratio of 28 percent.

The above figures suggest that under a special land tax the high-income taxpayers will typically bear a proportionately greater burden. But as we look into the *residential properties* alone, the *L/I* ratio disparities between residential suburbs and the municipalities in nonresidential categories are considerably narrowed. This is due to the fact that industrial properties scarce in residential suburbs are characterized by low *L/I* ratios. While in residential properties *L/I* ratio for high-income suburbs is still 48 percent, the ratio for the central city is a much closer one of 43 percent. The low-income suburbs trail the rest with the lowest ratio of 36 percent.

Table 6.1–Mean Land/Improvement Ratios[a] among Types of Municipalities in the Urban Area of Milwaukee, 1970

Municipality type	Total real estate	Residential real estate
Central city	38.3%	42.7%
Balanced	34.3	41.8
Industrial	28.4	44.1
Residential		
High-income	47.6	48.0
Medium-income	41.3	40.7
Low-income	36.7	36.3

[a]The unweighted means of the average for individual municipalities.

Sources: The figures were computed from the data available in the *County District Value Card 1970* (Madison: Wisconsin Dept. of Revenue 1970), which record state-equalized values of real estate by use and by municipality.

These figures are the averages and do not reveal the ratio variation among individual property owners, but the general pattern points to a positive correlation between the *L/I* ratio and the level of income. Thus, difference in the *L/I*

---

40 and 60 percent. Classification by income of residential units was based on the level of average adjusted gross income per tax return as reported to the Wisconsin Department of Revenue.

8. Our figures lend support to the earlier findings that the share of land in real estate tends to rise with value of holdings. See President's Commission on Urban Housing, *Report on Urban Housing* (Washington, D.C.: Government Printing Office, 1968), and Mason Gaffney, "Land Speculation," (Ph.D. diss., University of California, 1956), pp. 210-17.

ratio would cause, under a land tax, a bias against the high income and one may argue that the tax has a progressive quality.

Moreover, the "disadvantage" associated with large landholding should be considered along with the blessings of land ownership. Between 1962 and 1970, the increase in land value was a phenomenal 98 percent for the taxable land in the state of Wisconsin as a whole. The consumer prices during that period rose by 28.4 percent and the wholesale prices by 16.5 percent. Within the Milwaukee Urban Area, the land value rose by 44 percent in the central city, 97 percent in the suburbs within Milwaukee County, and 157 percent in the suburbs outside the county. The secular centrifugal trend accelerated by the large investment in expressways during the sixties should have contributed greatly to the larger value increase in the outlying areas. In the five selected urban counties of Wisconsin, which respectively contain the cities of Milwaukee, Madison, Racine, Kenosha, and Green Bay (the five largest cities of the state), the average land value increase during the same period was 85 percent in the central cities and 133 percent in the counties outside the cities.

Granted that there may be certain grievous cases of hardship under a special land tax, the greater cause of equity seems to demand a measure that claims a share in the fruit of collective social activities and externalities.

When a tax is levied for specific purpose, it should be noted, the propriety of the tax must be measured not only on its own merits but on the use to which the yield is placed. Recent research conducted on the Milwaukee Urban Area shows that under the Wisconsin school aid system the per pupil aid received by the central city of Milwaukee (which ranks among the lowest in per capita income and property valuation) was even less than the average per pupil aid received by many of its *high-income* neighbor municipalities.[9] The major reason for this perverse disparity was traced to the aid formula which used *per pupil* valuation as the measure of a community's ability to finance education. Though low in *per capita* property valuation, the central city, with its low-ratio school-age population, was placed among the group of municipalities with high *per pupil* valuation, thus qualifying for the low amount of school aid. In 1969, seven other states—Massachusetts, Michigan, New York, Pennsylvania, Rhode Island, Iowa, and Colorado—used market value per pupil as a major determinant in distributing funds to local school districts.[10] Recommending a substitute measure is beyond the scope of this paper, but the use of *per pupil* valuation as the measure of a community's ability to finance education neglects the fact that public functions of a community are not limited to education and that costs of

9. John Riew, "State Aid for Public Schools and Metropolitan Finance," *Land Economics*, 46, no. 3 (August 1970), pp. 297-304.

10. See Thomas L. Johns. ed., *Public School Finance Program, 1968-69* (Washington, D.C.: Office of Education, U.S. Department of Health, Education, and Welfare, 1969), pp. 2-329.

supporting these other functions typically bear no relationship to pupil populations. Use of per pupil valuation (or per pupil income for that matter) would be appropriate when public education is the only function of the local government.[11]

URBAN-RURAL EQUITY

The more important debate on the issue of equity involving a land tax concerns urban-rural comparison inasmuch as L/I ratios are expected to vary widely between urban and rural areas. For our analysis, we have selected the 9 most rural counties out of the total of 72 counties in Wisconsin (the farm land value exceeding ¾ of the total taxable land in each case). For these rural counties, the average L/I ratio in 1970 was 79 percent (unweighted mean of the averages of individual counties, the median being 65 percent) in contrast to 39 percent for the Milwaukee Urban Area and 37 percent for the five urban counties referred to earlier.

Thus, solely on the basis of disparities in the relative land holdings, a land tax may seem unduly penalizing to the farm segment. Some qualifications are in order, however. First, there are some indications that land is substantially underassessed (even in terms of equalized values) relative to improvements, especially in urban areas.[12] Moreover, the present assessment procedures in Wisconsin call for inclusion of improvements such as fence, irrigation works, etc., in land value. When various improvements (primarily visible ones) are separated from land value as they should be, the land component will be expected to fall further for the farm segment.

Secondly, higher L/I ratios are not an indication wholly adverse to farm land owners. As shown in Table 6.2, the highest L/I ratios are found in the three counties (Green, Iowa, and LaFayette) that lie near the rapidly growing high-income urban area of Madison, the state capital. The increase in the value

11. In the interest of giving more aid to poor school districts, the widespread use of "flat" aids (to which all well-to-do districts are entitled) might be eliminated. The larger the amount of flat aid, the lesser the fund available for the needy school districts. The study of the Wisconsin system cited above shows that the flat aid in that state, as it affected the Urban Area of Milwaukee, represented as much as 45 percent of the average school aid per pupil for the whole area (see Riew, "State Aid for Public Schools and Metropolitan Finance," p. 303). It should be pointed out that in the 1968-69 academic year all but six states in the nation had a flat grant of one sort or another incorporated in their school aids (see Johns, *Public School Finance Program*).

12. For a recent survey involving the city of Milwaukee that reveals a systematic relative underassessment of land value and a general discussion of the factors underlying such an underassessment, see Mason Gaffney, "Adequacy of Land as a Tax Base," in *The Assessment of Land Value*, Daniel M. Holland, ed. (University of Wisconsin Press, 1970), pp. 157-212, esp. pp. 173-80.

Table 6.2–Ratios of Agricultural Land Value to Total Land Values, Ratios of Land
Values to Improvement Values, Percent Increase in Land Values, 1962-70,
and Per Capita Land Values, 1970, for Nine Most Rural Counties in Wisconsin

County	Ratio of agricultural land to total land	Ratio of land to improvement	Increase in land value 1962-70	Per capita land value
Buffalo	81.5%	64.6%	68.6%	$1,804
Clark	85.0	55.2	41.9	1,454
Grant	81.5	64.8	51.4	2,025
Green	80.9	80.7	108.5	3,433
Iowa	91.0	122.2	97.0	3,626
La Fayette	93.1	168.4	79.4	4,897
Pepin	75.8	52.7	57.9	1,538
Trempealeau	76.2	44.3	68.9	1,393
Vernon	83.8	56.0	45.1	1,527
Average[a]		78.8	61.9	2,323

[a]Unweighted means of the averages for individual counties.

Sources: The figures were computed from the data available in *Property Tax 1962*,
Bulletin no. 462 (Madison: Wisconsin Dept. of Revenue, 1962), and *Property Tax 1970*,
Bulletin no. 470 (Madison: Wisconsin Dept. of Revenue, 1970).

of the total taxable land in the three counties ranged from 79 to 108 percent
during the 1962-70 period in contrast to more modest increases (ranging from
44 to 55 percent) in the other rural counties. Urban influences that include a
rising trend for urbanites seeking investment in farm land or a second cottage
home in the nearby rural counties have no doubt contributed to these higher
increments to their land value.

Thirdly, and perhaps more importantly, the farm land ownership is now
widely shared by those who are not farmers in the traditional sense. That this
is the case in Wisconsin as well as in the United States can be clearly seen in
Table 6.3. In Wisconsin, the smaller farms which comprise 41 percent (in number) of the total farms in 1965 earned only 8 percent of their net total income
(farm and nonfarm) from the farm sources. For those in a larger class which
comprised 27 percent of all farms, the farm income represented still only
about one-half of their total income. For the largest farms making up only 8
percent of all farms, the farm income exceeded 83 percent of the total income.
Farmers as a separate class are a very limited group. The large investment
poured into highway construction during the past two decades now allows
greater interaction between rural and urban areas in commuting, property
ownership, and in industrial location. The farm-nonfarm or rural-urban distinction in the present context of tax equity becomes less meaningful as so many
farm owners derive a large part of their income from nonfarm sources.

Table 6.3–Percent Distribution of Farms by Size and Ratio of Net Farm Income to Total Net Income for Farm Owners in Wisconsin and the U.S., 1964-65

Farms classified by annual sales of farm products	Percent of all farms		Ratio of farm income to total income (percent)	
	Wisconsin	U.S.	Wisconsin	U.S.
Less than $5,000	40.9	56.5	7.6	8.7
5,000- 9,999	27.1	16.0	52.6	48.3
10,000- 19,000	23.9	14.8	75.2	69.7
20,000- 39,999	6.6	8.2	82.9	79.5
40,000-100,000	1.2	3.5	85.7	86.5
Over 100,000	.3	1.0	96.5	94.2
	100.0	100.0		

Source: Computed from James B. Herendeen, *The Distribution of Agricultural Income by Economic Class of Farm: United States and Selected States,* Pennsylvania State University, College of Agriculture, Agricultural Experiment Station Bulletin no. 769 (University Park, Pa.: May 1970), pp. 10-11, tables 4 and 5.

The charge that farmers are unfairly treated under the property tax when their land is taxed on the market value rather than the use value should be examined in the light of the above observation. The alleged hardship ought not to be exaggerated for those small farmers who typically earn significant parts of their income from nonfarm sources. The owners of larger farms with "ripening land" seem to deserve no sympathy but only envy. Hardship, if there is any, ought not to be isolated from the gains they experience. It is indeed difficult to picture a farm owner who would object to a rise in his land value because it would cause an increase in property taxes.[13]

The system of a uniform rate tax on all land, farm or nonfarm, is preferable for its simplicity. It also avoids a potentially very difficult problem of classifying land in the urban fringes. The foregoing observation suggests that a statewide, uniform rate land tax will not pose serious problems of urban-rural inequity. Furthermore, considering the present pattern of school aid distribution and the prospect of continued rural advantages in the receiving end of the school fund, such a tax would seem eminently fair.

In the 1970-71 academic year, the per pupil state aid received by the nine most rural counties cited earlier averaged $347 in contrast to the much smaller average of $207 for the five urban counties (see Table 6.4). In spite of this and

13. The traditional overrepresentation of rural influence in the federal and state legislatures, one might note further, has led to various institutions (involving taxes and subsidies) favorable to the farm segment.

Table 6.4–Mean Per Pupil State Aid, Mean Per Pupil Expenditures, and School Tax Levy among Nine Most Rural and Five Most Urban Counties in Wisconsin, 1970-71

County	Per pupil[a] state aid	Per pupil[b] expenditures	School tax levy
Rural			
Buffalo	$420	$934	20.5 mills
Clark	406	896	22.6
Grant	327	883	21.0
Green	167	945	18.3
Iowa	319	924	19.6
Lafayette	253	842	18.9
Pepin	391	751	20.3
Trempealeau	417	845	21.3
Vernon	426	869	21.5
Mean[c]	347	877	20.4
Urban			
Milwaukee	172	1,003	20.1
Dane	230	1,043	20.5
Racine	275	926	21.8
Kenosha	236	910	21.6
Brown	190	837	18.9
Mean[c]	207	944	20.6

[a]Derived by dividing the number of pupils enrolled in September 1970 into the total school aid received by the school districts in each county in the 1970-71 academic year.

[b]Derived by dividing the September 1970 enrollment into the sum of the school aid and the aggregate school tax levies in each county. This somewhat understates the actual figures because our aid figures do not include state payments into social security and teacher retirement funds.

[c]Unweighted means of the averages for the individual counties.

Sources: For school aid, *Distribution of Wisconsin Public School Aid Dollars 1970-71* (Madison: Wisconsin Department of Public Instruction, 1972); for public school enrollment, *1970-71 Enrollment of Grades* (Madison: Wisconsin Department of Public Instruction, 1972); for school tax levies (amounts and rates), *Town, Village & City Taxes–1970* (Bulletin nos. 170, 270, and 370 combined) (Madison: Wisconsin Department of Revenue, 1971).

the fact that the school tax levies are nearly equal with 20.4 and 20.6 mills respectively for these rural and urban counties, per pupil expenditures are still lower for the rural counties. The expenditure disparities shown in Table 6.4, $877 versus $944 in favor of urban counties, understate the actual rural-urban difference in educational standard. The urban counties, with exception of Milwaukee County, include rural areas to varying degrees and this tends to lower the urban average expenditures. Moreover, urban advantage of scale economies,[14] rural disadvantage of high cost of transportation and the likelihood that rural areas and small towns can not attract teachers with higher training without "boredom pay" would further suggest that the rural-urban disparities in the resources used per pupil or the standard of education are considerably greater than indicated by the figures shown above.[15]

A need exists for a great deal more of resource equalization among public schools in Wisconsin.[16] With the school aid formula so adjusted as to largely maintain the present parity favoring rural areas, a state-levied, uniform rate land tax for school promises to be a measure that is fair and goes a long way in meeting this need.[17]

THE REVENUE POTENTIAL

In 1971, the property tax in Wisconsin with its average full value rate of 29.9 mills[18] provided an aggregate yield of $1,040 million, of which 56.8 percent or $591 million comprised school levies. Under the state aid program, $230 million were allocated to the school districts throughout the state. In that year, the total equalized *land* value reached $8,638 million (compared with $20,523 million for improvements). Had there been a 10-mill state land tax, the collections from the tax would have been over one third of the amount given out in school aid in the same year.

While a tax on land will be expected to be capitalized and tend to lower the

14. Recent studies indicate that there are significant scale economies in the operation of public schools, especially at the secondary school level. See Elchanan Cohn, "Economies of Scale in Iowa High School Operations," *Journal of Human Resources*, 3, no. 4 (Fall 1968), pp. 422-34, and John Riew, "Economies of Scale in High School Operation," *Review of Economies & Statistics*, 48, no. 3 (August 1966), pp. 280-87.

15. Living cost differences between rural and urban areas are a factor which favors rural areas, particularly where urban areas involve large metropolises. This aspect, in the case of Wisconsin, is not too relevant because, with the possible exception of Milwaukee, urban-rural living cost differences are relatively insignificant. For a related discussion, see Schultze et al., *Setting National Priorities*, pp. 328-33.

16. According to the Report of the President's Commission on School Finance cited in note 4, above, Wisconsin ranks high among the states in the equalization achievement (Report, p. 15). Even so, the state officials confide that the disparities in educational qualities among the state's public schools are a top priority concern.

17. The rural taxpayers who are already sensitive to their high school taxes may not consider the exchange of land tax for a better school as a fair bargain. While the taxpayer sentiment ought to be respected, other considerations must also enter in the determination of the proper standard of education for public schools.

18. This is the *effective* full value rate, reduced from the gross full rate of 33.9 mills under the system of property tax relief in Wisconsin (*Property Tax 1970*, Bulletin no. 470, Wisconsin Department of Revenue, Madison, pp. 2-3).

land value,[19] the external forces which have sustained the steady uptrend in land value will continue to prevail. The rapid increase in population and rise in the average income provide continually rising effective demand for housing and other goods and services which all require space. It is important to note that the effect of a tax on land value is a one-shot affair, whereas the rise in land value has been and is likely to be a continuing phenomenon.

Table 6.5–Equalized Values of Total Taxable Land and Improvements, Ratios of Land to Improvement Values in the State of Wisconsin, 1941-70

	Land (millions)	Improvements (millions)	Ratios of land to improvements
1941	$1,474	$2,474	61.0%
1946	1,727	3,146	54.9
1951	2,257	6,257	36.1
1956	2,915	9,780	29.8
1958	3,333	11,099	30.0
1969	4,369	13,065	33.4
1966	5,732	15,463	37.1
1970	8,638	20,523	42.1

Sources: The equalized values of land and improvements are available in *Property Tax Bulletin* published annually by Wisconsin Department of Revenue, Madison, since 1939.

Table 6.5 shows a consistent and accelerated pace of increase in land value during the past three decades. The land value during the last 15-year period (1956-70) tripled following a doubling of the value in the preceding 15 years (1941-56). The continued acceleration in the rate of appreciation in land value

19. Theoretically, the value of a capital asset is determined by capitalizing the earning of the asset. Thus,

$$V_L = E/r$$

where V_L, E, and r are respectively the value of land, its earning, and the discount rate. Now if we levy a land tax at the rate of t, the earning from the land falls to

$$E' = E - V_L \cdot t (1 - a)$$

where a is the marginal federal individual income tax rate—the term $(1 - a)$ to account for the deductibility of the land tax under the federal income tax. Thus the land value falls by

$$\Delta V_L = E/r - [E - V_L \cdot t (1 - a)]/r$$

or

$$\Delta V_L = V_L \cdot t (1 - a)/r$$

Thus, the magnitude of the decline in land value is directly related to the land tax rate and inversely related to the marginal federal individual income tax rate and the discount rate.

can be seen further by the doubling of the value during the last 8 years (1962–70).[20]

If it is assumed that the 1962-70 performance will continue and that a 1-percent land tax is levied, the value of the total taxable land in Wisconsin will reach approximately $16 billion by 1978.[21] In this situation, a modest 1-percent land tax will yield $160 million. The revenue potential of a land tax should not be judged under the mistaken premise that land is only a small and shrinking fraction of the total real estate.

The data in Table 6.5 exhibit a clear picture that defies this premise. As of 1970, land was 42 percent of the value of improvements,[22] or 30 percent of the total real estate, hardly a small part. Furthermore, the steady fall in the L/I ratio which characterized the first 15 years of the post-war period has been reversed by a steady rise since the mid-1950s. These then seem to challenge the view that a land tax can not substitute building tax, partially or otherwise, to materially reduce the burden on improvements without introducing a politically unfeasible tax rate on land itself. Introduction of a state-levied land tax, to the extent that its yield is used to lessen local fiscal pressure permitting an absolute fall or a reduction in the rate of increase in property tax, is in itself a partial substitution of land tax for building tax. Considering the steady trend of rising L/I ratio, such a substitution is likely to become increasingly potent in reducing the burden on improvements.

20. During the first 15 years of the postwar period, the improvement value quadrupled in contrast to a doubling of the land value in the same period, but over the subsequent 15 years, 1956-70, the improvement value only doubled while the land value tripled (see Table 6.5). That the increase in land value substantially exceeded that in improvement value is also indicated in the recent study by Allen D. Manvel, "Trends in the Value of Real Estate and Land, 1960-66," in National Committee on Urban Problems, *Three Land Research Studies,* Research Report no. 12 (Washington, D.C.: Government Printing Office, 1968), p. 1.

21. Assuming a discount rate of 10 percent, the average marginal federal income tax rate of 20 percent and a 1-percent tax on land, the value of the 1970 total taxable land ($8.6 billion) will theoretically fall by $\Delta V_L = V_L \cdot t\,(1 - a)\,/r$ or $688 million to approximately $7.9 billion. Doubling this amount as the figure projected for the land value in 1978 we get about $16 billion.

22. This is strikingly close to the L/I ratio of 41.5 percent based on Manvel's 1966 estimates of the market values of land and improvements for the United States (see Manvel, "Trends in Value of Real Estate," p. 1). But consider again the earlier reference (p. 83 and note 12, above) to the tendency for relative underassessment of land values plus Manvel's own admission that his estimates of separate land and structure values are less reliable than the total real estate values (Manvel, "Trends in Value of Real Estate," pp. 12-13).

7 Douglas Y. Thorson

Looking at Tax Choices in Statewide Finance of Education

Decisions on allocating state tax resources to education can be appraised both on grounds of efficiency and on grounds of distribution. And an important body of opinion has maintained that a complementarity exists between the objective of an optimum investment in human capital and the objective of reducing economic inequalities through education.[1] However, in the last few years, the distributional effects of education expenditures have been doubted.

Some studies conclude that children from minorities and from the lower income classes do not derive as much per pupil benefit as do other students.[2] Therefore, experts now disagree over the potential benefits of additional educational expenditures for the underprivileged. Several positions can be identified.

The optimistic argue that increased expenditures in jurisdictions with low per pupil expenditures will significantly alleviate the problem. By contrast, an opposite view maintains that enlarged outlays will have scant success in equalizing per pupil benefits due to the heredity based cause of low student achievement. Finally, there are the cautious who contend that innovational new

1. This is reflected in the human resources programs passed in the 1960's, such as the Economics Opportunity Act of 1964. An important tenet of this approach to poverty is that individuals are to be given sufficient human capital to raise them above the poverty line. Lester Thurow estimates the human capital poverty line for a family of four (1967) at $33,350, in his *The Impact of Taxes on the American Economy* (New York: Praeger Publishers, 1971), p. 15. The theory of this approach is that increments of human capital will help not only the impoverished, but that in addition there will be a spillover of benefits for the rest of society.

2. The following sources illustrate a large and growing literature: James S. Coleman et al., *Equality of Educational Opportunity* (Washington, D.C.: Government Printing Office, 1966); Lester Thurow, *Poverty and Discrimination* (Washington, D.C.: Brookings Institution, 1969); Thomas Ribich, *Education and Poverty* (Washington, D.C.: Brookings Institution, 1968).

educational programs and complementary expenditures on health, housing, and cultural enrichment are needed before schools can reduce economic inequality. This being the case, expenditure distribution cannot be used to justify the use of a regressive state levy to finance education.

Educational expenditures absorb about one-quarter of the budget of state governments and over two-fifth of the budget of local governments.[3] Nearly half of the funds for these expenditures at the state level come from sales and excise taxes, while over three-fifths of the funds for education at the local level come from the property tax.[4] A portion of the base of both these tax sources is expenditures for necessities of family life, but the portion is much larger in the case of most sales taxes.

Standard incidence analysis ignores the absolute burden of the tax upon the poor.[5] This is a matter of importance to this study and is given separate attention in the consideration of the incidence of individual taxes that follows:

PERSONAL INCOME TAX

Personal income tax laws now exist in forty-three states, plus the District of Columbia. Most of these states have broad based income taxes with graduated rates. But a few states tax capital income only, and four states have a proportional income tax.

In the 1920s, the individual income tax was never better than fifth among the major sources of state tax revenue. However, it has now climbed into second place, and in 1970 it supplied about two-fifths of total state revenue.

Empirical studies of tax incidence have found the state individual income tax to be moderately progressive.[6] We can sharpen this generalization by examining certain specific characteristics of the tax. These characteristics are based on data for September 1970.[7] More recent developments will be summarized later, where relevant.

3. *Facts and Figures on Government Finance: 16th Biennial Edition, 1971* (New York: Tax Foundation, Inc., 1971), pp. 157, 222, 246.

4. Ibid., pp. 173, 234; Advisory Commission on Intergovernmental Relations, *State-Local Finance: Significant Features and Suggested Legislation* (Washington, D.C.: Government Printing Office, 1972), p. 10.

5. Richard A. Musgrave, *The Theory of Public Finance* (New York: McGraw-Hill, 1959), chap. 10; Carl S. Shoup, *Public Finance* (Chicago: Aldine, 1969), pp. 7-19.

6. W. Irwin Gillespie, "Effects of Public Expenditures on the Distribution of Income," in Richard A. Musgrave, ed., *Essays in Fiscal Federalism* (Washington, D.C.: Brookings Institution, 1965), p. 136; *Tax Burdens and Benefits of Government Expenditures by Income Class, 1961 and 1965* (New York: Tax Foundation, Inc., 1967), p. 24; Richard A. Musgrave, "Incidence of the Tax Structure and Its Effects on Consumption," in *Federal Tax Policy for Economic Growth and Stability* (Washington, D.C.: Government Printing Office, 1955), p. 98.

7. *Facts and Figures on Government Finance*, pp. 182-83.

Looking first at personal exemptions, the median state exemption for a family of four is $3,000. The high is California and Iowa, where the figure reaches $6,600. The low is Wisconsin's tax credit that is equivalent to about $1,500 in income exemption. When deductions are added, the data suggests that the typical state grants an income exclusion that comes reasonably close to the poverty line. In short, the typical state income tax imposes a zero absolute tax burden upon the poor.

Turning to effective rate progression, according to one tax economist: "for the average state using a personal income tax, the 'effective' median rate at a taxable income level (adjusted gross income) of $25,000 was approximately six times greater than the 'effective' rate at the $5,000 taxable income level (in 1968), though at higher income levels the taxes tend to become regressive due to the deductibility of the federal personal income tax."[8] A review of certain specific features of rate and bracket structure will fill out this generalization.

First, there is the matter of the top bracket.[9] The top bracket in the median state for a family of four is slightly over $15,000. There is no nominal marginal rate differentiation beyond this point. Variance is high, however. In five states, the bracket differentiation carries up to the $200,000 level.[10] At the other part of the spectrum are the states with proportional income taxes whose effective rate progression comes from personal exemptions only.

A second determinant of effective rate progression is the marginal rate pattern. In this connection, the upper level marginal rate in the median state is 7 percent. For the top state, the upper level marginal rate is 20 percent.[11] On the bottom part of the spectrum is the Indiana proportional income tax with a rate of 2 percent.

Another aspect of the marginal rate pattern is nominal rate progression: the ratio of high to low marginal rate within a particular statute. In this regard the median ratio is four.[12] At the top of the range are California and North

8. Bernard P. Herber, *Modern Public Finance: The Study of Public Sector Economics* (Homewood, Illinois: Irwin, 1971), p. 154. Also see Violet J. Sollie, "Are Personal Income Taxes Regressive?" *Taxes* (February 1959), pp. 169-80.

9. In our calculations, exemptions have been treated as a zero bracket rate. Thus, the top bracket is equal to the taxable income level where marginal rate differentiation terminates plus the exemptions for a family of four. In this way, the role of exemptions as an instrument of graduation are included in the calculations.

10. These states are Alaska, Nebraska, New Mexico, Vermont, and West Virginia. In three of these states, the carrying of differentiation into the upper income levels is a by-product of the state tax being a supplement on the federal tax.

11. This figure is for the state of Vermont where the state income tax is 25 percent of the federal income tax, plus a 15 percent surtax on tax liability.

12. For example, in median states such as Arizona and Missouri, the rate advances from 2 percent to 8 percent, and from 1 percent to 4 percent, respectively.

Dakota with ratios of 10 (1 percent to 10 percent) and 11 (1 percent to 11 percent), respectively. At the bottom of the range, are the proportional rate structures with constant marginal rates.[13]

The conclusion suggested by the data we have reviewed is that under the typical state income tax the effective rate of tax advances in the $3,000 to $15,000 income range at a pace only slightly below that of the federal income tax. After $15,000, however, effective rate progression slows, and actually becomes regressive at high income levels in states that permit deductibility of the federal personal income tax. About 40 percent of the states allow such a deduction.

In general, marginal rate progression extends into high income ranges under state laws only when the state defines income tax liability as a percentage of federal income taxes payable.

The moderate yield of the typical state income tax limits its redistributional effect more than any other characteristic mentioned.[14] The yield in the median state is only about 18 percent of total state revenue. Oregon and New York are distinct exceptions, with yields of 50 and 41 percent, respectively. At the other pole, in states that levy taxes on capital income only, the yield is less than 5 percent.

CORPORATION INCOME TAXES

In 1970, forty-three states used the corporation income tax. The rates ranged from 2 percent in Indiana and Missouri, to 11 percent in Pennsylvania. Eight states use brackets and the remainder use a flat rate, except for Alaska where the levy is 18 percent of the federal corporation income tax. The percentage yield of the corporation income tax for fiscal year 1970 was about 8 percent of total tax collections, as compared with 19 percent for the individual income tax.

Although the incidence of the corporate income tax is a highly moot point,[15] a common assumption of incidence studies is that one-third of the tax is passed on to the consumer in the form of higher prices.[16] A U-shaped pattern of distribution of tax by income class follows.[17] The tax tends to vary between

13. These states are Alaska, Nebraska, and Vermont.
14. Richard Goode, *The Individual Income Tax* (Washington, D.C.: Brookings Institution, 1964), pp. 262-68.
15. See Perter Miezkowski, "Tax Incidence Theory: The Effects of Taxes on the Distribution of Income," *Journal of Economic Literature,* 7 (December 1969), pp. 1103-24, for a survey of the literature on the incidence of the corporate income tax.
16. Gillespie, "Effects of Public Expenditures," p. 134.
17. Ibid.; Musgrave, "Incidence of the Tax Structure," pp. 98-100; *Tax Burdens and Benefits,* p. 24.

regressivity and proportionality in the lower to middle income ranges, but it becomes progressive in the higher income ranges. The partial sales tax character of the corporate income tax creates the regressivity in the lower income ranges, while the concentration of capital income in the upper income brackets causes it to be progressive in this region.

RETAIL SALES TAXES

The retail sales tax is the single most important revenue source for state governments. During fiscal year 1970, it supplied about 30 percent of all tax funds. The median yield was 34 percent. On the bottom of the range is Massachusetts with a yield of 14 percent and New York with a yield of 17 percent. On the top is Hawaii with a yield of 48 percent and Mississippi with a yield of 47 percent. The median sales tax rate is 4 percent. The low is 2 percent in Indiana and the high is 6½ percent in Connecticut. Several states do not use the tax.

The following distributional characteristics are commonly imputed to the tax: it hits low income families hard; it is regressive; and it does not take account of family size.[18] These generalizations are based upon two assumptions. The first proposition is that the average propensity to consume is higher in the low income brackets and for large families than it is for the higher income brackets and for small families. The second assumption is that the tax is passed on to the consumer in the form of a higher price on the commodity taxed. Hence, those with a high average propensity to consumer (the poor and the large family) pay a larger share of their income in taxes. Basing their analysis upon these two assumptions, incidence studies confirm this pattern of regressivity for state retail sales taxes.[19] Though there are economists who challenge these conclusions, we believe the analysis we have summarized to be essentially correct.[20]

The typical retail sales tax fits the above model. It contains neither a food exemption nor a tax credit against income. The result is a tax that places a heavy burden upon the poor, a tax that is regressive, and a tax that hits large families harder than small ones.

18. Daniel C. Morgan, Jr., *Retail Sales Tax* (Madison, Wisconsin: University of Wisconsin Press, 1963), p. 131.

19. Gillespie, "Effects of Public Expenditures," p. 134; Musgrave, "Incidence of the Tax Structure," p. 98, and *Tax Burdens and Benefits*, p. 24.

20. One source of challenge is by those who employ the permanent income hypothesis. See David G. Davies, "An Empirical Test of Sales Tax Regressivity," *Journal of Political Economy*, 67 (February 1959), pp. 72-78. Another source of challenge has come from Earl Rolph, in his *The Theory of Fiscal Economics* (Berkeley: University of California Press, 1954), chaps. 6, 7.

The character of the retail sales can be affected by special provisions. Three special provisions are of particular interest: (1) inclusion of services in the base, (2) exemption of drugs and of food, and (3) a tax credit against the state individual income tax.

When state sales taxes first developed, most were applied exclusively to commodities. However, tax literature and tax practice have increasingly looked toward inclusion of services in the base. There are modest gains to be derived from such an inclusion, both in terms of yield and in terms of a reduction of regressivity. Yet, as of 1971, twenty-six of the forty-five sales tax states extended the sales tax base no further than the services of utilities, hotels, and admissions categories. Only two states, Hawaii and New Mexico, tax virtually all services. Grounds exist for extending the tax at least to a selected list of services: especially to those rendered primarily to individual consumers by commercial, as distinguished from professional establishments.[21]

Another special provision is exemptions. Many states have introduced exemptions into their retail sales tax, primarily to reduce regressivity. One such exemption is drugs and medicine. Such exemptions have spread rapidly in recent years. As of 1971, twenty-six states plus the District of Columbia exempted all prescription drugs and medicine.[22] This exemption, especially for prescription drugs, has the dual merit of reducing the burden on the poor, as well as eliminating an extra burden on those who are unfortunate enough to require large expenditures for medicine. For these reasons, there would be a social gain if the seventeen states who have no such exemption would exclude prescription drugs from the sales tax.

An interesting exemption is the one for food. As of January 1971, fifteen of the forty-five sales tax states exempted all or almost all food. In addition, North Dakota exempts a limited range of basic foods, and the District of Columbia and Louisiana tax food at a lower rate (2%) than the other goods.[23] Since a high percentage of family expenditures in the lowest income groups goes for food, the exemption clearly lessens food prices relative to other prices. A sales tax that includes food keeps the relative cost of food constant, whereas, with food exempt, additional food consumption is encouraged.[24] Furthermore, the food exemption lessens discrimination against large families. But the exemption does have drawbacks. For one, it results in a revenue loss of between 15 and 20 percent. This is of concern since it derives not only from excusing the

21. John F. Due, *State and Local Sales Taxation* (Chicago, Illinois: Public Administration Service, 1971), pp. 86, 302.

22. Ibid., p. 69.

23. Ibid., p. 66.

24. J. M. Schaefer, "Sales Tax Regressivity under Alternative Tax Bases and Income Concepts," *National Tax Journal,* 22 (December 1969), pp. 516-27; H. M. Somers, *The Sales Tax* (Sacramento: California Assembly Committee on Revenue and Taxation, 1964).

nonaffluent from a tax on food, but also from exempting the middle and upper classes who may choose to concentrate their luxury spending upon expensive foods. In short, it is a clumsy and costly means of reducing regressivity and of reducing the burden upon the poor. And to make matters worse, much burden remains upon the lowest income population even after the exemption. A second drawback is that the exemption creates administrative problems, such as the interpretive one of deciding whether certain items are food (e.g., vitamins).[25]

Some states exempt other necessities, such as clothing. These actions amplify the problems discussed. The experience we have had with the complicating and spreading effect of exemptions during the past thirty-five years suggests a strong presumption against exemptions and deductions of a special nature. They have a role, but it is too often abused.

An attractive substitute for the food exemption is the tax credit against the state income tax. The credit can either be flat, or vanish at higher income levels. As of January 1971, six states and the District of Columbia used such a credit against income tax. Four states used a flat credit, while Hawaii, Vermont, and the District of Columbia used a graduated credit that declines with income and eventually vanishes.[26]

The tax credit results in a cash payment when the income tax due is less than the credit. For a family of four with an income tax of zero, the cash payment value of the credit ranged from $24 in Massachusetts and the District of Columbia to $84 in Hawaii. The median value was $28.

Modest technical problems arise with the tax credit approach,[27] yet administration is simpler than with the food exemption. Furthermore, the revenue loss is less, discrimination against persons spending large amounts on food is avoided, and all burden can be removed from the poor. Finally, pressure to exempt clothing and other items is reduced.

In conclusion, the retail sales tax can be modified to meet the distributional objections mentioned earlier. The most important feature in this connection is the credit against income tax. For states that do not have a personal income tax, a food exemption becomes a second best choice.

SITE VALUE TAXATION

The American property tax does not distinguish between land and improvements; selecting out land for special taxation has a long history in tax literature,

25. Due, *State and Local Sales Taxation,* pp. 66-69.
26. Ibid., pp. 71-72.
27. Examples of these problems are interpretive questions about residence and the use of fictitious social security numbers. Also, some persons did not file to obtain refund (ibid., p. 72).

and land taxation also enjoys precedents in practice. The history of this subject is well known and need not be repeated. It begins with the Physiocrats, was given impetus by Ricardo, and reached a zenith with the single tax philosophy of Henry George. But our interest is not in a single tax on land in lieu of all other taxes; rather it is in the distributional consequences of land taxation, and its possible role in educational finance.

Recent theoretical and empirical work suggest that the property tax is more a wealth tax than an excise tax.[28] The inference drawn from this analysis is that the burden of the tax rests heavily with the owner of capital. In the second place, some studies have used a broader income concept in computing the incidence of the property tax. One study adjusts the money income base to include imputed rental income of home owners and subtracts federal income tax paid from income; using this approach, it finds the property tax to be proportional.[29]

We do not mean to give the impression that present knowledge denies that harsh distributional features exist in the property tax. But we do believe that modern analysis suggests the property tax is a much better tax than widely circulated studies of twenty years ago concluded.

Professor Carl Shoup has suggested that the property tax on business real estate is somewhat progressive when compared to a tax on residential property. His rationale is as follows: Because of the elasticity of demand for business products within a community, not much of the tax will be passed forward to the consumers. Also, the firm's demand for rental space will be very inelastic in many cases and so will bear the burden of the tax. Given this incidence analysis, the tax acquires progressivity (when compared to a residential property tax) due to the concentration of business property in the middle and upper income ranges.[30]

The real estate tax on housing can be improved by (1) exempting the first $5,000 or so of the value of owner occupied property and refunds to renters, and (2) providing public housing under tax-exempt provisions.[31] Of course, such an approach encounters the same objections as does the food exemption under the retail sales tax: it is an inefficient method of tax relief, and it is

28. J. M. Buchanan, "The Methodology of Incidence Theory: A Critical Review of Some Recent Contributions," in *Fiscal Theory and Political Economy* (Chapel Hill: University of North Carolina Press, 1960); J. M. Buchanan, *The Public Finances*, rev. ed. (Homewood, Illinois: Irwin, 1965), pp. 491-97; A. C. Harberger, "The Incidence of the Corporate Income Tax," *Journal of Political Economy*, 70 (June 1962), 70, 215-40; A. C. Harberger, "Efficiency Aspects of Taxes on Income From Capital," in M. Krzyzaniak, ed., *Symposium on Business Taxation* (Detroit: Wayne State University Press, 1966), p. 26.

29. James Morgan et al., *Income and Welfare in the United States* (New York: McGraw-Hill, 1962), pp. 292-99.

30. Shoup, *Public Finances*, p. 297.

31. Ibid., p. 392.

costly in terms of revenue loss. A more efficient means to the same end is a property tax credit against state income tax; this method is now used in some states. Not only does this alternative economize on revenue loss; in addition, it alleviates the burden both upon renters and low income home owners.

The incidence of the portion of the property tax upon land is likely to possess some elements of progressivity for two reasons. (Our statement is based on a comparison of the land tax to any of the following: the typical retail sales tax, a real estate tax on housing, or even a proportional income tax.) The first reason is that a tax on site value cannot be shifted, and the second reason is that there is little ownership of land by the lower income population.[32] Thus, taxing land at a higher rate than residential property would mitigate the regressivity of the general property tax. This argument is separate from the notion of using the land tax to appropriate windfalls and economic profits. Although the socially created nature of much land value is an added reason for a higher tax, such economic profits and rents are not unique to land; they also occur in the case of scarce labor services, and in the instance of a firm or a union that possess monopoly power.[33] Also, many who now own land have purchased it for a sum equal to the capitalized value of the flow of net rent. They are not the original owners who reaped the surplus of economic rent, but they will reap future benefits.

But returning to our main point, land is an important form of personal and corporate wealth, and it constitutes a larger share of the wealth of middle and upper income individuals than is true of the general property tax. This is the distributional grounds for having land play a larger relative role in the American property tax.

There are certain inferences to be drawn from our examination of the property tax. Interestingly, the property tax is again becoming a candidate for state revenue after serving as the mainstay of local government for many years. This is the situation that arises as states face the prospect of assuming a larger share of the burden for local expenditures.

As a possible choice for added state revenue, the property tax does not fare as badly in an evaluation as it once did. First, modern studies of incidence suggest that it is not regressive. Second, its burden on the poor can be reduced and its efficiency improved through a classification that taxes land at a higher

32. Ibid., p. 391; Mason Gaffney, "Adequacy of Land as a Tax Base," in Daniel M. Holland, ed., *The Assessment of Land Value* (Madison, Wisconsin: University of Wisconsin Press, 1970), p. 206.

33. Ervin K. Zingler, "A Critical Evaluation of Land-Value Tax Theory and Its Relationship to Price and Distribution Theory," in Arthur P. Becker, ed., *Land-Value Taxation and Contemporary Economic Thought* (Milwaukee: Boulder Conference Committee, 1964), pp. 14-16; James Buchanan, *The Public Finances,* 3rd ed. (Homewood, Illinois: Irwin, 1970), pp. 396-97.

rate than improvements. Third, even the absolute burden of the property tax upon the poor can be combated through a tax credit against state income taxes. This credit can be made to disappear above a specified income level.

CONCLUSION

Having completed our analysis, we are in a position to identify the judgments and conclusions that are implicit in the paper. Most of these points deal with tax and expenditure impediments to the objective of equality of educational opportunity, and with the tax choices that face the states.

Tax structures and tax arrangements can impede equality in educational opportunity when a jurisdiction has insufficient tax resources, or if the tax instruments used deny low income individuals essential private good complements to human capital formation.

Removal of these tax impediments to equality of educational opportunity entails greater state administration of tax systems as well as increased efforts to remove tax regressivity. However, even more important than the alleviation of tax regressivity is the elimination of the absolute tax burden upon the poor.

All of the alternative tax instruments available to state governments can be so designed and so modified as to be distributionally acceptable. However, the typical retail sales tax is not at present structured in a way that meets this condition. What is required is either a tax credit against state income tax, or a food exemption to overcome this regressivity. Concerning the property tax, we feel that it should not be discarded as a source of state revenue. Its distributional character can be improved by raising the tax on land above that on improvements, and by granting a property tax credit against state income tax. Though all taxes can be so tailored as to have a place in financing additional educational expenditures, the state individual income tax is the tax instrument that best meets the distributional criteria in its existing form. However, the extensive use of the base by the federal government as well as state and local governments reduces its availability as a source of new revenues.

8 Richard W. Lindholm

Hawaii and Oregon: Graded Property and Land Value Taxation

The desire of Hawaiian and Oregon voters to be taxed on a system based on ability to pay is a basic element in their interest in land value taxation (LVT). This interest resulted in the adoption of the graded property tax in Hawaii in 1963 and the recommendation of a uniform 2 percent land tax to finance kindergarten through 6th grade education in Oregon in 1971.[1] Because LVT would provide much of the revenue needed to carry out government services desired by residents of both states, its use would permit enjoyment of a given level of government services with a lower level of income and sales taxes. In addition, in both Hawaii and Oregon, LVT is seen to be a tax that would provide an economic prod to more intensive use of land. This would help preserve the beauty of the environment of the two states while increasing personal income of workers and businesses and the efficiency with which activities are carried out in cities and urban areas.

The political necessity that LVT be collected according to a commonly accepted and understood concept of ability to pay has been only partially understood in Hawaii and Oregon. In Hawaii, because the concentration of land ownership is so obvious, the need to demonstrate LVT was not a tax paid largely by ordinary families was of less importance than would be true of other states. Citizens of Hawaii are aware that much of the land of their state is owned by small groups, as for example, the Campbell Estate. The use of LVT under these circumstances is clearly a tax paid largely by those with great ability to pay. In Oregon, land ownership is concentrated in the hands of the federal government, wood products companies, ranchers, land companies, and the like. In addition, in Oregon many lower income people hold a few acres

This paper benefits from research undertaken in the Spring of 1972 for the Advisory Committee on Intergovernment Relations of Washington, D.C.

1. Richard W. Lindholm, *A Description and Analysis of Oregon's Fiscal System, Area 5, Land Taxation* (Salem, Oregon: State Executive Department, 1971), p. 20.

adjacent to urban areas. These conditions make the ability to pay aspect of LVT less apparent in Oregon than in Hawaii.

LVT AND EDUCATION

LVT cannot be solidly rooted as a tax based on ability to pay until the general voter understands a number of propositions, several of them of considerable sophistication. Even in Hawaii where the obviousness of land ownership concentration is very great, the relationship has been weakened since the original legislation was adopted and political support for expansion of LVT is lacking.

The first of the economic relationships that require explanation is that when it comes to tax burden, land is different from other capital and the income or rent arising from the control of land is different from other income. In other words, Rickardo was basically right about land rent. For the owner of land to understand this concept he must comprehend that what he pays in LVT he saves in interest costs on owning a given piece of land. He must understand that the cost of owning and controlling land consists of interest paid or forgone on amount invested plus taxes paid on the land. When the land tax cost goes up, interest cost goes down. The out-of-pocket cost of acquiring and holding land is the same with high taxes as with low taxes. The person not owning land and with little expectation of becoming a landowner needs to understand that the payment of land taxes to government increases efficiency of land use and expands opportunities for jobs. In addition, substantial use of LVT decreases need to pay taxes of other types, and this is accomplished without increasing the cost of land ownership or production costs and therefore will not increase prices of purchases.

The answer to why it is better for the state and its citizens to have a landowner pay a $1 of LVT than a $1 of interest needs research; a statement of the logic of the situation is not enough. The same situation exists in answering why it is better for a state to collect quite a few of the tax dollars needed from LVT and fewer dollars from sales, payroll, and conventional property taxes. The quality of the research is fundamental to the success of efforts to introduce LVT as the approach to bring about statewide finance of a uniform level of education.

A first research step is a statewide study that identifies the distribution of land ownership by income class estimations and use. The actual names of landowners in each city and county are not needed, but the data must be sufficiently complete to permit the development of a chart relating the percent of the population with the percent of total value of land owned. Some help can be expected from studies completed and now underway. If data already available give the correct picture, one can forecast that new studies will demonstrate the ownership of land of a state, county, or city above parcels of $4,000 or so are in only a few hands.[2]

A study of changes of land values as represented by sales is another research must. The study should be able to locate land sales by county and include the major use of land as well as current assessed values and previous values. Death tax data and land sale advertisements should be used in the study.

Finally, a study of the impact of LVT on the development of urban areas and investment in personal property and real estate other than land is needed. Again, studies have been made that will be helpful.[3]

Precedent for the need of research if progress is to be made comes out of the Hawaiian experience. The Hawaiian graded property tax legislation (a type of LVT) grew out of actual legislative interest, starting with the election of the reform legislature in 1954. The Hawaiian Legislative Reference Bureau of the state provided a general historical and theoretical underpinning of what was new to Hawaii but not new to the world. In 1948, the Bureau released a study titled the *Graduated Land Tax.* In 1954, the Bureau published *A Memorandum on the "Pittsburgh Plan" of Property Taxation.* In 1969, a careful study titled "Taxation as a Tool for Planning" was commissioned.[4]

Through the years the work of the Hawaiian Legislative Reference Bureau and the Hawaiian Economic Research Center have actively explored land use and taxation problems. Research leadership of this kind is found in very few states. It is perhaps a necessary portion of a conscious change of property taxation policy toward LVT.

ACCEPTABILITY

In addition to the problem of explaining the advantage of a tax that reduces capital requirements and therefore interest costs and makes the savings available to reduce other taxes, there is the business of fitting in with what might be called "applied tax psychology." LVT cannot develop a general following unless it does at least modestly well in this area.

It is accepted wisdom among state and local government tax practitioners that taxes are accepted or rejected by legislatures and voters on the basis of impact, i.e., who makes the payme t, and not on the basis of incidence, i.e.,

2. Mason Gaffney, "The Property Tax Is a Progressive Tax," *Proceedings of 64th Annual National Tax Association* (1971), pp. 408-26.

3. John H. Niedercorn, "A Negative Exponential Model of Urban Land Use and Its Implications for Metropolitan Development," *Journal of Regional   nce,* 2 (1971), pp. 317-26.

4. Leslie Carbert, "Taxation as a Tool for Planning," in *State of Hawaii's Land Use Districts and Regulations Review* (Honolulu: Hawaii Land Use Commission, 1969), p. 137.

location of economic burden. In both Hawaii and Oregon, this attitude is modified by a strong belief that a citizen can only make wise government spending choices if he knows what it is costing him. A third principle would be that taxes paid a little at a time and tied to a purchase or an income receipt are favored over a single large payment or a payment not associated with an economic transaction. Finally, taxes closely associated with a service considered of general benefit or closely related to an activity accepted as an area of government responsibility, will find legislative and citizen support easier to develop.

. With these points in mind, wise policymakers might find the introduction of LVT to be a good time to also introduce semi-annual property tax payments. The LVT, which is dedicated to school finance, would be paid in September. The tax on improvements to meet general government costs would be paid in March. Also, if the state replaced its retail sales tax or the lower income portion of its individual income tax with a value added tax at the time LVT is introduced, many voters would be relieved of direct tax payments.

In addition, down-to-earth political adjustments are required. For example, the first $1,000 of land owned by an individual needs to be exempt. Also, a procedure is needed to reduce LVT liability of persons in unusual circumstances that cause payment to be a great economic sacrifice or an apparent loss to society, e.g., aged in family home, railroad lands, and hospital parks.

The experience of both Hawaii and Oregon demonstrate that provision must be made to reduce agriculture opposition in any serious statewide LVT legislative proposal. The Hawaiian solution was to exclude land zoned agriculture from the graded property tax.

In 1963 legislation that placed the graded or Pittsburgh Plan property tax on the statute books of Hawaii limited the impact of the program to urban and resort property. Land classified as agriculture or conservation and the buildings and other improvements on this land were not affected directly by the legislation.

The Hawaiian approach to agriculture, or perhaps a modification of it, is a must to the adoption of a statewide LVT. One modification might be a guarantee that LVT paid by farmers would not be greater than under a uniform statewide property tax. Also, a farmer can be defined under the law as a person earning 50 percent or more of his income from farming. Another modification might be that a corporation could receive farmer treatment if 80 percent of the corporate profits arising in the state came from the sale of agricultural products grown on land cultivated in the state. Finally, farmer treatment could be dependent on a certificate issued by the State College of Agriculture stating agriculture was being carried out as intensively as the land and existing economic conditions made appropriate.

COORDINATING VAT WITH LVT

If a state introduced a value added tax (VAT) to replace its retail sales tax at the same time as the statewide uniform land tax to finance basic education was adopted, agriculture units could be required to pay the value added tax at the full rate or the uniform land tax, depending on which was the greater. (Michigan's value added tax (1954-67) collected only about 1 percent of its revenue directly from agriculture.) In addition to the uniform statewide LVT, agriculture would continue to be subject to the property tax on buildings, equipment, livestock, and crops as the laws of the state provided.

Under this approach, other business taxpayers would be subject to both VAT and the statewide uniform LVT. However, the general property tax on buildings and equipment would need only be high enough to raise funds needed to support local government services other than education, and the regressive retail sales tax would be gone.

The statewide uniform land tax would somewhat discourage scatteration of businesses and households. If used to finance schools, it would also reduce the local property taxes paid to support schools in the areas where property values were low and the number of children to be educated was high, and therefore meet objections raised by *Serrano* v. *Priest*—5 Cal. 3d 584, 487 P. 2d 1241 (1971).

The procedure outlined would grant agriculture as an industry, a tax advantage not available to other industries. At the same time, agriculture would not be granted special rates under either the value added tax or the uniform statewide land tax. The treatment accorded agriculture under conditions of the introduction of VAT and LVT has a number of economic impacts in addition to the obvious removal of agricultural resistance on economic grounds to both VAT and the LVT.

1. Land adjacent to rapidly growing urban and recreation areas would be subject to the uniform statewide land tax with value set at highest and best use, unless the lands were operated by a genuine farmer and produced a substantial value added.

2. Land holdings by corporations aimed largely at realizing capital gains while benefiting from deduction of current expenses from taxable income arising from other sources would become large payers of LVT.

3. Subjecting agriculture to the land tax only if the VAT liability at full rates is less, encourages production while causing some downward pressure to be placed on land prices because land not fully utilized would be more expensive to hold.[5]

5. John Shannon, "State-Local Tax Systems: Proposals and Objectives," *National Civic Review*, 61 (April 1972), 174.

ECONOMIC DEMOCRACY

"A good market in land, one built around prices, is of utmost importance in getting the most productive use of something we must all have, space."[6] Land is different from other broad categories of wealth because a high price or large profits from gaining control cannot stimulate more production. To assure "wise" use of land space, the user must pay the full economic productivity of the land, but it is not necessary that this payment be received by the owner. The owner need not receive the full payment because the payment is not needed to bring forth maximum supply. Quite a chunk of the price can go to government as an ad valorem land tax without reducing the owner's efforts to search out a productive use of the land or a buyer able to offer a high price.

The capitalistic system is constantly endangered by two basic problems: (1) too great a concentration of power to permit democracy to work, and (2) failure to distribute awards on the basis of effort and ability. The use of the land tax at uniform and substantial ad valorem rates helps capitalism overcome both of these weaknesses. Land value taxation, of course, cannot be expected to carry out this continuing battle alone. For example, tax shelters under the income tax also need to be destroyed. Also, all persons must have an equal opportunity for an education and employment. In addition, production and marketing monopoly need to be controlled.

The great usefulness of land taxation is that in making its contribution to an effective democratic-capitalistic economy it requires a minimum of interference with individual decisions through government fiat.

The close relation between power and large land holdings is well documented. Although the importance of owning land to possess economic power has shifted from the days of the great American land barons, it remains true that land ownership in a city, a suburb, or in a rural area is economic power. As population and land uses expand, the monopoly power that land ownership always provides increases. Desirable and efficient sites for housing and industry are always limited. The land tax through its reduction of increases in land prices as demand for land increases, pushes toward highest and best use. Under conditions of a substantial LVT ownership decisions that withdraw land from the market's determination of best use become too expensive because of out-of-pocket tax payments and of a reduced potential for capital gains.

Increases in the value of natural resources, including land, are created by society and are therefore an unearned increment.[7] The wealth arising in this fashion is a windfall. It is wealth that can be taxed away without decreasing

6. C. Lowell Harris, "Land Value Taxation: Pro," in *International Property Assessment Administration*, vol. 2 (Chicago: International Association of Assessing Officers, 1970), p. 62.

7. Richard Armstrong, "A Better Way to Pay for Schools," *Fortune*, 87, no. 2 (February 1973), p. 162.

general economic well-being. This is well recognized in economic theory and in practice. Application of a special tax to pick up all or a portion of windfall gains arising from a shift in government policy is considered equitable and justified. What has been created by the community through legislative action can also be in whole or in part taken away by legislative action.

This same basic concept of justice is applicable to increases in land values arising from legislative decisions such as changing zoning, changing transportation patterns, building schools, digging sewers, and the like. When LVT is used, increases in land values arising from above actions are reduced. Gains are partially reclaimed for social use. The unearned gains of the lucky, powerful, or wise landowner are partially shared when a uniform and a relatively substantial land tax is applied. Also, land with a falling value because of government actions or change of tastes finds this reduction reflected in reduced LVT liability. Therefore, during adversity the owner of land bearing a high LVT suffers less because he shares the loss with government.

OREGON STATEWIDE LAND TAX PROPOSAL

The Oregon land values that would be included in the base of a 2 percent statewide land tax to finance 100 percent of education costs of kindergarten through 6th grade would consist of:

Value of taxable locally assessed land	$4,450,000,000
Zoned land and other reductions from full cash value	425,000,000
Land of utilities	640,000,000
Undervaluation of vacant lots	375,000,000
Base upon which the federal government[8] would make payments in lieu of property taxes	600,000,000
Total land values to bear a 2 percent tax for a 100 percent finance of basic education (kindergarten through 6th grade)[9]	$6,490,000,000

The amount raised by the 2 percent state land tax and the in lieu of tax payments on Federal lands would be about $128.8 million.[10] The 1969-70 after tax relief school levy plus the county school levy, also after relief, was $298.60 million; about $130.4 million of this total was needed to cover education for grades K through 6.

8. 52.2 percent of Oregon's land is federally owned.

9. "Correct land assessment is necessary to close loopholes of federal income tax," quotation from Mason Gaffney, "What Is Property Tax Reform?" (mimeographed), Conference on Property Tax Reform, December 12, 1970 (Washington, D.C.: Resources for the Future, 1970), p. 7.

10. EBS Management Consultants, Inc., *Revenue Sharing and Payments in Lieu of Taxes*, Pt. 5, Public Land Law Review Commission Study Report (Washington, D.C.: Government Printing Office, 1970).

The revenues of a 2 percent land tax at $128.8 million are approximately equal to the $130.4 million total tax levy cost of education for grades K through 6 in 1969-70. The apparent revenue shortage could be covered by leaving to local money raising efforts some of the expenditures made in the richer districts and from savings arising from centralized purchase, and the reduced birthrate. Also land values are believed to have increased substantially during the 1970-74 period.

Examples

Average Residential Property School Finance Tax Liability Under Present System

Value of lot	$ 4,000
Value of house	20,000
Value of house and lot	$24,000
Current average rate used to raise funds to finance schools	1.73%
Average amount paid in 1969-70 on a $24,000 residential property	$ 415

Under the proposed 2 percent state land tax to cover *all* costs of education in K through 6, the property taxes on the same residential property work out as follows:

Value of lot	$ 4,000
Tax rate (consists of 2 percent state land tax to finance 100 percent of costs of education K through 6 and 0.92 percent rate applied to taxable values to provide revenues equal to those of 1969-70 to finance 7 through 12 schooling—land is not brought up to full value as it is for 2 percent state land tax)	2.92%
Tax due on lot to support all primary and secondary education	$ 116
Value of house	$20,000
Tax rate to support education 7 through 12	0.92%
Tax due on house to support education 7 through 12	$ 184
Total property tax on $24,000 residence to support primary and secondary education under the proposed 2 percent land tax	$ 300
Dollar reduction of property taxes on typical homestead to support education brought about by the introduction of a statewide land tax dedicated to support of education K through 6.	$ 115
Percentage reduction	27.7%

Business Property

Value of business property	$250,000
Current average property tax rate for education	1.73%
Property taxes for support of education under existing procedures	$ 4,325

Situation under a 2 percent state land tax to pay 100 percent of education K through 6:

Value of land	$125,000
Rate on land (includes broader base only for 2 percent state land tax)	2.92%
Total taxes on land	$ 3,650
Value of building	$125,000
Rate on building	0.92%
Total taxes on buildings	$ 1,150
Total school taxes under 2 percent state land tax to pay 100 percent of costs of education K through 6 and continuation of present procedure to finance 7 through 12	$ 4,800
Additional property taxes under 2 percent state land tax	$ 475

Agriculture Property

Value of total farm and farmstead	$200,000
Current average property tax rate for education	1.73%
Property taxes for support of education under existing procedures	$ 3,462
Value of land	$165,000
Tax rate	2.92%
Taxes due	$ 4,818
Value of buildings and personal property	$ 35,000
Tax rate	0.92%
Taxes due	$ 322
Total taxes for education	$ 5,140
Additional taxes under 2 percent state land tax to support education	$ 1,678

The adoption of a statewide land tax of 2 percent would:

1. Provide a very substantial increase in state support of primary and secondary education in Oregon.

2. Assure equal education opportunity during early formative years.

3. Decrease by about 27.7 percent the real estate taxes going for education paid by a typical urban family owning their home.

4. Decrease substantially the property taxes resting on commercial buildings, homes and personal property which would stimulate employment opportunities.

5. Set in motion forces that would reduce speculation in agricultural land, vacant lots and land adjacent to urban areas.

6. Increase use of federal landholdings as a tax base.

7. Return to the basic American idea that land values and basic education are closely related (see chap. 1).

Oregon's Land Inventory

It is estimated from information available from general property tax supervision in the Oregon Department of Revenue that the value of urban land allocated for residential use is $1.3 billion and for business use the value is $0.9 billion. This urban total of $2.2 billion is somewhat more than the private agricultural and grazing total of $2.0 billion. If the value of private forestry land is added to that of private agriculture and grazing, the total is $2.3 billion, somewhat greater than the urban total. There is a relatively small $80 million classified as urban but valued for agriculture and forest use. Also the agriculture and forest total consists of land held for urban development and should be added to the urban total.

It has also been learned that in Oregon, as perhaps in the rest of the nation, agricultural, grazing, and forest lands are relatively undervalued.[11] In addition, the tendency to allocate too large a portion of the total value of income-producing urban real estate to the structure continues because improvement value gives rise to depreciation deductions from realized income on real estate other than owner occupied residences, while this cannot be done with value allocated to land.

CONCLUSION

Although the value of land is largely created by society, land values are enjoyed by the owner and land taxes are paid by this owner. This situation creates a relationship between the level of land taxes paid and the general economic well-being of the owner that can be neglected only at great peril. Wherever LVT is being considered data are needed to demonstrate the distribution of the ownership of land. Reliance cannot be placed on the social desirability of better land use arising from LVT or the fact that total cost of holding land is no greater if land taxes are high than if they are low, and that therefore LVT is the best of all taxes because it does not increase costs or decrease take-home pay. The impact of tax payments on taxpayer well-being and the importance of ability to pay in measuring tax justice are too firmly imbedded in the minds of taxpayers to be avoided in the discussion of any tax change including a shift to LVT.

The need to relate LVT to the ability to pay of the taxpayer has too often been neglected by social scientists. Improved wealth data and particularly of land ownership distribution are improving opportunities to demonstrate LVT's strengths as a just tax because it is related to ability to pay. Also, LVT has a very real practical political plus in these days when property taxes on homesteads must be reduced as a portion of any tax reform. Data are now generally becoming available that demonstrate the average homeowner would

11. R. Charles Vars, "Area 23–The Property Tax Base," in *A Description and Analysis of Oregon's Fiscal System* (Salem, Oregon: State Executive Department, 1971).

find his taxes reduced if total property tax collections remained the same, but were collected with an ad valorem rate applied only to the land portion of real estate. Also, of course, rapidly rising land prices are visible to anyone who will look.

9 George M. Raymond

The Future of the Property Tax in Education Finance

During the 1968-69 school year, the Beverly Hills School District, which is located just outside of Los Angeles, California, spent $1,244 per enrolled child, while Baldwin Park, another district in the same area, spent only $595 per child. Surprisingly, however, Baldwin Park was taxing itself at a rate twice as high as that of Beverly Hills. That startling difference resulted from the fact that in the Beverly Hills School District each public school pupil was supported by taxable property market-valued at approximately $200,000, whereas Baldwin Park only had approximately $16,000 in property valuation for each child. Since, as is the case with school districts throughout most of the nation, both Beverly Hills and Baldwin Park relied primarily on the local property tax to finance their schools, the level of expenditure per child in each district was a function not of the educational needs of its children but strictly of "the wealth of the parents and neighbors."[1] In view of the prevalence of such disparities, Burke and Kelly, in a recent authoritative report, correctly state that the entire "present system of educational finance is one which regularly provides the most lavish educational services for those who have the highest income, live in the wealthiest communities, are of majority ethnic status."[2] It is no wonder, therefore, that the landmark *Serrano* v. *Priest* decision declared the state's school financing system to be unconstitutional.

REPLACING THE PROPERTY TAX

All things considered, the case for continuing the property tax in support of schools is demonstrably poor. Before its replacement can be seriously

1. *Serrano* v. *Priest,* California Supreme Court, 5 Cal. 3d 584, 487 P. 2d 1241 (1971).
2. Joel S. Berke and James A. Kelly, *The Financial Aspects of Equality of Educational Opportunity,* prepared for the Select Committee on Educational Opportunity, U.S. Senate (Washington, D.C.: Government Printing Office, 1972), p. 39.

considered, however, a good case must be made for a substitute. This paper will attempt a few steps in that direction, using New York State as a case study. In considering the detailed argument for an alternative approach to the support of schools, it should be emphasized that the appropriateness of continuing to finance all other municipal services through the property tax is not now being questioned.[3] The so-called "municipal over-burden," that is, the amount required to cover costs of all municipal services, also tends to rise at an accelerating rate, particularly since the advent of strong municipal civil service unions. But one question that must be answered as part of any analysis of the impact of a shift from property taxes to other forms of taxation in support of education, is whether the rapidly accelerating cost of local government will take up the slack. Were this to happen, the property tax burden on individual taxpayers could gradually again reach an intolerable level. For this reason a statutory maximum limit should be imposed on the property tax as a percentage of true property value, regardless of the purposes for which the revenue therefrom might be used, as was recently recommended in New Jersey.[4] A limit on the property tax would also lend political credibility to the proposition that what is offered is a *shift* of the school tax to other taxes, rather than a means of raising more taxes, overall.

Any cost of municipal services in excess of the amount which would be raised within such limits would have to be covered from other sources, such as state aid, or a local income or sales tax. A careful analysis of all municipal responsibilities is thus appropriate to determine the extent to which they, too, along with education, might be more appropriately discharged by, and paid for, at a higher level. Thus, for instance, in New York State's Nassau County much of the police function is discharged and paid for on a countywide basis; in neighboring Westchester County, on the other hand, there are almost as many police departments (40) as there are communities (45), serving a population only two-thirds as large as that of Nassau County. Fire protection in Nassau County is still largely performed on a voluntary basis, and the county is broken up into a multitude of sewer districts, garbage collection districts, and all kinds of other special districts, in addition to two small cities, over fifty incorporated villages, and three huge unincorporated townships. This hodgepodge of jurisdictional overlaps almost forces the conclusion that an assumption by the county of most municipal responsibilities would be more

---

3. Nor is any position taken as to the best method of levying a tax on property as between continuation of the tax on land and improvements or a substitution therefor of a tax on land value. The recent proposal of the New Jersey Tax Policy Committee that all local jurisdictions be given the option of using the traditional form or a modified land value form of taxation may well represent the most practical approach to this problem (see New Jersey Tax Policy Committee, *Report,* Summary, p. vii).

4. Ibid., p. vi.

efficient and economical, and certainly more equitable if as a result they would be supported by a countywide tax. Also, in dealing with a single jurisdiction of 1½ million people, which is the population of Nassau County, it is feasible to collect a local income tax in order to reduce property taxes; an income tax would not be equally feasible or even logical for each one of Nassau's local government and special district jurisdictions.

It is suggested that one possibly acceptable alternative to a statewide property tax for the support of schools, at least in states that now levy a broad spectrum of taxes including a reasonably progressive income tax, might be a proportional increase in all existing state-imposed levies. A study was performed for the state of New York to evaluate what would happen if the entire cost of education were shifted from the property tax to the aggregate of all other state taxes. Of course, state tax structures vary so much that the conclusions reached with respect to one state are not necessarily generally applicable; nevertheless, even a rudimentary analysis can shed light. Only one aspect of the problem was analyzed—the effect on other state taxes; other admittedly important economic dimensions of the shift, such as, for instance, the state's competitive position vis-à-vis other states, were ignored.

In the fiscal year ended June 30, 1970,[5] the grand total of all expenditures by all school districts throughout New York State amounted to $5,314,653,000. Of this amount, only $2,173,539,000,[6] or about 40 percent, was contributed by the property tax. The remainder came from state aid ($2,123,097,000), federal aid ($242,443,000), and miscellaneous other revenues and borrowings.

The $2.17 billion in property taxes for school purposes in 1969-70 equalled 37.3 percent of all state taxes collected in the fiscal year ended March 31, 1970, and 36.3 percent of those collected in the fiscal year ended March 31, 1971.[7] It is assumed, therefore, that in the fiscal year ended June 30, 1970, property tax revenues for school purposes throughout the state equalled approximately 37 percent of all the taxes collected by the state. (Since fiscal periods vary for different purposes, this study required approximations which, however, do not affect its basic conclusions.)

Thus, to shift responsibility for school financing to the state, the proceeds from all state taxes would have to be increased by 37 percent.

5. Data on school expenditures and distribution of financial responsibility are from *Financial Data for School Districts* for the fiscal year ended June 30, 1970, New York State Department of Audit and Control.

6. The Fleischmann Commission estimated the school property tax revenue at $2.28 billion. While this paper will use the official state data, its conclusions would be unaffected if the slightly higher figures were used.

7. Data on state taxes are from *Statistical Supplement to the Annual Report of the New York State Tax Commission* for the fiscal year 1970-71 (Albany: State of New York, 1972).

The state tax collections in the fiscal year ended March 31, 1971 were a composite of the following, in the proportions given:

Tax source	Percent of total tax (rounded)
Personal income tax	42.6
Business taxes (corporations, banks, insurance, and unincorporated business)	14.6
User taxes and fees (sales and use tax, motor vehicle and fuel, highway use, alcoholic beverage tax and license fees, and cigarette tax)	37.1
Revenues from other activities (estate tax, real estate transfer, pari-mutuel, racing admission, and boxing taxes, and the lottery)	5.7

If all state taxes were to be increased uniformly, of the $2.17 billion which would be transferred to the state from the local property tax, only 42.6 percent, or about $924 million, would have to be met out of the personal income tax. The remainder would be allocated as follows:

To business taxes	$317 million
To user taxes and fees	$805 million
To revenues from other activities	$124 million

For simplicity, it is assumed that the $924 million increment to the personal income tax would be levied in a manner which would not change the present relative tax burden on any class of personal income taxpayer. The latest available breakdown of personal income taxes, by total income class, is for the year 1969. The total tax, amounting to $2,186,445,000, was paid in the proportions shown in Table 9.1.

Table 9.1–Proportion of total New York State Personal Income Tax Contributed by Each Income Class, in 1969

Total income class	Percent of total tax
$ 1,000- 1,999	0.1
2,000- 2,999	0.5
3,000- 3,999	1.1
4,000- 4,999	1.9
5,000- 5,999	2.8
6,000- 6,999	3.4
7,000- 7,999	3.9
8,000- 8,999	4.3
9,000- 9,999	4.3
10,000-10,999	4.2
11,000-11,999	4.1
12,000-12,999	3.6

Total income class	Percent of total tax
$ 13,000–13,999	3.1
14,000–14,999	2.9
15,000–19,999	10.2
20,000–24,999	6.1
25,000–49,999	16.6
50,000–99,999	12.2
100,000 and over	14.7
Total	100.0

If the $924 million by which the total personal income tax would have to be increased as a result of a transfer of responsibility for school costs from the property tax were to be divided among all of the state's 6.8 million taxpayers in all income classes, in the same proportion as that which each is now contributing, the result would be as set forth in Table 9.2.

Table 9.2–Average Personal Income Tax Contribution by Total Income Class

Total income class	Percent of total contribution (from Table 9.1)	Total amount to be contributed (in thousands)	Total taxpayers[a]	Average contribution per taxpayer[a]
$ 1,000– 1,999	0.1	$ 924	370,294	$ 2.50
2,000– 2,999	0.5	4,620	469,725	9.84
3,000– 3,999	1.1	10,164	528,698	19.22
4,000– 4,999	1.9	17,556	611,695	28.70
5,000– 5,999	2.8	25,872	662,578	39.05
6,000– 6,999	3.4	31,416	640,309	49.06
7,000– 7,999	3.9	36,036	584,524	61.65
8,000– 8,999	4.3	39,732	535,988	74.13
9,000– 9,999	4.3	39,732	454,451	87.43
10,000–10,999	4.2	38,808	375,088	103.46
11,000–11,999	4.1	37,884	318,719	118.86
12,000–12,999	3.6	33,264	238,848	139.37
13,000–13,999	3.1	28,644	180,038	159.10
14,000–14,999	2.9	26,796	142,996	187.39
15,000–19,999	10.2	94,248	369,669	254.95
20,000–24,999	6.1	56,364	133,097	423.48
25,000–49,999	16.6	153,384	161,865	947.60
50,000–99,999	12.2	112,728	42,828	2,632.11
100,000 and over	14.7	135,828	13,532	10,037.54

[a]The amount needed in 1970 is distributed among 1969 taxpayers. The amount to be contributed by each income class and by each taxpayer may be overstated as a result, since the number of taxpayers in each class probably increased in 1970 compared with the previous year in line with the nation's economic growth prior to the recession in the fall of 1970.

The state sales tax would be called upon to produce about 19.5 percent, or $423 million, of the total amount which would have to be raised by the state as a result of the abandonment of the property tax for school purposes. Based on information supplied by the U.S. Bureau of Labor Statistics, this would call for an additional contribution per taxpayer, by total personal income class, in accordance with Table 9.3.

Table 9.3—Sales Tax Impact, by Total Income

Total income class	Additional contribution per taxpayer based on 37 percent increase in sales tax[a]
$ 1,000- 1,999	$ 14.43
2,000- 2,999	14.43
3,000- 3,999	18.87
4,000- 4,999	22.94
5,000- 5,999	26.64
6,000- 6,999	30.34
7,000- 7,999	33.67
8,000- 8,999	37.00
9,000- 9,999	40.33
10,000-10,999	43.66
11,000-11,999	46.99
12,000-12,999	49.95
13,000-13,999	52.91
14,000-14,999	55.87
15,000-19,999	64.38
20,000-24,999	73.73
25,000-49,999	87.65
50,000-99,999	111.15
100,000 and over	146.08

[a]Sales tax computed from 1971 Optional Sales Tax Table published by the U.S. Internal Revenue Service for a family size of 3 (in line with the median family size in the U.S. in 1969). Additional sales tax was derived by using median class interval.

Several conclusions applicable to New York State may be drawn from the above data:

1. Total financial responsibility for the support of public education can be transferred to the state without punitively taxing any one group of taxpayers or any single function within the state.

2. Such a transfer would directly benefit property owners with a modest fixed income (such as the retired) and enable many of them to maintain ownership of their home.

3. Such a transfer would also benefit all persons with incomes of under

$25,000, a group which in 1970 represented 96.8 percent of all personal income taxpayers. On the average, whether they are property owners or renters, members of this group probably pay more in property taxes for schools—either directly, or as part of their rents—than would be required of them in combined increases in personal income and sales taxes. Renters would, of course, benefit only if a compulsory rent reduction, equal to the reduction in the property tax, were instituted at the time of the changeover in school financing.

4. Such a transfer would enable renters to deduct their contribution to the support of education for federal income tax purposes. Since at present this privilege is extended only to property owners, landlords in effect, benefit from a deduction attributable to hidden property tax payments by tenants.

5. The sales tax, while somewhat regressive, is less so than the property tax, as the poor spend most of their limited funds on items which are not subject to sales taxes (rent, food, etc.).

6. The change in tax formulas would, of course, affect the wealthier taxpayers not only via the possibility that the increases in their state income and sales taxes would exceed their present property tax, but also via increases in the stock transfer, estate, real estate transfer, and various business taxes. Given these taxpayers' high tax bracket, however, much of their increase in the state personal income and sales taxes would otherwise be paid to the federal government. Indirectly, of course, the capture of this tax source has the same effect as a direct increase in federal aid to education for the purpose of reducing present inequities in school finance burdens. (Property taxes are also deductible.)

7. To a lesser degree, increases in business taxes would also affect the taxpayers in lower brackets via price increases for goods and services to cover the higher costs of doing business. But while business taxes would be increased by $317 million, this would be more than compensated for by the elimination of the nonresidential property taxes for education. Of the $2.17 billion in property taxes raised for the schools in 1970, only an estimated $1.13 billion came from residential property.[8] The rest came from vacant and farm land and from various businesses. It is important to stress that the increase in direct business taxes would be related to business profits as against the present system of taxing square feet of space occupied, regardless of whether a business operates in the black or in the red.

8. Windfall profits which may accrue to property owners as a result of the shift away from property taxes will be subject to income taxes, on both the state and federal levels. Increments in land values brought about through changes in the property tax structure could be taxed in the long run by adjusting the rate of capital gains taxes on land. Furthermore, income tax payments

8. Charles L. Schultz et al., *Setting National Priorities* (Washington, D.C.: Brookings Institution, 1972), p. 343, tables 10-11.

on other income will increase due to the end of deductions attributable to the school property tax.[9]

A blind shifting of tax burdens from the property tax onto other state taxes may create new imbalances, but many possibilities exist for preventing their occurrence. For example, the state could decide not to increase the income tax of any taxpayer whose income is under $5,000 per year, and perhaps for strictly political reasons, also not to increase the income tax of any taxpayers by more than 2.5 percent[10] of their income. Implementation of both segments of such a policy in New York State would require that the state raise an additional $40 million and $125 million respectively, or a total of $165 million, from other sources.

While this modification would exempt the poor from all direct education support burdens and would also avoid overly burdening the taxpayer at the most affluent end of the spectrum, it would leave a deficit of $547 million to be made up. A 37 percent increase in the alcoholic beverage tax and license fees and the cigarette tax would produce an additional $152 million. Under the blindly proportional reallocation scheme, the balance of nearly $400 million would have to come largely out of the motor vehicle and highway use taxes. Given the particular form of our civilization, motor vehicles are a necessity rather than a luxury for people in all income classes, including those in lower brackets. An across-the-board increase in auto use taxes, therefore, might be more regressive and unfair than the sales tax. The remaining deficiency, therefore, should preferably be made up by tapping some of the expected new revenues from federal sources (discussed below) or new sources of taxation, i.e., the various tax loopholes which favor taxpayers of one or another type on the federal level and in virtually every state. In New York State, for instance, which has no oil wells of any kind, it is difficult to understand why taxpayers are favored with an oil depletion allowance! In a recent national survey made for the Advisory Commission on Intergovernmental Relations (ACIR), nearly one-half of the respondents to a question on tax preferences indicated that, before any federal tax increases, they would like to see a reduction in all types of special tax privileges (such as for capital gains, charitable contributions, medical expenses, etc.).[11] It is entirely likely that these sentiments are shared on the state level.

9. Robert S. Benson and Harold Wolman, eds., *Counterbudget: A Blueprint for Changing National Priorities, 1971-1976* (New York: Praeger Publishers, 1971), p. 150.

10. This figure was selected as the average, assuming that the total property tax in New York State averages close to 4 percent of income, and that 1.5 percent or so would continue to be levied for municipal purposes.

11. ACIR, *Public Opinion and Taxes* (Washington, D.C.: Government Printing Office, 1972).

The above discussion assumed no increase in federal aid to education. It took no notice of the just adopted federal revenue-sharing program. It also ignored the possibility that the states might be relieved of all or a substantial share of their current public assistance costs. By ignoring the likelihood of a major revamping of federal responsibilities the above analysis was unnecessarily conservative. The amounts involved would represent a very large proportion of the local share of educational cost. Increased federal aid to the states would release state funds which, in turn, could be used to correct any imbalance caused by a shift away from the local school property taxes. If a large number of populous states decided to finance education through higher income and business taxes, the pressure on Congress to pick up the cost of welfare and an increased share of the cost of education might become irresistible because the people paying higher taxes possess political clout.

Indicative of the new freedom which increased federal participation in financing public assistance and education would bring are the following figures derived for the state of New York, the specific state that we have chosen to study. At the present time the federal government finances 6.9 percent of the total cost of public education. There is every indication that this percentage will be increased substantially, both in order to ease the transition from local to state financing and to reduce the increasing political liability which results from federal insensitivity to the continuing rise in the property tax. In his 1972 State of the Union message the President announced that the administration is considering a proposal to eliminate the *residential* property tax as a source of funds for schools by raising some $12 to 13 billion, possibly by means of a national value added tax.[12] From this source New York State could expect to receive over $1 billion. Even if federal aid to education were to increase by only $4 to $5 billion, as recommended by the President's Commission on School Finance, New York State could expect to receive between $400 and $500 million. The National Education Association has been consistently urging an increase in the federal share of public education costs to "at least one-third of the total." This recommendation, which would amount to approximately $14 billion, is considerably nearer that of the President than that of his more parsimonious commission.

As for the impact of a federal take-over of all public assistance costs, in 1970 this would have relieved New York State and its localities of a $1.4 billion[13] contribution. The state's share of this amount for family and adult

12. Schultze et al., *Setting,* p. 342. A recent Gallup poll reports that a majority of American adults are opposed to a value added tax, but favor a larger role for the states in meeting public school costs ("Value Added Tax Opposed in a Poll," *New York Times,* August 27, 1972).

13. ACIR, *State-Local, Finances: Significant Features and Suggested Legislation* (Washington, D.C.: Government Printing Office, 1972), p. 60, table 38.

programs, alone[14] (i.e., excluding programs of medical assistance) was nearly $400 million. Added to the $0.5 to $1 billion possible saving due to increased federal participation in education finance and to the $400 million which the state expects from the revenue sharing program, this would have freed some 15 to 23 percent of the 1970 state budget for reallocation to other programs. In addition, selected local governments would also have been relieved of having had to contribute some $400 million to public assistance, most of which was also raised through the property tax.

Any savings resulting from increased federal aid programs would be affected by the need to increase the total statewide cost of education in order to equalize school district expenditures nearer the level of the highest spenders. The national cost of equalizing to the ninetieth pupil percentile level, state by state, would amount to almost $7 billion. New York State's share of that cost would be $610.2 million.[15] The imperative need to equalize upward would thus reduce the spillover benefits of additional federal aid programs, but it would leave enough to assure that any negative impacts caused by the total elimination of the school property tax could be properly compensated for.

This exercise seems to prove that it is entirely possible to move to a system of taxation in support of schools that makes little use of the property tax. Many of the substitute taxes proposed bear a much more direct relationship to income than does the arbitrary ad valorem property tax. The recent survey performed for the Advisory Commission on Intergovernmental Relations[16] reported that, by margins of 3.4:1 and almost 2:1, respectively, the respondents preferred increases in state sales or income taxes to the institution of a state-wide property tax. Given these popular preferences and the relative painless-ness of the proposed shift, it is believed that, politically, an approach similar to that recommended in this paper would prove more acceptable than the establishment of a state-wide property tax. The difficulty of getting a state-wide property tax through state legislatures is indicated by the failure of seven consecutive proposals for the institution of such a tax to even reach a floor vote in either of California's legislative chambers since 1961.[17] Of course, the need to comply with the *Serrano* decision may change legislative attitudes, but chances are that most states will resort to some approach which will include major adjustments in other state taxes, whether or not they decide to

14. Family programs include aid to dependent children and one-person and family home relief. Adult programs include old age assistance and aid to the blind and disabled.

15. Schultze et al., *Setting,* p. 352, tables 10-14.

16. ACIR, *Public Opinion and Taxes.*

17. Betsy Levin, Michael A. Cohen, Thomas Muller, and William J. Scanlon, *Paying for Public Schools: Issues of School Finance in California* (Washington, D.C.: Urban Institute, 1972), p. 56.

keep any part of the property tax. The kind of research that would be most helpful to them in their painful stocktaking would trace to their ultimate ends the ripples in the overall tax system at the respective state and the federal levels, making as explicit as possible the share of the total new public education finance structure which every group and category of taxpayers will be expected to meet. This type of research is, unfortunately, still to be performed in spite of the urgency of the public issue which the nation is now confronting.

10 Ronald E. Grieson

The Finance and Allocation of Educational Resources

I eventually want to discuss the effects of, efficiency of, and misconceptions about property tax financing of education, but let us first turn our attention to educational finance in a perfectly optimal world.

NON-EXTERNALITY REASONS FOR GOVERNMENT INTERVENTION IN EDUCATION

Consider a world in which all education (not research) was financed and provided for privately by means of tuition payments levied on students! Would anything be unoptimal about this system?

First, there might be communitywide externalities from education, i.e., good citizenship. To the extent that education makes one a better citizen, it ought to be subsidized. We will return to this possibility later.

Conversely, if all education was strictly vocational and thereby produced no externalities other than a market for products produced, would there be any reason for its subsidy or public provision?

An argument could be advanced that the poor would not be able to purchase education to the point where its marginal benefit equaled cost. Why wouldn't the poor borrow? There might exist imperfect capital markets making it difficult for parents or children to borrow against future human capital. In that case a loan program could be established which spread the risk of such loans and extended repayment time à la FHA., making either the children or parents responsible for repayment.

Another argument might be that parents are not altruistic or do not have the ability to determine the optimal amount of education for their children.

Next, one might say that parents do not know the optimal amount of education for each of their children. It could also be asked whether the educational bureaucracy knows better. If it does know, or could find out at reasonable cost (since information is not free), parents could be informed of their children's prospects and the optimal amount of education for them whether funded by the parent or borrowed against the children's future income.

It may well be that parents' ignorance, if it exists, typically lies in over-estimating the benefit their children receive from education, hence overspending on their children's education and suggesting government intervention, taxation, etc. to reduce excessive expenditures. On balance, parents are probably both altruistic and optimizing.

Let us assume the worst and say parents are unaltruistic or uninformed of the value of education and would have their children receive too little even though the children would bear at least part of the cost of loan repayment. In this case, we might be able to take the decision from the parents and give (to the extent that it may be possible) the children the optimal amount of education, making the children liable for the costs. This would involve the same force levels currently contained in involuntary attendance requirements and the subsequent taxation. Another possibility, which we will discuss in much greater detail later, is that governments provide the optimal education to each child and finance it through general taxation, accepting the inefficiencies and deadweight losses of such taxes.

GENERAL GOALS OF EDUCATION

It may be that education is in part a consumption good for children and/or parents and society feels the poor have too little consumption. If so, the solution would merely be to re-distribute some income to the poor in the most efficient possible way.

It may also be argued that investment in education is a good method of combating poverty (by raising the future income of children), which poor individuals and families would not adopt themselves. In this context one might refer to the pessimistic reports on education as a cure for poverty done by Weisbrod, Smolensky, or Ribich,[1] or look at the Job Corps ineffectiveness at changing personality structure.

With regard to education and employment, it would seem that individuals would privately contract for the optimal amount of education either through schools (vocational or otherwise) or through on the job training unless one of the above problems is present, in which case information and loans would be all that is needed. Again, the failures of education cited by Ribich, Smolensky

1. Burton A. Weisbrod, "Preventing High School Dropouts," in R. Dorfman, ed., *Measuring Benefits of Government* (Washington, D.C.: Brookings Institution, 1965); Eugene Smolensky, "Investment in Education of the Poor: A Pessimistic Report," *American Economic Review*, 56 (May 1966), 370-78; Thomas I. Ribich, *Education and Poverty* (Washington, D.C.: Brookings Institution, 1968).

and Weisbrod would support this conclusion. The general finding is that short vocational re-training programs for the poor are the only ones with worthwhile benefit-cost ratios. There is no reason to believe that this type of retraining would not take place privately except for the aforementioned easily remedied imperfections (imperfect knowledge or capital markets).

Another argument put forward is that individuals will invest too little in education because of the existence of welfare and ability to pay taxes which reduce the perceived benefits of education to individuals, or similarly that this transfer creates pecuniary externalities for society to income and therefore education. In truth, the tax system as it exists creates disincentives to all types of investment (physical and human) and all types of work and productive effort. Increased expenditures per student have not been shown to result unambiguously in increased educational benefits equal to cost, never mind increased work effort, on-the-job training, or investments in human capital. The only way to eliminate the tax distortion would be to abolish the tax.[2]

In discussing whether education does reduce individual poverty and increase general economic well-being, we might stop to look at education's ability to produce private benefits or increased productivity which ought to be much more certain. Studies by Coleman, Bowles,[3] and others seem to show that expenditures per child and class size have little effect on educational output, thereby implying that merely providing per capita subsidies to students does not guarantee the funds will be used by schools to provide even significant private benefits, never mind public ones. These studies do, however, seem biased toward finding the results they did. They studied very small variations in class size for example, thereby not really testing the class size hypothesis. They also appear to contain errors in specifications and simultaneity, discounting the validity of their results.

To whom do the positive benefits from education or the negative ones from its absence accrue and to what extent? Eighty percent of all locally educated students eventually reside in a community other than that in which they are

2. In this vein it is worth noting that only net of tax income, adjusted for transfers, should be used in benefit-costing education lest we provide too much education relative to other productive factors, i.e., private education and physical capital, etc., since the private sector only looks at net (after tax benefits). Actually the theory of second best would indicate that we evaluate the benefits of education at something between gross and net increase in income. If we do not count only net of tax benefits, all private activities would be taken over by government since the private sector only counts net of tax benefits, while government counts gross of tax benefits.

3. James S. Coleman et al., *Equality of Educational Opportunity* (Washington, D.C.: Government Printing Office, 1966), and Coleman, "The Concept of Equality of Educational Opportunity," *Harvard Educational Review*, 38, no. 1 (Winter 1968); Samuel S. Bowles, *Education Production Function*, U.S. Office of Education (Cambridge: Harvard University Press, 1969).

educated. Much of the income expansion arising from education will not accrue to the locality in which a student is educated. Rather it will largely accrue to other localities within the state and nation. Therefore, the portion of educational expenditures paid for by localities is likely to be the private good portion of education. We must seriously question what the benefits of education subsidies are and to what extent they are affected by merely providing the aid independent of performance. A very good case could be made that education in reading, writing, arithmetic, and American History create large general benefits.[4] However, merely giving each district some amount of aid over a child's school lifetime or per day of attendance in no way gives the school any incentive to create the desired abilities. The school may merely use the subsidy to reduce the local cost of providing the private goods portion of education or waste it bureaucratically.

A more desirable method of bringing about this type of basic general education would be to give the school, or better yet the individual, a cash payment equal to the value of the benefits to society. School or students could be given a payment based upon their scores on standardized tests, etc. (as could adults if we really want to push citizenship capabilities), that is, if a literate earning $10,000 per year is preferred by society to an illiterate earning the same salary. These payments would probably not be proportionate to test scores but a declining proportion, perhaps $S = aT^{1/2}$, since going from illiteracy to literacy probably generates a much greater increase than going from literacy to an understanding of Yeats.

Paying these subsidies to all literates would involve taxes, which create distortions. Taxing someone $100 and giving him $100 will make him worse off unless the tax is a lump sum or a land tax. A better way to internalize the benefits to society would be by means of fines or ignorance taxes since these taxes would have almost no deadweight loss and could be made to have no (undesirable) effects on income distribution merely by giving poor individuals an increase in income equal to the expected value of their fine.

The most efficient system would be to fine or tax individuals so that they can produce the desired general education by means of the optimal combination of home education, self-study, and formal schooling. The system could contain federal, state, and local elements, though localities would have a relatively much greater interest in adult education (since less than 20 percent of the younger students will come to reside in their locality of education).

In summary, the citizenship benefits of education would largely accrue to the nation, and to the extent that education exists it ought be funded nationally,

4. Music and Art courses may create knowledge which leads individuals to create a more aesthetic environment, thereby creating some indirect general benefits, but so do many activities that are not internalized either, because of the difficulty of measurement or administration.

or conversely the nation could tax individuals who do not obtain it. The results would be the same except that taxing those who do not obtain an education would eliminate the deadweight loss of raising taxes for a general subsidy. Subsidizing everyone $1000 to learn reading, writing, arithmetic, and a little American History has the same effect as charging them $1000 if they do not, but charging them is better since you need not incur any deadweight tax losses in raising revenue for the subsidy.

Most important, general benefits resulting from education accrue to the student's state or nation; hence it is likely that localities would ignore them.[5]

CHOICE AND EFFICIENCY

The most efficient system for providing choice and controlling cost would be competing tuition financed private schools with subsidies for externalities and perhaps public scholarships for low income students. In this regard large city systems will be less responsive to local needs and less cost effective but may provide more variety (specialized) educational facilities. Decentralized private and public schools will have great incentives to meet consumer demand at optimum cost, whereas large systems will have some monopoly power (less elastic demand), at least in the short run, and therefore less pressure for efficiency. However, decentralized public schools serve students geographically and not by interest or ability; hence they cannot achieve the specialization— art, music, mathematics, science, remedial English, history, etc.—which can be obtained by private schools or a large public school system using cross registration.

New York City is a perfect example: on balance the citizens seem to feel it less well meets their needs than the more flexible competing suburban systems, though its expenditures per student are very high (and property taxes relatively low) and it provides specialized schools in science, art, music, etc. Thus it seems decentralized public schools may be more efficient on balance than centralized public schools even though the geographically tied provision of a good limits the economies of scale, specialization, and consumer choice possible.

EFFICIENCY OF PROPERTY TAX FINANCING

Property taxes as a means of funding the local costs of education cause substantial deadweight losses.[6] The property tax is a tax on the cost of structures,

5. The local general benefits from education would be internalized locally. They present no real problem and, as we shall discuss later, can easily be financed from local land or lump sum taxes and measured by means of local voting, etc.

6. We are again assuming that since few general benefits accrue locally, localities must basically fund the private goods portion of education.

which can have a capitalized value or sales tax equivalent of 50 percent or more (the sales tax equivalent equals the property tax divided by the rate of return on capital) on structural capital. It therefore causes individuals to substitute away from structural capital (mostly commercial and rental housing due to federal tax laws) toward other less taxed goods bringing about undesirable substitution effects and deadweight losses compared to a lump sum or land tax (or even general sales and income taxes).

A simple utility curve diagram can show the inefficiency (loss of utility) involved in taxing one good to obtain say $1000 from someone and giving the individual $1000 or $1000 worth of benefits. An undesirable substitution effect is created that would not occur as a result of land taxes (taxes on a totally inelastically supplied or demanded good), lump sum payments, or tuition payments of equal amount. It is interesting to note that the inefficiency of property taxes, adjusting for differences in local public goods, should cause them to be overcapitalized. Property taxes will reduce the value of land by the tax paid plus the resulting deadweight loss. If demand and supply of structures are sufficiently elastic the deadweight loss of property taxes could be greater than the tax itself.

Can the inefficiencies of property taxes be reduced without an outright recourse to land taxes or tuition payments? Zoning so that the quality and density of structure are required to be the same as they would be in the absence of property taxes has the potential, though not perfectly, since the exact optimal quantity and type of use, etc. for each piece of property would be difficult for zoners to determine. Another way would be to assess each residence equally, converting the property tax to a lump sum tax. I have demonstrated that varying property tax assessment ratios proportionate to elasticities of supply of each type of structure[7] would be the same as a land tax—perfectly efficient as a means of raising revenue.

Progressive legislation designed to force the use of fair market value for assessment purpose would prevent the use of fixed lump sum assessments or property tax assessment ratios based on and proportionate to land values. They would further prevent the bind of assessment ratio bargaining which goes on between localities and businesses, all of which reduce the deadweight loss of the property tax. Full value assessment and property taxation is not the most efficient kind of taxation and is probably worse than the existing system of differential assessment ratios.

---

7. The actual rule is that the assessment ratio (a_j) times the elasticity of supply of the particular structure, (ES_j), $a_j \cdot ES_j$, be equal for structures, all j, such that $a_j \cdot ES_j = a_i ES_i = C$ or $\dfrac{a_j}{a_i} = \dfrac{ES_i}{ES_j}$, which can be shown to be the same as an equal ratio tax on all land.

A statewide property tax has also been suggested as a means of financing the full (private and public) components of education. Statewide property taxes would end the ability of individual communities to use zoning and lump sum assessments as means of reducing the deadweight loss of property taxes. Statewide property taxes would also be likely to lead to fair market value assessment which would be another impediment to improving the efficiency (reducing the inefficiency) of property taxes.

A statewide property tax on industrial and commercial structures has been suggested as another tool for funding education, and it is undoubtedly the least efficient and worst possible tax this paper will consider. The deadweight loss of a particular tax is an increasing function of the elasticity of demand for the taxed goods. It is better to tax a more rather than a less inelastically demanded good. The demand for industrial location is certainly more elastic than the demand for structures in general. Therefore, switching from the taxation of all structures to just the more elastically demanded industrial sector would increase the deadweight loss of the tax, driving industry out of the state and preventing the above zoning and assessment methods of increasing the inefficiency loss of property taxes. Furthermore, property taxes, mortgage interest, and the imputed return on equity in owner occupied homes are deductible or not included in the personal income tax base, almost completely eliminating—and causing housing to be priced relatively lower than other goods for high income individuals (33 percent bracket or above)—the deadweight, or inefficiency, loss of property taxes levied on them. This alone would suggest that all property taxes be transferred to owner-occupied homes, commercial and rental structures being exempted from all property taxes used to fund education.

A statewide land tax has also been advanced as a method of funding education. Land taxes of any sort are an extremely efficient way of raising revenue for any purpose. A question has been raised about the ability of land taxes to replace the forty billion dollars now raised by means of property taxes. I have used a general equilibrium model of land values to estimate the effect of shifting from property to land taxes upon the price (not value, which would rise)[8] of land. I find that, given reasonable assumptions about the elasticity of supply and demand for structures, a total switch from property to land taxes would reduce the price of land less than 100 percent, and also reduce the prices and increase the quantities of all types of structures.

8. It is important to understand that the elimination of property taxes would cause all land to rise in value and be used more densely. See Ronald E. Grieson, "The Economics of Property Taxes and Land Values," M.I.T. Economics Working Paper no. 72, June 1971, revised April 1972, *Journal of Urban Economics* (July 1974).

OPTIMAL RESOURCE ALLOCATION AND TAXES

In the case of private goods the prices paid for them both fund their production and indicate the optimal quantities and types to be produced. Similarly the optimal amounts and types of education would be produced at minimum cost by means of competing education producers (schools) who charge tuition. As stated previously, the general benefits from education could be most efficiently internalized by means of subsidies or even more efficiently by taxes on the absence or failure to reach set goals.

Again tuition may not be a politically feasible method of financing the local private goods (investment and consumption) portion of education, giving us need to examine the ability of the various tax bases to reflect the private (and perhaps public) goods benefits of education, thereby guiding the allocation of resources in this area.

If demand for residence in a community is infinitely elastic and the benefits of living in the community are uniformly increased by \$300, demand for location in the community will rise by \$300; hence land values would rise by \$300. If property taxes were used to finance the benefit, land values would go up by \$300 minus the deadweight loss of the property tax (which would be greater than \$300 thus lowering land values).[9] The net increase in land values (net of the deadweight loss of property taxes) would reflect the benefit or gain in welfare from the service net of funding. Obviously, using property taxes of \$300 to finance a service worth \$300 would be undesirable, while using land taxes of \$300 to finance the expenditure would leave the community indifferent. The use of a property tax will mean that it is only worthwhile to fund education expenditures whose benefits exceed costs by the deadweight loss of the property taxes needed to fund them.[10]

This difficulty could be eliminated by zoning all areas of the community so as to require exactly the same pattern of allocation that would exist with land taxes or tuition payments. Exactly optimal zoning is an extremely difficult objective if the optimal pattern would involve a large multiplicity of land uses. The task would be greatly simplified if the optimal pattern was a relatively

9. If the good is a pure public good whose benefits exceed costs, the value of land will rise by the benefits minus the increased cost of occupying the community more densely, the net benefit of the public good. The greater density will be desirable in order to optimally utilize the public good (or economics of scale good). For an analysis of this mechanism, see Ronald E. Grieson, "Density, Local Public Goods, Taxation and the Tiebout Hypothesis" (mimeographed).

10. In the case of owner-occupied housing, property taxes, interest, and the imputed rental are all deductible or tax exempt while the rental value of the structure need not be reported as income. Hence, owner-occupied structures receive a subsidy S, the marginal personal income tax rate, yielding a cost of $(1-S)(1+t/r)P$ or a rent of $(1-S)(r+t)P$, which may not be significantly different than the untaxed cost of housing; where t is the property tax rate, r the discount rate and P the cost of a unit of structure, capital, and land.

homogenous land use. All of these methods would lead to the benefits of educational expenditures being reflected in changes in aggregate land values with little inefficiency.

Zoning of this sort has often been called snob zoning, but it may actually increase the efficiency of resource allocation. It prevents rising property tax rates, large inefficiencies, game theory type under maintenance, and attempts to underzone and underutilize the land in a community in order to obtain a financial transfer from high quality uses.

States, which would not be expected to have infinitely elastic demand curves for residence, could not therefore realistically expect the benefit of education to be fully reflected in land values, thus losing this valuable guide to the allocation of funds. Considering the large deadweight loss of property taxes, it would seem that if education is to be funded on a statewide basis, land, sales, or income taxes would be preferable.

Statewide property tax funding of education would be likely to bring about several further difficulties. Such a tax would lead to equal spending per student even though benefit cost calculation shows that many students would not benefit from so high a level of expenditures. Statewide property taxes and control might lead to greater homogeneity in education, thus limiting the ability of schools to meet differing needs of different students. Another difficulty is that statewide taxes could seriously deteriorate the financial position of major cities. New York City's Budget Bureau has estimated that equal per pupil expenditures throughout New York State funded by a uniform statewide property tax, at the level now prevailing in New York City, would lead to a 30 percent increase in New York City's property tax rate. Furthermore, equal per pupil expenditures would prevent parents who desire to spend more than the standard amount on their children from so doing, thus withdrawing a large measure of middle class support for the public school system and hastening its demise.

Most studies of the educational production function seem to indicate that the quality of education is not very strongly related to per pupil expenditure, pointing up the fact that differences in spending may merely be differences in the consumption component of education, not the investment part. Hence, equalizing expenditures may merely be the over equalization, relative to other goods, of one type of consumption, in which case the poor and rich would probably be better off with direct income redistribution.

Conference Review Hour

Harvey Brazer: As economists, we now know a little bit more than was understood when Seligman said that the property tax as actually administered in the United States is the worst tax known in the civilized world.

I once even quoted that with approval, but this is ignorance. Since I quoted that in print last, we have had studies by Jim Morgan and Harvey Brazer and others that suggest that the property tax as applied to residential property only may, in fact, not be regressive.

For example, in a book called *Income and Welfare in the United States,* which I now cite with approval, we find that if you include imputed rental income in the income base, the property tax doesn't turn out to be very regressive at all. It tends to look almost proportional. Moreover, if we are going to be consistent as public finance experts, we surely ought to insist that as a first reform, imputed rental income should be included in the income tax base.

In any case, in any measure of income we should include imputed rental income. We have the study by University of Chicago type economists, Reid and Muth and others, with findings suggesting that the income elasticity of the demand for housing is as high as 1.1, perhaps somewhat higher. If that is true, then, by definition, the real estate tax is progressive. You may say, "Well, yes, perhaps it is progressive in respect to permanent income." The record shows that there is such a view, and two additional studies using different procedures point in this direction.

I should say that if we had to start from scratch, if we had a clean sheet of paper on which to draft the tax structure for the United States, I would still argue that we probably would not want a property tax, or at least not much of a property tax. But that's not where we are.

We do have a tax system; however, in this tax system we exempt imputed rental income from the federal income tax. At the same time, we are foolish enough to allow the deduction of the property tax and the interest paid on mortgages. You cannot acknowledge this and at the same time argue that the

135

property tax is an efficiency destroying excise tax placed on housing. It just is not so.

As Milton Friedman has told us, when you have one set of excise taxes in a system, it may be that you can improve efficiency, by an offsetting tax. In the same vein, with respect to taxation of business property, we know that if we didn't have a heavy payroll tax, there might be little or no rationale for the offsetting tax on business capital; however, as long as we have heavy payroll taxes representing essentially an excise on inputs in the form of labor, we may actually improve efficiency by adding an excise tax on capital input.

Perhaps we have done the job too well in convincing the public and the politicians that the property tax is an obnoxious tax aside from its readily recognized administrative deficiencies in actual practice. However, each of us, I am sure, could revise that system of administration if only we were given the chance.

Daniel Holland: That recognition that we have done too well in denigrating the property tax has come home to many in a disquieting fashion. I think you were present at that recent meeting at the Treasury, Professor Vickrey. There were ten or fifteen of us who had often engaged in the standard forms of castigation of the tax that had constituted the consensus. This negative consensus was put to the test by President Nixon's suggestion that we get rid of a substantial portion of the property tax. Suddenly there was a general agreement of most of those present—most of the public finance people—that we weren't so certain we wanted to get rid of it.

In spite of all the statements that we had made against it having become common currency, now we weren't so sure they were true. We only believe our arguments when we make them, not when everybody does. It turned out that the greatest piece of knowledge that came out of the meeting was the fact that an investment in one's own home, given the nontaxability of imputable income from all sources and the deductibility of interest from taxable income, can be a profitable investment.[1]

Now I want to raise a set of questions in relation to the fundamental questions posed by George Raymond, who is not with us today. He raised some basic questions about the incidence of property taxation; he also performed an operation on the New York State tax structure that suggested all taxpayers in New York State (all but that insignificant portion that received over $25,000 a year in income) stood to gain by a proportional expansion of all other taxes by an amount sufficient to recoup a forgone property tax.

All those who receive over $25,000 a year are very small in number and in any sensible political structure, will be outvoted. So the elimination of the

1. Editor's note: It would be even more profitable if depreciation, insurance, and maintenance costs were deductible as it is in the case of commercial property.

property tax should be a very appealing prospect. It should be quite appealing, but I think, just on the basis of its not having yet been adopted, very suspect; I think we might address ourselves to these implicit suggestions of Mr. Raymond.

I think Mr. Raymond's position on the incidence of the property tax, should be used as a challenge to see if we can generate any additional broad consensus about that difficult matter. Let's see if we can start with this general area—the incidence of the property tax and Mr. Raymond's operations on the New York State tax structure.

Our program states we are to consider among alternatives a state administered property tax or a state administered land value tax in place of the present local property tax for the finance of education, or any other tax structures that we may design. Who would care to speak to this general range of considerations?

William Vickrey: The paper of John Riew does address this question of a state tax. It seems to me that it advanced at least two notions. One was that a state land value tax would avoid the traditional difficulty of competitive under-valuation for the purpose of reducing the community's share in state tax.

It wasn't quite clear to me how the land value tax avoided this.

John Riew: It is not correct to say that state land tax avoids the problem of competitive undervaluation. It does increase the need for improvement in the state equalization program. The local assessors, I expect, are competitive here in Wisconsin, and the state equalizers ought to be more careful and do a better job of equalizing.

William Vickrey: You will still have the equalization problem with a state property tax regardless of what the base of that tax is. The other questionable idea is that somehow a tax on land is more appropriate as a state tax whereas the tax on improvements is more appropriate as a local tax. However, at least in terms of interjurisdictional competition, improvements in the long run are more fugitive than land. Therefore, I would have been driven to the opposite conclusion, that since land cannot flee a jurisdiction it is most suitable for local taxation, and it is the tax on improvements which is the more suitable for state administration.

M. Mason Gaffney: I don't think there's anything wrong with your logic, Mr. Vickrey. I think, however, that you and Mr. Riew are addressing a different set of issues. You were talking about the fugitive nature of capital, and Mr. Riew had in mind something more like the fact that local governments have a particular interest or bias in excluding poorer population to avoid diluting the tax base. I think the thrust of what he said was that it would be desirable to shift the financing of schools in order to overcome this bias.

At any rate, I don't think there is a logical conflict here; you are discussing different issues. In order to resolve it, you'd have to get together on two or three other matters including the tendency of municipalities to behave in a monopolistic manner.

Eli Schwartz: I don't know why Harvey Brazer does not address himself to the question. He made some plea for keeping the property tax in our tax structure because if we had to replace it with something else, we would fall into worse problems. I would like to know what these problems are.

Harvey Brazer: I can just repeat that there are certain consequences in removing the property tax that you may not like. For example, Michigan's proposal on the ballot for November 7, 1972, will effectively remove the property tax for the purpose of operating its schools.

That is $1,200,000,000. The thing I worry about is what the Secretary of Revenue in the state of Wisconsin implied the other day. It is politically possible to get legislatures to raise taxes only by so much in any given period of time. When you give away $1.2 billion, the chances are that you will have an awful time replacing it.[2]

I am also concerned about the fact that we believe that taxes on land are capitalized and taxes on buildings are partly capitalized, and then we are willing to pass over the windfall gains that will accrue if we substantially reduce the property tax. I am not sure that removing the property tax does not damage distributional considerations.

I am also not sure that removing the property tax does not damage efficiency. Yet at the same time, if given my preference, I would certainly not want to *increase* the property tax. I think that under the circumstance where we can choose only in second best terms, the best choice is one where we freeze the property tax at its present level and go on from there to develop, perhaps, more rational tax structures.

Daniel Fusfeld: I would like to speak to the question of reducing or eliminating the property tax. I have been working with a friend who is a land speculator, and he is just waiting for the day when the property tax goes! He will then be able to buy up all this land, hang on to it indefinitely, let its value rise, and retire a far richer man than he is now.

Of course as of now, he pays very little property tax because our assessors are wise enough to keep taxes on open land very, very low so as to keep our speculators getting wealthy rapidly. However, when you think about the question of property tax and the dynamic environment of growing population, spreading urban areas, and the ability of land speculators to hang onto land and make capital gains, I think I would have to differ with Harvey Brazer.

Perhaps if we look at the income distribution effects of the property tax in a dynamic urban environment, perhaps we do want to raise the property tax

2. Editor's note: Because of this problem a package including replacement taxes as well as property tax reductions is often developed.

and get some of this land into use instead of allowing it to sit as weedy fields making land speculators rich.

Eli Schwartz: Do you mean the property tax or land tax, Mr. Fusfeld?

Daniel Fusfeld: It's the property tax in Michigan.

Eli Schwartz: From the way you talk, you would prefer the property tax base shifted over much more heavily on land?

Daniel Fusfeld: Oh, yes, it would be very nice if it were shifted in that direction. As it is now, the property tax falls more heavily on improvements relative to the land.

Ronald Grieson: In reference to the comment that speculators will buy up land *after the property tax is lifted* and make windfall gains, I must say that the gains at the time the property tax is removed will accrue to the owners. Speculators will have to pay the old price for land plus the capitalized value of the annual property tax abated.

Harvey Brazer: His friend is speedy!

Ronald Grieson: Fusfeld reported his friend is going to buy it up when the property tax is taken off.

If the previous tax was $100 per year on the land and the tax is abated, the value of the land will rise by the capitalized value of the tax, perhaps $1,500. The supply of land is fixed (totally inelastic), and any increase or decrease in tax will be capitalized as soon as it is announced.

Speculators, anyone holding land, will gain if the land tax is lowered while they are holding the land and lose only if land taxes are unexpectedly raised.

The speculators' profits are not affected by the existence of land taxes— only by unanticipated changes in the taxes.

Moreover, land taxes or changes in land tax rates will not significantly affect the timing of land development. A land tax on the actual or best use potential rent of land will have no effect on the timing of development.

There is the valid objection that the removal of the overall property taxes will create windfall gains. However, a land tax could be set at the same absolute level as the present property tax based on the site plus structures. Additional taxes would then be imposed on any future increments to the basic land value.

Harvey Brazer: I don't care too much about how you fix the present level of tax, but I would probably prefer your modification that leaves the tax on a particular parcel unchanged.

Noel Edelson: We haven't taken up Daniel Holland's challenge of Mr. Raymond's thesis yet. I have no answer to it. On the face of it, it seems like an absurd result. However, I think the paper may not be sufficiently clear as to methodology.

William Vickrey: I have the feeling that this notion that the property tax is regressive is a little of an artifact. I don't really see the inhabitants of a ghetto as being property owners in any tax incidence sense, and I don't really see the tenant farmers, the sharecroppers, the migrant workers as being bearers of much of the incidence of the property tax.

To the extent that there are poor people who own farms or who own property, this is likely to be in areas where the tax rates are fairly low—in rural areas—as compared with property in the city. I have a feeling somehow that we have taken a distribution of property ownership by income class and applied a uniform rate of taxation, whereas there is likely to be a correlation between income levels and the rate of taxation that has not been taken into account.

Daniel Holland: Isn't it true that a standard accusation is that rental property is taxed particularly heavily, and the inhabitants of the ghettos are, in fact, renters?

William Vickrey: To the extent that the tax falls on improvements, that could conceivably be true. I think a good deal of the argument follows from the assumption that the landlord considers the tax as a cost and sets the rent accordingly. However, it is not made clear what it is that enables him to raise the rent. If he could not have done it before, why didn't he? The implication must be that somehow the landlord is in the position of a monopolist and is restraining himself from maximizing his monopoly profit on some kind of "just price" notion. When you tax him, he exerts himself to recover more of his monopoly profit.

I don't think landlords are like this, and I don't think the market in ghetto real estate is that monopolized.

Seymour Sacks: We have 500,000 people living in public housing in New York City alone; the regressivity assumption of Mr. Raymond does not consider them. The public housing element in New York City is a rather major one, so we should at least recognize that factor. If we followed Raymond's suggestion we would move them from a situation where they are not paying any tax at all to one where they are going to be picked up on the other end of the tax structure.

Could I ask one other question, though? There is a feeling here that there is an independence between land taxation and taxation on improvements. I really don't feel this is completely real. If you change one tax relative to the other, there may be a tendency by the assessment process, or by a number of other processes, to pick up the additional revenues that you want.

What I want to know is, What are the feelings of the people here who have worked on the problem of the independence of the land and improvement taxation? Ultimately, doesn't the land taxation only have meaning in terms of the improvements or vice versa?

Ferdinand Schoettle: I am not an economist, but Netzer gives figures that seem to indicate poor people do pay property taxes. Certainly the Oldman and Aaron study in Boston[3] indicated that poor renters were discriminated against in two ways: (*a*) by paying taxes and (*b*) by the fact that for a variety of reasons, the owners of slum dwellings tend to bear a relatively higher assessment ratio. I do know that the tax gets capitalized; the standard studies I have seen indicate that the tax is considered one of the numbers in the capitalization value in buying urban property.

Maybe if the tax is all capitalized, you are right, the renter wouldn't bear it.

William Vickrey: I am ambivalent as to the effect of the tax on improvements. Certainly to the extent that, for instance, high property tax rates in places like Newark led to high abandonment rates, there is pressure on the supply side, which raises rent.

Noel Edelson: Should we be speaking of the effect of a rise in tax rates on the whole rent structure? There is the position of the individual landlord who may not have the monopoly power to raise his rent; however, when you raise the tax, you raise it for the whole housing industry.

William Vickrey: To the extent that the tax is on improvements (i.e., buildings) rather than on land and to the extent that the increase in taxes on improvements makes it difficult for new low income structures to be built, yes; however, there are very few low income structures that are being built by private enterprise. If there are none being built and all that's being done is that a supply of old houses trickles down, the effect of the tax on the supply is limited almost to the effect on abandonment.[4] While a full ten years ago, you could have brushed that off and said the result was negligible, I think in the last five years this has become a fairly serious problem.

William Oakland: The evidence I have been able to find and gather in Baltimore suggests that the conversion of rent into market value in slum property occurs at higher capitalization rate than that of the rents on luxury apartments. Frequently the methodology used in formal incidence studies is to assume that a person pays a given rent because the property contributes to the property tax.

However, if you live in a slum, you pay a given rent, but the value of the house which you live in may be very close to zero. In this case you are not going to pay much in the way of a property tax on structure.

A second comment is that the property tax might actually help the poor in the sense that conversion of new slum housing, the opportunity for low-priced housing, may be actually accelerated. We know that the property tax

3. O. Oldman and A. Aaron, "Assessment-Sales Ratios under the Boston Property Tax," *National Tax Journal*, 18 (March 1965), 36-49.

4. Editor's note: Would not the tax affect the whole supply of housing? And to the extent there is some competition for housing across all income groups, all groups would share in the increased rents.

works to aid the creation of new slums; it discourages maintenance of existing property. The whole conversion process may actually improve the lot of the poor. I think Dick Muth has also mentioned this.[5]

Harvey Brazer: I should like to respond briefly to Mr. Schoettle again. When you cite Dick Netzer's data or figures on property tax incidence, you have to indicate which of Dick Netzer's estimates you are referring to. Dick Netzer, at the time of publication of the *Economics of the Property Tax,*[6] included in his chapter on incidence at least four or five alternative estimates which differ considerably from each other.

Ferdinand Schoettle: The one I remember shows about 7 percent for the lowest income bracket.

Harvey Brazer: The one I remember is the one that I developed that he reproduced, and that, of course, is very different.

Ferdinand Schoettle: Would you agree with the statement that the property tax is regressive for those with the lowest income?

Harvey Brazer: I would prefer to say at this stage we don't know very much about the incidence of the property tax. It may or may not be regressive; I have yet to see convincing evidence that it, in fact, is. A lot depends upon the concept of income that you use as the basis for your estimation—and upon the kinds of assumptions you make about whether or not a tax is shifted. The evidence cited with respect to the assessment ratio for low value·versus high value properties can readily be countered with other evidence drawn from other assessing jurisdictions. The overassessment of low value properties is not consistent across assessing jurisdictions.

There is the point that William Oakland has made in his paper about the ratio between rentals and property values. I think it is a well-taken point, and it does relate to the question of how you arrive at the estimates of incidence of property tax.

If you look closely at Dick Musgrave's estimates made some years ago,[7] look at the footnotes; what you find is that he has very little evidence upon which to base his estimates of incidence that any of us would now accept. He used old Federal Reserve consumer finance survey data on household expenditures. Household expenditures are a very different number as they are distributed among income brackets—very differently from assessed value for property occupied by different income groups.

5. Editor's note: Richard F. Muth, "Capital and Current Expenditure in the Production of Housing," in C. Lowell Harriss, ed., *Government Spending and Land Values* (Madison: University of Wisconsin Press, 1973), pp. 65-78.

6. Editor's note: Dick Netzer, *Economics of the Property Tax* (Washington, D.C.: Brookings Institution, 1966), pp. 32-85.

7. Editor's note: Richard A. Musgrave and others, "Distribution of Tax Payments by Income Groups: A Case Study for 1948," *National Tax Journal,* 4 (March 1951), 37.

M. Mason Gaffney: Mr. Oakland stole my thunder. He and Harvey Brazer have torn the regressive incidence argument apart in much the same way I would have, only in a much more gentlemanly fashion. I would like to add one supporting note to what William Oakland said. George Peterson at the Urban Institute has come up with this clincher to the effect that poor live in dwellings whose capital value is very low relative to the rent. He is in the process of providing elaborate statistical verification of a situation based on my limited experience in the ghetto of Milwaukee. The findings will show a dwelling unit in the ghetto sells for two and a half years' rent.

Wealthy people tend to live in residences of long future life expectancy and in areas where land value is appreciating. As a result of both these factors, they live in dwellings whose capital value is high relative to the rent. Thus property tax based on capital value and not on rent is automatically progressive, even without taking into account Margaret Reid's findings that the income elasticity of demand for residential housing is 2.0. This elasticity number has been challenged, of course, and bandied about as not true, but the critics, at that, left out second homes.

Eli Schwartz: At the moment, I am surprised that there should be any argument that, by and large, the tax on improvements is shifted to the renter. It is clear under any kind of market theory this would be the case. There is a certain expected return to capital. In the short run, before the changes in supply can take place perhaps the owners may absorb a rise in tax. In the long run, a tax on improvements that could not be shifted forward in the rent would cut into the supply of new housing. (Far better to get new housing built, even under the trickle-down theory, than to allow old housing to deteriorate rapidly so as to provide poor people with the most miserable shelter.) I find the evidence that the capitalized value is low relative to rent in poor districts is just another indication that the property tax is shifted; or where it can't be shifted, it brings about the deterioration of the property.

The reason that your evidence shows the capitalized value of slum housing to be low is that when all the expenses are considered, the net rent is very low. The net rent is capitalized, not the gross rent. With a high property tax, you reduce the net rent very sharply. Old housing is not assessed on its capitalized value. Anyone who knows about assessment practice knows that downward assessment is very slow in taking place; some long-term historical figures stay on the assessor's books.

All these factors lead me to believe that the property tax on improvements probably has some regressive effects. I do not blink this away. However, on the other hand, you can think of all sorts of tax "reforms" which you could argue will improve everyone's position (at least in the short run) but those people who have incomes over $25,000 per annum. The fact that a given tax could be taken off, replaced with something else and that everybody under $25,000 a year would gain, is not a sufficient reason for removing the tax.

In New York City you could make subways free, place the costs on an income tax. I am sure that initially this would help many poor people; the effect will be progressive. (It may even be a good idea, but not solely on this basis.) We could change the income tax (raise the family exemption allowance, increase the upper brackets rates to make up the difference), and statistically you could prove that everybody under $25,000 would be benefited.

However, our tax system never was formulated purely on the basis of progressivity. There are other factors we have to consider. I still think that at least part of the property tax could be justified as a *quid pro quo* for local functions performed.

Charles Waldauer: First, I believe the evidence is that the assessed values on slum housing are far in excess of the market value.

Second, at the end of Ron Grieson's discussions, Harvey Brazer raised an interesting question: that is, given the model that Ron worked with, if you replace the property tax with an income tax or higher income tax rates, what would be the effect, if any, on property values?[8]

---

8. Editor's note: The second question was not answered.

Part III
Legal Adjustments and Restrictions

11 Seymour Sacks, Ralph Andrew, Paul O'Farrell, and Jerry Wade

Competition between Local School and Nonschool Functions for the Property Tax Base

There are only a few cursory remarks on "municipal overburden" in the property tax literature, apart from those found in the alternative literature in school finance, which deal explicitly with the relationships between the various purposes of local property taxation. Neither literature, however, deals with how the purposes for which property taxes are raised affect the level or distribution of property taxation. This is a serious oversight because neither the amount nor proportion of the local property tax base devoted to education can be discussed independently of the base's other noneducational demands and the alternative nonproperty tax sources which substitute, in some cases directly and in other cases indirectly, for the property taxes. This analysis focuses on the large city areas and assumes that for national policy to be meaningful, account must be simultaneously taken of interstate and intrastate variations in demands made upon the property tax. This will enable us to focus on both the large city problems and the noncity areas where school finances dominate property taxation to a much greater extent than they do in the cities. The goal is to provide both a meaningful framework for analysis and a set of results which are appropriate to a current understanding of the competition between school and nonschool uses of the property tax bases.

LARGE CITY PROPERTY TAXES

As has been noted elsewhere, the property tax in the United States is now dominated by its use for school purposes. The advisory Commission on Intergovernmental Relations has reported that the school share of total property taxes in the aggregate has risen from 32.9 percent of the total in 1942 to 42.8 percent in 1957 to 51.4 percent in 1970 (see Table 11.1). This general trend is due to the increase of school expenditure relative to other local property tax financed expenditures during a period of increasing use of nonproperty taxes to finance nonschool expenditures at the local level.

Table 11.1–School Share of Local Property Taxes, Selected Years, 1942-69

Fiscal year	Local property taxes (millions)	Percent distribution by type of government			
		School districts[a]	Cities[b]	Counties[b]	Townships and[c] special districts
1942	$ 4,347	32.9	39.0	20.1	8.0
1952	8,232	39.2	32.7	19.8	8.3
1957	12,285	42.8	29.7	19.2	8.3
1967	25,418	48.9	24.8	18.5	7.8
1969	29,692	50.0	24.1	18.1	7.8
1970	32,963	51.4	23.7	18.1	7.9

[a]Includes estimated amounts allocable to dependent city, town, and county school systems.

[b]Excludes estimated amounts allocable to dependent school systems.

[c]Township property taxes in several states are used in part to support dependent school systems.

Source: Advisory Commission on Intergovernmental Relations, *State-Local Revenue Systems and Educational Finance* (Washington, D.C.: Government Printing Office, 1971).

The large cities represent a sufficient portion of education expenditures and property tax collections that their inclusion and exclusion alter the patterns and levels of property taxation dedicated to education. With a national average of 51.4 percent, 43.1 percent of large city property taxes are for local school purposes in contrast with 54.6 percent for the rest of the nation.[1] This difference in percentages is not the result of a lower level of school property taxes, but of a higher level of nonschool property taxes.

The tax problem of the large cities is understated because of the far more extensive use of nonproperty taxes by these cities than by the rest of the nation. Unfortunately, only the most crude guess can be made about the use of school nonproperty taxes outside the large cities so a comparable analysis is not presented for this category. Nevertheless, the general picture is clear as well as the specific one for large cities. Of the national total of nonproperty urban taxes of $5.9 billion, the large cities raise in excess of half that total, $3.2 billion, and the remaining smaller cities, suburbs, and rural areas only $2.7 billion. In per capita terms this means an additional $70.26 to local property taxes for a total tax level of $270.59 in the large cities and an

1. The difference between the 50.3 percent reported by the Advisory Commission on Intergovernmental Relations in Table 11.1 and the 51.4 percent in Table 11.2 is due to a slightly different reporting technique. See Seymour Sacks, "The Interaction of Local School and Non-school Finances: A Systems Analysis," *Proceedings National Tax Association* (1971).

Table 11.2–Distribution of Per Capita Property Taxes, 1970

	Per capita total property taxes	Per capita school property taxes	Per capita nonschool property taxes	School property taxes as percent of total property taxes
Nation as a whole	$162.39	$83.48	$ 78.91	51.4
Large cities in the sample	200.33	86.34	113.99	43.1
Rest of nation	151.42	82.68	68.74	54.6

Source: Computation of Syracuse University Research Corporation: Policy Institute.

additional $17.01 for a total tax level of $168.43 in the rest of the nation. In the case of the large cities a very small proportion of the total of nonproperty taxes is used for school purposes (7.8 percent), but often, where they are used, their effect appears to be substantial. On an individual area basis it is therefore important to take into account the interaction between property and nonproperty taxes before any conclusions can be drawn concerning the interrelationship (or the competition) between school and nonschool property taxes.

Because the primary unit of analysis in this paper is the large city, the basic sample was drawn from the 95 central cities of the 72 largest Standard Metropolitan Statistical Areas. Alternative approaches have analyzed the large school districts within a state or the large school districts within these cities, however. These have been unable to analyze the relationship between the school and nonschool fiscal behavior in a consistent fashion. This is a function of the lack of coterminality and/or the multiplicity of school districts in some of the largest cities in the nation. The inclusion of only the major districts would underestimate, in some cases by a serious amount, school taxes within these cities. Therefore, all school districts in the large cities were included on the basis of 1970 enrollments available from the Office of Education and the use of allocators provided by the Government's Division of the Bureau of the Census for the year 1966-67. Changes in school district boundaries or annexations by municipalities since then could have seriously distorted only a few of these figures. These computed enrollments were then compared to the enrollments of public schools as shown in the 1970 Census of Population to determine the comprehensiveness of the analysis. Major disparities were located along with their causes and appropriate adjustments in the data were made.

School taxes were allocated on the basis of enrollment percentages and were accordingly totaled for those cities which were made up of more than one district or for those which were not coterminous. An alternative method, i.e., to allocate taxes on the basis of the proportionate share of property valuations, could not be undertaken at this time because of the limitations in time and the available data. The overlying counties' and special districts' nonschool taxes were allocated on the basis of proportionate shares of populations. During the process of allocation inadequate data forced the removal of some cities from the analysis because of the absence of data. These include the triple cities of Anaheim-Garden Grove-Santa Ana, California, and Riverside-San Bernardino-Ontario, California, as well as Everett, Washington, Easton, Pennsylvania, and Honolulu, Hawaii.

Table 11.3–Distribution of Local Taxes in Large Cities, 1969-70

City	School property taxes / Total property taxes	School nonproperty taxes / Total nonproperty taxes	Total school taxes / Total taxes
Northeast			
Hartford	37.5%	.0%	37.2%
Wilmington	29.4	.0	21.8
Washington, D.C.	31.7	31.7	31.7
Baltimore	43.9	43.9	43.9
Boston	28.7	.0	28.3
Springfield	50.4	.0	50.1
Chicopee	53.3	.0	52.8
Holyoke	51.0	.0	50.6
Jersey City	49.5	.0	40.6
Newark	41.5	.0	37.2
Paterson	41.0	.0	37.9
Clifton	52.9	.0	48.1
Passaic	48.6	.0	45.5
Albany	44.6	.0	34.3
Schenectady	37.7	61.9	38.6
Troy	30.3	.0	29.7
Buffalo	22.1	28.6	23.2
New York	42.3	.0	25.9
Rochester	43.7	.0	41.3
Syracuse	35.5	.0	28.2
Allentown	51.8	33.7	47.3
Bethlehem	53.3	36.0	49.0
Harrisburg	52.2	21.5	44.5
Philadelphia	19.5	26.8	21.1
Pittsburgh	34.9	38.5	36.0
Providence	47.2	.0	46.6
Midwest			
Chicago	51.6	.0	36.8
Gary	42.3	.0	42.0
Hammond	47.0	.0	46.9
East Chicago	31.4	.0	31.3
Indiana	36.3	.0	36.2
Wichita	46.0	.0	43.4
Detroit	41.3	.0	30.6
Flint	67.7	.0	54.4

City	School property taxes / Total property taxes	School nonproperty taxes / Total nonproperty taxes	Total school taxes / Total taxes
Grand Rapids	57.9%	.0%	45.3%
Minneapolis	43.3	3.4	41.9
St. Paul	45.5	.0	42.7
Kansas	58.9	.0	41.7
St. Louis	49.2	.0	30.1
Omaha	53.6	.0	49.6
Akron	72.1	.0	56.1
Cincinnati	79.7	.0	52.4
Cleveland	52.4	.0	43.0
Columbus	46.4	.0	38.1
Dayton	63.3	.0	45.7
Toledo	74.8	.0	50.9
Youngstown	64.6	.0	46.5
Warren	82.8	.0	59.4
Milwaukee	37.7	.0	37.3
South			
Birmingham	51.5	.0	20.4
Mobile	41.0	.0	16.7
Jackson	45.8	.0	35.6
Miami	32.3	.0	25.8
Tampa	33.9	.0	25.0
St. Petersburg	37.6	.0	28.5
Atlanta	43.7	.0	36.7
Louisville	42.2	11.0	27.3
New Orleans	38.2	25.9	31.2
Greensboro	25.9	.0	25.1
Winston-Salem	29.1	.0	28.2
High Point	33.9	.0	33.0
Oklahoma City	51.1	.0	39.8
Tulsa	54.9	.0	44.5
Knoxville	23.7	46.4	29.9
Memphis	29.9	50.0	42.0
Nashville	41.0	50.4	43.9
Dallas	43.3	.0	36.4
Fort Worth	45.8	.0	38.8
Houston	44.8	.0	37.3
San Antonio	34.1	.0	25.6
Norfolk	48.5	48.8	48.5
Portsmouth	70.6	70.6	70.6
Richmond	56.4	56.4	56.4
West			
Phoenix	52.3	.0	41.9
Fresno	45.0	.0	36.4
Los Angeles	44.0	.0	37.3
Long Beach	49.7	.0	43.4
Sacramento	41.7	.0	34.1

City	School property taxes / Total property taxes	School nonproperty taxes / Total nonproperty taxes	Total school taxes / Total taxes
San Diego	51.1	.0	43.4
San Francisco	28.1	.0	24.9
Oakland	43.8	.0	37.1
San Jose	55.9	.0	49.4
Denver	67.6	.0	49.6
Portland	51.7	47.8	
Salt Lake City	49.8	.0	38.9
Seattle	52.4	.0	40.8

Source: U.S., Bureau of the Census, *Local Government Finances in Selected Metropolitan Areas and Large Counties, 1970-71* (Washington, D.C.: Government Printing Office, 1972).

The general pattern as shown in Table 11.3 indicates a sizeable variation in the proportion of local property taxes that are utilized for schools. The unweighted average is 46.1 percent with a standard deviation of 12.4 percent (coefficient of variation = 26.8 percent). The weighted average (by population) is 42.4 percent with a standard deviation of 10.6 percent (coefficient of variation = 24.0 percent). The highs are in Warren and Cincinnati, Ohio, where they reached 82.8 percent and 79.8 percent respectively of all property taxes. These extreme values are a reflection of the uses of alternative local sources and the political and legal reasons for the placing of education generally on the property tax rolls. For example, the fact that Warren, Ohio, uses 82.8 percent of its property tax dollars for schools is due to the fact that the other functional categories make exceptional use of nonproperty tax sources and that they provide only a minor competition in the proportionate sense to school districts. Thus, in Ohio the school districts use the property tax base and the non-school governments make very extensive use of nonproperty taxes. Generally where the school proportion is low, as in Buffalo, Knoxville, and Washington, D.C., extensive use is made of nonproperty taxes for school purposes, thus lowering the observed pressure of schools on the property tax base. In many of these cases the explicit reason for the use of nonproperty taxes for school purposes is to reduce school pressure on the property tax base.

The unweighted average of school taxes as a percent of total is 39.2 percent with a standard deviation of 9.9 percent. In only a very small number of cases is the school proportion higher for the total taxes than for property taxes and that reflects an extensive use of nonproperty taxes for school purposes (where the proportion used for schools is greater than for nonschools). The fraction that school property and nonproperty taxes make up of total local taxes is a direct reflection of the level of taxes for other purposes.

To permit intercity comparisons the taxes were converted into per capita

Table 11.4– Regression Coefficients and Simple Correlations for School Property Taxes, Using Selected Variables (Weighted and Unweighted by Population)

Dependent variable—percent school property tax	Simple correlations				Regression coefficients[a]			
	N=86		N=63		N=86		N=68	
	Unweighted	Weighted	Unweighted	Weighted	Unweighted	Weighted	Unweighted	Weighted
Percent nonschool property tax	.38	.40	.36	.32	0.202[b]	.164[b]	.196[b]	.153[b]
					(.049)	(.047)	(.060)	(.049)
Percent school nonproperty tax	-.32	-.37	-.39	-.44	-.447[c]	-.581[b]	-.426[c]	-.589[b]
					(.180)	(.135)	(.192)	(.140)
Percent nonschool. nonproperty tax	-.04	-.07	.13	.08	.056	.122[c]	.061	.106
					(.081)	(.055)	(.089)	(.058)
1970 enrollment ratio (percent)	.01	.03	-.12	-.04	1.81[c]	2.40[b]	1.96[c]	2.76[b]
					(.805)	(.829)	(.887)	(.877)
Percent personal income	.44	.45	.58	.56	.030[b]	.036[b]	.032[b]	.039[b]
					(.007)	(.006)	(.008)	(.007)
Statewide school fraction of the property tax (percent)	.47	.43	.22	.20	1.095[b]	.985[b]	.989[b]	.763[b]
					(.204)	(.219)	(.240)	(.240)
Statewide local tax assignment (percent)	.50	.48	.35	.34				
Nonresidential fraction of assessed value (percent)	—	—	-.30	-.18			-.498	-.690[c]
							(.292)	(.253)
					.74	.78	.76	.81

[a]Standard errors in parenthesis
[b]Significant at .01 level
[c]Significant at .05 level

amounts. For the sample, all school property taxes averaged $82.25 per capita with a standard deviation of $30.96. The higher weighted averages were discussed earlier. The level of school property taxes, as shown in Table 11.4, reflects a variety of factors, including the level of state aid, the enrollment ratio, and the use of school nonproperty taxes, as well as the taste for education as measured by the income characteristics of the community. The range, as already indicated, inclusive of Honolulu is from zero in that city to $142.94 in Flint, Michigan. This is the highest total in the sample, except for Washington, D.C. where the addition of the property and nonproperty taxes raises the specially circumstanced local total to $163.80.

THE EFFECT OF COMPETITION BETWEEN SCHOOL AND NONSCHOOL USES ON THE LEVEL OF TAXATION

One of the important questions is how the competitive uses of property tax levies influence the level of school finances. As already noted, the level of school expenditures financed from the local property tax base is not only a function of the competition of other property tax levies, but of differential requirements of local school finances themselves. The use of nonproperty school taxes has already been recognized as providing a method of escaping legal and voter limitations on property tax rates and probably should be so considered. In addition to the formal circumstances involving the local school property tax, there are the basic determinants which differentiate areas.

School nonproperty taxes are assumed to be inversely related to the level of school property taxes such that for every one dollar of nonproperty tax for schools the level of the school property taxes should decline by one dollar. Similarly, if nonschool nonproperty taxes are perfect substitutes for nonschool property taxes, the regression coefficient should have the opposite sign from and same value of the nonschool property tax coefficient (+ one dollar).[2]

Both the proportion of the population enrolled in public schools (the enrollment ratio) and the level of income should be significantly and positively related to the level of property taxes for school purposes. The enrollment ratio should also be an important determinant of the proportion of property taxes for schools.

Some of the differences in state aid for education and in the utilization of the property tax are considered by the introduction of the statewide average share of property taxes for school purposes. The parameter value for this variable is hypothesized to be such that a 1 percent increase in the pro-

2. S. Sacks, David C. Ranney, and Ralph Andrew, *City Schools-Suburban Schools: A History of Fiscal Conflict* (Syracuse, N.Y.: Syracuse University Press, 1972).

portion should be associated with a 1 percent increase in the level of school taxes. The correlation should be very significant, although this may be reduced by the influence of large cities in our sample since they are less likely to reflect their statewide patterns relative to the smaller cities.

Density is hypothesized as being negatively correlated with the level of per capita school property taxes and positively with per capita nonschool property taxes. This variable reflects the degree to which cities assume suburban characteristics in their demand for locally financed public services. That is, lower densities reflect higher relative demands for education and lower costs due to state aid formulas.

One final variable has been introduced to determine if the character of the property tax base is related to the observed competition for the property tax. It is presumed that the greater the nonresidential portion of the tax base, the greater the level of per capita nonschool property taxes and the lower the level of school property taxes reflecting the nonschool needs of this segment of the base. Because a high nonresidential tax base facilitates levying very high per capita school property taxes at very low rates, this variable will have a positive regression coefficient. In this sample of cities the likelihood of this is very small. This pattern might be expected in an industrial enclave within a metropolitan area, but not for the central city as a whole.

The analyses are designed to determine the extent of the competition between school and nonschool taxes for the property tax base. The order they will follow will be similar throughout. First, the observed simple correlations will be presented and their consistency with the hypothesized values will be ascertained. Second, the simple regression of per capita nonschool property taxes on per capita school property taxes will be presented, thus recognizing its traditional importance for school finance. Following this, the entire model is fitted by the method of multiple regression, thus considering the complicating influence of the school nonproperty taxes, the nonschool nonproperty taxes, the enrollment ratio, the local level of income, and the statewide average of local property taxes for schools.

The model will be presented in two versions. The first is the traditional unweighted model in which every observation is considered equally influential whether it be New York City with almost eight million persons or East Chicago with slightly less than fifty thousand persons. The second version is population weighted, with proportionally more weight being assigned to high population observations. This version is more appropriate for national policy decisions since its conclusions actually yield per capita results, not "per observation" results.

Two additional variations of the basic model have been considered. The first variation emphasizes the relationships from the perspective of the share rather than the level of property taxes. In this case the local taxes are expressed as the per cent of the local property taxes going to school purposes versus the per cent going to nonschool purposes and the per cent of nonproperty taxes going to these functions. The second variation considers the elasticity of the school property taxes with respect to nonschool property taxes. This second variation omits nonproperty taxes for school purposes because the inclusion of this variable reduces the sample size drastically, since only sixteen cities in the sample utilize this tax instrument for schools.

In both the unweighted and weighted versions of the model, the observed simple correlations only partly confirm the initial hypotheses. The major and important exception in sign is a significant positive correlation between per capita nonschool property taxes and per capita school property taxes. The simple regression shows that an increase in property taxes for the school function is significantly associated with an *increase* in taxes for the nonschool functions. The simple regression coefficients are +.223 with a standard error of .060 in the unweighted version and +.196 with a standard error of .056 in the weighted version.

Surprisingly the simple correlation shows neither the nonschool nonproperty taxes nor the enrollment ratio to be significantly related to school property taxes as hypothesized. Further, there is no fundamental difference between the weighted and unweighted versions of the model.

The results of the multiple regression which appear in Table 11.4 reaffirm the positive association between the per capita property taxes going to schools and the nonschool functions. Instead of the expected trade-off between school and nonschool property taxes, the positive and significant net regression coefficients of +.202 and +.164 in the unweighted and weighted versions respectively indicate the existence of a reinforcement effect and contradict the hypothesyzed negative relationship. The results of the multiple regression show that the relationship described by the simple regression holds even if income, the enrollment ratio, the school nonproperty taxes, and the differences between states are taken into account. Stated in terms of tax burdens, these findings mean that cities that have high taxes in one domain also have high taxes in the other.

While signs of the remaining variables are consistent with the hypotheses, it is particular parameter values and their significance levels that are of interest. The use of nonproperty taxes for schools has a reducing effect on the school property tax but the coefficients of −.447 and −.581 in the unweighted and weighted versions respectively are significantly different from the expected value of minus one. The nonproperty school tax is only half replacive. An increase of one dollar per capita in the nonproperty tax for schools will result in a reduction of the property tax for schools by approximately one half dollar per capita.

The nonschool nonproperty tax continued to be insignificant in the unweighted model but emerged as significant when the observations were weighted by their population. The sign implies that if the increases in the nonschool taxes are made through the nonproperty tax, the school function makes increased use of the property tax.

The enrollment ratio and the level of income were positive and significantly related with income appearing quite strongly. As indicated earlier, these results verify again the findings of a number of previous studies dealing with the determinants of educational finance.[3]

SCHOOL AND NONSCHOOL PROPERTY TAXES OUTSIDE THE LARGE CITY AREAS

To a much greater extent than is generally the case in the large cities the property tax in the rest-of-state areas is primarily a school tax. But there are important interstate differences reflecting the size of state aid for education, the assignment of the welfare function to local governments, and the use of nonproperty taxes for school and nonschool purposes. These not only influence the relative shares of school and nonschool property taxes, but also influence the per capita levels as well.

Using the national norms of $82.68 and 54.6 percent as guides (see Table 11.2), the pattern of property taxes may be divided into a number of groupings. In the first are those states in which the local governments outside the large city areas allocate a significantly larger per capita amount or larger share of the property tax base to school taxes than the national average for the areas outside of the large cities. Similarly there are those in which local governments in the rest-of-state area allocate a smaller amount or smaller shares to the school property tax base. The ranges for high, low, and normal are drawn from the means and standard deviations of the weighted large city data. Those which will be considered as high are those in the upper 10 percent of the large city distributions. This means in proportional terms:

High—greater than 57.9 percent
Low—less than 30.5 percent
In per capita terms:
High—greater than $122.49
Low—less than $50.05.

3. The structure of the model invites comparison to the preceding expenditure determinants literature. First, the total coefficients of multiple correlation are sufficiently high to attribute significant explanatory power to our models. Second, state aid, the often criticized and misunderstood variable of the literature, is not included in the model. Rather, system variables were used to reflect its indirect influence. Finally, first-order multicollinearity was not a problem in the analysis, as was seen by the rather low simple correlations of the independent variables.

States which fall into the upper end of the distribution are Pennsylvania (61.9 percent), Maryland (69.4 percent), Michigan (66.9 percent), Ohio (77.4 percent), Indiana (62.9 percent), Minnesota (68.2 percent), Missouri (65.9 percent), Virginia (62.1 percent), Kentucky (61.5 percent), Georgia (66.9 percent), Oklahoma (68.9 percent), Arizona (68.9 percent), Utah (64.7 percent), Washington (66.2 percent), and Oregon (73.9 percent). In fact all those in which the proportions were in excess of 66.6 percent had school taxes which were more than twice the total of all other property taxes put together (see Table 11.5).

At the other extreme were the states devoting less than 30.5 percent of local property taxes to schools. The only region represented in this group were some southern states. Indeed, these would be the only states included on a comprehensive national analysis. Specifically, they are the states of North Carolina (20.8 percent), Alabama (21.8 percent), and Louisiana (21.0 percent). The latter two states used school nonproperty taxes. This distribution is obviously skewed to the upper end.

The second step in the analysis involves a comparison of the per capita amounts of school taxes. The picture at the upper end is quite different, since most states include a mixture of suburban and rural areas which are the principal recipients of state school aid. The only three states which are included on this basis are New Jersey ($129.92), Oregon ($129.74), and California ($122.22). At the other end of the distribution there were a large number of states in which school taxes were less than $50.05. Once again these are the states which make very extensive use of state aid and/or nonproperty taxes. They include Delaware ($31.20), Kentucky ($34.43), Tennessee ($29.26), North Carolina ($14.28), Alabama ($6.50), Louisiana ($11.97), and Florida ($48.96).

The state of Pennsylvania just misses the cutoff point at $51.32, and other states in which the figure is less then $60 include Virginia ($58.05), Georgia ($53.73), Oklahoma ($56.18), and Texas ($55.01). These states are very surprising because they all contain relatively wealthy suburban areas, with the exception of Oklahoma.

The major question, whether the level of nonschool property tax has a substitutive, independent, or reinforcing effect on property taxes, will now be analyzed on a rest-of-state basis.

The dominance of school taxes in the local property tax system outside of the large cities alters some relationships between school and nonschool property taxes. Increases in the level of per capita nonschool property taxes are significantly and positively associated with changes in school property taxes (+.5879). On the simple level there is a reenforcement between the two and, surprisingly, this reenforcement is stronger in the outside city areas than in the cities themselves.

Table 11.5–Local Property Tax Behavior, Total, School, Nonschool, and School as a Proportion of Total, in Selected States, Outside of Cities, 1969-70

State	Per capita total property taxes	Per capita school property taxes	Per capita nonschool property taxes	School taxes Total taxes
Northeast				
Massachusetts	$240.84	$ 97.36	$143.48	40.4%
Rhode Island	157.88	73.39	84.49	46.5
Connecticut	209.27	119.91	89.36	45.4
New York	243.68	113.81	129.87	49.7
New Jersey	229.18	129.92	99.26	56.7
Pennsylvania	82.96	51.32	31.64	61.9
Delaware	70.09	31.00	38.89	44.5
Maryland	143.14	99.40	43.74	69.4
North Central				
Michigan	170.90	114.36	56.54	66.9
Ohio	152.65	110.57	42.08	77.4
Indiana	148.69	93.53	55.16	62.9
Illinois	211.62	113.80	97.82	53.8
Wisconsin	185.03	98.68	86.35	53.3
Minnesota	157.66	107.48	39.28	68.2
Missouri	126.13	83.12	43.01	65.9
Nebraska	216.01	119.53	96.98	55.2
Kansas	197.36	112.50	84.86	57.0
South				
Virginia	93.47	58.05	35.42	62.1
Kentucky	55.95	34.43	21.52	61.5
Tennessee	59.96	29.26	30.70	48.8
North Carolina	68.52	14.28	54.24	20.8
Georgia	80.21	53.73	26.48	66.9
Florida	110.37	48.96	61.41	44.4
Alabama	29.83	6.50	23.33	21.8
Louisiana	56.89	11.97	44.92	21.0
Oklahoma	81.10	56.18	24.92	68.9
Texas	114.65	55.01	59.64	48.0
West				
Arizona	129.08	88.94	40.14	68.9
Colorado	171.57	88.36	83.21	51.5
Utah	115.06	74.44	40.62	64.7
Washington	115.71	76.55	39.16	66.2
Oregon	175.53	129.74	45.78	73.9
California	209.77	122.22	87.55	53.1

Source: Advisory Commission on Intergovernmental Relations, *State-Local Revenue Systems and Educational Finance* (Washington, D.C.: Government Printing Office, 1971).

In the rest-of-state areas, an increase in the level of school property taxes is positively and significantly associated with an increase in the school's share of total property taxes. While the reenforcement between the level of school and nonschool property taxes may be noted, an increase in the nonschool function does not lead to a reduction in the school's share of property taxes as is found in the case of the cities. The coefficient of correlation between the level of nonschool property taxes and the share of total property taxes for schools is neither large nor significant at $-.179$. That is, an increase of $1 in nonschool property taxes is associated with about a $1 increase in property taxes for schools in the rest-of-state areas. It is not that school and nonschool taxes do not move together, but that an increase in nonschool taxes in the rest-of-state areas is not associated with a reduction in the school proportion of the total property tax.

CONCLUSION

The nature of school property taxes has been analyzed for both large cities and for the rest-of-state areas in those states in which the large cities in this sample are located. There are two basic conclusions about the nature of the competition between school and nonschool taxes for the property tax base. First, in both the city and rest-of-state areas an increase in school property taxes is associated with an increase in nonschool property taxes. This relationship was more systematically analyzed in the large city areas where nonproperty taxes are used more extensively for both school and nonschool purposes. Second, when specific account is taken of the effect of nonschool property taxes on the school fraction of total taxes, there is a major difference between the two areas. In the large city areas an increase in the level of nonschool property taxes is associated with a significant decline in the school fraction of total property taxes. This is true after other variables which influence both the levels of nonschool and school property taxes are taken into account as well as in the simple regression between the two variables. This is not the case in the rest-of-state areas where an increase in the level of nonschool property taxes is not associated with any significant decline in the school fraction of total property taxes. This latter result is very important because the level of nonschool property taxes is much higher in the central city areas than in the outside areas. *This model implies that the reduction in the nonschool sector occasioned by the General Revenue Sharing bill should be accompanied by a more than equivalent increase in the school share of the total property tax.*

Other findings of significance involving the use of the property tax indicate that the nature of the property tax base as measured by the fraction of the base which is nonresidential is related primarily to the nonschool uses of the property tax. If one assumes that income is consistently related to the residential portion of the property tax base then we find school property taxes primarily responding to differentials in income and the enrollment ratios.

The cross sectional analysis, while appropriate to national policy, does not provide the more detailed structural information that would be available from a time series analysis in which the changes in nonschool property taxes and school property taxes could be analyzed in a more operationally meaningful fashion. Finally, the analysis was carried on without specific consideration of the legal constraints, the political processes, and the exact purposes for which the levies are raised. Some of the extreme cases involving the school use of property taxes, reflect more legal circumstances than underlying fiscal realities. A similar omission in the analysis involves the question as to whether the levies are for current operations, over which there is at least nominal control, and in most cases de facto control, or for the very large portion of the school property tax which is often a reflection of debt service charges and the payment of interest and principal. In this latter case, the local political decision making unit has very little control over the observed levels of school taxation or the relationship between school and nonschool property taxes.

The major conclusion of the analysis is that school and nonschool property taxes are mutually reenforcing as to level. There is competition, however, between the two if explicit account is taken of the influence of nonschool property taxes in the large city areas on the proportion which school districts make up of the total. This aspect of competition takes on additional significance because the same situation does not exist in the rest-of-state areas where an increase in nonschool property taxes is not associated with a decline in the school proportion.

12 W. Craig Stubblebine and Ronald K. Teeples

California and the Finance of Education: Alternatives in the Wake of *Serrano* v. *Priest*

In what may come to be regarded as a landmark decision in the field of educational finance, the Supreme Court of the State of California in the case of *Serrano* v. *Priest* has found that the present system of funding primary and secondary public school education in the state "invidiously discriminates against the poor and violates the equal protection clause of the Fourteenth Amendment."[1] Extensive reevaluation of school financing now appears both inevitable and imperative.

INTRODUCTION

The existing system of California public school finance is complex. Ignoring the University, State College, and Community College systems, school districts expended some $3.87 billion on current account, plus another $150 million for capital and debt service during 1970-71. Of current expenses, 6.4 percent, or $0.25 billion, was federally funded; 35.8 percent, or $1.38 billion, was state funded; and 57.8 percent, or $2.23 billion, was locally funded. The range of current expenditures per unit of average daily attendance (hereafter a.d.a.) among school districts is summarized in Table 12.1.

The source of school district generated funds is the property tax. The range of assessed valuations per a.d.a. is summarized in Table 12.2.

Legal Status

The case of *Serrano* v. *Priest* was initiated in the Los Angeles County Superior Court as a class action on behalf of pupils and parents residing in school districts offering inferior education opportunities. Defendants to the suit argued, and the Superior Court concurred, that the plaintiffs' claims were

1. *Serrano* v. *Priest*, 5 Cal. 3d 584, 487 P. 2d (1971).

Table 12.1–Current Expenditures per Unit of Average Daily Attendance, 1970-71

Type of District	Low	High	State average	Total a.d.a.
Elementary school	$420	$3447	$733	1,082,396
High school	766	1879	973	525,444
Unified school[a]	597	2448	830	3,084,455
Total	–	–	–	4,692,295

[a]Unified School Districts raise and expend funds for both elementary and high school grades.

Source: California, Legislature, Joint Legislative Budget Committee, *Analysis of the Budget Bill of the State of California for the Fiscal Year July 1, 1972 to June 30, 1973, Report of the Legislative Analyst to the Joint Legislative Budget Committee*, 1972 Regular Session (Sacramento: 1972), pp. 785-86.

Table 12.2–(Modified) Assessed Valuations per Unit of Average Daily Attendance, 1970-71

Level of education	Low	High	Median
Elementary school	$ 75	$1,053,436	$20,083
High school	8,836	335,513	42,777

Source: California, Legislature, Joint Legislative Budget Committee, *Analysis of the Budget Bill of the State of California for the Fiscal Year July 1, 1972 to June 30, 1973, Report of the Legislative Analyst to the Joint Legislative Budget Committee*, 1972 Regular Session (Sacramento: 1972), p. 786.

insufficient to constitute a cause for action. The decision was sustained by the Court of Appeals, then reversed and remanded by the Supreme Court to the Superior Court "with direction to overrule the demurrers." The case now awaits retrial, a situation which is expected to continue until the U.S. Supreme Court has ruled on a similar case now before it, *Rodriguez* v. *San Antonio (Texas) Independent School District.*

In rendering its decision, the California Supreme Court established no specific conditions for constitutionality. It argued merely that, as a result of the disparities observable in Table 12.2, "wide differentials remain in the revenue available to individual [school] districts and, consequently, in the level of educational expenditures."[2] Inasmuch as assessments reflect wealth *and* wealth is judicially recognized as an "inherently suspect classification which may be justified only on the basis of a compelling state interest"[3] *and* education is a "fundamental interest" *and* the present funding system is "not necessary" to

2. Ibid., p. 607.
3. Ibid., p. 624.

accomplishing this interest, it follows that the system "denies to the plaintiffs and others similarly situated the equal protection of the laws."[4]

In assessing the implications of *Serrano* v. *Priest,* several aspects should be noted. First, the court voided only the present *system* of educational financing. It did *not* declare that property taxation is an unconstitutional source of school funds.[5] Second, the court did *not* establish a constitutional standard of equal expenditure per (public) school enrollee. At the same time, the court did not foreclose the possibility that such a suit might be pleaded successfully under equal protection auspices.[6] Any such pleading, however, could not use the instant case as precedent. Finally, the court specifically ("unhesitatingly") rejected the argument that "if the equal protection clause commands that the relative wealth of school districts may not determine the quality of public education, it must be deemed to direct the same command to all governmental entities in respect to all tax-supported public services."[7] It did, however, take note of a decision by the Court of Appeals for the Fifth Circuit which "intimated that wealth discrimination in the provision of city services might also be invalid."

ALTERNATIVE ADJUSTMENTS

In the wake of *Serrano* v. *Priest,* any number of alternatives to the present system are being promoted. Broadly speaking, they fall into five major categories although the number of variants within any given category are limitless: expansion of the state role within the present system, redistricting, full state funding, power equalizing, coordinated tax base sharing and tuition grants.

Expansion

One proposed response to the court's decision is a substantial increase in the Basic Aid-Equalization Aid contributions to local districts from the state

4. Ibid., p. 623.
5. Although no judicial notice was taken, there is some statistical evidence that a negative correlation exists between the degree of reliance on (local) property taxation and per pupil expenditures. See D. G. Edwards and J. M. James, "Major Determinants of Public Educational Expenditure: A Cross Sectional Analysis," mimeographed (Dallas, Texas: Department of Economics, Southern Methodist University, August 1972), and the literature cited therein.
6. "We need not decide whether such decentralized financial decision-making is a compelling state interest, since under the present financing system, such fiscal free will is a cruel illusion for the poor school districts" (5 Cal. 3d 620).
7. "Although we intimate no views on other governmental services, we are satisfied that, as we have explained, its uniqueness among public activities clearly demonstrates that *education* must respond to the command of the equal protection clause" (ibid., p. 622; italics in original).

general fund. For example, the State Board of Education has proposed foundation levels of $687 per elementary pupil and $900 per high school pupil.[8] Such an expansion reasonably may be expected to reduce the disparities existing in per pupil expenditures among school districts, and *might,* on this account alone, survive a constitutional challenge.

However, it would do nothing to meet the dominant logic of *Serrano* v. *Priest,* for it would leave intact the very system to which the court took exception. Whether the state aid be large or small, it comes to the district as a fixed grant unaffected by local decisions. At the *margin* of local choice, the disparities among districts in the funding of *additional* educational purchases would persist.[9] To fund an additional expenditure of x dollars on each of m public school pupils in a district with an assessed valuation of Z dollars requires an increase in the district's tax rate of $t_z = \frac{m}{Z}(X)$. Since m/Z merely is the inverse of assessed valuation per pupil, Z/m, the larger is m relative to Z, the larger is the required tax rate increase. To the extent they gauge their tax burden by t_z, the more perversely unequal will voters in low valuation districts perceive to be their opportunities to provide educational support over and above the level of state aid. Moreover, the argument would apply to any locally oriented tax base—personal and/or corporate income, or sales.

Although the court did not make it explicit, this distinction between state aid and local opportunities at the margin appears to have dominated its reasoning. On this point at least, the court's intuition seems soundly based. *For this reason, one has the feeling that only a level of state aid which reduced to zero local support would be upheld under this system.*

Redistricting

Some proposals have looked to redrawing school district boundaries. Their advocates seem to have in mind districts large enough to share the poorest areas in the state so that discrimination by residence can be made tolerably insignificant, far short of full statewide control of tax-expenditure decisions for public schooling. Under one plan, the number of school districts would be reduced from the present 1070 to 58 countywide districts; another envisions 12 regional districts—the same districts now being used for vocational education planning. Both plans would reduce, but not eliminate, disparities in per pupil assessed valuations as shown in Table 12.3.

8. California, Legislature, Joint Legislative Budget Committee, *Analysis of the Budget Bill of the State of California for the Fiscal Year July 1, 1972 to June 30, 1973,* p. 791.

9. The disparities might narrow: as the level of state aid increases, the penalties (rewards) for living in a low (high) per pupil valuation district decrease; in turn, this should lead to some bidding up (down) of property values in low (high) districts as households move around in response to the changed pattern of penalty/rewards.

Table 12.3—Estimated Effect on Assessed Valuations per Unit of Average Daily
   Attendance among Elementary Schools

Plan	Low	High	Median
Present districting	$ 75	$1,053,436	$20.083
County districting	8,346	81,229	18,155
Regional districting	12,743	28,869	15,368

Source: California, Legislature, Joint Legislative Budget Committee, *Analysis of the
Budget Bill of the State of California for the Fiscal Year July 1, 1972 to June 30, 1973,
Report of the Legislative Analyst to the Joint Legislative Budget Committee,* 1972
Regular Session (Sacramento: 1972), p. 796.

This approach would seem compatible with *Serrano* v. *Priest* if, and only if,
district boundaries were drawn strictly to equalize assessed valuations per pupil,
the total number of districts being determined in accordance with some un-
specified criterion or criteria—perhaps compactness or convenience or neighborhood affinity or ethnic balance. Large districting surely would destroy whatever good still comes from local control of local education—interest, pride,
adaptability. As matters now stand, this must be relatively weak in districts
such as Los Angeles Unified with some 650,000 students. With smaller, more
numerous districts, periodic restructuring would be necessary to correct whatever imbalances arise from the inevitable unequal growth rates experienced by
various parts of the state. Although certainly possible, anyone familiar with
congressional and legislative redistricting to distribute voters equally will
recognize the pitfalls. Inauguration of such a plan inevitably must lead to frag-
menting some communities and antagonizing parents and pupils in the process.

Full State Funding

The ultimate in large districting would be creation of a single statewide
school district with whatever regional/local subdivisions are appropriate for
administration. The essential feature of a statewide district is to bar localities
from raising—whether from local tax sources or private donations—and expend-
ing monies on schools within the locality. To hold otherwise surely would
contravene the court's ruling in *Serrano* v. *Priest*. This means, in effect, that
per public pupil expenditure throughout the state also would be equalized
whatever the tax base source of state educational funds.

To the extent local school boards were permitted to survive, they could
hire personnel and allocate state provided funds among various local educational programs. One suspects, even then, that pressures both from within and
without the district would force legislative action where a district departed
from widely held norms. It seems likely that parental/community interests

in differential education would be channeled wholly to the private sector.

Whatever its form, full state funding goes far beyond the findings of *Serrano* v. *Priest*.

Power Equalizing

Of relatively recent origin is a class of proposals to establish a relationship between the tax rate levied by any school district on its tax base and the expenditure per pupil permitted the district. The precise relationship would be determined by (periodic) action of the state legislature, but could take on almost any complexion.[10] The schedule of Table 12.4 may be taken as illustrative. Should the district's tax base produce less (more) revenue at a given rate than the spending permitted at that rate, the difference presumably would be supplied from (to) the state general fund either as equalization aid or a combination of basic aid and equalization aid.

Table 12.4–Illustrative Power Equalizing Schedule[a]

Locally determined tax rate applied to local tax base	Permitted spending per a.d.a.
$1.00 (minimum)	$ 900
1.01	950
.	.
.	.
.	.
2.00	1,400
.	.
.	.
.	.
3.00	1,900

[a]Other schedules may be found in J. E. Coons, W. H. Clune, and S. D. Sugarman, *Private Wealth and Public Education* (Cambridge: Harvard University Press, 1970), pp. 204-6.

Source: J. E. Coons, "Financing Educational Variety for the Poor," An Address to the National Tax Association, Kansas City, September 28, 1971, p. 9.

Such a plan would appear to satisfy the dictates of *Serrano* v. *Priest* while retaining local expression of preferences for educational expendi-

10. See J. E. Coons, "Financing Educational Variety for the Poor," An Address to the National Tax Association, Kansas City, September 28, 1971; J. E. Coons, W. H. Clune, and S. D. Sugarman, *Private Wealth and Public Education* (Cambridge: Harvard University Press, 1970); and Charles S. Benson, *The Economics of Public Education,* 2d ed. (Boston: Houghton Mifflin, 1968).

tures.[11] Yet, charging the legislature with responsibility for setting the relationship between local tax rate and permitted local spending introduces a decided power centralizing element. Legislative majorities could use their power over the schedule to thwart the ability of localities to express their preferences.

Coordinated Tax Base Sharing

There is a variant of this class which satisfies *Serrano* v. *Priest* while reducing substantially the power centralizing elements both of the present financing system and of power equalizing.[12] Under it, the state's role could be reduced to that of data collection/calculation. Prior to the school districts' budgeting period, the state would estimate for the coming fiscal period: (*a*) the state's total number of a.d.a. units, (*b*) the a.d.a. units of each district, (*c*) the state's total school tax base, and (*d*) the tax base of each school district.[13] Based on these estimates, the per pupil revenues raised statewide by each tax rate would be calculated. With knowledge of the calculated relationship between tax rate and per pupil revenues, each district would turn to the task of choosing that tax rate—with its implied district budget—appropriate to voter preferences within the district.

A state school fund would be established to which surplus districts would contribute, and on which deficit districts would draw, to make up the difference between per pupil revenues raised within the district and the calculated statewide revenues per pupil raised by the district's tax rate. Any net school fund deficit or surplus would be shared among all districts proportionate to district tax bases through a state mandated adjustment to district tax rates in the next fiscal year.[14] The present system of state aid would be eliminated.[15]

11. There has been some suggestion that schedules could be highly progressive in the burden placed upon high valuation districts. However, there may be less freedom than proponents realize: to the extent education is funded publicly, *Serrano* v. *Priest* requires that the burden of financing additional educational expenditures be uniform for all similarly situated voters everywhere in the state. The progressive schedules contemplated here surely would violate this rule.

12. The plan as conceived by one of the authors seemed a natural extension of the state's present equalization aid program. He developed the plan prior to becoming conversant with the notions of "power equalization" explored above.

13. The base could be income, sales, property, or any other source capable of being allocated to local districts.

14. If the school fund is expected to operate at a net annual deficit, there would be a one-time state mandated levy to provide the fund with working capital.

15. Should federal school programs dictate participation by statewide revenue sources, the state portion could be funded through the school fund. Certain programs which under the present system are or would be funded statewide or by state categorical aid grants— e.g., vocational education or education of the handicapped—could be handled here by creation of special (regional or statewide) educational districts which would participate on an equal footing with all other districts. Special districts either could operate their own

In addition to satisfying *Serrano* v. *Priest,* the advantages of this variant are several: (*a*) it permits viable local control of fiscal decisions; (*b*) it requires no periodic updating of schedules; (*c*) it is computationally simple and straight-forward; (*d*) it avoids the fiscal distortion commonly associated with local sharing of state tax sources; and (*e*) it may serve as a model for local funding of a wide variety of local programs—police, fire, streets, sewers, etc.[16]

Tuition Grants

Consideration of the problems associated with education from time to time has spawned proposals to provide publicly funded vouchers with which parents would pay some or all of their children's education at public or private schools.[17] Though the whole notion deserves a substantial treatment, only the funding aspects need consideration here. Assuming parents and others retain the right to fund privately additional (or substitute) educational purchases,[18] *Serrano* v. *Priest* would seem to dictate that the publicly funded portion be based either on some statewide tax system or on some variant of power equaliz-ing.[19] On this ground, no new aspects would seem to be introduced by a con-version of the present system to a tuition grant program.

At the same time, recent court decisions suggest that such grants could not be used in any school which attempted to discriminate among admission candi-dates on the basis of race or religion or which infused religious instruction into

---

facilities or contract with regular districts for the special services sought. Teacher retire-ment would be funded entirely by localities.

Community college districts also would participate on an equal footing with primary and secondary school districts.

16. Indeed the only exception might be welfare programs—and then only because there would be incentives for the eligible poor to take over a welfare district in order to vote themselves unlimited benefits. A statewide welfare district, however, would be feasible.

17. Perhaps the most stimulative of modern discussions is that by M. Friedman, "The Role of Government in Education," *Economics and the Public Interest,* R. A. Sc' , ed. (New Brunswick: Rutgers University Press, 1955), pp. 123-44, reprinted in his *pitalism and Freedom* (Chicago: University of Chicago Press, 1962), pp. 85-107.

18. Serious and difficult constitutional questions may be on the horizon as interested parties seek equality of educational opportunity rather than equality of access to *basic* education—however these terms might come to be defined. *Serrano* v. *Priest* does not appear to offer any guide as to how a high court would resolve a challenge in this area. Tuition grants may seem to raise this question explicitly, but it applies with equal force both to the present system and any of the alternatives considered above.

19. Including family power equalizing. See J. E. Coons and S. D. Sugarman, *Family Choice in Education: A Model for State Voucher Systems* (Berkeley: Institute for Gov-ernmental Studies, University of California, 1971), partially reprinted in *California Law Review,* 59 (March 1971), 321-438.

the curriculum. Just how religious academies—parochial or other—would respond to this constraint remains to be seen.

Private Education

Although not now receiving serious attention, one response to *Serrano* v. *Priest* could be complete removal of public funding of education. The quantity and quality of education provided would then be left entirely to private demands—along with such important categories as housing, clothing, food, entertainment, etc.[20]

SIMULATION MODEL

Some appreciation for the implications of the various funding alternatives is possible through a simple simulation model of California educational finance. The nature of the model is summarized in Table 12.5, which delineates four school districts composed of four or six different family units varying in income, residential property, number of school-age children, and the proportion of commercial-industrial-agricultural property located in the district. The four school districts may be described briefly as follows:

$k = 1$ urban, relatively low income commercial-industrial
$k = 2$ urban, relatively average income
$k = 3$ urban, relatively high income
$k = 4$ rural/agricultural, relatively low-average income

As one might expect in such a model, the numbers are chosen to be manageable.[21]

20. Welfare recipients could have their aid payments increased as necessary to assure their children of access to some minimum educational opportunities.
21. For comparative purposes, actual California data show:

	Actual	Model
Number of Households (1970)	5.0	5.4 million
Number of School Children (1970)	5.0	5.6 million
Personal Income (1970)	$88.8	$60.6
Adjusted Taxable Income (1969)	$60.9	
Assessed Valuation of Property (1970)	$54.7	$59.0 million
Per Household Personal Income (1970)	$17765	$11222
Per Household Assessed Valuation (1970)	$10940	$10926
Per a.d.a. Assessed Valuation (1970)	$11891	$11569
Per a.d.a. Assessed Valuation by School District		
$k = 1$		$ 7500
$k = 2$		$11250
$k = 3$		$16667
$k = 4$		$12857

Based on this model, equilibrium tax prices per $100 of public school expenditure per public school enrollee were calculated for each family unit under each funding alternative using a two-stage process. In stage one, all children were assumed to be enrolled in public school and the implied tax rate appropriate to each school district was applied to each family's holding of the tax base to compute the family's tax price—a procedure more or less complicated depending on the fiscal institution under consideration. Thereafter, each family was voted in a school referendum to determine the number of $100 educational units preferred by the median family based on the set of assumed demand-for-education curves.[22] If the median educational expenditure was more than $200 less than what the family would prefer at a private price of $100 per $100 of school expenditure, the family was assumed to enroll its children in private school, expending in tuition the number of dollars appropriate to the family's demand for education curve.

In turn, the second stage calculated tax rates appropriate to funding the education of those children who remained enrolled in public school. The new tax rate/tax prices were used to determine the new, or equilibrium, median educational expenditure per public school pupil, as reported in Table 12.5.

Equilibrium Tax-Prices

In examining Table 12.5 on equilibrium tax prices, three relationships stand out:

1. The higher a family's income/residential-property class, the higher is its tax price for public education, whatever the tax funding alternative.

Given the nature of the tax institutions under consideration, this was to be expected. They did differ, however, in the degree of progressivity measured by the ratio of tax-price to family income. Only the statewide income tax (column 2) was uniformly proportional—.84 percent of family income over all classes. For the others, because residential property holdings were assumed to be regressive relative to income,[23] the ratio of tax-price to family income declines as family income increases. Whether this is good or bad lies well beyond the purview of this study.

2. The greater the extent to which school districts are dependent upon their local tax base(s), the wider is the disparity among taxprices to families situated similarly with respect to income-residential property class.

22. See p. 173.
23. Among other sources, data made available to the authors by the *Los Angeles Times* supports this assumption. However, studies here and there are coming up with the finding that the property tax is income proportional and income progressive.

Table 12.5 – Equilibrium Tax Prices per One Hundred Dollars per Pupil Enrolled in Public School[a]

Family class f_i^k	School district k	State foundation program (equalization aid portion only) (1)	Statewide income tax (2)	Statewide property tax (3)	Coordinated property tax base sharing (4)	Statewide tuition grant program (5)	School district property tax (6)	Comparative private price (for families with children) (7)
$i=1$	$k=2$	$147	$210	$200	$124	$220	$126	$100
	$k=3$	109	210	200	101	220	84	
$i=2$	$k=1$	65	84	85	64	94	84	200
	$k=2$	64	84	85	55	94	56	
	$k=3$	47	84	85	45	94	37	
	$k=4$	57	84	85	51	94	47	
$i=3$	$k=1$	30	34	38	30	42	40	300
	$k=2$	30	34	38	26	42	27	
	$k=4$	27	34	38	25	42	23	

[a]Tax price as percent of family income, statewide income tax only, for comparative purposes: 0.0084.

Uniformity within any given income class was achieved only by full state funding—statewide income (column 2) or property (columns 3 and 5) taxation. At the opposite extreme, school district property taxation (column 6) produced a tax price for a middle-income family ($i = 2$) in the lowest per pupil assessed valuation district ($k = 1$) which was 2.25 times the tax price to a similar family in the highest per pupil assessed valuation district ($k = 3$). Inasmuch as state aid under the present state foundation program comes to individual school districts as flat or fixed grants, the tax prices relevant to any district's choice as to additional or marginal expenditures on public education were those computed for column 6.

In essence, the model bore out the central relationship under which *Serrano* v. *Priest* was prosecuted successfully in the state supreme court. Indeed, the model went somewhat further in that the "disparity notion" was seen to apply as well to middle- and upper-income families in districts other than the very wealthiest. Since education is not unique among publicly funded services, this suggests one force motivating the formation of relatively homogeneous wealthy residential enclaves.

3. A shift to full state funding of public education tends to increase the tax price to all families.

As long as individual school districts are not fully self-contained economic units, the choices made within any given district will impact on families located in other districts. Specifically, in the context of the present model, district property taxation imposed burdens on commercial-industrial-agricultural (C-I-A) property which were not borne entirely by families residing within the district. The C-I-A effect shifted—or "exported"—a portion of the district's expenditure burden onto families residing elsewhere. By contrast, no group lay outside the economic boundary of choice, and no portion of the financing burden could be exported, under the model's full state funding alternatives.[24] Imputed tax prices, therefore, were higher.

Some appreciation for the impact of publicly funded education may be gained by comparing the private supply price of education—column 7: $100 per child per educational unit, or $300 for a family with three children—with the tax prices under each of the school financing alternatives. It makes abundantly clear that child-rearing families have a substantial stake in furthering public funding of education (see p. 173).

24. In reality, of course, the California economy is interdependent with the economies of other states, and nations. Hence, some "out-state exporting" is possible. There is no reason to believe, however, that this possibility affects the relation stated here between the degree of state funding and tax-prices since the ability of individual districts to export burden surely exceeds the ability of the state as a whole.

Summary

If the logic of *Serrano* v. *Priest* is followed, the funding institutions characterized in Table 12.5 as state foundation program (column 1), school district
property taxation (column 6), and private financed school system (column 7)
are removed as viable alternatives. Of the four remaining, three statewide
income taxation (column 2), property taxation (column 3), and tuition grants
(column 5)—imply a substantial reduction in the level of education being
funded in districts other than the very lowest under the present system.

If this downward pressure on per pupil and total expenditure is to be miti-
gated, the only option remaining is coordinated tax base sharing either to
fund public schools exclusively, or to fund district tuition grants. It is the
most powerful response to *Serrano* v. *Priest*. It is the simplest to inaugurate
and the least disruptive to state and school district budgeting.

MODEL ANALYSIS AND QUALIFICATION

The simulation model was able to produce results in terms of which one
might evaluate the relative impact of various funding options for California
school finance. Notwithstanding its simplicity, the model's results were powerful in the sense that they were not refuted clearly by available observations.
Moreover, its creators believe that further research and experience will tend
to confirm, rather than reject, its implications. It remains, then, to indicate
the direction in which further research might proceed.

Variety

Without altering its basic analytical structure, the model's discriminatory
power could be enhanced by increasing the number of family classes and
school districts. The model assumed a simple relationship among family
income, residential property, the number of school-age children, and the
family's demand for education. Increasing family classes from six to twelve
or twenty would permit a much wider variety of relationships among these
key variables. Similarly, increasing the number of school districts two- or
fourfold would permit greater variety in the composition of district electorates and in the range of per pupil assessed valuations especially at the
lowest and highest ranges.[25]

---

25. For example, more family classes would permit small and large family sizes in
each income category. In turn, this would permit a better modeling of the private school
sector especially of parochial schools.

Incidence

The model recognized no residential rental property. This may be interpreted under either of two assumptions: (1) that all residential property is owner-occupied, and any property taxes imposed thereon are borne fully by the owner; or (2) that renters occupy residential property bearing the same relation to income as owner-occupied housing, and any property taxes imposed thereon are passed on fully to the renter as if he were the owner-occupier. A more elaborate model would incorporate rental property together with its own distribution of assessed valuation by income class and among school districts.[26] As well as adding variety in the composition of district electorates, this would permit calculation of family tax-prices under various assumptions with respect to the shifting of property taxes—e.g., borne partially by the renter and partially by the owner.

No business or firm can bear any portion of a tax. Rather, it must be borne by individuals in their roles as business owners, employees, or customers. In the absence of definitive data as to the income distribution of ownership of commercial-industrial-agricultural property, and in the absence of any definitive arguments to the contrary, the model was run under the assumption that the entire burden of C-I-A property taxation was borne proportionately to family income.

In addition to property taxation, the model incorporated a proportionate family income tax. In fact, California revenues are derived from various sources, each of which would have its own pattern of incidence. Presumably the burdens of sales and excise taxes are distributed regressively relative to income, while corporation taxation is distributed progressively—based on the notion that corporate ownership is related progressively to family income. Taken together with the moderately progressive personal income tax, the burden of nonproperty taxation was distributed proportionately to family income in the model.

The model also assumed implicitly that any change in the level of school financing from state funds would lead to equivalent changes in rates of taxation such that the proportion of revenues raised from each tax source would remain unchanged. In fact, the options here are many and varied, ranging from concentration of the change on one tax source to changing the level of expenditure in some nonschool category.

Federal Relations

Ignored completely in formulating the model were relationships among the

26. There is some evidence that renters occupy space having a lower ratio of assessed valuation to income than do owner-occupiers.

California and other economies. To the extent decisions by California state government and school districts affect the prices of goods produced in California for sale elsewhere or produced elsewhere for sale in California, or the relative attractiveness of employment and investment in California, a portion of the burdens associated with these decisions will be exported to households in other parts of the world. Similarly, an increase in state and local taxes will decrease the federal tax liability of at least some Californians, and either increase the liability of taxpayers elsewhere or decrease the funds available for federal expenditure programs. Both tend to reduce the tax prices to Californians of providing additional units of public education.[27]

Neither did the model incorporate the flow of federal funds to support California primary and secondary education, whether by categorical aid or general revenue sharing. To the extent such funds are made available, they exert income and/or substitution effects on education decisions at the margin of state and school district choice.

Whether or not a model incorporates these federal features in and of itself is of no importance. What would matter is whether there are significant differential effects among the funding institutions. As far as can be judged, in the absence of an explicit model, any differences would be relatively minor.

Multi-period Model

A shift from one fiscal institution to another could be expected to be relatively permanent. In turn, institutional shifts in relative tax rates among the various revenue sources could be expected to lead to changes in the relative prices of assets. In stepping outside the single-period focus, a multi-period model would seek to capture the effect of institutional choice on the market value of property and securities, the location of population and of commerce-industry-agriculture, the formation of human capital and its allocation among occupations, and the resulting distribution of income/wealth among households.

Each fiscal institution yielded an outcome which may be characterized in terms of per pupil and total expenditure, and cost of education to the various family units. At the level of constitutional or institutional choice, the electorate must weigh the outcome expected from one institution against that of another. The instant model neither permitted predictions as to which institutional combinations of expenditure and family cost would be preferred by family units, nor offered any explanation of electorate choice among fiscal

27. For a careful treatment of federal tax liability effect, see N. M. Edelson, "Budgetary Outcomes in a Referendum Setting," chap. 19 of this volume. Also compare this approach with that of chap. 10.

institutions.[28] It is here that incorporation of family preference functions could offer significant additional insights for students of California educational financing.[29]

28. Thus, for example, under the state foundation program, the model does not explain the size of the state basic grant or of the guarantee level.

29. For further discussion, see W. Craig Stubblebine and Ronald K. Teeples, *California and the Finance of Education: Alternatives in the Wake of Serrano v. Priest,* Claremont Economic Papers, No. 44 (Claremont, California: Claremont Men's College, October 1972).

13 Morris Beck

Fiscal Reform in New Jersey: Proposals Affecting School Finance and Property Taxation

Although tax reform has been a topic of debate in New Jersey for many years, public discussion of fiscal issues was never greater than in the first half of 1972. Within weeks after the state's method of financing public education was declared invalid in the *Robinson* v. *Cahill* decision, a comprehensive plan to restructure the entire fiscal system was submitted by the governor to the legislature.

The core of the plan was a sharp reduction in the role of the property tax, but virtually every part of the fiscal structure came under scrutiny. By mid-July, when the plan was subjected to its first legislative test and soundly defeated, the debate came to an end. This paper will review those features of the plan, and those parts of the fiscal system of New Jersey which are central to the theme of this conference.

RECENT DEVELOPMENTS

A century-old provision of the New Jersey Constitution requires the state to provide "a thorough and efficient system of free public schools." In recent years the state has met that responsibility by supplying about a quarter of school funds, channeled to local school districts via 25 categories of state aid. Modernized in 1970, the present system of state aid was declared unconstitutional in January 1972, and a search is on for an alternative method of school finance.

Unlike other states that are under court pressure to find an alternative, New Jersey is in the fortunate position of having done its homework in advance of the court decision. A five-volume study by a blue-ribbon tax policy committee has proposed state funding of public schools as part of a comprehensive program of fiscal reform. Of particular interest to this conference, also, are the committee's recommendations for a statewide property tax, a form of site value taxation for urban centers, and a state-local tax structure in which the property tax furnishes not more than a third of tax revenues.

179

In May 1972, the governor submitted to the legislature some 50 bills implementing nearly all of the committee recommendations, plus an "excess gains" tax proposal to recapture from owners of business property all or most of the benefit of property tax reduction. In the case of apartment property, 75 percent of the benefit would go to tenants in the form of credits against income tax liability. Moreover, in arriving at taxable income, the tenant would be permitted to deduct the portion of rent attributable to property taxes. To my knowledge, the proposed excess-gains tax is unique in the annals of property taxation, and the rental allowance would be the first to place all tenants on an equal footing with homeowners in regard to property taxes.

On July 17, 1972, the New Jersey Assembly rejected the income tax and thus shelved the entire reform package. No action on revising the state's tax structure or system of school finance was taken during the legislative session of 1973, an election year, although the New Jersey Supreme Court has since affirmed (April 1973) the superior court verdict.[1]

NEW JERSEY SITUATION

New Jersey's system of financing public education was challenged primarily on the ground that it discriminates against pupils in poor districts. The plaintiff alleged that equalization factors in the state-aid formula do not compensate adequately for variations in local resources, and pupils from low-value school districts are therefore denied equal access to educational opportunity. Tax inequities caused by the present financing scheme will be reviewed in the next section; here, the emphasis is on the issue of unequal opportunity for the recipients of public education.

As Table 13.1 shows, school expenditure per capita in New Jersey is about equal to the national average, but the locally raised share of school funds is well above average, whether or not federal funds are included in the computation of shares. The state government's share, excluding federal aid, is approximately a quarter of school revenues despite a new law, effective July 1, 1971, aimed at raising the state level of support to 40 percent.[2]

Among the state's 600 school districts the 1969-70 per pupil expense for

1. *Robinson* v. *Cahill,* 118 N.J. Super. 223, 187 A.2d 187 (1972). On April 3, 1973, the New Jersey Supreme Court unanimously upheld the superior court decision, but did not specify the characteristics of a constitutionally valid system of school finance. Moreover, the New Jersey decision is based exclusively on the state constitution, which guarantees the right to a thorough education, and is therefore unaffected by the U.S. Supreme Court decision of March 1973 in the *Rodriguez* case.

2. State School Incentive Equalization Aid Law, N.J. Laws ch. 234, pp. 823-33 Laws (1970), commonly known as the Bateman Act. In its first year of operation, 1971-72, Bateman Act funding supplied 25.1% of school revenues. From approximately a fifth in the early sixties, the state's share of school funds rose abruptly in 1966-67 to 28.6 percent and fell gradually thereafter as budget growth outpaced state aid.

Table 13.1–School Finances and Other Fiscal Measures, 1969-70

	New Jersey	Average of all states
Sources of school funds		
Including federal share		
Federal	8.2%	10.1%
State	22.1	38.8
Local	69.8	51.1
Excluding federal share		
State	24.0	43.2
Local	76.0	56.8
State-local tax receipts contributed by		
Property tax	54.1%	39.1%
General sales tax	11.1	16.4
Personal income tax	0.5	10.7
All state-level taxes	41.5	55.2
All local taxes	58.5	44.8
State-local revenue as percent of personal income		
Taxes	10.6%	11.7%
General revenue from own sources	12.5	14.6
Total general revenue	14.3	17.6
Per capita amounts		
Local school expenditure	$186	$184
Property tax	242	168
State aid for local schools	54	84

Sources: U.S. Bureau of the Census, *Governmental Finances in 1969-70*; and Advisory Commission on Intergovernmental Relations, *State-Local Finances* (Washington, D.C.: Government Printing Office, 1972).

current operations ranged from less than $500 in 4 districts to more than $1,200 in 27 districts. Median and (unweighted) average cost per pupil was approximately $800. Total expenditure per weighted pupil, a more comprehensive measure which explicitly recognizes cost differences based on grade level, shows approximately the same range of variation and a median value of $826.[3]

Apparently, also, as note 3 indicates, cost is affected by size of enrollment. Among the 300 comprehensive districts—offering programs from kindergarten through the twelfth grade—expenditure per pupil is lowest in large districts (enrollment over 6,000), for both weighted and unweighted data. In medium-sized districts (Type 3) cost tends to be higher than in small districts (Type 2), but the evidence on this point, especially from unweighted tabulations, is ambiguous.

3. Current expense per pupil is published in annual reports of the New Jersey Commissioner of Education. The weighted measure, developed by the New Jersey Education

Expenditure per pupil is a rough proxy for the quality of education which a school district is able to offer. No serious student of public education will argue that substandard schools can be transformed into high quality educational institutions simply by increasing expenditure per pupil. Larger budgets, however, present administrators of low quality schools with an opportunity to reduce class size, hire better teachers, and provide compensatory education for disadvantaged pupils. In New Jersey, this opportunity is thwarted by a school-financing system which relies mainly on locally raised revenues and which makes only a half-hearted attempt, by means of state aid, to overcome local variations in fiscal capacity.

In almost every state, local fiscal capacity is a key determinant of school expenditure. This factor is particularly important in New Jersey because of the heavy reliance on local financing, the weakness of equalizing factors in the state-aid formula, and the extremely wide variation in taxable resources per pupil.

For purposes of distributing state aid to local school districts, New Jersey uses a measure called "equalized valuation per pupil." Since 1968, when personal property was removed from the local tax base, equalized valuation has consisted almost exclusively of real property at true (market) value. Small amounts of railroad and telephone company equipment—carried at assessed value and representing less than two percent of aggregate value—remain in the local tax base. From a level of 30 percent in the early sixties, the statewide assessment ratio for real property rose to 62 percent—nearly twice the national average—as of the 1967 Census of Governments, and is now above 70 percent. The Table of Equalized Valuations, by municipality, which is annually transmitted to the Commissioner of Education for state-aid purposes, is a highly reliable measure of local capacity to support public schools.

In 1969-70, equalized valuation per pupil ranged from less than $10,000 in four school districts to more than $100,000 in 37 districts. The median value was approximately $38,000 and the high was $56 million—in Teterboro,

---

Association, assigns to secondary pupils a weighting factor 30 percent higher, and to kindergartners 50 percent lower, than the base weight for elementary pupils. Results for 1969-70, from the Association's Bulletin, no. A71-2, are shown below:

| Type of district | Number of districts | Total expenditure per weighted pupil | | |
		20th percentile	Median	80th percentile
1. Elementary	337	$663	$791	$936
2. K-12: enrollment below 3,000	71	721	814	975
3. K-12: enrollment 3,000-6,000	72	749	855	993
4. K-12: enrollment over 6,000	57	742	835	954
5. Secondary	66	834	1,014	1,274
All districts	603	698	826	976

an industrial park with one pupil. Although local capacity is not the only factor accounting for differences in the size of school budgets, data for recent years show a "central tendency for districts with greater equalized valuation per pupil to budget the highest expenditures per pupil."[4] At the lower end of the range, "the system discriminates against pupils in districts with low real property wealth . . . and violates the requirements for equality contained in the State and Federal Constitutions."[5]

The New Jersey Legislature is obligated by the state's constitution to provide a thorough and efficient system of free public schools. This obligation is discharged through a complex system of state aid which supplied in 1969-70 about $205 per pupil. Equalization aid, however, is diluted by provision of minimum aid of $110 per pupil in 363 wealthy districts, plus a flat grant since 1970 of $25 per pupil in all districts.

These provisions, according to Judge Botter's opinion, cannot be reconciled with the education clause of the constitution. The legislature has until January 1, 1974, to devise a nondiscriminatory system of state aid or face redistribution of minimum-aid funds under the equalization formula. Presumably, the constitutional standard of a thorough education for all would be temporarily satisfied by this measure. Eventually, however, the Superior Court decision appears to call for a fundamental revision of the present method of financing public schools.

ROBINSON v. *CAHILL* DECISION

The preceding discussion has emphasized issues affecting the recipients of public education in New Jersey. Judge Botter's decision, however, condemns the present method of school finance on two grounds: "The system discrimi-

---

4. New Jersey Tax Policy Committee, *Report* (Trenton: February 1972), Pt. 3, p. 34.
5. *Robinson* v. *Cahill,* 118 N.J. Super. 223, 187 A.2d 187 (1972), 62 N.J. 473 (1973). The New Jersey decision parallels that of the California Supreme Court which found that California's school financing system "invidiously discriminates against the poor because it makes the quality of a child's education a function of the wealth of his parents and neighbors . . . such a system cannot withstand constitutional challenge and must fall before the equal protection clause."—*Serrano* v. *Priest,* 5 Cal. 3d 584, 487 P. 2d 1241 (1971).

Similar opinions have been handed down in Texas—*Rodriguez* v. *San Antonio Independent School District,* 337 F. Supp. 280 (1972), U.S. Sup. Ct. No. 71-1332 (1973)—and in Minnesota—*Van Dusartz* v. *Hatfield,* 334 F. Supr. 870 (1971). A class-action suit, charging unequal educational opportunities and challenging New York's financing system, was recently filed by 16 children from various school districts in that State. (*New York Times,* August 3, 1972, p. 36). Similar suits are pending in many other states.

nates against pupils in districts with low real property wealth, and it discriminates against taxpayers by imposing unequal burdens for a common State purpose. The State must finance a 'thorough and efficient' system of education out of State revenues raised by levies imposed uniformly on taxpayers of the same class."

Judge Botter's decision makes it clear that tax-rate inequality to provide a thorough education for all pupils is unconstitutional: "There is no compelling justification for making a taxpayer in one district pay tax at a higher rate than a taxpayer in another district, so long as the revenue serves the common State educational purpose." The administration has already proposed an alternative to the present method of financing schools, but the initial attempt to implement the plan failed on July 17, 1972, when the legislature rejected the administration's income tax proposal. A statewide property tax, to replace the 1972 school tax levy (local) of $1.4 billion would require an effective rate of 2.00 percent on an estimated property tax base (full value) of $70 billion.

State funding of a thorough education does not preclude local supplements, at least not now: "If monies are supplied to local districts from general State revenues sufficient for a 'thorough' education, some districts may still desire to add to that sum by local property taxes. This may reintroduce inequities of various sorts; however, the issue was not argued, and my decision is not intended to reflect upon it."

REFORM PROGRAM

A month after the Botter decision the New Jersey Tax Policy Committee published its plan for replacing the present system of school finance. Key elements of the committee plan, embodied in bills placed before the legislature, include the following:

1. State funding of a uniform, high-quality standard of education, with the commissioner of education determining annually the expense per pupil needed to achieve that standard

2. Local school districts now spending more than the state-supported amount per pupil, and districts receiving voter approval to exceed the standard expenditure, may supplement the state program and, subject to various constraints, receive from the state a share of the cost tapering down to zero for districts with more than twice the average wealth per pupil

3. Staffing of schools, development of curricula, and all other matters now controlled by local boards of education shall remain under local control

4. State property tax, at one percent of full value to finance that portion of school costs not funded from other State sources

The committee estimated that in the 1972-73 school year its standard (basic quality) program would cost about $1.5 billion, or $843 per pupil. The state's share of local leeway expenditures, based on 1971-72 data, would be a mere $37 million because (a) the state's contribution is a decreasing function of tax base per pupil and (b) sharing is limited to expenses not exceeding one-third of the standard cost per pupil.

In summary, the committee's plan calls for full state funding of a standard quality education, from a uniform statewide property tax, plus modest state sharing of local leeway expenditures. Local variations in taxable wealth would no longer produce unequal tax burdens for the support of a standard program, but local districts could elect to tax themselves for supplementary expenditures. Finally, the plan appears to overcome, at least for the present, the superior court's principal objection to the existing system of finance, namely, that it discriminates against both pupils and taxpayers in the less affluent school districts.

Besides the introduction of a personal income tax, estimated to yield $550 million in its first year, the following elements of the committee's program of fiscal reform tend to lessen regressivity:

1. The uniform statewide property tax, levied at 1 percent on equalized valuation, to replace $608 million of local property taxes levied at widely varying rates
2. General-purpose grants of $100 million to municipalities with per capita ratables below the statewide average, subject to state audit of expenditures and appropriate sanctions for improper or wasteful use of funds
3. State assumption of welfare costs now borne by local governments ($75 million) and of county judicial costs ($30 million)
4. State payments to municipalities for state-owned property ($13.5 million)

These and other measures add up to an estimated $863 million, almost 40 percent of the 1971 property tax levy—$2.2 billion. In addition to providing a balanced tax structure—between state and local levies, as well as among the three major types of taxes—the committee's proposals would enhance the equity and efficiency of New Jersey's fiscal system, and reduce the incidence of fiscal crises at both the state and local level of government.

Under the committee's plan, the property taxes would contribute a much smaller fraction of state and local revenues. The committee nevertheless saw fit to recommend changes in the administration and structure of the property tax, one of which is of particular interest here. Subject to voter approval, the principal urban centers would be permitted to substitute site-value taxation for the present real estate tax. Over a five-year transitional period, while land continues to be assessed at full value, the assessed value of improvements would gradually be reduced to 50 percent of full value. The regular tax base, however, would be used to apportion county and state taxes. Site-value taxation, it is hoped, would stimulate new construction and housing rehabilitation in the older cities.

PROPERTY TAX REDUCTION WINDFALLS

Property tax reduction for homeowners is offset by new liabilities under the personal income tax. Opponents of the committee's program were quick to point out, however, that owners of commercial and apartment property would reap a tax windfall without necessarily incurring additional tax liabilities. To prevent this, the administration devised a scheme for recapturing the windfall from landlords and transferring it to tenants.

The committee's income-tax proposal would allow tenants to deduct 20 percent of annual rental payments in computing taxable income. In his Master Plan for Tax Reform, Governor Cahill proposed instead that the tenant be allowed to deduct the full amount of his rent attributable to property taxes. Landlords would be required to document for each tenant the property tax component of his rent bill, on the basis of square footage, and renters would then enjoy parity with homeowners—at least with respect to this feature of the income tax.

The committee's program of tax reform was strangely silent, however, on the subject of short-run benefits to landlords stemming from reduction of local property taxes—about 40 percent, on the average.[6] The governor's plan therefore called for a transfer of these benefits from landlord to the tenant via a 75 percent excess-gains tax on the landlord's savings—the difference between his old and new tax liability. Proceeds from the excess-gains tax would be returned proportionately to each tenant in the form of an income-tax credit or a cash rebate, if the credit exceeded his liability. The untaxed portion of excess gains is, presumably, in recognition of the landlord's compliance costs.

To my knowledge, this levy is an innovation in state-local tax policy. The tenant gets an immediate benefit from a tax reduction, rather than an eventual reduction in rent reflecting the strength of his bargaining position with the landlord. After three years, the excess-gains tax would be discontinued.

The excess-gains tax would apply to commercial as well as apartment property. In the case of leased commercial property, the excess gain would be taxed at 75 percent and proceeds returned to the tenant. Owner-occupied

6. Tax windfalls would be particularly large in high tax jurisdictions where rental housing for low- and moderate-income families is concentrated. The committee's view was that "tenants should be in the position of negotiating rent reductions based on the degree of property tax relief provided to owners." (N.J. Tax Policy Committee, *Report*, Pt. 5, p. 92).

property would be subject to a 100 per cent excess-gains tax, with proceeds accruing to the state. However, businesses located in jurisdictions where the (effective) tax rate exceeds the statewide average by 25 percent or more are exempt from the excess-gains tax. The exemption is intended as an incentive to keep firms from leaving the cities, although it applies to property in any high-tax jurisdiction.

Banks, insurance companies, and public utilities are subject to special imposts designed to neutralize any excess gains resulting from local property tax reduction.

THE NEWARK PROBLEM

This review of New Jersey's fiscal structure and of proposals to reform the fiscal system would be incomplete without some reference to government finances in the state's metropolitan areas. The comparatively large role of local government is responsible for severe imbalance between the central cities and suburbs of metropolitan areas. Illustrative data are drawn from the Newark Standard Metropolitan Statistical Area (SMSA), the population of which was 1.9 million in 1970.

In 1970, the area's tax base (equalized valuation) was $14.9 billion, or slightly more than $8,000 per capita. In the city of Newark, the per capita value of taxable property was $4,047, less than half that of the outlying (suburban) territory—$9,062. The city's share of the SMSA's tax base had declined from 14.5 percent in 1960 to 9.9 percent in 1970. The effective tax rate on all property in Newark in 1971 was 7.22 percent, or 7.40 percent if calculated for real property only; the suburban (weighted) average, or ratio of property taxes to equalized valuation in the rest of the Newark SMSA, was 3.73 percent.

From its relatively small tax base, the city of Newark in 1969-70 spent $550 per capita for all purposes—municipal, school, and country—about 28 percent more than the suburbs ($429 per capita). Health and welfare, hospitals, housing, and public safety are among the functional categories in which the city's outlay per capita is significantly greater than in the outlying portion of the Neward SMSA. Woo Sik Kee's study of 22 large SMSA's shows that poverty-related spending, per capita, by the central cities is generally twice as high as in the Newark SMSA.[7] The ACIR tabulation for 1966-67, latest available on a nationwide basis, shows the city of Newark spending $290 per capita—twice the suburban average of $144—for all functions other than education.[8]

7. Woo Sik Kee, "City-Suburban Differentials in Local Government Fiscal Effort," *National Tax Journal*, 21, no. 2 (June 1968).
8. U.S. Advisory Commission on Intergovernmental Relations, *State and Local*

The metropolitan mismatch of needs and resources is found in nearly all of the nation's metropolitan areas; but fiscal disparities between city and suburb are particularly acute in New Jersey because of the disproportionate responsibilities borne by local government. The fiscal reforms proposed in 1972 would redress the imbalance between state and local government and materially reduce the disparities within New Jersey SMSA's.

Finances—1967 to 1970 (Washington, D.C.: Government Printing Office, 1969); N.J. Tax Policy Committee, *Report* M-50, p. 70.

14 Daniel L. Rubinfeld

Property Taxation, Full Valuation, and the Reform of Educational Finance in Massachusetts

This paper is concerned with school finance in Massachusetts. Consideration is given to the existing situation and possible reforms.

Normative implications as to who should control educational provision and decision-making should not be drawn from this paper. Numerous proposals were simulated, but it was decided that the simplest and most straightforward proposals were best suited for expositional purposes.[1] It will be assumed, for example, that all revenues for the reform of educational finance come from the state administrated property tax. It is likely that when and if reform does occur in Massachusetts and in other states, alternative tax tools will be used. Focus on the property tax does not imply that it need be the sole source or even the source of a large portion of the revenues. Alternative reform procedures worthy of serious consideration include the use of income and sales taxes, redefinition of school district boundaries and the direct federal takeover of substantial portions of school funding.

THE MASSACHUSETTS SYSTEM

There are large variations in local school expenditures in the state of Massachusetts. For example, in fiscal year 1970 Brookline spent $1280 per pupil while Malden spent only $643.[2] Part of this inequality in school finance is due to the existing disparities in the wealth of the communities in the state. Brookline has an equalized valuation per pupil of $74,797, while the corresponding amount for Malden is $22,834.[3] Clearly, it is easier for Brookline to raise a

---

1. Massachusetts does rely more heavily on the property tax than most other states. To that extent it serves as a good case study, because the redistributive effects of reform are likely to be greater than in most other states.
2. Despite the low spending level the tax rate was among the highest.
3. Equalized valuation is the estimated total valuation of the aggregate property

189

given level of expenditures per pupil than it is for Malden. Table 14.1 presents a clearer picture of the existing disparities in local school finance. These disparities are quite important in Massachusetts, in part because a good deal of the educational cost is financed locally and partly because the system of state

Table 14.1–Disparities in Public School Finance, Massachusetts, 1969-70: Relative Values of School Tax Rates and Expenditure per Pupil by Decile Groups According to District Fiscal Capacity per Pupil
(index of 100 = state median)

Decile	School tax rate	Expenditure per pupil	State aid per pupil	Fiscal capacity per pupil (thousands)
		Actual figures[a]		
1	27.28 mills	$706.22	$247.24	$15.60
2	26.11	740.59	249.08	17.86
3	23.70	728.71	229.52	19.51
4	23.64	761.48	231.98	21.34
5	21.36	742.58	215.08	23.10
6	21.54	738.91	178.58	25.97
7	19.27	743.28	170.06	28.62
8	20.02	807.62	161.82	32.42
9	17.26	866.02	124.17	40.98
10	7.61	944.42	133.37	99.70
State median	21.19	762.90	200.57	24.57
		Relative figures[b]		
1	128.7	92.6	123.3	63.5
2	123.2	97.1	124.2	72.6
3	111.8	95.5	114.4	79.4
4	111.6	99.8	115.7	86.8
5	100.8	97.3	107.2	94.0
6	101.7	96.8	89.0	105.7
7	90.9	97.4	84.8	116.5
8	94.5	105.9	80.7	131.9
9	81.4	113.5	61.9	166.8
10	35.9	123.8	66.5	405.7

[a]The figures are median values for decile groups arranged according to the state's measure of district fiscal capacity per pupil (based on "equalized valuation").
[b]Ratios of decile medians to the medians for the state.

Source: Steven J. Weiss and Deborah Driscoll, "Comparative School Finance Data–New England States vs. California," in *Financing Public Schools* (Boston: Federal Reserve Bank of Boston, January 1972).

subject to local taxation. (Personal property is a small portion of the local property tax base.)

and federal aid is not very redistributional across jurisdictions. This latter point can be clarified by an examination of the workings of the state aid system in Massachusetts.

State aid to education in Massachusetts consists of two types: Chapter 70 aid and categorical aid.[4] Categorical aid, consisting of items such as aid for vocational and special education, transportation, and school lunches, makes up a small portion of total state aid. Chapter 70 aid is distributed through a formula which appears on the surface to be redistributive. In the Chapter 70 formula local wealth is measured by the level of taxable property value per school attending child (SAC).[5] The amount of state aid received by the community is the product of reimbursable expenditures and a school aid percentage. Reimbursable expenditures include all school costs with the exception of Chapter 70 aid, categorical aid, and federal aid. The school aid percentage is defined as 100 percent minus 65 percent of the ratio of equalized valuation per school attending child in the community to the average level of equalized valuation per school attending child in the state. Two difficulties become immediately apparent even before complications in the system are mentioned. First, the level of wealth and the school aid percentage is a function of the number of school attending children while the reimbursable expenditures depend upon the number of public school children only. Second, since state aid is not included in reimbursable expenditures, a so-called yo-yo effect is produced. One year state aid is high and reimbursable expenditures are low, while the next year state aid is low and reimbursable expenditures are high.[6]

Before the Chapter 70 aid system went into effect, numerous amendments were added to the law, most of which served to diminish the amount of redistribution taking place. Among these restrictions were limitations on variations in local reimbursable expenditures as well as a save-harmless clause, which allowed no community to receive less aid under Chapter 70 than it did under the previous state plan. Examination of Table 14.1 makes it clear that

4. For more detail on the system of Massachusetts state aid, see Charlotte Ryan, *The State Dollar and the Schools* (Boston: Massachusetts Advisory Council on Education, 1970); and Steven Weiss and Deborah Driscoll, "Comparative School Finance Data— New England States vs. California," *Financing Public Schools* (Boston: Federal Reserve Bank of Boston, January 1972). Two additional works in this area are David Stern, "The Effects of Alternative State Aid Formulas on the Distribution of Public School Expenditures in Massachusetts," *Review of Economics and Statistics,* 55 (February 1973), pp. 91-97, and Martin Feldstein, "Wealth Neutrality and Local Choice in Public Education," Discussion Paper No. 293, Harvard Institute of Economic Research, July 1973.

5. School attending children include those of school age who reside in the jurisdiction, whether they attend private or public school.

6. The yo-yo effect has been eliminated as a result of recent amendments to Chapter 70 of Massachusetts law.

variations in state aid across deciles are much smaller than variations in local wealth. Weiss actually calculates from initial data from all state aid programs (categorical as well as Chapter 70) that the correlation between local wealth and state aid is .04.[7]

When the effect of all categorical aid programs has been taken into account, it is difficult to generalize about the redistributional effects of all state aid. It is for this reason that it is necessary to be extremely careful in interpreting simulated reforms for educational finance. The outcome of such reforms involves the net effect of first eliminating part or all of the existing state aid system and then replacing it with the new reform. Any such reforms should involve changes or elimination of the Chapter 70 portion of state aid, and should also seriously consider reforms of the existing categorical aid system.[8]

MEASURING EQUALIZED VALUATION

The process by which the Massachusetts State Tax Commission determines its biennial list of equalized valuations can best be placed in perspective by considering the extent to which the results of this process can affect the finances of local jurisdictions in the state. Of primary importance is the present Chapter 70 aid system. Although there is not a substantial amount of redistribution overall, it is still true that in individual cases a change in the level of equalized valuation can alter local revenues to a large degree. The incentive here is quite clear: it is in the best interest of the locality to have the state's measure of equalized valuation lower than any "true" statistical measure that might be determined. Other distributions in the state are also tied to the state's measure of equalized valuation, but at present these are quite small numerically and so are likely to have less effect on policy. (For example, payments from local jurisdictions to counties vary directly with the level of equalized valuation.) Additional cost considerations may arise because cities and towns face debt limits of 5 percent and 10 percent of total valuation, respectively. If these limits become constraining, communities will have to trade off the appearance of wealth (high equalized valuation) to raise new debt issues, with the appearance of "poverty" (low equalized valuation) so as to receive additional educational grants from the state. There is also reason to believe that the level of equalized valuation can affect the credit rating which the community receives, and thus indirectly alter its borrowing cost. Communities which have high

7. Steven J. Weiss, "The Need for Change in State Public School Finance Systems," *New England Economic Review* (Jan./Feb. 1970), pp. 3-22. Weiss's correlation was for 1966-67 and is not directly comparable to the data in Table 14.1.

8. School construction grants and other aid affecting the capital budget of communities is left out of the present study. There is no reason why construction grants as well as categorical aid could not be allocated on a matching basis with substantially different distributional effects than those implied by the existing structure.

ratios of debt to assessed valuations are considered to be poorer credit risks than communities with low ratios.[9] The importance of each of these incentives must be empirically determined, but it should be clear that local jurisdictions have strong incentives to influence the process by which equalized valuation is determined.

The actual method used by the State Tax Commission must of necessity be pieced together from discussions with the state and with those familiar with the workings of the Tax Commission. As well as can be determined, the State Tax Commission initially receives data from local assessors about recent sales in the community and assessments on the properties sold. Work sheets for the state divide all property in the community into four categories: residential land, commercial land, industrial land, and vacant land. The percentage of land in the community allocated to each use is given, along with estimated assessment ratios for each of the four categories.[10] An overall assessment ratio is calculated as a weighted average of the individual land use assessment ratios. The estimated assessed valuation of the taxable property in the community, when divided by the assessment ratio, yields the state's initial estimate of equalized valuation. Initial estimates of equalized valuation are presented to the localities for comment before the actual figures are made publicly available, and an official appeals process is available to the localities after the formal results are published.

An attempt was made to analyze statistically the extent to which political or other forces may have influenced the process by which equalized valuation is determined. Such an attempt is difficult because little is known about the actual process utilized by the state and because none of the state's data sources were made available. The issue in question is the extent to which the state's determination of the assessment ratio varies across jurisdictions. If all communities were assessed by the state at 50 percent of true market value, none of the distributional effects described previously would occur. Assessment ratios were calculated using sale and assessment data for twenty-one communities in the Boston metropolitan area.[11] These "true" assessment ratios are the average of assessment ratios on each of the individual properties sampled. While there are important data problems associated with the calculation of these ratios, most of these difficulties are faced by the State Tax Commission as well. Analysis involving only sale data is also limited because it is impossible to

9. For a detailed analysis of the process by which credit ratings are determined and their effect on borrowing costs, see D. Rubinfeld, "Credit Ratings and the Market for General Obligation Municipal Bonds," *National Tax Journal*, Vol. XXVI, March, 1973.

10. Assessment ratios are the ratio of the value of locally assessed property to the estimated full market value of that property.

11. Details relating to data sources and limitations as well as more specific results are not presented here. They are described in a more complete Institute of Public Policy Studies, University of Michigan working paper under the same title.

separate political and administrative influences from influences involving imperfections in the workings of the market.

A comparison of the state assessment ratios (AR_s) and the true assessment ratios (AR_t) makes it clear that in every community the state's determination of the assessment ratio is higher than the "true" counterpart. Conversely, the state's measure of equalized valuation is always lower than the true market value of all taxable property. Of primary importance for policy purposes is the extent to which the ratio of these two equalized valuation measures varies between jurisdictions. Boston and Braintree, with the highest ratio of state to true assessment ratios (2.09 and 2.04), gain the most in the way of educational aid (in percentage terms), while Belmont (1.25), Arlington (1.20), and Wellesley (1.23) are adversely affected. Several statistical calculations were made to test the hypothesis that the state was determining equalized valuation properly. One test assumed that the state attempts to determine full market value, while a second test assumed that the state attempts to reach only 90 percent of market value.[12] In the first case, we rejected the hypothesis that the state is doing its job properly in 18 of the 21 cases used. The corresponding figure for the second hypothesis was 11 out of 21 cities and towns. If the analysis is reliable, then the State Tax Commission's determination of equalized valuation is either poorly done and/or subject to political influence. Based on the rather small sample, some patterns begin to emerge. Political power appears to rest more in the hands of the larger more commercialized communities than it does in the hands of the wealthier bedroom communities. The suburban communities spend a larger portion of their budgets on education, but the larger cities stand to gain more in dollars of educational aid and are likely to have more direct legislative and other political influence in the state.

STATEWIDE PROPERTY TAX AND UNIFORM SPENDING REFORM

The reform model discussed at this time is quite simplistic in nature; it assumes that the state raises revenue from the property tax and then distributes that revenue in such a way that all communities spend exactly $800 per pupil. Despite the simplicity, this model serves to illustrate property tax issues associated with many of the reform plans under consideration by state governments across the nation. Under this plan, property tax revenues to finance the chosen expenditure level are raised by the state through a levy of a given number of mills per dollar of equalized valuation in each and every community.

12. There is reason to believe that the goal of the Tax Commission is not 100 percent valuation, despite a state law to this effect. This might be due in part to lags in the valuation of property, but it might also be the result of a reluctance to invite litigation if property is valued at greater than 100 percent.

Table 14.2–Simulation of State Property Tax Raising $800 per Pupil Tax Rates, Selected Communities Using State Assessment Ratios (AR$_S$)

City or town	State full value tax rate[a]	Percentage of total taxes to schools	New full value tax rate[b]	Percentage change in tax rate
Boston	101.40	17	105.90	+4.4
Everett	38.80	36	46.53	+19.9
Somerville	75.30	25	78.17	+3.8
Brookline	58.30	33	60.76	+4.2
Revere	61.10	37	60.19	−1.5
Malden	65.10	29	67.91	+4.3
Medford	57.60	37	57.99	+0.6
Belmont	36.80	41	43.41	+18.0
Watertown	53.70	38	54.99	+2.4
Newton	58.20	49	51.38	−11.7
Arlington	47.70	44	48.24	+1.8
Milton	34.40	44	40.91	+19.3
Quincy	53.30	43	52.08	−2.3
Melrose	46.30	47	46.24	−0.1
Stoneham	48.10	48	46.71	−2.9
Waltham	44.40	48	44.79	+0.9
Dedham	32.00	63	33.54	+4.8
Braintree	42.20	48	43.64	+3.4
Lexington	54.20	59	43.92	−19.0
Wellesley	38.60	54	39.46	+2.2
Weston	44.80	65	37.38	−16.6

[a]Rate at which taxes would have been assessed if property in the municipality were valued at its estimated full value. Includes tax rate to finance all local expenditures.

[b]Rate after changing school tax rate to the rate necessary to finance $800 per pupil in the state, given no change in state or federal aid.

Careful examination of Table 14.2 and 14.3 allows one to reach several important conclusions about reforms which involve equal expenditure per pupil, or about reforms which involve expenditures per pupil which come close to that goal. Of primary importance is the fact that central cities (with relatively low incomes) tend to face substantial tax increases, while wealthier suburbs face smaller increases and even declines in some cases. There are two important reasons for this occurrence. First, suburban communities tend to spend a substantially higher portion of their budgets on schools than do central cities, other things being equal, so that aid to education yields more benefits (percentagewise) to these localities. Second, almost all of the suburban schools opted to spend at a level above the $800 per pupil target before the reform was simulated. The subsequent forced decline in expenditures leads, other things being equal, to a lower tax rate.

Given that expenditure levels have changed, tax rate changes should not be

Table 14.3–Simulation of State Property Tax Raising $800 Per Pupil Tax Rates,
Selected Communities; Using "True" Assessment Ratios (AR$_t$)

City or town	True tax rate[a]	Percentage of total taxes to schools	New "true" tax rate[b]	Percentage change in tax rate
Boston	46.70	17	52.01	+11.4
Everett	23.09	36	28.01	+21.3
Somerville	50.31	25	50.96	+1.3
Brookline	43.94	33	42.67	−2.9
Revere	40.73	37	38.89	−4.5
Malden	40.30	29	41.84	+3.8
Medford	39.15	37	37.89	−3.2
Belmont	29.35	41	30.55	+4.1
Watertown	32.51	38	33.39	+2.7
Newton	37.54	49	32.38	−13.7
Arlington	39.71	44	35.47	−10.7
Milton	25.22	44	27.35	+8.4
Quincy	37.46	43	34.58	−7.7
Melrose	32.07	47	30.23	−5.7
Stoneham	36.74	48	32.33	−12.0
Waltham	27.85	48	27.71	−0.5
Dedham	19.59	63	20.48	+4.0
Braintree	20.70	48	23.99	+15.9
Lexington	36.28	59	28.10	−22.5
Wellesley	31.24	54	27.60	−11.6
Weston	29.38	65	23.51	−20.0

[a]This is the full value tax rate times the ratio of AR$_t$ to AR$_s$.

[b]After changing the school tax rate to the rate necessary to finance $800 per pupil in state, given no change in state or federal aid.

taken as a pure measure of benefit changes.[13] However, the relative change in tax rates does have important policy implications with respect to interjurisdictional migration. If one believes that effective tax rates (as well as public service benefit levels) are a factor in the location decision of individual households and firms, then such a reform is likely to encourage the suburbanization process. A complete answer to questions relating to this issue necessitates the development of a model of metropolitan location decision-making in which the effects of the reform on land prices, land use, migration, etc. is determined.

13. A measure of the net change in resources (the increase in school spending minus the increase in taxes paid for schools) would be suitable for this purpose.

14. Some preliminary attempts have been made to determine empirically whether taxes do affect location decisions and land values. See, for example, Wallace Oates, "The Effects of Property Taxes and Local Public Spending on Property Values: An Empirical Study of Tax Capitalization and the Tiebout Hypothesis," *Journal of Political Economy*, 77 (Nov./Dec. 1969).

Such a model would need to consider issues relating to the possibility of commercial and industrial taxes being exported outside the community in the form of lower wages and/or higher prices, as well as issues relating to urban-suburban interjurisdictional externalities.

The use of equalized valuation per pupil as a wealth measure in the equal expenditure reform also contributes to the potential difficulties facing the central cities and inner suburbs. One set of issues relates to the use of public school pupils in the denominator of the wealth measure. Central cities and inner suburbs in the Boston area tend to have a much smaller percentage of their population in public schools relative to the suburbs. This results from the fact that there are fewer school age children in the population and that a relatively large proportion of school age children living in the city attend private schools (primarily parochial schools in the Boston area). If one were to use school attending children or total population in the denominator rather than the number of public school pupils, central cities would be better off financially, while suburbs would be worse off.

The use of equalized valuation as a wealth measure should also be questioned. Complications arise, not only because of variations in statewide assessment practices, but also because the composition of taxable and nontaxable property varies substantially across the communities included in the study. In any case, urban communities which are poor in equalized valuation relative to the other communities in the metropolitan area are often not very poor on an absolute scale when rural areas enter the picture. The situation would be improved if median family income or other related data were used as a wealth measure, but even this would not account for problems arising because some communities have substantially different income distributions than others.[15]

At the basis of all of the previous discussion is the implication that educational reforms should be evaluated in part because of their interjurisdictional income effects. The implied concern lies not simply with poor communities, but with communities which are apparently faced with substantial burdens in the provision of all public services, not simply education. It is quite clear that reforms of the type discussed do little to aid these communities and it is natural to ask why these communities should receive aid in the form of interjurisdiction grants.

15. Income measures of wealth have not received additional attention here, primarily because under the existing legislative system the property tax base is the only tax base which is accessible to local school boards. Obtaining income figures for jurisdictions such as school districts can be difficult, especially if school jurisdictions are not coterminous with municipalities.

MUNICIPAL OVERBURDEN

It is popular in the literature to describe the "municipal overburden" facing central cities. The idea is that educational finance problems in central cities are especially difficult because of the unusual demands on taxpayers to meet non-school needs. Because of this added financial pressure, central cities are limited in their consumption choices of public service bundles. The term "municipal overburden" is quite misleading, however, because it does not reveal the explanation for the high tax rates faced by central cities. A combination of factors help to explain this phenomenon and each explanation suggests an alternative policy solution. For example, if the provision of public services in central cities is more expensive in the central city area than in suburbs because of higher input costs and diseconomies of scale, then revisions in the level of aid/pupil or other forms of municipal aid should be considered along with changes in jurisdictional size. If, on the other hand, central cities have higher tax rates than suburbs because they must service commuters who reside outside their jurisdiction, then a solution must involve taxes or subsidies between the jurisdictions in question. If individual or family poverty is the issue, then the negative income tax or other income maintenance proposals need to be considered. Finally, the higher tax rates might be to some extent the result of increased demand for public rather than private consumption in the community. In this case, tax rate differentials must be considered in light of differentials in housing and land prices. High tax rates and land values in one community in coordination with low tax rates and low land values in another community might be seen as the outcome of a competitive market process. To this extent, one could argue that market intervention is unnecessary. In any case, it is clear that reform of educational finance through the use of a single policy tool as the one described here cannot hope to resolve inequities arising from impacts of other quite distinct policy goals.

Within the context of the use of equalized valuation per pupil as a wealth measure, several variations are possible. If one wishes to include implicit aid of a categorical nature, for example, then distributions can be allocated on a weighted pupil basis, where pupils are weighted greater than one if they have important health, vocational, remedial, or transport needs. Allocations using alternative measures of fiscal capacity such as family income, household income for households with children, etc., also are worthy of further consideration.

PERCENTAGE EQUALIZATION REFORM

A large variety of plans for educational reform involve the notion of per-

centage equalization.[16] Under percentage equalizing plans a levy of one mill
in each school district is allowed to raise an identical amount of expenditures
per pupil. Communities which are poorer than a chosen key district receive
subsidies from the state, while wealthier communities contribute to the state
(this assumes that all redistribution occurs through the property tax system).
More explicitly, the aid received from (or donated to) the state is the product
of the level of expenditures per pupil and the state aid percentage, where the
state aid percentage is defined as 1 minus the ratio of equalized valuation per
pupil in the community to the equalized valuation per pupil in the key district.
In all of the models that were simulated as a part of this study, the key district
was determined by an iterative procedure so as to assure a balanced state
budget after reform takes effect.

Simulation of percentage equalization reforms is difficult because of the
complications associated with the existing Massachusetts state aid system.
The results assume that all present state and federal aid is used by the state
as a funding base for the new reforms. The state balances its budget only when
existing state and federal aid is included as a source of revenue. In addition,
the simulation model allows for the fact that changes in municipal tax burdens
under reform systems are likely to lead to district responses in the form of
changes in the level of public educational expenditures and/or in the form of
options to alter spending on private education. Given the lack of concrete information about the demand response of localities to a percentage equalizing
plan, it was decided to simulate the model under alternative assumptions about
the local price elasticity of educational expenditures.[17] While there is little
reason to believe that the price elasticity would not vary with wealth and
other variables, sufficient prior information was not available to allow for such
refinements. Given the difficulty of estimating the expenditure levels to be
chosen by communities, as well as the possibility of a massive shift to private
education, a phase-in process of several years would seem more reasonable than
an immediate introduction of the new system.

The results of the simulations suggest that a pure percentage equalization
plan would be generally redistributive. Under the assumption of no expenditure
adjustment to the new reform, Wellesley, Weston, Brookline and Milton (for
example), face substantial increases in tax rates, while tax rates fall in Boston,

16. See chapter 12 for a consideration of percentage equalization plans applied to
California data.

17. Leigh Marriner provided excellent assistance in gathering data and formulating the
simulation model, which utilized data from 351 Massachusetts school districts in Fiscal
Year 1970. Details about the data and specifics about the simulation model are available
from the author.

Somerville, Revere and Malden. When we allow for adjustment to changes in tax price, tax rate differentials between communities diminish somewhat, but the overall redistributive effect is still present. The fact that wealth as measured by equalized valuation per pupil varies substantially between communities implies that there are likely to be important equity effects in the form of positive and negative changes in the level of state financial support.

In an attempt to provide summary averages of key variables for all of the school districts in the state, all districts were placed into one of four categories: central city (center of SMSA), slow growing cities and towns (generally near to central cities), faster growing cities and towns, and rural areas. A somewhat surprising result is that rural communities are on average the richest in taxable value per pupil, while slow growing communities are more wealthy than faster growing suburbs. The presence of numerous rural resort areas as well as the fact that slow growing areas in Massachusetts tend to have large industrial bases helps to account for this result. This suggests that reforms which equalize property valuation per pupil between communities are more successful in equalizing school expenditures for central cities and the faster-growing cities and towns compared with rural areas and the slow-growing areas.

ADMINISTRATION

Leaving the measurement of equalized valuation directly under the influence of the local assessor is clearly undesirable. Reform of educational finance should be complemented by legislation to improve the assessment process in states such as Massachusetts. More and better information about commercial and industrial property must be obtained by assessors who must receive better training in their vocation. Sampling of all properties should be done each year by appraisal as well as by accurate sale information. Such data should be collected, analyzed, and made available for public consumption. This would do a great deal to eliminate some of the present incentives facing local assessors and other administrators.

CONCLUSION

The use of equalized valuation per pupil as a measure of local wealth involves several distinct problems. If redistribution between central cities and suburbs is desired, then equalized valuation per capita or an income measure would be a more suitable proxy for wealth. Central cities would also be aided if a proper pupil weighting scheme were utilized in the redistribution formula. Central cities tend to have larger health, special education, and vocational needs than do suburbs, although suburbs often benefit substantially under the existing grants set-up. Part of the large variation in fiscal capacity could be eliminated in Massachusetts if some of the smaller jurisdictions were encouraged to consolidate, but this brings about important issues with respect to control over decision-making which are beyond the context of this paper.

The goals of educational reform need substantial clarification before the actual policy instrument or set of instruments can be selected. Issues such as individual poverty, central city financial burdens, interjurisdictional externalities, scale economies in production of public services, categorical versus untied aid, etc. all appear in one form or another in discussions of the reform of educational finance. One should not assume, for example, that a new system of educational reform of a revenue-sharing nature obviates the need for a carefully designed system of categorical aid or for a system of individual grants which works towards the elimination of poverty.

Conference Review Hour

Daniel Holland: I think I would like to call on a volunteer. First, Daniel Rubinfeld, who suggested to me that some of the issues that emerged in the course of the discussion of his paper were less than fully dealt with and had a generality of interest that went beyond Massachusetts.

That might be a good basis for starting our general discussion. Would you care to say something, Dan?

Daniel Rubinfeld: To some extent my comments were dealt with in the discussion on California (chap. 12). However, perhaps one should make it clear that when one is discussing power equalization or percentage equalization all that it implies is an attempt to meet the *Serrano* decision *by equalizing* the tax price of education across jurisdictions. It does not imply anything about local or state control.

However, if in fact one is worried about rich districts withdrawing from the public school system, one should consider ways of keeping them in. One might consider a system in which the tax price of education would vary with the level of wealth in the community.

If the tax price of education fell as the level of wealth increases, there is less incentive for wealthy districts to withdraw from the system. One could supposedly finance the cost of that kind of subsidization by another tax system.

Noel Edelson: If we are really concerned about rich districts copping out, the Stubblebine-Teeples plan has little disincentive. On the other hand, some of the deficit under the *power equalizing plan* is shared next year by all districts in proportion to their wealth. If the wealthy districts cop out, it tends to raise the deficit, and the wealthy districts can forecast that they will bear part of that burden.

However, I would have thought a more direct way of doing it might not require that the deficit be borne by this one tax. One could, if one wished, put a further tax for the financing of education which would satisfy *Serrano.*

Such a tax would be a lump sum tax which would hold whether you are in or out of the public school system. Such a tax will have an income effect which deters high-income voters from walking out. It behaves exactly like the local school model where a high-income voter has to decide: "If I stay in my district, if I do not physically move, I will continue to bear the taxes regardless of whether I use the school for my children. I will make a simple customer surplus calculation to see if the extra value of the public education I could use is worth taking up."

Charles Waldauer: For a point of information, what is the lump sum tax you would use? A head tax?

Noel Edelson: It is a lump sum tax only from the point of view that it is fixed whether you leave or stay in the public school system. The tax is still borne no matter if you use the public schools or the private schools.

The effect of this tax on a high income district is comparable to the situation of a high-income voter located in a heterogeneous district.

Charles Waldauer: The same result could be accomplished by statewide methods.

Noel Edelson: Yes, but I want to preserve the local option. I think that's important.

William Vickrey: One gets to the situation where the dollar tax cost of expenditure can be greater than one. In effect, we ask the wealthy community to tax itself a $1.50 for each additional dollar it wants to spend on education. This goes in the face of what we used to think of as the case for state matching of local expenditures on the grounds of externalities. Even the wealthy community ought to have some incentive to accept these spillouts; the local tax dollar price of a dollar of education ought to be less than one for all communities. How do you meet this stipulation within the rubric of tax price equalization? It may be rather difficult. Perhaps excluding some cutoff point, it would be possible to devise a formula that would meet both the tax price equalization notion and the lack of dollar price in excess of one.

Douglas Thorson: I came to this conference with a good deal of interest, more I suppose, on the expenditure side of the problem. I was especially interested in the matter of equalizing expenditures per pupil, equalizing input. We briefly touched upon that the first day; there are certain kinds of finance questions that arise, such as the extent to which the tax structure poses impediments and the question of the regressivity of the tax structure. But as I have sat here, the heavy hand of reality has come down upon me. I have become impressed with the difficulty of doing very much substantively in terms of equalizing, at least as I define the concept of equalizing.

I have been impressed with the difficulties that may come from the constituencies of the wealthy communities. I have been impressed with some of the philosophical objections, and some of the uncertainty of our knowledge on the incidence of the tax structure.

I have concluded that there is likely to be more action in education finance in terms of some concept of minimum; this is a much more modest sort of thing, but the thoroughgoing education foundation minimum grant may be a more realistic goal. Points such as John Shannon has raised about the absolute burden on the poor of the retail sales tax and the property tax have become more important to me. As the conference has gone on, I have gotten sort of a different impression about the realities of this whole area.

W. Craig Stubblebine: It seems to me that developments in public finance in the last twenty years have been decidedly along these lines. There isn't an incidence of a tax system or an incidence of an expenditure. There is an incidence of fiscal institutions. The institution contains both the tax and the effect of the expenditures.

In our paper, we attempted a look, not just at tax incidence, but at the whole incidence.

Richard Lindholm: I think a point worth raising is a confusion between local option in the type of education and central financing. From the available New York studies and the Hawaiian experience, it is apparent that state financing doesn't preclude (in fact, it may encourage) local control, local interest in education, local varieties of education. Perhaps we have somewhat too readily assumed that financing from a central source is going to mean that central dicta are to be sent down to the community. Perhaps, the political and social trend is in the other direction. At the moment, we don't wish this social institution or other social institutions, despite central financing, to be directed lock, stock, and barrel by a central government.

Another point of importance ties in with Arthur Lynn's paper at the start of the conference. Mr. Lynn pointed out the relationship between land value and social and economic development. A good deal of this development shows up in land values and, therefore, land has some unique characteristics. In this sense, the rent from land becomes a relatively desirable source of financing of general education.

Finally, a point relative to flat grants, equalization problems, etc. One hundred percent financing at the state level avoids these problems and all the difficulties that arise under any procedure to deal with them.

There is at present a proposal in Oregon for 95 percent state financing. The legislature hasn't been elected yet, and we don't know what is going to happen.[1] We have gone through the problems of trying to work with various substitutes for 100 percent, and they turn out to be relatively impossible. There is a problem that the 100 percent financing doesn't avoid; that is the question of compensating districts for the capital cost of schools that have been built previously. This is something that needs to be worked out.

1. Editor's note: The proposal was referred to the people and defeated, May 1, 1973, by a 3 to 2 vote.

However, over a period of years this problem would disappear gradually. For capital construction from now on, there would be a capital budget relating to the needs and the growth of the various areas.

Ferdinand Schoettle: I have been playing with this as a lawyer, trying to take the court's mandate and work it into some actual tax systems.

The first alternative I thought of was: if the court requires an equal tax price for public education in each local jurisdiction, one could say, "All right, we will make every jurisdiction as well off as the most favored jurisdiction." However, when you think about that, it implies state expenditure for education at levels which are just impossible.

Another option is to say, "Well, we are going to level down the most favored jurisdiction." However, here you go into the problem of tax power equalizing. Then you have the problem that Mr. Vickrey mentioned where one locality has to raise $5 in taxes in order to keep $1.00 for local education.

Another alternative is redistricting. However, many of the papers at this conference show that differences in assessed valuation per pupil are still quite high. I have concluded that a completely equal tax price is improbable under any system I could visualize, other than total state financing.

Nevertheless, you can reach something that has substantial equality, along with some local option in tax expenditures, by taking the entire industrial and commercial tax base and assigning it to the state level. Of course, that presents some legal problems of definition on what to do with apartments, shopping centers, stores, etc.

The residential property tax base would be left to the local level, so that there is some opportunity cost when they make a decision on local spending. I have checked the rough data in conversation with John Shannon. They indicate that once you take the commercial and industrial property out of the local base, the local tax base per pupil would be approximately equalized. The amount the state would have to reallocate is estimated to run about 25 percent and 35 percent of the tax base. I think this would come the closest of any system I can think of to equalizing the tax price per jurisdiction, although it would not be absolutely equal.

Ronald Teeples: I share the enthusiasm for Craig Stubblebine's proposal. I have been talking to John Shannon about the possible application of the same plan at the federal level since the federal government is wrestling with similar issues of how to help states deal with the federal government's role in education in light of these types of court decisions.

We could in effect make each state a district faced with tax rates and expenditure levels raised from a base defined by the federal government on a national basis. The Stubblebine plan has implications for this problem too.

W. Craig Stubblebine: Actually a coordinated tax base sharing could be applied to any local service—fire, police, or public protection—anything you want. The state could be divided into various districts. You might have a board for each function or a single board; each of these functions would be financed from this coordinate base. Each community would get back funds relative to their tax spending opportunities.

The only function that creates a problem is welfare. However, all you would do is create a state welfare district. There would be so much money to be raised off the base for each person on welfare according to whatever welfare standards the district should decide.

The role for the state legislature in handling public decisions could be brought back almost entirely to the local level. The state legislature could go back to its function of about 1900.

Daniel Holland: And meet every five years.

W. Craig Stubblebine: The system would work automatically.

Charles Waldauer: I wanted to ask something of Mr. Lindholm. You mentioned state financing to cover the flat grant. Would you envision the flat grant as it is now, some minimum or foundation level of education, or rather an attempt to try to capture some average level of expenditure for the state as a whole?

Richard Lindholm: No, rather the amount is determined by need as determined in the budget process. For example, in the state of Hawaii expenditures per student for the island of Hawaii are relatively large. Education is more expensive there because of student travel distance. Also you have to pay more to the teacher because it's a less desirable place to live (you have to furnish housing for the teachers). Also, where the people are located right along the uncrowded beach, they have a very different sort of education program from the type of education in downtown Honolulu, a city crowded with people with different interests. The students are trained for different types of life, and the education is very different.

The Hawaiian program of state financing probably varies as much from place to place, and perhaps even more, than is the case in states where a considerable portion of the financing is done by a flat grant and the remainder of the money is raised through a local property tax assessment.

It is true that the Hawaii system has brought about, perhaps, more private schools than typically exist elsewhere. However, you can't be certain that this is not because of the Hawaiian environment and the racial mix, rather than the tax system.

Charles Waldauer: One last point, about the proposal that Mr. Schoettle raised about the state taxation of industrial and commercial property. This could be a poor mechanism if only the state were allowed to tax this property. After all, commercial and industrial businesses use other local government services—fire, police, and what not; it would be wrong to deny the localities the right to tax property for these services, which are pretty well related to property.

Ferdinand Schoettle: In my model, the right to tax this property would be given to the state for education only. Actually my analysis holds that welfare and health are also the same as education. There should be no legal obligation on the local community.

William Vickrey: Tax power equalization takes care to some extent of the industrial property problem. Comparing the situation in Beverly Hills, California, for example, with that of Teterboro, New Jersey, suppose under the formula in both cases the local community has to tax itself for $4 for each $1 it can devote to its own educational or other purposes. In the case of Beverly Hills, that could result in very serious movements in the direction of opting out of the public system or of trying to separate out and provide frills privately rather than publicly. In the Teterboro situation, however, the private individuals who vote are not the industrial taxpayers who pay. In a sense, they may be quite willing to charge the industries the $4; their share is still only going to be one-for-one in terms of what they get.

In that sense, I think the power equalization formula might take care of the problem without having to go through explicit state taxation of the industrial property. In effect that is what the tax power equalization does. It takes away the extra revenue that you are getting from taxing on the extra industrial property in your area.

Arthur Becker: I am responding to Mr. Schoettle's comment about attaching the education function to commercial/industrial property. I can't really imagine anything worse from the economic point of view. I could envision expanding this concept so that each class of property is responsible for financing a particular service.

It is very likely that we will have to raise a lot more money if we are going to meet the requirements of recent court decisions, either to meet the "thorough education" standard required by New Jersey's constitution or to eliminate the fiscal disparities as required in California. If we are going to have to raise a lot of money, and if we are going to raise it through the property tax, then perhaps we ought to think of raising it from the property tax in a way which would do the least violence to the allocation of resources. This would be the case if we taxed land values alone and not buildings, thereby maintaining efficiency as well as a certain amount of equity. However, I would hate to see another barrier develop in the movement of land from one kind of use to another.

Ferdinand Schoettle: I think you may misunderstand. Commercial and industrial properties will pay the local rate for noneducation purposes. The school board will set its budget. Part of that budget will go to a county auditor for local collection on residential properties. Part of that budget will be satisfied by the allocation from the state tax on industrial properties.

Ford and General Motors, two identical plants in the same state, would pay the same amount of taxes as far as education goes. I don't see why from the economist's point of view it is efficient to say, "Like Ford and General Motors, you should pay the amount of tax that is dependent upon the impact of educational financing on the property tax base in the area where you put the plant." I don't see how the current system is efficient, as far as horizontal equity goes among business taxpayers, in distinguishing between those who do not consume educational services in the same way they consume police and fire protection.

William Vickrey: I think that in the matter of discrimination, the issue is not as to whether a firm is going to locate in one community rather than another. Perhaps again one should distinguish between the tax on improvements and the tax on land. A higher tax on improvements in one community will influence location. A tax on land will not, because if there is a difference in the tax on land, there is also a difference in the price of land.

Of course, if you do have state assessment of industrial property and a uniform state rate on the industrial property, and if there is a variation in the local rates, there will be a difference between the rates applied to property that is industrial and property that is not industrial. This may lead to some sort of distortion when it comes to a decision whether a particular property is to be devoted to industrial or residential use.[2]

A distortion can also arise if an exemption is applied to agricultural land. Perhaps the way to handle this, if one really feels that it is politically necessary to exempt agricultural land from the land value tax, might not be to exempt agricultural land as a category, but after the land value is assessed, to deduct a given amount from the assessment per acre and apply the tax only to the remainder.

This deduction could be set at a level which will affect most agricultural land, but wouldn't make all that much difference to urban land. In effect, if you did it this way, it wouldn't make any difference in tax whether the land was classified agricultural or otherwise. There would be no distorting effect introduced into the situation from that source.

Mason Gaffney: It seems to me that if a statewide land tax is best, advocacy of this approach should not be reduced because of farm opposition. I'd like to take exception to the idea that we have to go to bed with these pitchfork guys in order to get anything across. The farmers in the United States are the most spoiled children that we have, fiscally speaking, at every level. It would be a serious mistake to perpetuate this. John Riew has pointed out to us that agriculture is not homogeneous. There are a number of examples in purely agricultural areas where farmers have used the site value tax.

2. Editor's note: It may however lead to less distortion when industrial location is considered between one city or another within the state.

The irrigation district movement in California is the most outstanding case. I think the highest effective rates of taxation on land that I have ever observed are those which obtain in certain irrigation districts. The state of North Dakota under the old Nonpartisan League had a strong land tax movement, which was primarily agricultural, and even today, I believe, farm dwellings in North Dakota are not taxed.

The fact that we have farmers objecting at meetings where statewide land taxation is discussed, I find very suspect. I suspect that many of these were phony farmers. They may represent the kind of farmer that John Riew described to us, who is a speculative holder of land in an area surrounding a rapidly growing city.

Allen Manvel found (in his study) the value of farm land in the United States to be about $200,000,000,000 compared to $300,00,000,000 of urban land value. I think he may have overstated the relative share of farm land, but if he was anywhere near right, to exempt this enormous reservoir of land value from the tax base will not be a small matter. It would be a very high price to pay for presumed political advantage, which has yet to be demonstrated, and it would make the whole system quite inequitable.

I feel that a statewide site value tax should certainly include agriculture.

John Riew: We have talked about regressivity, progressivity, and in connection with this, we have also talked about rental value imputation. I think that imputing rental value to the income of the elderly retired would be a little unfair. Their mobility is severely restricted. If an old person lives in a $40,000 house, to have him include the rental in his income, might be too much for him to pay. Perhaps we can avoid this by providing a circuit-breaking thing.

I am impressed with John Shannon's emphasis on the high absolute value of the burden on the poor. That kind of a situation can be avoided by circuit breaking (i.e., selective exemptions). Professor Vickrey's suggestion to exempt agricultural land value up to a certain level might be too costly. The exemption would apply to everybody, poor and rich, and there are proportionately more rich landholders than poor. Here again we could use the concept of circuit breaking to apply to the farm land.

Part IV
Metropolitan Area and City Fiscal Environment

15 William H. Oakland

Social, Political, and Economic Analysis of the Finance of Education in the Baltimore Area

INTRODUCTION

A wide and growing divergence exists among geographical regions with respect to property tax rate dedicated to education and the level of expenditures this permits per public school pupil. As a result, the system is said to violate the principle of equal educational opportunity and/or the basic principle of tax equity, i.e., one's tax burden depends upon where he lives rather than his ability to pay. In practice, divergences often occur with respect to both dimensions, particularly between central cities and their suburbs. This has brought forth demands for higher levels of government to play a greater role in education finance. Among the proposals for reform are (a) a consolidation of small school districts into something resembling a countywide education system (b) an increased role by the state in equalizing the costs of education (c) direct assumption of the full costs of education by the state (d) equalizing federal aid to local school districts.

This paper explores the problem of education finance in the Baltimore metropolitan area. Besides being of interest in its own right, it is believed this study can offer valuable insights into the nature and quantitative significance of the education finance problem for large urban areas in general. Much of the dissatisfaction with present education financial arrangements appears to stem from a failure to cope adequately with the problem facing large central cities.

FISCAL SETTING

The Baltimore Standard Metropolitan Statistics Area (SMSA) is defined as Baltimore City and its five surrounding counties.[1] Its population, slightly in excess of two million, makes it the ninth largest metropolitan area in the

This study was partially financed by the Baltimore Urban Observatory.
1. Anne Arundel, Baltimore, Carroll, Harford, and Howard Counties.

213

country. Its per capita personal income in 1970, $4,167, places it between the average for the U.S. as a whole, $3,920, and the average SMSA, $4,283. In these terms, it ranks 52nd out of 253 SMSAs. In terms of growth, the Baltimore SMSA's performance has been average. Its population growth and per capita income growth during the sixties were 20 percent and 81 percent, respectively. The average SMSA experienced a population growth of 20 percent and enjoyed a 76 percent increase in per capita income during the same period.

Budget Structure

Current expenditures by local governments in the Baltimore SMSA during the fiscal year 1970 amounted to nearly $900 million or $430 per capita. Of this amount, outlays upon education accounted for nearly 40 percent while public safety, welfare, and debt service, taken together, account for another 33 percent. Thus, these four categories account for nearly 75 percent of all local expenditures. On the revenue side, 40 percent of current revenues were obtained from higher level governments—i.e., state and federal. Less than one-third of current revenues were provided by the property tax, while a local income tax and charges provided slightly more than 20 percent. The remaining 7 percent or so of current revenue was obtained from miscellaneous sources.

In Baltimore, property taxes as a *fraction of personal income* did not advance during the sixties. The popularly held belief that property taxes have grown increasingly oppressive does not stand up for the Baltimore area as a whole. A second noteworthy feature is the fact that per capita current expenditure grew at nearly twice the rate of personal income, indicating a very rapid expansion of local government during the sixties. Third, revenues from higher levels of government accounted for nearly 45 percent of all revenue increases during the sixties, raising the share of such revenue in total revenue from 30 percent to 40 percent. Without such an expansion in intergovernmental aid, property taxes as a fraction of personal income would have increased sharply. Finally, the most important source of expenditure growth was education, accounting for over 40 percent of the total increase in current spending. However, the growth of school expenditure only slightly exceeded that of total expenditure, indicating that other categories also played an important role in local budget expansion.

Comparison With Other SMSAs

On the whole, the Baltimore SMSA is reasonably representative of the average large SMSA. There are certain differences, however, which call for comment. First, 1969 census data indicate that Baltimore area governments spent $66 less per capita than the average large SMSA—a difference of 15 percent. However, nearly $38 of this represents lower utility expenditures and can be dismissed as being due to differences in institutional arrangements (e.g., private versus public ownership of gas and electric companies). The remaining $28 can be explained by differences in per capita income, which is 7 percent less in Baltimore than in the average SMSA.

The second significant area of difference is intergovernmental revenue. The Baltimore SMSA receives nearly 10 percentage points more from this source than the average SMSA. This is reflected in a smaller share of the property tax in the revenue structure and therefore a smaller property tax burden. This has caused the property tax to be of less importance in Baltimore than in most large SMSAs.

Finally, the share of increased expenditure accounted for by education is greater in Baltimore (50 percent versus 41 percent). Since per capita expenditure upon education is virtually equal to that of other SMSAs, the faster growth in Baltimore may simply reflect a catching up with other areas. If this is so, the role of education in future budget growth in Baltimore should not depart significantly from average.

Intra-Baltimore SMSA Disparities

The most interesting features of the Baltimore SMSA fiscal landscape lie in the disparities that exist within the area itself. Underlying these fiscal disparities are differences in the socio-economic characteristics of the population.

First, 56 percent of the SMSA's population resided outside Baltimore City in 1970 compared with 48 percent in 1960. The decline in the city's share of the total population was the result of a small decrease in its population coupled with a 35 percent increase in suburban population. Per capita personal income in the suburbs was 30 percent higher than in the city in 1970, up from a 12 percent differential in 1960. The corresponding figures for change in per capita taxable property are 38 percent and 1 percent, respectively. Though the city had only 44 percent of the area's population in 1970, it had 89 percent of the welfare cases, reflecting a six-fold difference in the incidence of welfare. Finally, in 1970, nonwhites comprised 47 percent of the city's population compared with 35 percent for 1960. The corresponding figures for the suburbs are 6 percent and 7 percent, respectively. These racial differences are magnified for public schools—65 percent versus 9 percent. In all major respects, therefore, the Baltimore SMSA exhibits the characteristics of the classic model of urban development (or decay)—a declining central city, increasingly occupied by economically disadvantaged minorities, and surrounded by a growing and affluent white population.

The impact of these socio-economic differences upon fiscal behavior are clearly demonstrated by a comparison of the budget structures of Baltimore City and its suburbs. Comments here are confined to those differences which are the most striking.[2]

First, the city spends nearly twice as much per capita as the suburbs. Furthermore, the city spends more on all categories save debt service. However, the three categories, public safety, public welfare, and hospitals, account for 70 percent of the difference. Presumably, there is a strong association between the latter and the differences in socio-economic characteristics noted above. Second, the composition of expenditure and expenditure growth differs sharply between the areas. Education expenditure accounts for over 50 percent of total spending and growth of total spending in the suburbs but only 30 percent in the city. This is not due to differences in per capita spending on education, nor in its growth; these magnitudes are virtually equal for the two areas.

A third major difference exists with respect to revenue structure. The city, in 1970, received nearly half of its total revenues from state and federal sources, whereas the suburbs received less than 30 percent. Furthermore, grants financed nearly 60 percent of all increases in city current expenditures but only 28 percent of those of the suburbs. Nevertheless, in 1970, taxes were much higher in the city than in the suburbs. As a fraction of personal income, taxes were 50 percent higher, and the effective property tax rate stood 75 percent higher.

Finally, we call attention to differences in the growth of tax bases. In Baltimore City, the assessable base per capita did not keep pace with the price level, growing only at 1.3 percent per year. In the suburbs, the figure was considerably higher—4.4 percent per year. Thus, not only is the city saddled with a slower growth of personal income, but its property taxes respond much less to growth.

The State: Budgets and Subareas

Our description of the fiscal setting would be incomplete without a discussion of the major economic and fiscal characteristics of the state in which our SMSA is located.

The state of Maryland is an affluent, highly urbanized region. Its 1971 per capita income of $4522 was 9 percent above the national average and ranked 11th among the states. Nearly five-sixths of its population resides within the boundaries of an SMSA, making it the fifth most urbanized state according to this measure.

Maryland has experienced sharp economic growth over the recent past. During the sixties, its population expanded by 26.5 percent compared with

2. For a detailed discussion of intermetropolitan disparities, see my "Using the Property Tax to Pay for City Government: A Case Study of Baltimore," in *Property Tax Reform,* ed. G. Peterson (Urban Institute and Lincoln Foundation, 1973), pp. 141-73.

13.3 percent for the country as a whole. This made it the sixth fastest growing state during that period. Personal income growth in Maryland during the sixties also exceeded the national average—8¾ percent versus 7.2 percent. However, in per capita terms, Maryland personal income just kept pace with the country as a whole, growing at a 6 percent annual rate.

The rapid rate of economic growth experienced by Maryland was not equally shared by its subregions. For these purposes we can divide the state in three regions: (1) the Baltimore SMSA, making up 53 percent of the state's population; (2) the Washington suburbs with 30 percent of the population; (3) rural Maryland encompassing the remaining 17 percent. In the Washington suburbs, per capita income is 25 percent above the state average, while in the Baltimore SMSA and rural Maryland it is 6 percent and 24 percent below, respectively. Thus, the level of economic well being differs markedly between the regions.

The Washington suburbs accounted for 59 percent of the state's population growth during the sixties, while the Baltimore SMSA and rural Maryland accounted for 32 percent and 9 percent respectively. Expressed as decennial rates of growth, these came to 69 percent, 15 percent, and 11 percent, respectively. Together with their greater economic resources, the resultant increase in the share of population residing in the Washington suburbs means that considerable shifts have occurred in the distribution of political power within Maryland. This fact will be of importance when considering reform in the present system of education finance.

State expenditures grew rapidly in response to the expansion in population and income. During the 1963-71 interval the state's general fund expenditure increased at an average 17.5 percent annual rate. This was achieved by an increase in state taxes from 5 percent of personal income to over 7 percent. For the U.S. as a whole, on the other hand, state taxes rose from 5 percent to 6.5 percent over the same period.

Comparisons of tax burdens should be made with respect to the combined total for state and local governments. However, this does not change the picture given by considering the state alone. In 1963, state and local taxes were 8.43 percent of personal income. By 1971, they reached 12.33 percent, an increase of almost 50 percent. For the U.S. as a whole, on the other hand, state and local taxes averaged 9.61 percent of personal income in 1963 and 11.66 percent in 1971 Thus, Maryland tax effort went from considerably below to considerably above average in only eight years. Whereas Maryland ranked 23rd in per capita taxes in 1963, it ranked 9th in 1971; this was achieved despite the fact that in terms of per capita income, Maryland's ranking remained unchanged.

Whatever measure is employed, therefore, state and local government activity has undergone a vigorous expansion in the past decade. Despite this fact, Maryland ranked only 17th in terms of tax effort in 1971. It would appear that sufficient revenue capacity remains for Maryland to continue to expand its governmental activity at a rapid pace. Nevertheless, when it is considered that Maryland ranked 45th in tax effort in 1963, one must conclude that the rate of expansion in the near future will necessarily be curtailed.

Short-Term Fiscal Outlook

We conclude this section with a summary of the findings of two recent budget projections. One study, completed in 1971, concludes that by fiscal 1975, the state and local governments of Maryland will experience a combined annual deficit of $450 million, or about 10 percent of total spending.[3] Two-thirds of the projected deficit is anticipated to occur at the local level, and one-half of this is expected to occur in Baltimore City. To put these magnitudes in perspective, $450 million is roughly equal to the yield of the state income tax, while to close the Baltimore City's budget deficit would require a doubling of its property tax rate.

The assumptions underlying the above study are "a modest improvement in the quality of public services" and no major change in tax rates or state aid to local governments. The definition of "modest quality improvements" is the same rate of improvement as experienced in the 1962-68 period. In order to close the state portion of the deficit, the study recommended an increase in the progressivity of the state's income tax. Furthermore, it recognized that Baltimore City's fiscal problem can be resolved only "by a substantial increase in state aid or by state assumption for some services, now performed by the subdivisions."

The second study, completed in 1972, restricted its attention to the Baltimore SMSA.[4] Two sets of projections were made for 1975. The first assumed no "quality" improvement in the level of public services above that of the 1965-70 period. Under this, the "constant quality" assumption, Baltimore City was projected to suffer a deficit in excess of $30 million, or roughly 20 percent of its property tax collections. The suburbs, on the other hand, were projected to enjoy a modest surplus. The second projection was based upon an improvement in the quality of public services paralleling that of the 1965-70 period. Under the "continuing improvements" assumption, the city was projected to suffer a deficit in excess of $100 million—or an increase in property tax assessed values or rates of two-thirds. The suburbs were projected to experience a shortfall requiring only marginal adjustments in tax rates. The study concluded that without a substantial shift in state aid, a substantial

3. *Report of Study Commission on the State Tax Structure* (Baltimore, 1971).
4. *Baltimore Municipal Finance Study* (Baltimore Urban Observatory, 1972).

differential in property tax rate and/or government service levels would arise in the near future. This result will hold even with the passage of federal revenue sharing, for the latter will not significantly reduce the disparities between central city and suburbs. What makes these findings of particular importance to this paper is the fact that all of the city's deficit under the constant quality projection and 60 percent of it under the "continuing improvements" projection is attributable to increased spending for schools. It would appear, therefore, that the resolution of the city's envisaged fiscal crisis must necessarily involve changes with respect to school finance.

In summary, the near future is likely to witness considerable pressure upon the state to increase its tax rates to *maintain* existing programs. In addition, revenue shortfalls at the local level coupled with their unequal division between jurisdictions will lead to increased demands for greater state assistance. This is at present the case with respect to elementary and secondary education, where reform proposals range from modest increases in state aid to full state assumption of costs. Since education plays such a major role in the expenditures of local governments, the current drive for greater state participation in educational finance may stem less from a concern for equal educational opportunity than from a practical means to eliminate the imminent fiscal crisis for certain local governments.

PRESENT SYSTEM OF SCHOOL FINANCE

During the 1970-71 school year, Maryland local governments spent an average of $974 per pupil upon current expenses for elementary and secondary education. Although this figure is only about 12 percent above the national average, it is fair to say that Maryland is a relatively big spender upon public education. This is brought out by Maryland's rank with respect to per pupil expenditure, 10th, and by the fact that education spending in Maryland is 25 percent above the median figure for all states. These figures are summarized in Table 15.1.

Maryland also ranks above average with respect to school spending per $1000 of personal income. Table 15.1 shows that the Maryland figure of $56.40 exceeds the national average by approximately 10 percent and is sufficiently high to rank Maryland 14th among all states. On the other hand, the table clearly reveals that, in terms of per pupil spending and fraction of income devoted to schools, Maryland is well below the highest state. The same is true of teacher's salaries as shown in column (3).

In columns (4) through (6) of the table the shares of current expenditure by each source—state, federal, and local—are shown. The state share in Maryland falls approximately 15 percent below and the local share stands 13 percent above the national average. Maryland ranks slightly above the median for local share and slightly below the median for state share.

Table 15.1 – Education Finance, Maryland versus Other States

	Total current expenditure per pupil, 1970-71 (1)	General expenditure for local schools per $1000 of personal income, 1970 (2)	Average teacher's salary, 1970-71 (3)	State share of (1) (4)	Local share of (1) (5)	Federal share of (1) (6)	Ratio of highest spending school district to lowest, 1969-70 (7)
U.S. average[a]	$ 868	50.31	$ 9,690	41.1%	52.0%	6.9%	–
Median state	780	51.35	9,088	38.2	53.6	7.3	2.78
High state	1,401	73.05	14,124	89.4	86.2	27.8	23.55
Low state	523	40.06	6,518	15.1	2.9	2.1	1.37
Maryland	974	56.40	10,463	35.3	58.9	5.8	1.63
Maryland rank	10	14	7	29	20	34	46

[a]50 states and District of Columbia.

Sources: for columns (1), (3), (4), (5), (6), NEA Research Division, *Estimates of School Statistics*; for column (2), *Governmental Finances*, 1969-70, table 24; for column (7), *President's Commission on School Finance* (calculation of low state did not include Hawaii, which has a state system).

Finally, in column (7), the degree of intra-state variation within Maryland is compared with that of other states. Whereas the highest-spending school district in the median state outspends the lowest-spending school district by a factor of 2.78, in Maryland the figure is only 1.63, ranking it 46th in this respect. This clearly indicates that extreme inequalities of educational spending that has brought successful court challenges in some states does not characterize Maryland. To a large measure, this owes to the large size of the Maryland school district and offers a rough estimate of the reduction in inequality that might be expected should a state adopt the Maryland pattern. Nevertheless, a ratio of 1.63 is still considered by many to be intolerable and has led to policy proposals which would narrow disparities.

In Table 15.2 we compare the Baltimore SMSA with the 72 largest SMSAs in the United States with respect to three important education magnitudes: (1) current expenditure per pupil; (2) local share of current expenditure per pupil; (3) current expenditure for schools as a fraction of total local expenditure. To make the comparisons more meaningful, the data for the SMSAs are broken down into their central city and suburbs components.

Table 15.2–Comparison of Baltimore with 72 Largest SMSAs, 1969-70 School Year

	Current expenditure per pupil		Local share of current school expenditure		Local school expenditure as percent of total expenditure	
	CC	OCC	CC	OCC	CC	OCC
Weighted average–all areas	$ 817	$ 775	.51	.53	n.c.	n.c.
Unweighted average–all areas	775	707	.55	.49	.38	.58
Median–all areas	734	723	.60	.51	.37	.57
High–all areas	1,267	1,227	.81	.81	.55	.93
Low–all areas	445	401	0	.13	.24	.30
Median–east only	931	776	.55	.58	.34	.55
Baltimore	822	759	.57	.52	.35	.62
Baltimore rank–72 SMSAs	28	23	41	32	40	18
Baltimore rank–19 eastern SMSAs	16	12	8	12	7	3

CC = Central City
OCC = Outside Central City
n.c. = not calculated

Source: U.S. Census Bureau as shown in Seymour Sacks and Ralph Andrew, *State Aid and the System of School Finance: The Metropolitan Dimensions of Revenue Sharing* (Syracuse University, 1972).

The table reveals that the Baltimore area stands about equal to the national average with respect to per pupil spending, being slightly above average for the city and slightly below for the suburbs. In terms of median values, the Baltimore SMSA is 5 percent to 10 percent above the norm for large SMSAs. However, when compared with only eastern SMSAs, Baltimore City ranks near the bottom and the suburbs slightly below the median. Thus, with respect to per pupil expenditures, Baltimore City stands somewhat above the national norm for large cities, but considerably below the levels prevailing in other eastern cities. The suburbs, on the other hand, stand close to the norm in both comparisons.

How do we reconcile the relatively weak showing of the Baltimore SMSA with the strong showing of the state as a whole? The answer lies with the Washington suburbs, which spend considerably above the state average, raising the figure for the state as a whole. We shall return to this important point later in the discussion.

Turning to the share of school expenditures financed locally, we find Baltimore SMSA governments quite close to median values for all SMSAs in the sample. Compared with only eastern SMSAs, Baltimore City is close to the median with the Baltimore suburbs falling slightly below. These results are surprising since our earlier discussion of local government budgets as a whole revealed that the Baltimore SMSA obtained a considerably greater proportion of its operating revenues from higher government levels. What our findings here reveal is that such greater aid occurs in other budget categories.

Finally, Table 15.2 indicates that the Baltimore SMSA follows the national pattern with respect to the share of total budgets devoted to education. The share of education in suburban government expenditures is considerably greater than for central cities. This pattern is repeated in Baltimore, but is even more pronounced. Its significance for reform of education finance appears obvious but seems often to be overlooked—suburban governments may have almost as much to gain by state assumption of the full costs of education as central cities. The findings reported below bear this out.

Behavior Over Time of State Totals

Partially in response to the rapid growth of spending and partially responsible for it, state aid to education in the Baltimore area grew at an annual rate of 11.8 percent from 1959 to 1970. The growth was not rapid enough to prevent the state share of current expenses from falling. This reduction has been used by the critics of the present system as a major deficiency of the existing aid program. To some extent, however, the reduction in the state share is a statistical artifact. In 1967, the state assumed a considerably larger share of the cost of school debt service and school construction activity. If we consider the state share of current expense plus debt service, the apparent reduction in state share vanishes. Furthermore, even if noncurrent expense state aid is ignored, the expansion of federal aid over the period kept the expansion of the local share to modest proportions.

The root of the difficulties facing local governments with respect to education finance lies not so much with an increased local share of current expense but with increased levels of local spending for current expense. Local spending upon education quadrupled in the 1959-70 period—an implied annual rate in excess of 13.5 percent. Since the backbone of local finance in Maryland, as elsewhere, is the property tax, and since the total assessable base grew only by 6.75 percent per year over the period, the increased local expenditure could only be achieved by substantial increases in the property tax rate. The magnitude of the required increase can be put into perspective by considering the fact that the increase in locally raised school outlays from 1959 to 1970 required two-thirds of all property tax collections in 1970.

The rapid increase in education expenditure would not have posed as great a problem if the growth of the property tax base per pupil were fairly uniform across school districts. However, this was not the case. Considerable variation existed in the rate of growth of the property tax base among subdivisions. We find absolutely no correlation between growth of the property tax base and per student expenditures as of 1970-71. The growth of taxable property did not take place where it was most needed nor decline where it was least needed.

On a per pupil basis, taxable wealth actually decreased in Baltimore City during the sixties. Since it is widely believed that Baltimore City's need for improved educational services grew more rapidly than other areas during the sixties, this could be accomplished only if its tax rates were increased substantially faster than other areas or if the state would finance larger shares of its education costs. As we saw in the section on fiscal setting, property tax rates in Baltimore City grew no faster than in its suburbs, while, as we shall see in the next section, the growth of per pupil receipts in Baltimore City actually outstripped that of its suburbs. Hence, a tremendous increase in intergovernmental aid must have occurred. That this is the case is brought out by Table 15.3, which shows the behavior of the sources of finance for Maryland's subregions from 1959 to 1970. Baltimore City is seen to have enjoyed a sharp increase in its state share despite the fact that the average state share showed a considerable decline over the same period. This was accomplished at the expense of other regions, as the table shows. Federal aid to Baltimore City also expanded sharply over the period, from virtually nothing to over 11 percent. The combined increase in state and federal share meant that Baltimore City's share of its current education expenses fell from 72.3 percent to 49.8 percent.

Thus, a crisis in education in Baltimore City during the 1960s was averted by a reshuffling in state aid and a rapid expansion of federal aid. This

Table 15.3—Source of Education Finance in Maryland Subregions, 1959-70

	State	Federal	Local
1959-60			
SMSA	32.1%	3.4%	64.5%
Baltimore City	26.2	1.5	72.3
Baltimore suburbs	38.0	5.3	56.7
Washington suburbs	36.6	7.3	56.1
Rural	57.7	4.3	38.0
State	39.2	4.6	56.2
1964-65			
SMSA	35.6%	3.5%	60.9%
Baltimore City	33.6	0.9	65.5
Baltimore suburbs	37.2	5.6	57.2
Washington suburbs	29.7	8.7	61.6
Rural	55.0	5.0	40.0
State	37.3	5.4	57.3
1967-68			
SMSA	36.7%	8.1%	55.2%
Baltimore City	38.6	9.2	52.2
Baltimore suburbs	35.1	7.2	57.7
Washington suburbs	29.6	10.4	60.0
Rural	44.5	13.0	42.5
State	35.8	9.7	54.5
1970-71			
SMSA	34.8%	8.0%	57.1%
Baltimore City	38.8	11.4	49.8
Baltimore suburbs	31.9	5.6	62.5
Washington suburbs	26.6	8.2	65.2
Rural	40.9	11.7	47.3
State	32.9	8.7	58.3

Source: Maryland Department of Education, *Annual Report.*

reshuffling of state aid had a cost, however. As the next section demonstrates, the reduction in state aid to rural Maryland was accompanied by widening disparities in education expenditure between urban and rural areas in Maryland.

Since Baltimore City's property tax base is expected to grow as slowly as it did in the sixties and since education outlays per pupil can be expected to continue their rapid advance, expansions of state and federal aid at a rapid pace will be necessary. However, it is unlikely that future expansions of state aid to Baltimore City will continue to be at the expense of rural Maryland. Indeed, it is likely that to reduce disparities, rural Maryland will also require an expansion of its state share. Given the growing political strength of suburban areas in Maryland, the expansion of Baltimore City's aid is also unlikely to occur entirely at their expense.

Variations Among Local Governments

Table 15.4 shows key characteristics of education finance for each of Maryland's 24 subdivisions and subareas for the school year 1970-71. In column (1), current revenue receipts per pupil, a figure akin to current expense per pupil, is given. In column (2), the relationship of the figures in column (1) to the statewide average is given. Current revenue receipts are seen to vary from $766 per pupil or .80 of the state average to $1202 per pupil or 1.25 of the state average. Alternatively, current revenue receipts vary from .90 of the state average in the rural areas to 1.11 of the state average. On a county basis, the ratio of high to low is 1.56 whereas on a regional basis, the ratio is 1.22. Inspection of the table, however, reveals Montgomery County, a Washington suburb, to be an outlier. If it is excluded from consideration, the ratios of high to low drop to 1.29 and 1.11, respectively. More than one-half of the range of variation in per pupil receipts, therefore, is caused by one county.

There is a good reason to believe that the range in variation shown in column (1) overstates the true variation in inputs per pupil. This is because average teachers' salaries vary widely among local governments, as is shown in column (3). In part, this variation reflects quality differences among teachers, but in part it reflects cost of living differentials between areas. As the bottom of column (3) shows, teachers' wages are lowest in rural areas and lower in the Baltimore SMSA than in the Washington area. It is generally agreed that living costs in rural areas are lower than in urban areas, and evidence provided by the U.S. Bureau of Labor Statistics indicates that living costs are lower in the Baltimore than in the Washington area. In order to make a crude adjustment for such differentials, per pupil receipts were deflated by the salary index shown in column (3). The results of this adjustment are rather startling. Not only is the ratio of high to low county reduced to 1.43, but the outlier county becomes a rural county—one which pays the lowest salaries in the state. Furthermore, the Baltimore SMSA shows per pupil receipts equal to those of the Washington suburbs. Most striking of all, however, is that disparities between subregions virtually disappear.

While the figures shown in column (4) are suggestive as to the impact of living costs, their validity as measures of relative input into education is extremely doubtful. As was mentioned above, much of the salary differentials are due to differences in qualifications, experience, etc. Furthermore, our deflation procedure was tantamount to assuming that all current receipts were used for salary purposes. While differences in living costs can be expected to have an impact on salaries, they have no relationship to other costs. Indeed, there may be a negative relation in this regard. Rural counties, although having lower living costs, have higher per pupil transportation costs. Thus, as measures of relative inputs into education, the figures shown in column (4) are seriously

Table 15.4—Maryland Local Government Public School Finance Significant Features

	Current revenue receipts per pupil 1970-71 (1)	(1)/state average (2)	Salary per teacher relative to state average (3)	(2) corrected by salary index (4)	Index of need[a] (5)
Allegany County	$ 861	.90	.92	.97	1.21
Anne Arundel County	823	.86	.98	.87	1.21
Baltimore City	938	.98	.95	1.03	1.23
Baltimore County	990	1.03	1.02	1.00	.84
Calvert County	882	.92	.95	.96	1.44
Caroline County	827	.86	.78	1.10	1.71
Carroll County	785	.82	.89	.92	1.17
Cecil County	796	.83	.91	.91	1.36
Charles County	926	.96	.87	1.10	1.42
Dorchester County	912	.95	.84	1.13	1.26
Frederick County	902	.94	.91	1.03	1.02
Garrett County	876	.91	.78	1.16	1.43
Harford County	819	.85	.87	.97	1.28
Howard County	992	1.03	1.01	1.01	.92
Kent County	963	1.00	.80	1.25	1.01
Montgomery County	1,202	1.25	1.15	1.08	.65
Prince George's County	953	.99	1.04	.95	1.04
Queen Anne's County	857	.89	.81	1.09	1.11
St. Mary's County	845	.88	.81	1.08	1.94
Somerset County	776	.81	.74	1.09	1.81
Talbot County	949	.99	.86	1.15	.75
Washington County	887	.92	1.01	.91	1.15
Wicomico County	766	.80	.81	.98	1.23
Worcester County	814	.85	.85	1.00	.89
State	957	1.00	1.00	1.00	1.00
Baltimore SMSA	923	.96	.97	1.00	1.08
Baltimore City	938	.98	.95	1.03	1.23
Baltimore suburbs	913	.95	.98	.98	.93
Washington suburbs	1,063	1.11	1.09	1.01	.77
Rural Maryland	864	.90	.87	1.00	1.20

[a]County taxable wealth plus taxable income as a fraction of state average.

Source: Education taken from Maryland Department of Education, *Annual Report;* personal income taken from *U.S. Census of Population 1970.*

Percent of (1) from state (6)	Percent of (1) from federal (7)	Percent of (1) from local (8)	Local education revenue as a percent of personal income (9)	(1)/state average 1964–65 (10)	(1)/state average 1959–60 (11)
39.9	8.6	51.5	.035	.87	.91
36.4	8.6	55.0	.032	.85	.85
38.8	11.4	49.8	.033	.91	.97
27.4	3.1	69.5	.036	1.03	1.02
46.3	12.7	40.9	.040	.96	.90
53.1	13.6	33.3	.030	.98	1.01
41.5	5.4	52.9	.032	.88	.90
41.6	9.2	49.2	.031	.94	.96
40.9	14.0	45.1	.042	1.01	.98
41.2	14.9	43.8	.034	.90	.91
30.8	9.8	59.4	.042	1.04	1.01
55.6	17.6	26.8	.030	.91	.93
40.5	10.7	48.8	.030	.96	.97
31.3	6.9	61.8	.043	.99	.93
31.9	13.0	54.8	.046	1.01	.99
24.0	6.2	69.5	.037	1.28	1.28
29.1	10.2	60.4	.036	1.01	.94
40.8	8.5	50.7	.041	.95	1.06
52.9	22.8	24.3	.019	.90	.90
55.9	16.9	27.1	.020	.87	.90
29.7	12.2	58.1	.035	.91	.95
36.6	10.1	53.3	.037	1.01	1.08
47.1	7.9	45.0	.030	.87	.85
36.6	9.8	53.5	.046	.92	.99
32.9	8.7	58.3	.035	1.00	1.00
34.8	8.0	57.1	.034	.94	.96
38.8	11.4	49.8	.033	.91	.96
31.9	5.6	62.5	.035	.97	.97
26.6	8.2	65.2	.036	1.14	1.12
40.9	11.7	47.3	.035	.95	.97

deficient. Nevertheless, they do suggest that the unadjusted figures may substantially exaggerate input differentials among school districts.

In column (5), an index which is inversely proportional to relative economic well-being is shown. The index is the ratio of the sum of taxable real property and taxable income per pupil for the state as a whole to that for each locality. This index of relative well-being is employed because it is the measure employed by the state in calculating education aid. However, the results would not change significantly if some other index, such as per capita income, is employed. Two things stand out about column (5): (1) a negative association exists between need and education spending; (2) the range of variation is much larger for the need index than for education spending. These will be treated in turn.

As the figures for the subregions indicate, those areas of greatest need are also those with lowest spending for education. However, the relationship, at the county level is rather weak. A number of instances occur (one-third of all counties) where a county with greater than average need spends a greater than average amount per pupil. The simple correlation between the two indices is only -.44. Thus, while significant, differences in need are not of overwhelming importance in explaining education spending.

Turning to intercounty variation, we find that the range of high to low is 3 as compared to 1.56 for education spending. Comparing the figures for subregions, we obtain 1.55 and 1.22, respectively. In either case, the range of variation of economic well-being is much greater than for per pupil receipts. Two circumstances could give rise to this difference: (1) poorer localities tax themselves relatively more than rich localities; (2) higher-level governments finance a greater proportion of poor communities' education activities.

Comparing the figures shown in column (9), locally raised education revenues as a fraction of personal income with the relative need figures of column (3), indicates that the first condition stated above does not hold. Local revenue effort for schools is virtually the same in each of the subregions. Furthermore, at the county level, the correlation between local school revenue effort and need is negative at -.63. This is precisely the opposite of what condition (1) requires. Rather than reducing disparities in education spending, local revenue effort exacerbates them.

Thus, we are left with condition (2) to explain the narrowing of disparities. Inspection of columns (5) and (6) of Table 15.4 clearly reveals a positive association between state share and need. The Washington suburbs, the wealthiest subregion, obtain only 26.5 percent of their school revenues from the state while the rural areas obtain 40.5 percent of their revenues from this source. At the county level, the simple correlation is .68, indicating a significant association. It follows, therefore, that state aid plays a significant role in reducing disparities among Maryland's school districts. Whether the system has gone far enough in this direction is another matter, and one which we shall treat at a later point.

Finally, we show in columns (10) and (11) relative per pupil receipts for 1959-60 and 1964-65 in order to determine whether the amount and range of variation has been changing over time. In terms of the ratio of high county to low county, there as been little change. The *level* of variation has increased since the mid-sixties, however. Using a crude measure of variation, the average absolute deviation about the state-wide average, we find it to have risen from 7.2 in 1959-60 to 10.0 in 1970-71. Much of this is a result of the fall in the relative standing of the rural counties. From the subregion average it will be noted that rural Maryland has fallen from 97 percent of the state average in 1959-60 to 90 percent in 1970-71.

Also worthy of note is the fact that Baltimore City education outlays fell relative to the state and its suburbs during the early sixties but recovered sufficiently in the late sixties to overtake its suburbs in per pupil spending.

In summary, the sixties have witnessed a growing disparity between urban and rural areas of the state. This occurred despite the fact that rural areas experienced a more rapid growth of taxable wealth per pupil than the state as a whole. What may have caused the rural areas to lag in education spending is the fact that the state share of their expenditure has dropped sharply over time, from a figure of 58 percent in 1959-60 to 40 percent in 1970-71. In addition, in 1967 the state allowed local governments to add a piggyback to the state income tax. Since rural areas have lower taxable income-wealth ratios than urban areas, the piggyback provided the rural areas with relatively less additional revenue. Finally, the late sixties witnessed a rapid expansion of Baltimore City education outlays relative to their suburbs and relative to the state as a whole. This spurt has enabled Baltimore City to overtake its suburbs with respect to per pupil spending and was accomplished by a rapid expansion of intergovernmental aid.

The Present System of State Aid

The Maryland system of state aid to education represents a composite of individual programs which were enacted in a seemingly ad hoc fashion to address particular needs. It consists of five major components.

1. A foundation program designed to equalize the costs of current expenses for education. This program amounted to $163 million in fiscal year 1971 or 60 percent of state aid for current expenses.

2. Transportation costs. The state pays the entire cost of transporting students to and from school. This cost the state $31 million in 1971.

3. Teacher retirement. The state pays the entire employer contribution to the Teacher Retirement Program and Social Security. This program cost $48 million in 1971.

4. Aid for handicapped children. The state pays the full cost of education

for the severely handicapped. For those who are mildly mentally retarded, the state contributes $200 per student. Finally, the state contributes $50 to the education of students who attend regular classes but, because of hearing, seeing, or speech difficulties, require special services. The total cost of this program was $20 million in 1971.

5. School construction costs. Prior to the school year 1971-72, the state paid the same fraction as its share of the foundation program, of 80 percent of debt service cost on debt issued prior to June 30, 1967. It also provided the same share of $1200 for each pupil housed through new construction. In 1970-71, the cost to the state of this program was $68 million, all of which was paid out of current state funds.

Beginning July 1, 1971, the state assumed the *full* cost of constructing new educational facilities or modernizing existing facilities. Furthermore, the state assumed in full the responsibility for school debt incurred prior to June 30, 1967. Although the current fund saving to the local government amounted to an estimated $45 million, the additional current fund cost to the state was negligible. The latter was accomplished by the issuance of $100 million per annum in state bonds to finance construction, part of which had been paid by current state funds. However, by the mid-eighties the annual cost of servicing the resulting debt was projected to grow to $140 million. Thus, the impact of the new program upon the state's general budget will not be apparent until several years hence. This must be kept in mind when considering expansion of other forms of state aid to education.

The Foundation Program

This program, begun in 1922, is the core of the state's aid to education program. Its diminished relative importance has played no small role in producing dissatisfaction with the present system. Like most foundation programs, it consists of two major ingredients: (1) the foundation, or level of educational expenditure established by the state in corresponding with some minimal educational standard; (2) the share of the foundation to be provided by the locality, generally a positive function of the locality's economic well-being. In Maryland, the latter is measured by the sum of assessed value of real property for property tax purposes and taxable income for income tax purposes. To avoid competitive underassessment, the state requires the average assessment ratio to fall within the 50-56 percent range. The use of the combined bases of the property tax and income tax is due to several considerations. First, in Maryland, the localities are able to employ a surcharge of up to 50 percent to the state income tax. On average, local income taxes provided 40 percent as much as the property tax, while taxable income was slightly less than 50 percent of assessed property. The two bases are aggregated roughly in proportion to their revenue productivities; hence, it does a good job of measuring the ability of the local government to raise tax revenue. A second, and perhaps more compelling reason, is that Maryland has a resort community which has two-thirds more than the state average taxable wealth per capita while having less than 70 percent of the average taxable income per capita. The presence of such an exceptional community makes the application of a single standard undesirable.

In order to calculate the state share of the foundation, a choice of a local offset to be applied against taxable wealth and taxable income must be made. In effect, this offset determines the average local share of the cost of the foundation.

The foundation program can be summarized by the linear homogeneous equation

$$S_i = fN_i - bW_i$$

where S_i is the state grant to the ith community, f is the foundation level, N_i is the number of students, b is the offset and W_i is the taxable wealth. In Maryland, the statutory level of f equals $370 while b equals .01228. It will be noted that the offset b is the same for all localities. This means that the fraction of taxpaying ability required to support the foundation will be the same in all communities. It is easy to show that b is proportional to the average local share, the factor of proportion being the ratio of statewide wealth per student to the foundation level. Over time we can expect wealth per student to grow. Hence, if the foundation is fixed, a constant b implies that the local share of the foundation will rise. To keep its share of the fixed foundation constant, therefore, the state must reduce the local offset at the same rate that wealth per pupil rises. Broadly speaking, this is essentially the policy followed by the state since 1968. Hence, the local offset in the foundation aid formula has been reduced from 1.228 percent in 1968 to 1.047 percent in 1971.

Although the preceding describes the basic foundation program as it currently stands, there are several important and many minor exceptions. The most important exception is seen to be the minimum guarantee. State law provides that no locality will receive less then $128 per student under the foundation program. Since $128 is the figure arrived at by applying the foundation formula to average wealth per pupil for 1967-68, the minimum guarantee produces equal aid for all localities with above average wealth. The principal beneficiaries of the minimum guarantee are the wealthy suburbs surrounding Washington and Baltimore, particularly Montgomery County and Baltimore County.

Next we have density aid. This amounts to $50 per pupil and is given only to those localities whose population density exceeds a certain figure. Oddly enough, Baltimore City is the only locality to qualify. A cynic might arrive at the conclusion that density aid is Baltimore City's equivalent to the minimum guarantee, especially since Baltimore City, Baltimore County, and Montgomery County constitute a majority in the state.

Incentive aid, amounting to an average of $12 per student, is a program whereby the state shares in the cost of additional professionals between 45 and 50 per 1000 students. The share is to be the share determined by the *Hypothetical* foundation but with a minimum of 35 percent. Since virtually every locality hires 50 professionals per 1000 students, incentive aid amounts to a lump-sum grant, proportional to the distribution of total foundation aid.

Next we have Section 128(b). This program allocates a flat grant of $22 per pupil, multiplied by the ratio of average state wealth per pupil to the locality's wealth per pupil. Other than the hypothetical foundation, this is the only program which systematically relates aid to need.

Finally, we have a series of miscellaneous provisions, such as $50 per increased enrollee, amounting to less than 2 percent of the total foundation program.

Table 15.5—Distribution of Foundation Aid among Maryland's Subregions, 1970-71[a]

	Hypothetical foundation (1)	(1)/state average (2)	Actual foundation (3)	(3)/state average (4)	Index of need (5)	Aid if allocated according to (2) (6)
Baltimore SMSA	133.46	1.14	211.46	1.07	1.08	224.58
Baltimore City	164.84	1.41	258.63	1.31	1.23	277.77
Baltimore suburbs	111.34	.95	178.18	.90	.93	187.15
Washington suburbs	62.46	.54	158.49	.80	.77	106.38
Rural Maryland	164.03	1.41	223.30	1.18	1.20	277.77
State	116.70	1.00	197.00	1.00	1.00	197.00

[a] All figures are in per pupil terms.
Source: Maryland Department of Education.

The impact of these exceptions upon the relative amounts of state aid is substantial. This is shown in Table 15.5, which gives the absolute and relative amounts of aid for each of Maryland's subregions under the hypothetical foundation program and actual foundation program. As would be expected, the various exceptions serve to substantially reduce the differences between wealthy and poor regions. This can also be seen in another way. The following regression was estimated:

$$S_i = aN_i + bW_i$$

where S_i, N_i and W_i are the ith locality's total state aid, total pupils, and total wealth respectively. In other words, we tested the total foundation program to see whether it could be described by a normal foundation formula. The resulting equation was

$$S_i = 320.5\, N_i - .00498\, W_i$$
$$(10.16) \qquad (-4.02)$$

where R^2 was .96 and the figures in parentheses give the t statistic. Thus, despite numerous amendments, state aid to education behaves as if it were allocated according to a foundation formula. The parameters of the foundation formula change substantially, however. The basic foundation is $50 less and the offset drops to ½ of 1 percent. The drop in offset means that the differences in aid caused by differences in wealth are substantially reduced. This is evident if we compare columns (2) and (4) of Table 15.5. It is also reflected in the elasticity of state aid with respect to wealth. A large absolute value of this elasticity implies that state aid responds sharply to changes in relative wealth. Under the hypothetical foundation program, the elasticity, evaluated at average wealth, is -2.17. In other words a 1 percent increase in per pupil wealth is accompanied by a 2.17 percent reduction in state aid per pupil. Under the actual foundation, this elasticity is reduced to -.63.

The difference that the drop in elasticity makes can be seen from Table 15.5. If the additional state aid associated with exceptions were distributed in the same proportions as the hypothetical foundation, the results would be as in column (6). It is interesting to note that even the Baltimore suburbs would have profited from such an allocation. The big loser, of course, would have been the wealthy Washington suburbs, particularly Montgomery County.

Other Current Expense Aid

As was pointed out above, the foundation program accounts for 60 percent of the state's aid for current expenses. The remaining 40 percent is made up of aid for handicapped children, transportation, and teachers' retirement. Each of these programs was tested for the existence of a systematic relationship with economic well being. The results of correlating wealth per pupil and aid per pupil are as follows: retirement aid +.80; transportation cost -.43; aid for the handicapped +.24. Retirement aid is strongly and positively correlated with wealth; thus it serves to reduce the elasticity calculated in the previous section. Aid for transportation is weakly, but significantly correlated with wealth; however, the direction of association is the reverse of that for retirement aid. Finally, the correlation between wealth and aid for the handicapped is positive, but not statistically different from zero.[5] Thus we have one program which tends to reduce aid elasticity, one which increases it, and one which should have no effect.

The combined impact of these programs upon the distribution of state aid by subareas is such that other current expense aid is distributed more heavily

5. Significance is measured at the 95 percent confidence level.

to the suburbs of Baltimore and Washington. The result is a narrowing of a relative aid for the total program as compared to the foundation program.

The combined impact of all aid for current expenses can also be measured by fitting a foundation formula to total aid for current expenses. As before we find that such a formula provides a remarkably accurate description of Maryland's program of aid to education. The fitted regression is

$$S_i = 416.47 \, N_i - .00422 \, W_i$$
$$(28.2) \qquad (-3.83)$$

with an R^2 of .98.

The combined impact of the other current expense aid programs is to raise the implied foundation by nearly $100 and to further reduce the local offset. Evaluated at average wealth per student, the elasticity of state aid with respect to wealth falls to $-.325$. Thus, the combined impact of other programs of aid for current expense is similar to that of the exceptions to the hypothetical foundation program—they serve to lessen the relative differences in state aid among school districts of different wealth.

Table 15.6–Distribution of State Aid for Current Expenses among Maryland's Subareas, Actual and Hypothetical, 1970-71

	Actual state aid (1)	(1)/state average (2)	Hypothetical foundation (3)	(3)/state average (4)	(3)-(1) (5)	Deviation of current receipts per pupil from state average (6)
Baltimore SMSA	$317.76	1.02	354.48	1.14	36.72	−34
Baltimore City	358.76	1.16	437.82	1.41	79.06	−19
Baltimore suburbs	288.16	.93	295.73	.95	7.57	−44
Washington suburbs	278.32	.90	165.90	.54	−112.42	106
Rural Maryland	344.36	1.11	435.67	1.41	91.31	−93
State	309.96	1.00	309.96	1.00	0	0

Source: Maryland Department of Education.

In Table 15.6, we show the difference in the distribution in state aid which would have resulted if state aid for current expenses had been distributed according to the hypothetical foundation.[6] The difference is shown in column (5) of the table. The effect of the exceptions to the hypothetical foundation program and other forms of current expense aid is clear. The wealthy Washington

6. The hypothetical foundation yields an average state aid of $116.70. Since actual aid was $310, the parameters of the hypothetical foundation were adjusted upwards by the same proportion.

suburbs gain considerably relative to other areas. The Baltimore suburbs essentially share in the same proportions as they would under the hypothetical foundation, although not all counties are equally affected. The big losers are Baltimore City and rural Maryland.

As of July 1, 1971, the state assumed full responsibility for the finance of all new construction, including modernization of existing facilities. In addition it assumed full financial responsibility for school debt issued prior to June 30, 1967. This represented a major departure from previous practice where only partial funding for debt service and construction came from the state.

The effect of the new state construction finance program is very likely to cause a further reduction in the sensitivity of state aid to differences in wealth. Furthermore, the program will prove quite costly in the long run, and may thus preempt funds which would have been made available for current expenses.

Evaluation of Present System of State Aid for Current Expense

As we saw in the preceding section, Maryland's system of state aid to education can be described as a foundation program. As of 1970-71, the foundation was $416 and the average local share of the foundation was 25 percent. We offer an appraisal of this program.

Foundation programs can be thought of as having three objectives: (1) to guarantee a certain minimal education level to every child in the state, (2) to promote locational neutrality, (3) to redistribute income.

Clearly, the present system of state aid fails to achieve the first objective stated above. The implied foundation in 1970-71 of $416 was only 43 percent of average spending and 54 percent of the figure for the lowest spending district. Hence, the present foundation is not binding in any of Maryland's school districts. Since foundation programs do not reward spending above the foundation level, the only effect the present state program has upon spending levels is through its effect upon the localities' income. Furthermore, the latter impact cannot be measured by the amount of state aid for education since the locality's residents must contribute to the finance of the program through state taxes. As we shall demonstrate below, such net income effects are of negligible magnitude Thus, the present program can be said to have a negligible impact upon the level of education spending in the state. If it is felt that an acceptable minimum is not being at present achieved, the state can bring it about by raising the foundation level with or without changing the state share of the foundation. As we shall see below, the state at present funding levels could support a foundation of $983, which is above current state average spending.

The second objective of a foundation program arises from the fact that education is not financed entirely by the users of such services. This is as it should be, since education is widely regarded as having spillover benefits. Such spillovers, however, are not confined to the residents of a particular school district. To cover the full costs of education by local taxation will be viewed as redistributive by nonusers and those users with above-average tax shares—generally those in higher income groups. There will be, therefore, incentives for these two groups to migrate to those communities which redistribute less—often, in practice, relatively wealthy counties, though this need not be the case, particularly for nonusers.

The state, by equalizing the costs of a particular package of educational inputs across communities through subsidies, makes the tax cost to the individual citizen invariant to the community in which he resides. The larger the equalized educational package relative to what communities actually spend, the more locationally neutral the system of education finance becomes. In the limit, perfect neutrality could be achieved if the state were to set a foundation level which no community would care to exceed or would be permitted to exceed. This would be tantamount to full state responsibility for the finance of education. We do not wish to discuss the merits of such an arrangement at this point. Suffice it to say that greater locational neutrality is achieved as the foundation approaches actual levels of education spending.

Since, in 1970-71, the effective foundation stood at only 43 percent of average current spending, it goes without saying that the present system of state aid falls far short of the optimum with respect to locational neutrality. This is particularly serious in the education field because of two considerations. (1) The costs of educating a child are high and vary, if at all, negatively with the income level of a child's parents. However, tax revenues show considerable sensitivity to income. Hence, there is considerable redistribution to poor families through education. It is safe to say that, from the standpoint of local taxes, public education is the most redistributive activity local governments engage in. (2) Local taxes to support education amount to 35 percent of all local taxes in Maryland. This means that a substantial portion of a locality's taxes are used to support a heavily redistribution program. This creates considerable incentive for families who are redistributed against to relocate.

If the foundation level were made a substantially higher fraction of average education costs, local income redistribution through education could be sharply curtailed. We shall demonstrate below that the foundation can be substantially increased without increasing present state funding levels. Hence, the present nonneutrality does not owe to the lack of state funds to support education.

We turn now to the last objective of a state aid to education program to redistribute economic resources from rich localities to poor localities. Even if there were no locational distortions or no significant differences of per pupil spending between localities when education were entirely locally financed, there would still be a case for spreading the cost of public education more equitably throughout the state. State aid redistributes income among localities if the proportions used in distributing the aid are different from the proportions in which the funds are raised. Since we know the former, we need only determine the latter to determine the redistribution involved in our present structure. This proves to be somewhat of a problem since the state obtains its funds from many different tax sources. Thus, our results will depend upon which taxes we assume are used to finance the state aid system. Limits on resources, however, limit us to consider only one state tax source—the state income tax. The advantages of this assumption are that data are readily available on income tax payments by locality and the incidence of the tax is not open to serious debate. Furthermore, it is the largest single state tax instrument and is by far the most visible.

Table 15.7 shows the redistributive impact of the present system of state aid. Redistribution is seen to vary from a negative 12 percent of state aid in the Washington suburbs to a positive 8 percent in Baltimore City and rural Maryland. In per student terms, the redistribution to Baltimore City amounts to about 13 percent of total current spending for education and to rural Maryland about 16 percent. When viewed in per capita terms, however, the effect is seen to be of much more modest proportions. This justifies ignoring the income effects of the program. Furthermore, more than one-half of the redistribution is due to the effects of the state tax structure. This can be seen in column (8), which shows the effect of allocating aid strictly in terms of relative numbers of pupils.

Summing up, the present state program is only modestly effective in redistributing income and quite ineffective in achieving locational neutrality or promoting minimum education spending levels in the localities.

PROPOSALS FOR REFORM

One obvious possibility for consideration is restructuring the present program along the lines suggested by the hypothetical foundation discussed above. Recall, the basic foundation in Maryland is

$$S_i = 370\,N_i - .01047\,W_i$$

Since this yields average state aid of $116.70, and since actual state aid is $309.96, the foundation could be increased from $370 to $983 and the offset from .01047 to .02781. Note that these figures are derived by multiply-

Table 15.7—Redistributive Impact of State Aid for Current Education Expenses

	Share of state income tax (1)	Share of state aid (2)	(1)–(2) (3)	Redistribution per pupil (4)	Amount of redistribution ($000's) (5)	Per capita redistribution (6)	Share of pupils (7)	Redistribution if (7) used instead of (2) (8)
Baltimore SMSA	.4797	.5212	.0415	25.27	$11,440	$ 5.52	.5091	8,104
Baltimore City	.1623	.2437	.0814	119.88	22,440	24.77	.2105	13,314
Baltimore suburbs	.3174	.2775	-.0399	-41.44	-10,999	-9.44	.2985	-5,210
Washington suburbs	.4013	.2809	-.1204	-119.32	-33,191	-28.05	.3128	-24,397
Rural Maryland	.1190	.1979	.0789	137.33	21,750	32.54	.1781	16,293

ing the parameters of the hypothetical foundation by a factor of proportion ($309.96)/($116.70). This would yield a distribution of aid as shown in column (3) of Table 15.6.[7]

This particular set of foundation program parameters was selected because they produce the same elasticity of state aid with respect to wealth as the basic foundation. The latter, in turn, had the property, at the time of its inception, of yielding the maximum aid elasticity consistent with nonnegative shares for all school districts. We recognize, however, that the choice of foundation level should involve educational as well as economic criteria. We merely intend this exercise to be instructive as to what might be achieved by rearranging state aid to education.

By combining its many programs of aid of education into one, the state would raise the effective foundation level from $416 to $983, a figure not only above the present average but exceeded significantly by only one county. Table 15.8 shows how the program would affect the distribution of aid, the level of spending, and local spending for public schools. State aid is transferred from the Washington suburbs to Baltimore City and rural Maryland. Mandated increases in education spending, however, uses up all of the increased aid in rural Maryland. Only Baltimore City is afforded local tax relief, while significant local tax increases are required in the Baltimore and Washington suburbs. These amount to a reduction of 12 cents on the property tax rate in Baltimore City, and an 18 cent and 27 cent increase in the Baltimore and Washington suburbs, respectively. In the Baltimore SMSA, this is enough to close nearly 20 percent of the property tax rate differentials.

By redirecting its present aid, therefore, the state can overcome most of the weaknesses of the present education finance program. Clearly, state aid has a measurable impact upon local spending since a large number of counties would have to significantly increase their spending under the program. Furthermore, the higher foundation level means a much larger fraction of education costs are equalized than at present. In addition, by substantially increasing the elasticity of state aid with respect to local wealth (from -.33 to -2.17), the redistributive character of the program is strengthened. Finally, disparities which currently exist with respect to per pupil expenditures will be sharply reduced. In part this owes to the relatively high foundation, but most significantly it reflects the raising of low spending counties to somewhere near the state average. Whether the foundation is $900 or $983 makes little quantitative differences in this regard.

7. Such a formula, however, yields a small negative aid for Montgomery County ($50 per pupil). While in principle, this poses no particular difficulties, it may prove politically infeasible. To implement this formula may require a small increase in state funding −2.1 percent or $5.9 million. The Washington suburbs figure should be raised $21.31 under the hypothetical program and the state figure should be raided by $6.67.

Table 15.8—Impact of Adoption of the Foundation Formula $S_i = 983\,N_i - .02781\,W_i$ [a]

	Change in state aid (1)	Required change in spending (2)	Required increase in local spending (3)	Percent change in local spending (4)
Baltimore SMSA	$37	$60	$23	4.4
Baltimore City	79	45	-34	-7.3
Baltimore suburbs	8	80	72	13.1
Washington suburbs	-91	17	108	15.6
Rural Maryland	91	119	28	6.8

[a] All figures are on a per pupil basis.

We turn next to the question of how the system would behave over time. Periodically, preferably each year, the foundation should be increased so that the state share does not fall. The rate of increase could be the rate of increase of wealth as it is currently measured. This would make per pupil expenditures expand at the pace of wealth per pupil for the state as a whole. By and large, this should prevent the development of excessive disparities over long periods of time. Furthermore, it will maintain the average elasticity of state aid with respect to wealth.

One consequence of such policy with respect to time is that the share of state aid will fall and even become negative in those areas with above average growth, and rise in those lagging areas, such as Baltimore City. The fact that aid may become negative is simply a reminder of the basic character of foundation programs—a proportional tax on the wealth of the state as a whole is used to finance the local share of the foundation. Thus, we should expect situations where a county contributes more than it gets back. The outcome would be exactly the same as if the foundation program were financed in full by the state but where the source of funds stemmed from two separate sources, one of which is a proportional tax on wealth in the state.

To repeat, the offset amounts to a uniform tax rate on taxable wealth and taxable income. However, because the latter are measured only with a lag and only a portion of taxable property is included in the measure of wealth, and because of federal aid, the effective tax rate is more likely 2 percent as compared with 2.78 percent. The local piggyback income tax averages 2.25 percent of taxable income; hence, school finance under the present proposal requires nearly all of it. For the property tax, the percentage preempted by school finance is nearly 50 percent. Since taxable property per pupil in Baltimore City is expected to show little growth in the future, much of its growth-induced revenue from the income tax will be needed for education. Thus, while state aid would finance increasingly larger fractions of Baltimore City's education costs, it would not totally eliminate the pressure on the city's finances caused by higher education costs.

While the reform proposal offered above has many advantages, its chances of passage are slim. The regional totals shown in Table 15.8 understate the extent to which state aid is reshuffled. For example, the table does not show that Montgomery County would receive no state aid whatever, or that Carroll County, a Baltimore suburb, would have to increase its local spending on education by 25 percent. The property tax increase in Montgomery County would be in excess of 50 cents—an increase of 30 percent, while in Carroll County the figure would be 28 cents, an increase of 20 percent. Other major shifts would occur in Baltimore County, Talbot County, and Worcester County. With the exception of Carroll County, the source of difficulty is above-average wealth—precisely the objective of the reform. However, political realities are such that reforms which rock the boat too vigorously, have little chance of passage. Only reform proposals which contain "save harmless" characteristics may be feasible.

Percentage Equalization

As an alternative to the foundation approach it has been proposed that the state adopt an aid program which equalizes the costs of any particular spending level, sometimes referred to as percentage equalization.[8] This differs from a foundation in that the levels of spending are not specified with the possible exception of upper and lower limits. In effect, therefore, state aid is open-ended, having the effect of reducing the price to local communities of additional education services. Furthermore, the extent of the price reduction is inversely proportional to the wealth of the community.

The advantage of this approach is that it allows localities much greater freedom in selecting their level of educational spending. By insuring that a given fraction of wealth will support the same level of educational services in all communities, it attempts to eliminate disparities in spending that would be wealth induced. Any remaining differences would reflect differences in needs or tastes and hence produce a superior allocation of resources.

The disadvantages of this approach is a consequence of its principal advantage—the level of education spending may vary excessively among communities. Hence, the quality of educational services rendered a family of given tastes would depend upon the tastes of others living in its community. More serious, however, is the fact that pure tax rate equalization will eliminate the effect of wealth differentials only if the price elasticity of demand were exactly equal to and opposite in sign to the wealth elasticity of demand. If the latter outweighed the former, we would find wealthier communities spending more than poorer ones. Whatever the cause, however, there is some risk that state

8. See Paul D. Cooper, "State Takeover of Education Financing," *Proceedings of National Tax Association Seminar on Balancing our Federal-State-Local Fiscal System* (July 1971). Also see *Report of Commission to Study the State's Role in Financing Education* (Annapolis, May 1970).

aid per student would be greater in wealthier localities than in poorer localities. This would violate most people's sense of justice.

In a large meaure the relative merits of percentage equalization hinge on the response of local communities to the incentives it offers. If all communities chose the same expenditure level, the result would be identical to a foundation program. Beyond this there is little that can be said without a knowledge of the parameters of communities' demand function for education. Without a suitable measure of output, such knowledge appears beyond our reach. The best we can do, therefore, is to calculate the distribution of aid under somewhat arbitrary assumptions concerning local tax effort for schools.

In Table 15.9, we show how present aid would be redistributed if allocated according to a percentage equalization formula. The result of redistributing aid through a pure foundation, as calculated in Table 15.6, is shown for comparison purposes. It is apparent that the relatively high local effort in the Washington suburbs and low effort in rural Maryland weakens the redistributive impact of the percentage equalization scheme. This is precisely the difficulty with percentage equalization; they may actually redistribute in favor of wealthy areas. In column (5) of the table we show the impact of a recent commission proposal, which would increase the state share of the present foundation program through a percentage equalization formula.[9] It is apparent that unless relative spending patterns are drastically reversed, the wealthy subdivisions will profit from the reform.

What are the prospects for a relative shift in expenditure levels? As column (2) of Table 15.9 show, all localities have an incentive to expand their tax effort since the state will share part of the cost of improving educational services. Although the state will share a larger proportion of the costs in the

Table 15.9–Impact of Distributing State Aid According to Percentage Equalization

	State share actual (1)	State share equalization (2)	Change in per pupil aid (3)	Change in per pupil aid under foundation (4)	Change in per pupil aid under commission recommendation (5)
Baltimore SMSA	34.8	39.6	$44	37	203
Baltimore City	38.8	43.2	41	79	192
Baltimore suburbs	31.9	37.2	48	8	212
Washington suburbs	26.6	23.9	-29	-112	184
Rural Maryland	40.9	42.4	13	91	143

9. *Report of Commission to Study the State's Role in Financing Education.*

poorer areas, the wealthier areas have the wherewithall to take advantage of the lower price they face. The final distribution of state aid will depend upon the relative strength of these two forces. No such uncertainty clouds the potential outcome under the foundation approach. Although localities may augment the foundation, they do so completely at their own expense. Thus, the distribution of state aid is known with certainty. Given our state of knowledge, this is perhaps the most compelling reason in favor of the foundation approach.

What is the likelihood of substantive reform of the present system of education finance in the near future? Unfortunately, the prospects are dim. The state is faced with the prospect of a large budget deficit in the upcoming fiscal year. Indeed, the state recently initiated a hiring freeze in order to avert a budget deficit in this fiscal year—despite the recent passage of federal revenue sharing. Thus the deficit forecast by the study commission nearly two years ago, is apparently coming to pass. Without adopting new programs, therefore, the state fiscal outlook is grim.

Matters will be even worse by 1975. By then, the costs of the recent state takeover of responsibility for school construction will become apparent. Such outlays are projected to be $20 million in 1975 and will increase by $8 million each year thereafter.[10] Since state aid to education has been increasing at an annual rate of $25 million, the costs of the new program will absorb nearly one-third of such funds.

That little will be done to substantially revise the state aid program has become evident in recent months. The governor has ruled out any change which will increase state costs by more than $20 million per year.[11] Thus, it appears that the only avenue for reform is through redistribution of present state aid. However, recent attempts in this direction have been successfully beaten back. It has become increasingly clear that redistribution will only be possible at the margin—i.e., using the annual increments in state aid. If the governor is successful in holding such increments to $20 million, it will take many years until something resembling the hypothetical foundation is achieved.

CONCLUSION

Dissatisfaction with the current system of education finance stems from two related consequences of present arrangements: (1) wide disparities among areas with respect to resources devoted to education and/or (2) wide disparities with respect to tax burdens and/or level of other public services. These are

10. Ibid.
11. *Baltimore Evening Sun,* September 21, 1972.

related in the sense that attempts by local governments to reduce one disparity may simply increase the other.

In this paper we have examined these disparities within the Baltimore SMSA, and, to a lesser extent the state of Maryland. Our aim was to determine the extent to which these disparities exist and how they can be expected to behave in the near future. In addition, we investigated the impact upon these disparities of present and proposed systems of state aid to education.

Our major findings are as follows: (1) At present, serious disparities among localities with respect to education spending do not exist; however, without a significant change in financing arrangements, serious disparities will emerge in the near future, particularly within the Baltimore SMSA. (2) At present, tax burdens within Baltimore City are significantly higher than in its suburbs; the difference is expected to grow in the near future, particularly if Baltimore City attempts to avert disparities in education spending. (3) The present system of state aid to education achieves a modest redistribution of resources to the poorer areas of the state, particularly Baltimore City; however, much of the redistribution stems from the tax side rather than from the way in which aid is redistributed. (4) The present system of state aid to education has little impact on the level of education spending within localities; thus it cannot prevent serious disparities from arising in the future. (5) By redistributing present state aid according to a foundation formula based on present state aid levels, the redistributive properties of state aid would be improved, locational neutrality enhanced, and disparities in spending levels narrowed; however, the reform does not completely or even substantially eliminate fiscal disparities between Baltimore City and its suburbs. (6) Because of budget stringency at the state level, substantive reform of the present system in the near future appears unlikely.

We conclude with the observation that the issues surrounding education finance are indeed complex. We do not claim to have treated all relevant facets of the problem. Some issues were omitted by design, others because of oversight. However, the analysis does make clear the limitations of reform of education finance for resolving fiscal disparities in urban areas. Even the most extreme reform, full state funding, closes only a fraction of present gaps between city and suburban tax burdens.

16 Robert N. Schoeplein

The Impact of Changes in Local Property Taxation and School Finances on Metropolitan Development

Three contemporary issues can be identified in the school finance controversy over allocating resources to education:[1]

1. Improving the quality of education for all pupils, within budget constraints
2. Providing for more equal access to quality education for every pupil
3. Simultaneously reducing the degree of reliance on local property taxes to finance education.

A look at these problems seems to indicate that a conflict may be developing. If average spending per pupil were to rise in poorer districts and none of the wealthier districts were mandated to reduce their current spending per pupil, then total educational spending on a per-pupil basis would increase in the state. This possible net increase in aggregate school expenditures also may be significant, if the various state commission recommendations were adopted. In the three states of California, New Jersey, and New York alone, study proposals call for a combined increase of $4.5 billion in state taxes, to be offset only in part by reductions in local property taxes. The Tax Foundation notes that this proposed $4.5 billion increase for the three states can be placed in perspective when one appreciates that the combined budgetary requests for immediate program needs other than education reform in all the 41 states holding legislative sessions in 1972 totaled $2.5 billion.[2]

These changes in financing public education may have significant effects on society, depending, of course, on the extent of fiscal reform. Changed

---

1. Three of the most prominent cases are (a) California: *Serrano* v. *Priest,* 5 Cal. 3d. 584 (1971): 487 P. 2nd 1241 (1971): (b) Texas: *Rodriguez* v. *San Antonio Independent School District,* 299 F. Supp. 476 (1971), U.S. District Court W. D. Texas, Civil Action No. 68-175-SA; and (c) Minnesota: *Van Dusartz* v. *Hatfield,* 334 F. Supp. 870 (1971), U.S. District Court, 2 Minnesota, Order No. 3-71, Civ 243.
2. Tax Foundation, *Tax Review,* 33, no. 3 (March 1972), pp. 9-12.

school finance can affect both the tax structures and the distribution of many categories of public services at the state and local levels. Education fiscal reform also can affect the organization and structure of educational services. Clearly the scope of proposals already made would affect the distribution of income and wealth, in rural areas as well as urban complexes. Changes in school offerings coupled with altered property tax burdens can affect population migration and movement, and in doing so, affect the rates and patterns of future metropolitan development.

CHANGING METROPOLITAN PATTERNS

Metropolitan areas exhibit dynamic change. One illustration is the Chicago Standard Metropolitan Statistical Area (SMSA). The 12.2 percent total population increase for the Chicago SMSA in 1960-70 was irregular within the area. The city of Chicago realized a 5.2 percent population decline, while the balance of the SMSA outside Chicago increased 35.3 percent. This suburbanization movement represents 330,000 households moving into the metropolitan area outside Chicago between 1960 and 1970. On the average 18,000 new homes and 17,000 multiple-dwelling units were constructed annually during this period in the SMSA outside the core city.

This dynamic intraurban movement of households continues, thereby affecting education resource needs and education policies both within and outside the core city. Given this dynamic setting, significant changes in local tax structures and school finances may affect the rates and patterns of future metropolitan development. Each major state reform proposal contains the critical elements that (a) school property taxes ought to be significantly reduced in some, perhaps most, school districts; and (b) education spending per pupil ought to rise sharply in many districts, at least to some average of current statewide district spending per pupil. Moreover, the same school districts that realize the greatest relative reduction in school tax rates also could be the districts with the most significant consequent increases in spending per pupil.

Changes in school finance and property taxes will have an irregular, or checkerboard, impact among residential communities circling the core city. Some communities will realize a very moderate fiscal impact; other communities could enjoy the reinforcing effects of significantly reduced taxes coupled with increased school offerings. This uneven local fiscal bonus will affect population stabilization or expansion among the numerous existing and potential suburban communities. Given the differential impact, the patterns of single family dwellings may change vis-à-vis multiple-dwelling units. The population densities in some communities may be affected by consequent shifts in land use. Moreover, population characteristics such as race may change in the central city as well as residential communities, in response to different patterns of new residential construction. Reduced reliance on local property taxes and increased state support for schools could affect the location and construction of federally sponsored low-income housing programs, in addition to the maintenance and renovation of existing low-income housing units. As the patterns of metropolitan development are affected, so also are the varying needs for extended public services among the communities. Some communities may experience excess capacities of certain services, while others must expand at an unprecedented local rate.

The initial solution to school finance and local property tax relief conceivably could even loop back in some school districts and create additional fiscal problems because of changes in rates and patterns of population movement in a metropolitan area. The rate of housing construction in previously undeveloped outlying areas could be accelerated, for example, creating a need for new school construction at the same time that select school districts close in may realize school excess capacities because of being bypassed or experiencing a residential exodus of young couples with school-age children. Educators may find that solutions to one problem may create other education finance dilemmas, as a policy decision to alter education in one fashion acts as a catalyst to multiple changes thereby affecting education in other ways.

LOCATION THEORY

The popular basic location models generally are adaptions of rent and land value theories to a spatial setting.[3] The analysis is in the framework of comparative statics. Income and wealth distribution is accepted as a parameter, and within these constraints households strive to maximize their satisfaction in residential location decisions. This is a consumer satisfaction problem in the abstraction of a market economy. Household income, transportation costs, and costs of other items in the household budget determine the demand for housing. Aggregate demand for housing throughout an urban area in turn determines land values, given the stock of total available land. In a comparative statics solution, the individual household residential location decision is a function of land rent outlays and transportation costs. Increased density is a consequence of more intensive use of higher rent lands.

These basic location models in a most abstract form can be visualized as an urban cone. The ordinate of a vertical cross-section of this urban cone is

3. See William Alonso, *Location and Land Use* (Cambridge: Harvard University Press, 1974); John F. Kain, "The Journey-to-Work as a Determinant of Residential Location," *Regional Science Association Papers and Proceedings,* 9 (1962), 137-60; Ira S. Lowry, *A Model of Metropolis* (Santa Monica: Rand Corporation, 1964); Lowdow Wingo, Jr., *Transportation and Urban Land* (Washington, D.C.: Resources for the Future, 1961).

the population density, on the premise of a single employment-production (or dominant employment-production) activity center for the metropolitan area.[4] The horizontal plane is distance from the activity center, measured either in miles or in travel time. One then has density rings spun concentrically around the activity center, with lower and lower densities further out from the employment pole.

The concentric zone models that dominate spatial location theory minimize or assume away consideration of the numerous local governments in a metropolitan area. Personal income and wealth distributions are accepted as given. Density as a correlate and consequent proxy for land rent, the location of the activity center, and the time plus explicit travel costs to commute to the activity center then are the three determinants of residential choice among the rings. Yet we appreciate in reality that each concentric ring may be comprised of scores of incorporated cities and villages, and other residential clusters. Each community can have a different quality of life, reflecting in part varying levels of local government services and local resident tax burdens.

Why have local government effects been assumed away in location theory? First, these theoretical location models frequently are applied to transportation problems, and the levels of abstraction employed may be adequate to provide general data for transportation policy.[5] Second, urban writers frequently have treated local government services and the supporting local property taxes as though they were mutually offsetting in a complementary "benefits received" fashion. This premise is generalized as the Tiebout hypothesis: households have the metropolitan-movement option of choosing from among communities the residence where they can purchase through local taxation that mix or quality of public services that best reflects their wants.[6] If the Tiebout hypothesis were empirically valid, one would predict a strong correlation between measures of local tax effort and the levels (or quality) of local public services. Public elementary and secondary education is about one-half of total annual direct spending by all units of local government, and educators have demonstrated for some time that greater than average school offerings and spending per pupil can be paired with less than average school tax rates in many school districts because of wealth clustering.[7]

4. This single-center abstraction of urbanization can be modified to include multi-centered urban areas. In both cases, one has density or activity rings around one or more employment centers. For an elaboration of multicentered urban centers, see Hugh O. Nourse, *Regional Economics: A Study in the Economic Structure, Stability, and Growth of Regions* (New York: McGraw-Hill, 1968), pp. 114-23.

5. R. F. Engle et al., "An Econometric Simulation Model of Intra-Metropolitan Housing Location," *American Economic Review,* 62, no. 2 (May 1972), pp. 87-97.

6. Charles M. Tiebout, "A Pure Theory of Local Expenditures," *Journal of Political Economy,* 64, no. 5 (October 1956), 416-24.

7. The school finance analysis receiving widespread publicity is contained in John F.

Third, one must appreciate an identification problem in static location theory: the economic status of the relocating family (and other such families clustering to form a new community) will affect the determinants of quality of local governmental services, and likewise the levels of existing or anticipated local governmental services and tax rates will affect the location decision of the moving family.[8] The identification problem property can be dealt with only in a time dimension, as movement itself is a dynamic process.[9]

A separate comment by Bryan Ellickson in a recent article on this subject serves both as a postscript and link: "Although we have no satisfactory theory of urban local government, economists have not been reluctant to propose reforms in existing institutions."[10]

LOCAL PUBLIC ECONOMIES

The school finance issue has blown the lid off the subject of variations in the quality and mix of local government services among communities in a metropolitan area. Economists previously have been proceeding at a leisurely pace both in (a) the study of equity and efficiency considerations because of wide metropolitan ranges in local fiscal capacities, local tax efforts, and local government needs; and (b) the construction of more meaningful analytical frameworks to appreciate the interrelationships between variations in local government finances and metropolitan population movements.

Coons, William H. Clune, and Stephen D. Sugarman, *Private Wealth and Public Education* (Cambridge: Harvard University Press, Belknap Press, 1970). Economists discovered this consequence of balkanization as recently as 1962, several years after educators had been complaining of gross fiscal inequities. For an economist's observations, see Dick Netzer, "The Property Tax and Alternatives in Urban Development," *Regional Science Association Papers and Proceedings*, 9 (1962), 191–200.

8. John F. Kain has made several contributions to spatial residential location theory, concentrating in part on the "journey-to-work" facets. Kain's following comment reflects static community settlement rather than the dynamics of marginal household moves: "It is an empirical fact that the mean quality of the housing stock, and most likely of government services, increases with the distance from the central business district. My intuition, based partially on the findings presented here and those of related research, are that an explanation of residential location in these terms is at best an oversimplification and at worst may be basically incorrect. It is my belief that housing quality is less of a determinant of residential choices than are collective residential choices a determinant of the quality of housing services and of the quality of governmental services." See John F. Kain, "The Journey-to-Work as a Determinant of Residential Location," p. 223.

9. Bryan Ellickson has commented on the seriousness of this simultaneous interaction of residential location decisions and the local political process in building a basis for empirical analysis (see Bryan Ellickson, "Jurisdictional Fragmentation and Residential Choice," *American Economic Review*, 61, no. 2 (May 1971), 334–39.

10. Ibid., p. 334.

The school finance controversy has highlighted the situation that the concentration of assessable real property in wealthy enclaves has afforded the residents of these communities the option of providing superior local school offerings at local school property tax rates below the metropolitan average. Or to explain this situation another way, the residents of wealthy communities presently have the option of providing quality educational service at a significantly lower "average community unit price" than can residents of poorer communities. This favorable position is heightened by the treatment of property taxes under the federal income tax.

The school finance controversy indeed is a Pandora's box. If some communities have a more desirable local government sector than others, can we be more specific in weighing desirability, other than as one element of local amenities? If quality local services and local tax effort are not directly and closely related in many relevant instances, then local government desirability must consolidate both elements. With regard to local public education, we initially would describe a desirable community as providing a program offering represented by expenditures per pupil significantly greater than the metropolitan average and at the same time assessing a school tax rate that is significantly less than the metropolitan average. An undesirable community for households with school age children is one with program offerings or spending per pupil significantly below the metropolitan average coupled with school tax rates above the average. What is this range of desirable communities in various metropolitan areas, and would some index of desirability be related to average value of residential dwellings, average household incomes, or per capita incomes among the respective communities?

Do any discernible relationships and patterns in school finance within a metropolitan area also hold for other local government services and corresponding property taxes? Local public services as a group in the past have been a superior good; empirically household income elasticity of demand for local government services has been greater than an elasticity coefficient of 1. But the income elasticity for improved local government services need not be constant throughout the range of household income classes. Moreover, the school finance issue has demonstrated that the average community unit price can decline with increased average community wealth, so that in the past varying community demands for local government services have combined price and income (or, wealth) effects.

The issues in school finance raise the possibilities that in the near future the qualities of local educational services may be sharply increased in select communities, and that the community unit prices, or property tax rates to finance schools may be affected across the board. Moreover, some proposals (such as resource equalization) for changing the basis of school finance in a state may have significant impact on the marginal community prices, or incremental tax increases, necessary to add to local school budgets. Given such changes in education services and relative prices for local school allocations, can one anticipate any complementary or substitution effects among other classes of local government services? Separate estimates of current income elasticities and cross-elasticities of demands for major local government services would contribute to a greater understanding of the governmental facets of the suburbia process. All levels of government are partners in providing local services, because the federal and state governments in constantly altering grant-in-aid and equalization grant formulae and modifying higher level programs affect the local tax requirements and service options of individual communities.

If issues of school finance lead to considerations of changes in other local government services and possible corresponding changes in a host of local average and marginal property tax rates, and this action in the local government sector affects patterns of metropolitan growth and land development, where does the process end? No doubt an urban modeling effort can best proceed by a careful step-by-step development of the theoretical relationships involved in residential choice and demands for local government services and then refining these sector relationships before fitting them into an overall urban model, keeping in mind all the time that the whole may not be equal to the sum of its parts. We now appreciate more than ever that the assertion of the Tiebout hypothesis that households in an urban setting can "vote with their feet" in selecting a community with a preferred mix of government services and corresponding local tax rates is essentially an abstraction concentrating on issues of allocative efficiency. Clearly there are horizontal and vertical equity facets to this abstract process of "voluntary clustering" in suburban residential communities. Moreover, even the general conclusions by Tiebout within the limited efficiency perspective recently have been challenged by Buchanan and Goetz.[11]

I believe in structuring a study of the impact of local government services in a metropolitan area so that the area is segmented into relevant rings around the city core. I believe this to be the best approach even though employment opportunities are increasing in suburban areas. The ring framework provides a constructive basis for many specific analyses of household residential choice among communities with significantly different desirable local government services. An initial constraint of studying communities only within a specific time or distance ring essentially minimizes the commute cost consideration, to the extent that the metropolitan area has one *dominant* employment pole.

11. James M. Buchanan and Charles J. Goetz, "Efficiency Limits of Fiscal Mobility: An Assessment of the Tiebout Model," *Journal of Public Economics*, 1, no. 1 (April 1972), 25-43.

As one moves out from the city core, the typical residential communities become younger with each successive ring. In addition to community age (and varying average ages of residents), one can anticipate different land densities and different land use problems as one expands a study out of successive rings. One has a basis for comparing local government service levels among communities of similar socio-economic characteristics but located in different rings. An initial confining of analysis within rings may be more manageable and productive than tackling an entire metropolitan area and compensating in some fashion for distance or location. The Chicago Standard Metropolitan Statistical Area alone, for example, includes 276 cities and villages and 436 school districts outside the city of Chicago. When one structures rings around the Chicago city limits in 8- or 10-minute peak-hour commuter travel-time widths, one encompasses about 50 residential communities in each ring, with corresponding school districts about twice that number.

The stratification of a metropolitan area such as Chicago into rings is meaningful. Deferring detailed discussion of requisite data for the moment, the 1970 U.S. Census of Population and Housing, the 1967 and 1972 Censuses of Construction, and annual financial reports filed by respective units of local government provide basic data sources for analyses of changing government finances and population movements in a metropolitan area during the last decade. Given this setting, our project will provide a basis for answering some questions posed initially in this section and raising some more fundamental issues in the impact of changing local government services on metropolitan population movement.

First, one must resolve the question of the range of desirable communities in a ring and of whether desirability, taking into account both public services per capita and the local property tax rates, indeed is a function of income and wealth of households in the respective communities. A desirability index in itself can be constructed.[12] But one may have an identification problem in relating this desirability index to wealth, if wealthy households are drawn to a community because of its desirability, which is a function of local public spending and tax rates, which in turn depend on wealth. This identification problem can be resolved by simultaneously estimating the local tax-and-expenditure budgets, the desirability index, and the relationship between desir-

---

12. If D_j = index of public education desirability of community j
$\quad\quad E_j$ = current school expenditures per pupil
$\quad\quad T_j$ = rate of school tax levy in community j

and $\bar{E} = \frac{1}{n} \sum_{j=1}^{n} E_j \quad\quad \bar{T} = \frac{1}{n} \sum_{j=1}^{n} T_j$

Then $D_j = 100 \left[\frac{E_j}{\bar{E}} + (1.00 - \frac{T_j}{\bar{T}}) \right]$

ability and household income for the respective communities in each urban ring. This will provide a more rigorous test of the public service-and-wealth relationships among communities in rings, as distinct from the alternative quartile analyses used by educators which compare wealth and offerings in all school districts within a suburban or entire metropolitan area.

The subsequent issues of the availability of specific local government services and the options afforded relocating households follow the findings of desirability and wealth among communities. The Tiebout hypothesis in general form argues that households have the option of different mixes of government services among communities. The dominance of a wealth, or income, effect in demands for all categories of local public services by residents of wealthiest communities probably would swamp any considerations of substitution effects and options of different mixes of local services for all communities. One alternatively can group communities in each ring by household income or wealth subclasses. Given these subclasses, one can categorize major local spending programs on a per cpaita or per pupil basis, such as health and safety, recreation, and school spending. Do households have options for different mixes of local government services within income or wealth subclasses, and if so, do discernible differences in local services reflect relevant character differences in the respective communities, such as a concentration of elderly persons or households with young children?

These wealth or income subclasses of communities in each ring also provide a format for estimates of income elasticities and cross-elasticities of demands for major local government services, as previously mentioned. Time series data can be prepared for per capita spending by major service categories for each community, together with an index for changes in community average household incomes. The time series necessarily must be of short duration because the implicit assumption that changes in spending levels reflect correlate changes in service units and in service quality becomes more tenuous over longer periods of time because of technological innovation. In any event, the possibility of some consistent coefficients of complementarity and substitutability may provide much needed insights into short-run community responses to significant changes in local school spending per pupil and local school tax rates.

Another issue basic to the voluntary clubs perspective of Buchanan and others in appreciating the balkanization of suburbia is an analysis of aggregate local spending levels for communities in income or wealth subclasses on a metropolitan ring. Do the residents of any particular communities show a significant preference for aggregate public goods over private goods? Aggregate public spending and/or spending by relevant categories may be so clustered for communities within each income or wealth class that a household does not have a choice, say, of certain high school spending per pupil, within that particular income or wealth class. In other words, a household may be doubly frustrated in trying to realize a particular level of local public services: empirically, there may be a tight cluster of sets, or points, within their wealth constraint line, while the desired level or quality of public services is provided only by wealthier communities. Such a situation if validated would be incongruous in the sense that poorer households would not in reality have the option of trading off private consumption for superior local public goods and services, while wealthier households have the option of reduced levels of local government services in any event if they are willing to accept adverse neighborhood effects of poorer communities. The frustration experienced by lower income households in stretching their wealth constraints in attempts to buy into desired wealthy communities is a controversial vertical equity situation. Households with unequal wealth constraints would be bidding for quality local public services.

The equity issue is fundamental and cannot be ignored, but the arguments become irrelevant if in fact the voluntary clubs that are wealthy enclaves are virtually closed to all but exceptional latecomers regardless of their wealth. Established communities can impose various institutional constraints that in effect create very formidable barriers to further entry. Buchanan and Goetz reasoned on an efficiency basis that pioneers in the community would accept latecomers only if certain conditions were satisfied: for example, if a newcomer's tax dollars generate public goods inputs for others in the appropriate sharing group as well as for himself and allow the per-unit cost of public goods to fall for each individual as group size expands; or if the addition of more residents does not add an element of congestion or other private-goods feature into the distribution of the local government goods. Otherwise, the pioneers have personal cause to erect barriers against newcomers.[13]

How accessible are desirable communities today, before consideration of changes in school finance and property taxes? What is the variance of residential home values about the mean for these desirable communities? What has been the ratio of moderate-value homes relative to expensive homes in these communities since 1960 or 1964, relative to the residential housing mix in prior years? Do black households who are newcomers have a higher ratio of income-to-house value than recent white household arrivals?

Both availability and accessibility of housing in specific established communities are significant in the impact of changing school finance and local property taxes. Barring further challenges that voluntary club wealthy residential communities deny equality of opportunity, any induced new residential construction may continue to be located in previously unincorporated or sparsely populated areas.[14]

13. James Buchanan and Charles Goetz, "Efficiency Limits of Fiscal Mobility," pp. 28-32.
14. The entire zoning ordinance of Madison Township, New Jersey, was struck down

RESEARCH POSSIBILITIES

Such questions may seem far afield from the original concern about changing school finances and property taxes, but all these issues are inexorably linked in the provision of quality governments at the local government level when a metropolitan area is fragmented into hundreds of separate communities.

Much of the data necessary to evaluate and appreciate the specific issues raised can be located in the 1970 Census of Population and Housing, particularly the Fourth Count. There are some problems in application; for example, the Bureau of Census provides some demographic data by blocks (approximately 1,000 inhabitants) and socio-economic data by place (cities and villages) only within their specification of an urban area. This arbitrary boundary in the instance of Chicago is about 20 miles from the city core. Data beyond the urban area are aggregated by tracts of about 8,000 inhabitants. This means that one would have little difficulty accumulating requisite socio-economic data on those new communities in the outermost rings with populations of 8,000 or more, but information on some of the newest, smaller subdivision communities may be difficult to identify.

A second common problem is that school district boundaries in many states do not coincide either with city boundaries or census tract lines. These data acquisition problems are difficult and rather costly, but not insurmountable. When accomplished one has a basis to anticipate the impact of actual changes in school finances on property valuations, land development, and subsequent metropolitan development.

---

in 1971 by the Superior Court of Middlesex County on the grounds that the provisions of the ordinance interact to discriminate economically against 90 percent of the general population. This decision is the first time the standing of persons residing outside a community has been recognized as challenging the community's laws which exclude them. See Geoffrey Shields and L. Sanford Spector, "Opening Up the Suburbs: Notes on a Movement for Social Change," *Yale Review of Law and Social Action* (Summer 1972), pp. 300-333.

17 Terrie Jean Gale

Land Value Taxation and the Finance of Education in Metropolitan Areas

The effect that a land value taxation system (LVT) would have on public school finance depends upon two basic factors: (1) the influence of the tax upon the residential location of families with school-age children; and (2) the influence of the tax upon the revenue-raising capacity of the various school taxing jurisdictions.

The discussion of these factors in this paper is limited geographically to metropolitan areas and assumes a fragmentation of governmental and tax-levying authority. The terms "site value taxation," "land value taxation," and "land taxation" will be used interchangeably. It will be assumed that a site value tax would be based on highest economic use value of the land. Current or present tax systems will refer to ad valorem taxation of land and improvements. This paper will presume a situation in which both land and improvements have previously been taxed, with existing housing stock and land use patterns influenced by that tax system.

CURRENT SITUATION

Statistical, factual, and historic information on land value taxation is sparse. The analyses of this tax are long on theory, but short on actual proven effects.[1]

Empirical evidence of the effects of land taxation on family residential patterns within metropolitan areas is practically nonexistent. None of the American land-tax colonies is of metropolitan proportions. The Fairhope Single Tax Corporation owns and leases only about 20 percent of the land area of the city of Fairhope, Alabama. Arden, Ardentown, and Ardencroft are enclaves within the Wilmington, Delaware, metropolis. Free Acres, New Jersey, is a small, exclusively residential area.

The graded tax system in Pittsburgh and Scranton applies within center city boundaries only, and even there the overlapping school and county

1. Editor's note: In fact, this is far too true for all taxes.

taxes are not graded. Hawaii's experience with a graded tax is very limited, but has proven to have had a greater impact than the degree of differential between rates on land and improvements would indicate. This arose because the construction of many high-rise hotels forced a high value onto the land, even though the additional percentage of total value of the property allocated to land is not large. The California Irrigation Districts include mostly farmland, and the land tax they levy is for water service only, with other public services financed from property tax collections based on both land and improvements.

A. M. Woodruff and L. L. Ecker-Racz concluded that local ratings based on unimproved capital value in Australia and New Zealand had no significant effect on community development patterns there because of the very low levels of rates.[2]

Thus to understand the effects of land value taxation on residential location—within the metropolitan area—of families with school-age children, we must depend on fragments of related information and to a great extent on deduction.

First, there must be acknowledgment of the presently existing (pre-land-value taxation) building stock and location. This immediately raises the question as to whether it is already too late to curb suburban sprawl. Certainly whole subdivisions and shopping centers would not simply disappear under land value taxation, but LVT combined with higher fuel costs could stimulate fill-in of urban areas.

SLUM HOUSING

Much of existing residential building stock in the central cities is found in the ghetto areas of the urban core. These would be the first residential areas to be affected by land value taxation. Particularly if a ghetto were near the central business district, its high land values would mean tax increases which, together with the inducement to rebuilding brought about by the untaxing (or decreased taxing under a graded plan) of improvements, would result in redevelopment of the area to uses more consistently profitable than slums.

Land economic theory would indicate that a slumlord or any landlord would lose the ability to shift part of his tax—the part based on improvement value—to his tenants. Land, which Paul Samuelson describes as "price-determined rather than price-determining," theoretically cannot demand a higher rent than that indicated by the supply of land suitable for given uses. And the supply will not be reduced by a higher tax.

2. A. M. Woodruff and L. L. Ecker-Racz, "Property Taxes and Land-Use Patterns in Australia and New Zealand," *Tax Executive,* 28, no. 1 (October 1965), 16-63.

However, there is one circumstance wherein a land tax could be shifted, and the nature of this circumstance is such that slum dwellers might be particularly vulnerable. That is the case of tenants "having no knowledge of powers of moving and nowhere better to go," a situation described by Ursula Hicks in reference to India.[3]

It is doubtful that central city slum dwellers would be able to absorb the shifted increase in taxes, and a landlord who tried this route would soon face conditions forcing him toward abandonment of his property. But if slum dwellers felt they had nowhere else to go, they might further double up within their apartments to meet increased rent demands. Or in an area with land value low enough, the poor could absorb the shifted taxes.

In the long run although provision of housing for low income families might remain a problem, a land tax system would make it easier for at least some persons at the upper limits of this income stratum to obtain better housing via the private market. The increased tax on vacant land would result both in lower land prices, through the capitalization of the tax,[4] and in greater availability of land, as the speculative advantages of land holding are diminished. More land, at lower prices, together with the untaxing (or decreased taxing) of improvements, may fairly be expected to precipitate an acceleration of building and rehabilitation activity. Landlords would be stimulated to expand the number of living units by the construction of new apartment complexes. The increase in supply of living units could work toward better living quarters for reduced rent payments.

Under the present form of property taxation, private housing for the very poor abides in the best of all tax worlds: low tax assessments of both land and buildings, not to mention Federal tax breaks for depreciation, mortgage interest, property taxes, etc. For those families whose income is so low that they could not possibly sustain rent or mortgage payments within the private market, even with a land tax that decreases land prices and encourages increased housing construction volume, land value taxation will mean a decreased supply of affordable housing. Under land taxation, with land assessed at highest use value and improvements untaxed (or taxed at lower rates), landlords will no longer pay artificially low taxes and will no longer be discouraged from improving their structures. As the profitability of slum holding disappears, so will the slums themselves which, however unpleasant, have been the chief source of housing for the poor.

3. Ursula K. Hicks, "Can Land Be Assessed for Purposes of Site Value Taxation?" in *The Assessment of Land Value,* Daniel M. Holland, ed. (Madison: University of Wisconsin Press, 1970), p. 12.
4. The heavier tax burden on land initially would be capitalized into lower land prices. But the removal of the tax burden on improvements would increase the demand for land on which to build, with resulting higher prices.

Government assistance for both new construction and rehabilitation will still be required to assure adequate housing for low income families.

Whether new government-assisted housing would be built in the central city or in the suburbs would depend on several factors, not all of them economic, including land prices, space availability, local government cooperation, and local zoning regulations.

In the provision of low income housing, as in so many other ways, gradualism in the introduction of a site value tax would alleviate many problems. Gradualism would eliminate the possibility of large numbers of slum residents being turned out of their neighborhoods at once as the owners or purchasers of slum properties begin redevelopment of their properties. Gradualism would give the government time to subsidize, build, and/or rehabilitate housing for the poor.

FAMILY HOUSING

Taxation of high central city land values at full economic use levels, together with the untaxing (or decreased taxing) of improvements, would encourage the development of high-rise apartment buildings as well as commercial buildings in the city. It is likely that residents of these apartments would be affluent, from upper and upper-middle income groups, causing a reduction of the concentration of these households in the suburbs. Residential opportunities for middle income families in centrally located, high-rise structures would become available only as demands for commercial and luxury apartment space were filled. But whether upper income or middle income, residents of these buildings are likely to be predominantly older persons, couples without children, and unmarried men and women. For understandable reasons, these groups seem to be attracted to the city, while most families with children have shown a disinclination for high-rise living.

Older but still substantial single-family homes within the city would be filtered down to low income families in some cases. But in many cities such homes are enjoying a growing popularity. Young couples especially are buying these homes and practicing do-it-yourself renovation. Site value taxation would provide a definite stimulus to these private rehabilitation and new construction activities. In encouraging such efforts, site value taxation would be a "golden key to urban renewal . . . and not at public expense" as characterized by Mary Rawson.[5]

In the suburbs land taxation might stimulate the construction of apartment developments for the same reasons as in the city: to concentrate as much un-

5. Mary Rawson, *Property Taxation and Urban Development* (Washington, D.C.: Urban Land Institute, 1961), p. 28.

taxed (or low-taxed) improvement value over as little high-taxed land as possible. Similarly, there might be an increase in row-house and other small-lot development.[6]

In any case the effect of land taxation in increasing the availability of land for purchase would probably act to make home ownership more widespread. The high cost of land under the present low-land-tax conditions is one of the main factors responsible for putting homeownership out of reach for many middle and lower-middle income families today.[7]

As stated previously, evidence of the effect of a land tax on residential patterns is very scarce. But two examples, from Australia and from Canada, support the conclusion that land value taxation would lead to more widespread homeownership. The August 1960 special issue of *House and Home* stated that "the pace of home building in those Melbourne suburbs that tax only land is much faster than in the suburbs where houses are taxed, too."[8] And the International Research Committee on Real Estate taxation quoted a former mayor of New Westminister, British Columbia, where land values were taxed at 100 percent and improvements at 20 percent: "Since this system was adopted, New Westminister has reaped considerable benefit by way of increased population and additional property owners resident within the municipality. Gradually more persons were encouraged to purchase property and become homeowners."[9]

LAND TAX REVENUES IN CITIES AND SUBURBS

It is generally agreed that a system of site value taxation would improve the revenue-raising capacity of most center cities. If needed, tax rates could be increased to assure that there would be at least no lessening of revenue. Such tax rate increases would not discourage redevelopment and growth in

6. Max Neutze, however, has suggested that site value taxation would discourage large-scale developments, because of land value increases generated by the developments—see Max Neutze, "Property Taxation and Multiple-Family Housing," in *Land and Building Taxes,* Arthur P. Becker, ed. (Madison: University of Wisconsin Press, 1969), pp. 122, 127. Neutze adds that "this effect would be felt only when the rules of assessment for site value taxation were applied to units smaller than the complete development."

7. A recent report indicates that both higher land prices and higher construction costs have boosted housing costs in the last few years to the point where families have had to economize on floor space, bathrooms, air-conditioning, and other extras. Home buyers are paying more and getting less. See J. A. Livingston, "A paradoxical boom: More homes, yet less," *Louisville Courier-Journal and Times,* September 3, 1973.

8. *House and Home,* 18, no. 2 (August 1960), 133.

9. International Research Committee on Real Estate Taxation, H. Bronson Cowan, Research Director, *Municipal Improvement and Finance as Affected by the Untaxing of Improvements and the Taxation of Land Values* (New York: Harper and Brothers, 1958), p. 7.

the city, for two reasons. First, via the capitalization effect, higher land taxes would mean lower land prices. Second, the untaxing of improvements would provide an impetus to construction and rehabilitation. Cities would benefit from increased revenues from redeveloped areas and from vacant land, which constitutes a substantial proportion of many cities' land areas.

The value of land on the urban-rural fringe continues to increase as metropolitan populations expand. Under the present form of taxation (of both land and improvements), with low taxation of land, this value increase is profiting mainly speculators. Meanwhile, the public, whose joint actions have given the land its value, loses on at least two counts: the public treasury does not recoup the values created by the public; and land held off the market by speculators forces leapfrog development and suburban sprawl, resulting in greater public and private expense and inconvenience in providing utilities, transportation, and other services plus reduced land for producing food and reduced land for other purposes.

The major source of increased tax revenues in suburban areas under land value taxation would be the empty of underused, ripe-for-development land presently being held for rises in market value. Land taxation, via the capitalization effect, would lessen the profits of land speculation, and thus would hasten the development of many of these vacant parcels. But whether or not the institution of a land tax system brought a parcel of land into development, the revenue from the parcel would be greatly increased from pre-land-tax levels.

While suburban land value is increasing, suburban population is increasing also. But, as Mason Gaffney has written, "the suburbs probably have more land value per capita than the central city."[10] Unfortunately, this per capita value is not necessarily distributed proportionately among suburban taxing jurisdictions.[11]

The various suburbs of any metropolitan area are often marked by wide differences in development patterns. There are large-lot residential suburbs of affluent families, small-lot subdivisions full of middle-class and lower-middle-class families, industrial suburbs with few, if any, homes, and other suburban jurisdictions which are largely undeveloped.

Many large-lot residential suburbs have instituted zoning ordinances requiring that lots be of a certain minimum size. This not only makes for homogeneity of the neighborhood, but effectively holds down the number of chil-

10. Mason Gaffney, "Adequacy of Land as a Tax Base," in *The Assessment of Land Value*, p. 173.
11. Gaffney's land value study of Milwaukee and its suburbs concluded that "The land share is low in tight, fully built bedroom suburbs . . . It is low in industrial suburbs with blue-collar housing . . . The land share is high in sprawled suburbs with empty land . . ." (ibid., pp. 178-79).

dren in local schools. The amount of land per house (and per family) is large and the value of the land is high, partly due to the exclusive "preferred" nature of the area.

Small-lot, densely settled suburbs have less land per house (and per family) and generally lower land values. (It should be pointed out that because current assessment practice often assesses smaller lots at a higher value per acre than larger lots, the differences in actual land value between exclusive large-lot suburbs and middle-class small-lot suburbs are not as obvious as they would be if the land were assessed uniformly.)

Residents of suburban developments are often burdened for many years after completion of building with additional tax liability besides that needed to support schools and other on-going public services. Though it is the extension of transportation and utility lines that makes an area of land suitable for development and thus provides the developer with his opportunity to profit, the cost of these extensions is usually borne by the residents of the development as well as other residents of the taxing jurisdiction in which the development is located. A recent case involving a Levitt planned community to be built in Loudoun County, Virginia, outside Washington, D.C., related to this point. The County Board of Supervisors issued a new regulation that Levitt and other developers must pay the costs of schools, sewers, parks, libraries, and other capital projects to the extent that these costs exceed the amount that the county would have to pay if there were no rezoning for increased population.

These regulations, while safeguarding the interests of older residents, will probably cause the costs to be borne by the new residents, by way of increased prices. One of the effects of land value taxation would be to decrease suburban sprawl and the lengthy utility and transportation extensions necessitated by it, thus reducing speculation and bringing closer-in land onto the market. This would mean a savings, to be reflected in tax rates or purchase prices for the suburban homebuyer.

Industrial suburbs with little residential development may not produce as much revenue under site value taxation as under the current tax system, depending on the relative value of the plants and other improvements.[12] Where the jurisdiction includes few families, public expenditure levels may be so low that lesser revenues may not matter.

It has become more and more common in recent years for suburbs which are largely residential to make special efforts to attract office buildings and industry to increase the local tax base. To the extent that office and industrial property value is in improvements rather than land, such development in

12. Dick Netzer has written that "the ratio of improvements to land value is generally much higher for industrial than for residential development . . ." *Economics of the Property Tax* (Washington, D.C.: Brookings Institution, 1966), p. 130.

residential suburbs would be a less attractive prospect. Under land taxation, with improvements untaxed (or taxed at lower rates) a greater share of new office buildings may well be attracted back into the center city. A heavy industry needing horizontal layout and much land, however, would find the suburban regions more appropriate.

In an independent taxing jurisdiction with much empty land and little development requiring few public expenditures, it would be possible to maintain such low rates even within a land tax system that it would be possible for landowners to maintain large undeveloped parcels whether for personal use or for speculative purposes. This potential points to state-wide or at least county-wide LVT rates.

LAND BANKS AND OPEN SPACE

Any discussion of land taxation must consider the effect of the tax on open space and land use patterns.

Certainly, careful and comprehensive planning would be at least as important under a land tax system as under current tax systems. Possibly it would be more so, because the tax would encourage the full economic use of every privately owned land parcel. To assure open space, parks, and greenery as well as other nonlucrative but essential land uses, there must be planning. A persuasive argument can be made that the cause of open space would be better served by land value taxation accompanied by planning than by present tax systems. Dick Netzer has written: "And if the goal is the preservation of open space, then an unneutral property tax is a clumsy instrument indeed to guarantee this . . . It cannot assure that the appropriate types and locations of open space are preserved, only an entirely accidental selection."[13]

The preservation of open space at the fringes of the metropolis would be aided by land taxation through the encouragement of development of empty land closer to the central city. Throughout the metropolis land might be reserved both for open space and for other public purposes through government ownership or some form of option for future use. There is even now government-owned land in many cities by way of the urban renewal program. A well-planned system of land banks could assure not only green space, but land for schools, hospitals, and other public facilities. Land banks may be the best method of maintaining a supply of low-priced land in cities and suburbs for the low-income housing which would be at least as necessary under site value taxation as under current tax systems.[14]

13. Ibid., p. 207.
14. Grace Milgram, *U.S. Land Prices—Directions and Dynamics,* Research Report #13, prepared for the National Commission on Urban Problems (Washington, D.C.: Government Printing Office, 1968), pp. 63-66.

Many foreign countries have land bank systems, including especially the Scandinavian countries. In this country it may be expected that public land ownership would stir political opposition; but land value taxation, by bringing many parcels of vacant land onto the market, could lead to an oversupply of available land which could be conveniently resolved by public purchase.

On the question of possible congestion resulting from overdevelopment under a land tax, James Heilbrun has written that arguments to this effect "should be regarded skeptically. Most of them completely overlook the general-equilibrium nature of the land use problem: people moving into one block necessarily move out of another."[15] The increased availability of land for purchase and use, resulting from land value taxation, would provide many new blocks into which people might move.

Land use planning and land banks would do much to assure the success of site value taxation in revitalizing the central city and encouraging appropriate land use. But certainly these objectives are necessary whether or not land taxation is instituted. They do not represent any extra expense or effort related to land value taxation.

CONCLUSION

The higher economic use of land which would be stimulated by a land tax, as well as the taxation at full use value of underused land parcels, would improve the school revenue situation of the center cities of metropolitan areas. School finance conditions in large-lot residential and predominantly industrial suburbs would continue to be favorable. In small-lot residential developments, where there is a greater concentration of children, the situation would be less auspicious.

The problem of inequality of financial resources for education under land value taxation would be thus similar to the problems under present forms of taxation based on both land and improvements; so it is not surprising that the frequently proposed solution would be similar. This proposal is for larger, metropolitan- or statewide property tax collection jurisdictions.

Larger school-taxing jurisdictions may be even more needed under land value taxation than under present tax systems. Land value varies less among properties in the same vicinity than does improvement value (which explains why land value would be easier to assess than land and improvement value together),[16] so jurisdictional boundaries are even less likely under land taxation to enclose properties with a variety of revenue-producing levels.

15. James Heilbrun, *Real Estate Taxes and Urban Housing* (New York: Columbia University Press, 1966), p. 127.

16. See statement by A. M. Woodruff, *Hearings before National Commission on Urban Problems*, vol. 1 (Washington, D.C.: Government Printing Office, 1968), pp. 286-90.

School finance, in particular, might suffer from this lack of variety of land value. It has been stated that "the property tax of households tends to decline under a land tax."[17] This assumes a taxing jurisdiction which includes industrial and/or commercial as well as residential property. But it points out that the land share is not high for most residential properties. Residential areas, especially those with smaller-lot development, have less land value but more children to educate.

Equitable distribution of resources for educational finance necessitates large taxing jurisdictions with varied land uses, whether the tax is based on land and improvements or on land only.

17. Richard W. Lindholm, "Twenty-one Land Value Taxation Questions and Answers," *American Journal of Economics and Sociology,* 31, no. 2 (April 1972), 159.

18 Charles Waldauer

Local Impacts of Alternative Methods of Financing Education

This study examines the impacts on local finances of several alternative methods of federal-state sharing of basic education costs. School finances in New Jersey, New York, and Washington are aggregated on a countywide basis to see how the various methods would affect local fiscal structures in comparison with existing federal and state grant programs for education.

These three states are selected for study because (1) as shown in Table 18.1 they are representative of relatively high (Washington), moderate (New York), and low (New Jersey) levels of state sharing of local education costs; (2) their local costs of education are financed primarily from real property taxes; and (3) the fiscal data were available on a countywide basis.

Table 18.1 – Relative Shares of Local, State, and Federal Finances for Elementary-Secondary Education, 1968-69

State	Percent local share	Percent state share	Percent federal share	State-local finances as a percent of state personal income
U.S. Average	52.0	40.7	7.3	4.6
New Jersey	67.9	27.5	4.6	4.3
New York	47.9	47.8	4.2	5.1
Washington	32.5	60.8	6.7	4.7

Source: Advisory Commission on Intergovernmental Relations, *State Aid to Local Government,* Report A-34 (Washington, D.C.: Government Printing Office, 1969), pp. 53, 54.

The author wishes to thank the following people for assistance in providing him with data and data sources: Mr. Louis Bruno, Superintendent of Public Instruction for Washington; Mr. Frank Haines, Executive Director of the New Jersey Taxpayers Association; Ms. Betsy Levin, Director of Educational Studies, The Urban Institute; and Mr. Harold Pellish, Director of the New York State Bureau of Planning and Research.

DETERMINING FEDERAL AND STATE SHARES OF BASIC EDUCATION COSTS

The need for minimum national and regional standards in education, and the necessity to adjust for educational costs and benefits that are external to states as well as localities, call for some federal and state sharing of basic education costs. These basic costs should represent the expenditures necessary to provide a foundation program in education: one which would provide every child with the level of education necessary to ensure that he or she has the chance to become a useful and productive citizen. However, this foundation program should not preclude additional state and local financing, or even additional federal financing in very special circumstances, so that educational expenditures and standards could be raised well above the prescribed minimum levels.

For administrative feasibility, the foundation program should be defined in terms of a per pupil (or a per classroom instruction unit) level of expenditures. This expenditure level should be adjusted for regional differences (e.g., urban-rural, north-south) in the costs of education. Median teacher salaries[1] or a government services price index could be used for this purpose. Additional adjustments, involving the weighting of pupil enrollments, should be made to reflect cost differentials associated with different types of educational programs (e.g., kindergarten, elementary, and secondary school instruction; vocational education; classes for mentally and physically handicapped children).[2] These expenditure levels could be further adjusted, again using weighted pupil enrollments, to reflect differences in educational needs that are associated with very sparsely or densely settled school districts, or with districts that have a high proportion of educationally disadvantaged (low-income) children.[3] No attempt at such weighting differentials is made in this study because the necessary data were not available.

Based on the 1968-69 national average for total school expenditures per pupil in average daily attendance (see Table 18.2), an $800 level is arbitrarily selected to represent the national costs of a foundation program in education. Only Maine, some of the Great Plains states, and the Southern states had expenditure levels considerably below $800. In general, the Northeastern and Great Lakes states had expenditures well above this level. This figure is not intended to be a measure of a national minimum standard for basic costs of

1. E.g., Lester Thurow, "Aid to State and Local Governments," *National Tax Journal,* 23, no. 1 (March 1970), 23-35.
2. Roe Lyell Johns, *Financing Education: Fiscal and Legal Alternatives* (Columbia, Ohio: Merrill, 1972).
3. Ibid.

Table 18.2–Statewide Expenditure Levels per Pupil in Average Daily Attendance for Elementary and Secondary Schools, 1968-69

State	Expenditure levels per pupil in a.d.a.			
	Total	Current	Capital	Interest on school debt
U.S. Average	$ 834	$ 696	$113	$25
New Jersey	1,018	852	133	33
New York	1,306	1,140	129	37
Washington	808	673	108	27

Source: U.S. Office of Education, *Digest of Educational Statistics, 1967 Edition* (Washington, D.C.: Government Printing Office, 1969), p. 56.

education; it is used solely to see how alternative methods of federal-state sharing in education costs would affect local finances.

The federal and state shares of these basic education costs should be based on an efficient use of resources in the face of geographic externalities in educational costs and benefits. Unless these externalities are taken into account in the fiscal decision-making process, an underallocation of resources for education is likely to result.[4] The federal share should reflect the degree of cost-benefit spillovers among the states, while the state share should reflect the degree of spillovers among localities within the same state.

One simple measure of these cost and benefit spillovers is the extent of the population migration among the states and among local areas within the same state. The interstate migration ratio could be taken as representative of the federal share, while the migration ratio among localities in the same state (e.g., intercounty migration) could be used to reflect the state share.[5] Recent Census of Population data indicate that the interstate migration rate is about 28 percent, while about 70 percent of adult Americans have lived in more than one

4. Werner Z. Hirsch, Elbert W. Segelhorst, and Morton J. Marcus, *Spillover of Public Education Costs and Benefits* (Los Angeles: Institute of Government and Public Affairs, University of California at Los Angeles, 1964); and Burton A. Weisbrod, *External Benefits of Public Education,* Research Report series no. 105 (Princeton: Industrial Relations Section, Princeton University, 1964), present detailed analyses of the effects of spillovers on fiscal decision-making for education.

Weisbrod formulates the hypotheses that benefit spill-ins (represented by immigration of education adults) are ignored in school expenditure decisions, while benefit spill-outs (represented by outmigration of locally educated persons) will reduce local financial support for education. The results of a multiple regression for the 48 contiguous states, using 1960 fiscal data, tend to support the hypotheses.

5. At the Madison Conference, Professors Edelson, Oakland and Stubblebine pointed out that one-time migrations might not have a great impact on school fiscal decisions at the margin. Theoretically, there is justification for their view, but, ultimately, it is an empirical question subject to statistical analysis.

county. This understates the migration rate among local schools since most school districts cover an area smaller than a county.[6] Based on these migration patterns, the federal share is arbitrarily set in this study at 30 percent of the basic costs[7] with the states picking up the remaining 70 percent. That is, of the $800 per pupil, the federal government would finance $240 and the state government $560.

ALTERNATIVE FINANCING PLAN

A flat grant approach, with no consideration of local (or state) fiscal capacity and effort, would be warranted only if there were no concern with providing adequate fiscal resources to achieve equality of educational opportunity. This desire for equalization would require some variable sharing of education costs that would be inversely related to fiscal capacity and directly related to fiscal effort.

Such equalization could be carried out by appropriately weighting the federal share of costs by the ratios of each state's personal income and state-local tax effort (defined, say, as state-local taxes as a percent of personal income) to the corresponding national averages.[8] This approach would guarantee that there always would be some federal funding of a foundation program in education. No attempt is made in this study to include a variable funding formula among the states, since the impacts on local finances are being examined in only three states.

Equalization also could be achieved by similar weighting of the state share of basic costs by the ratios of each school district's fiscal capacity and effort

6. Weisbrod, *External Benefits,* p. 62, estimates that upwards of 90 percent of the financial returns of a high school education in Clayton, Missouri, a suburb of St. Louis, will be realized by other localities because of the high mobility of young adults. Other research indicates that Milwaukee, Wisconsin, and its suburbs do not retain more than half of their high school graduates ten years after graduation: U.S., Congress, House, Committee on Ways and Means, *Is There a Metropolitan Alternative to Revenue Sharing? Hearings on General Revenue Sharing,* by Gary Gappert, 92nd Cong., 1st sess., June 1971, p. 1492.

7. U.S. Representative Roman C. Pucinski introduced on March 16, 1971, the *National Partnership in Education Act of 1971* (H.R. 6179, 92d. Cong., 1st sess.) which calls for substantially increased federal financing of state-local current expenditures per pupil. The proposed federal share is to rise from 10 percent in 1972 to 33 percent in 1974, with these proportions adjusted for each state by the ratio of national to state per capita personal income. Thus, one-third federal financing is intended to be the norm.

National Education Finance Project, No. 5, *Alternative Programs for Financing Education* (Gainesville, Fla.: University of Florida Press, 1971), p. 229, calls for 30 percent federal funding of education costs.

8. This approach is incorporated in several of the proposed plans for federal financing that are put forth in ibid., pp. 212–29. It also is contained in the proposed *National Partnership in Education Act of 1971* (H.R. 6179).

to the corresponding statewide averages.[9] In practice, the great bulk of equalization at the state level is carried out through the use of a Strayer-Haig formula approach (34 out of 42 states use it). Here, the state's share of a foundation program is equal to a per pupil level of expenditures, unweighted or weighted for differences in program costs and needs, less the local share which usually is expressed in terms of some tax rate or percentage of local wealth. In a majority of instances, there is a minimum state funding regardless of the school district's wealth.[10] Of course, this should be the case so long as there is a need for a statewide minimum standard, and there exist local spillovers in education costs and benefits.

Some local funding of foundation program costs could be defended on the grounds that local responsibility for providing an educational program ought to carry with it some local responsibility for its financing. However, more than a modest local share may violate the equal protection clauses of the federal and state constitutions as they apply to equality of educational opportunity.[11]

9. Iowa, Massachusetts, New York, Pennsylvania, Rhode Island, and Vermont all employ a variation of this approach, called "percentage equalization." The state's proportional share of foundation costs is weighted by the ratio of the district's per pupil wealth to the state average for all districts. In several cases, a minimum local tax effort also is required in terms of a tax rate millage on the full value of taxable property. U.S. Office of Education, *Public School Finance Programs, 1968-69* (Washington, D.C.: Government Printing Office, 1969). New Jersey recently shifted to a percentage equalization approach.

10. Ibid., and *Alternative Programs for Financing Education*, pp. 234-37.

All three states studied here define and support a foundation program in education in terms of weighted per pupil expenditure levels. For current operations this level is $400 in New Jersey, $860 in New York, and $368 in Washington for the 1968-69 school year. For capital purposes the per pupil level is $45 in New Jersey, and variable rates in New York and Washington depending, partly, on a construction cost index. There are additional aid programs for transportation and for special programs for highly urbanized and rural school districts.

These foundation program grants attempt to equalize the difference between the foundation level of expenditures and the local share of the costs defined as minimum tax rate efforts ($10.50 mills in New Jersey, $11.00 mills in New York, and $14.00 mills in Washington). Schools are guaranteed a minimum flat grant per pupil of $75 in New Jersey, and $304 in New York, as long as they are expending at the foundation level and picking up their tax effort share of the costs. There is no guaranteed minimum aid level in Washington.

11. Ferdinand P. Schoettle, "Judicial Requirements for School Finance and Property Tax Redesign: The Rapidly Evolving Case Law," *National Tax Journal*, 25, no. 3 (September 1972), 455-72.

The "district power equalizing" approach represents one way to avoid such possible unconstitutional practices and yet retain local prerogatives in financing education. Under this method, school districts would set the tax rate they desire and the state would guarantee them a given revenue yield per pupil, irrespective of local wealth. In general, wealthier districts would tend to end up paying a surplus into the state fund, while

Because of the prevalent state practice, including that in the three states analyzed, this study utilizes the Strayer-Haig approach to equalization by deducting a uniform local share from the $800 per pupil level of basic education costs. As is explained below, one method bases the local share as a tax millage on the full value of taxable property, while the other sets the local share as a percentage of personal income. Under both methods, there is no minimum federal-state funding of foundation expenditures for wealthy school districts. When the local share is based on taxable property, there are several instances in which rural and resort areas with relatively few pupils would receive no aid.

Three alternative plans of federal-state financing are examined: (1) a flat grant of $800 per pupil in average daily attendance (a.d.a.), with no local share required; (2) a flat grant of $800 per pupil in a.d.a. minus a uniform local share defined as a tax rate of 12 mills on the full market value of taxable property—no aid would be received if the local share exceeds $800 per pupil (i.e., when the full value of property is $66,666 per pupil or greater); and (3) a flat grant of $800 per pupil in a.d.a. less a uniform local share expressed as 2 percent of personal income—again, no aid would be received if the local share exceeds $800 per pupil (i.e., when personal income is $40,000 per pupil or greater).

The local shares of education costs are based on two different measures of fiscal capacity and effort: (1) the full market value of taxable property, reflecting its use as the primary, if not the sole, tax base in raising local revenues for education; and (2) personal income, out of which ultimately must come the local share of education costs.[12] In general, there is no close association between the full value of taxable property and personal income.[13]

A tax rate of 12 mills is based on the average for a sample of 222 school districts, from 8 states, analyzed by the National Educational Finance Project (NEFP)[14]—this tax rate also is used in several NEFP proposals for state financing of education.[15] The 2 percent of personal income figure is based on half the NEFP rate for the state share of education costs in a proposed plan for federal financing of a basic foundation program in education.[16]

---

poorer districts would tend to be subsidized from this fund. For a discussion of this approach, see President's Commission on School Finance, *Final Report: Schools, People, and Money—The Need for Educational Reform* (Washington, D.C.: Government Printing Office, 1972), pp. 32-33.

12. To the extent that local property or other taxes are levied on businesses, the tax burdens could be shifted forward onto nonresident consumers in the form of higher output prices, shifted backward onto nonresident suppliers of the factors of production in the form of lower input prices, or capitalized on nonresident owners in the form of lower after-tax earnings or market prices for shares of stock.

13. E.g., *Alternative Programs for Financing Education,* p. 90.

14. Ibid., p. 92.

15. Ibid., pp. 282-85.

16. Ibid., p. 213. The use of personal income as a measure of fiscal capacity to sup-

PLAN 1: FLAT GRANT PER PUPIL[17]

The flat grant of $800 per pupil in ADA provides for equalizing differences in local fiscal capacities and efforts. It does not attempt to compensate for differences in educational program costs and needs by appropriately weighting pupil attendance figures. As a result in all three states the more heavily urbanized areas, possessing greater population density and wealth, would receive the greatest *absolute* increases in aid under Plan 1, although the more rural areas would receive somewhat larger *relative* increases.[18] This aid pattern would help reduce any municipal overburden on the local tax base that might exist in these urbanized areas, as reflected by property taxes for municipal purposes relative to school purposes.[19]

Localities in New Jersey would experience the greatest absolute and relative increases in aid under Plan 1, in the aggregate receiving about a fourfold rise, while those in New York would experience the smallest increases—about 10 percent in the aggregate. In fact, in a majority of counties in New York the aid received would actually decline; for the most part, only the heavily urbanized counties would experience an increase. All areas would receive substantial increases in federal aid (the proposed $240 per pupil is far in excess of the minuscule amounts actually received).

Thus, these differential impacts reflect state aid patterns and are the result of two conditions: (1) New Jersey has a low level of state sharing of local education costs (27.5 percent), with only a modest level of foundation program expenditures to be aided ($400 per pupil); and (2) New York State shares a

---

port education does not take into account differences in personal taxes paid to federal, state, and local governments for noneducation expenditures. An alternative NEFP plan uses "net personal income," defined as personal income less federal personal taxes paid and less $750 per capita for subsistence consumption expenditures (pp. 217-18).

17. Editor's note: The detailed county-aggregated local school finances, including the actual and proposed shares of federal-state aid, under the three alternatives for New Jersey, New York, and Washington are available from the author or the editor.

18. This outcome is in line with the findings of the simulation study by the National Educational Finance Project, *Alternative Programs for Financing Education,* p. 346, in which the major beneficiaries of a flat grant program would be the wealthy suburban districts surrounding the central cities. The central cities also would benefit, but they would be disadvantaged by the failure of this aid formula to adjust for their higher educational program costs and needs.

A similar result is found in the simulation study of New York schools by the Syracuse University Research Corporation, *Revising School Finance in New York State: Final Report* (Syracuse, N.Y.: Syracuse University Research Corp., August 1971), pp. iii-2.

19. There is some controversy over whether such municipal overburdens do in fact exist. For example, the National Educational Finance Project, *Alternative Programs for Financing Education,* p. 98, can find no persuasive evidence of its existence, while the Syracuse University Research Corporation, *Final Report,* pp. ii-16, 17, finds this overburden to be a major cause of inadequate local financial support of schools in New York State cities.

moderate level of local education costs (47.9 percent), but aids a very high level of foundation program expenditures ($860 per pupil, well in excess of the contemplated $560). The intermediate position occupied by Washington, with only modest increases in state aid, results from the state's very high share of local costs (60.8 percent) combined with a fairly low level of foundation program expenditures to be aided ($368 per pupil).

These results demonstrate some of the problems posed by using a flat grant, based on national averages, for federal-state financing of education. First, states and localities with higher educational costs are penalized, as there are no adjustments for regional cost differentials. Clearly this is the case for New York, which has one of the highest per pupil expenditure levels in the nation. In general, the Northeastern states have higher costs for both public and private sector services.

Second, states supporting per pupil levels of foundation program expenditures well above the national average would not be relatively as well off as those whose support is below the national average. The federal share of aided program costs would be proportionately less for these higher-than-average aid states, and this could act as a disincentive for greater state funding of foundation program costs. Again, New York provides a good example of this, as the federal grant of $240 per pupil is a far smaller proportion of foundation costs ($860) than that in either New Jersey ($400) or Washington ($368). High per pupil aid states would find it to their fiscal advantage to have the national standard for basic education costs set as closely as possible to their levels; this would maximize the relief for their state-local tax burdens. Conversely, low aid level states would find it in their interests to have the national standard set as close as possible to their foundation program costs, since any mandated increases in their financial support would increase state tax burdens and these might not be offset at the local level by increased federal aid.

One way to avoid discouraging states from aiding foundation program expenditure levels above the national average, in addition to adjusting for regional differences in program costs, is to weight the per pupil federal grant by the ratio of each state's per pupil level of aided expenditures to the national average—up to some specified maximum of, say, 1.50. This weighting factor also could be used to penalize states with per pupil levels of aided expenditures below the national average; i.e., the per pupil federal grant would be reduced by the proportion that the state level falls below the national average.

In order to avoid any disincentive for states to finance a greater share of education costs, the per pupil grant also could be weighted by the ratio of each state's percentage share of state-local finances for education to the corresponding national average. This approach could even eliminate the need to establish a per pupil level of state aid, relying solely on encouraging the states to assume a greater proportion of education costs.

PLAN 2: FLAT GRANT LESS UNIFORM LOCAL SHARE BASED ON PROPERTY VALUE

The flat grant of $800 per pupil in average daily attendance is reduced by a uniform local share of education costs measured as a tax rate of 12 mills on the full value of taxable property. This financing method does provide for equalizing differences in local fiscal capacity, but not for local fiscal effort; also, it does not compensate for differences in local educational costs and needs. Consequently, for all three states Plan 2 does result in greater equalization among the localities,[20] but the federal-state shares of basic education costs are sharply reduced when compared with Plan 1. In New Jersey and New York less than half the amount is received under Plan 2, while in Washington slightly more than half is received.

In general, the urban counties, which are the wealthiest, stand to lose relatively more aid than the rural ones when comparing Plan 2 with Plan 1; the most extreme example of this is New York City. The major exceptions are the five rural and/or resort counties (one each in New Jersey and New York, and three in Washington) with relatively few pupils compared to the full value of their property, since they would receive no aid under Plan 2. The per pupil values of their property all exceed $66,666.

When contrasted with the actual aid received, fewer funds would be distributed under Plan 2 in New York (a decrease of more than 50 percent) and Washington (about a 17 percent reduction), but more would be distributed in New Jersey (about an 85 percent increase). All counties in New York would experience reductions, with the urban ones receiving the greatest decreases—again, New York City provides the most extreme example. In Washington, a majority of counties would receive less aid, with King County, containing the city of Seattle, the biggest loser. All counties in New Jersey except Cape May, which would receive no aid, would experience increases.

The fiscal impacts of Plan 2 point out the advantages and disadvantages of using this method for financing the federal-state share of a basic program in education. First, as discussed in the evaluation of Plan 1, the failure to adjust for differences among school districts in program costs and needs will penalize those with high costs and needs—primarily urban districts and Northeastern states.

Second, also as discussed in the criticism of Plan 1, states supporting per pupil levels of expenditures well above the national average would be disad-

20. As pointed out in the National Educational Finance Project, *Alternative Programs for Financing Education,* pp. 346-47, complete equalization can be realized only with this approach if "negative" aid payments are possible; i.e., school districts contribute to the state education aid fund that portion of their uniform local share that is in excess of their actual costs of education.

vantaged by a formula that relies solely on this average. States such as New York would be discriminated against. This objection could be overcome by use of a ratio of the state level to the national average as a factor for weighting the federal grant. Further weighting could rely on the ratio of each state's percentage share of state-local finances for education to the national average of all state's shares.

Plan 2 does offer the advantage over Plan 1 of taking local fiscal capacities into account in order to equalize for the differences in these capacities. Plan 2 also establishes a uniform local share of basic education costs; this is an advantage if it is felt that some local share in these costs is desirable. However, consideration for both economic efficiency and equity probably would require only a modest local share—far less than the local shares that otherwise would be borne in New York and Washington. The fact that no aid might be received under this method certainly would be undesirable in view of the extensive educational costs and benefits that are external to localities, as well as the need to establish a minimum national standard in education.

The local share of financing basic education can be kept modest, and some federal-state share of these costs can be guaranteed for all schools, if local fiscal capacities are equalized on a relative basis. That is, the base federal-state share could be weighted by the ratio of each school district's wealth to the statewide and/or national average for school wealth. This weighting factor also could be used to adjust the federal share for differences in state fiscal capacities, by employing the ratio of each state's wealth to the national average.

Finally, Plan 2 possesses the disadvantage that it does not attempt to equalize for differences in fiscal efforts. Schools making greater than average efforts would go unrewarded, while those making below average efforts would not be penalized. Fiscal equity would call for suitable compensation for these differences. This equalization also could be best handled on a relative basis. The federal-state grants could be weighted by the ratio of each school's local fiscal effort (measured, say, by the tax rate on the full value of taxable property, or by taxes as a percentage of personal income) to the statewide and/or national average for local effort.

Again, this type of weighting factor could be used to adjust the federal share for differences in state fiscal efforts, taking the ratio of each state's effort to the national average for all states. The Syracuse University Research Corporation study of schools in New York indicates that central city schools would have their aid decreased if only school taxes were used to measure local effort, but that their share of aid would increase if total local (municipal and school) taxes were used to define local effort.[21] This most likely is true of central city schools in New Jersey and Washington, as well as in other

21. Syracuse University Research Corporation, *Final Report,* pp. ii-37 to 41.

states, and is the reason for the great concern about municipal overburden in school finances.

PLAN 3: FLAT GRANT LESS UNIFORM LOCAL SHARE BASED ON PERSONAL INCOME

This approach to federal-state financing of basic education costs differs from Plan 2 only in that personal income is used rather than taxable property as the basis for the uniform local share of these costs. The impacts of Plan 3 vary from those of Plan 2 only as county personal income levels vary from the full values of taxable property, and as 2 percent of personal income represents a different sum than a tax on property of 12 mills. The use of personal income rather than taxable property as the measure of local fiscal capacity, would reduce education aid more for urban than for rural areas;[22] the only major exceptions would be industrial and commercial enclaves, where property values greatly exceed the income of residents, and the exurban estate country, where resident incomes exceed property values.

Again, the financing method does promote equalization of fiscal capacities, but it ignores variations in fiscal efforts and fails to recognize differences in educational costs and needs. Plan 3 distributes more aid to all three states than does Plan 2 (New Jersey would experience an increase of about 40 percent, New York about 33 percent, and Washington about 35 percent), with the urbanized areas receiving a relatively larger share. This is most pronounced in New York and least so in New Jersey.

Unlike Plan 2, all counties would receive aid under Plan 3 (i.e., in no county does personal income equal or exceed $40,000 per pupil in average daily attendance). This guarantees that there will be at least some federal-state sharing of basic education costs. However, Plan 3 provides less aid than Plan 1 for all three states. In New Jersey and Washington, Plan 3 results in more funds than the actual federal-state aid received; the actual aid distributed is greater than that provided by Plan 3 in New York.

The advantages and disadvantages of federal-state financing under Plan 3 are quite similar to those already discussed for Plan 2. The only exceptions are that Plan 3 offers the advantages of (1) providing some federal-state funds in all counties, at least for the three states studied; and (2) using personal income, rather than taxable property, as the measure of local fiscal capacity (income is a better measure of current ability to pay than is wealth).

Again, the disadvantages of Plan 3 could be minimized if (1) per pupil enrollment figures were weighted for differences in program costs and needs; (2) the per pupil grants were weighted by the ratio of each state's share of

22. Ibid., p. iv-3, indicates this pattern for school districts in New York.

local costs relative to the national average; and (3) the grants were weighted by the respective ratios of each school district's fiscal capacity and effort to the statewide and/or national averages—the federal grant could be appropriately weighted by the ratio of each state's fiscal capacity and effort to the national averages for all states.

CONCLUSION

Ideally, any federal-state financing of basic education costs should reflect (1) the need to establish minimum standards for a foundation program in education; (2) educational costs and benefits that are external to localities and to states; and (3) the desire to guarantee adequate fiscal resources to provide a foundation program (one dimension of equality of educational opportunity). This can best be achieved by defining the minimum national standards in terms of per pupil levels of expenditures, suitably weighted to adjust for school district differences in program costs and needs. The respective state and federal shares of these expenditure levels should be based on the degree of educational benefit and cost externalities among localities within a state and among the states.

Greater equalization among the counties takes place when the flat grant is adjusted by deducting a uniform local share of education costs based on local fiscal capacity. With few exceptions, this equalization causes the urban areas to lose more aid than the rural ones. When the full value of taxable property is used as the measure of fiscal capacity, rather than personal income, some rural/resort counties would receive no aid at all. Their very high per pupil values of taxable property eliminate any federal-state financing. This result runs counter to the very purpose of federal-state assumption of at least some education costs when a minimum standard in education is desired, and when cost and benefit externalities must be taken into account. Basing the uniform local share of costs on personal income, rather than taxable property, is somewhat more beneficial to urban than rural areas. In almost all cases, counties would receive more aid when income rather than property is used.

19 Noel M. Edelson

Budgetary Outcomes in a Referendum Setting

Consider a local government which levies taxes on all its constituents (voting units) and supplies services that are consumed in equal amount by all who use them. We call such services "pure communal goods," in contrast to "pure public goods," and assume that doubling the population served with a constant budget halves the amount received by each user. This will be the case either if there are no economies of scale in purchasing the communal good or if all communities are of sufficient size to have exploited such economies of scale as do exist. Clearly, efficiency considerations favor individual rather than collective purchase unless the good involves either economies of scale or externalities.

The size of the government budget is determined by "sincere" majority voting: each voter proposes his choice of budget based on his preferences and tax price. Voting equilibrium occurs at a budget level where more than 50 percent of the voters oppose any further increase. This means that the preferences of the median voter are decisive, where the identity of that voter is determined by the distribution of incomes and tax burdens. This model would predict budgetary outcomes accurately even if referenda were not actually held, provided decisions are made by elected officials responsive to majority rule (e.g., school boards).

We assume that (1) taxes levied by the local government have a constant income elasticity; (2) the income distribution of voters is 2-parameter lognormal; (3) preferences can be represented by marginal valuation curves with constant income and price elasticities. A tax base that permits deductions

Space limitations prevented Part II of "Budgetary Outcomes in a Referendum Setting" from appearing in this volume. Part II is available from the author on request, and is entitled "Implications of the Voting Model for Property Taxes and Public Education." The specific topics considered are: full state funding of public education; tax credits for parents of nonpublic school pupils; and limiting federal deductibility of state taxes and mortgage interest payments to the larger of $700 or a tax credit of $25.

The paper is related to the work of Yoram Barzel, "Two Propositions on the Optimum Level of Producing Collective Goods," *Public Choice,* 6 (Spring 1969), pp. 31-37. However, Robin Barlow, "Efficiency Aspects of Local School Finance," *Journal of Political Economy,* 78 (September/October 1970), 1028-40, appears to have been the first to confront the model with actual data.

and exemptions is incompatible with assumption 1, but, except for homestead concessions occasionally extended to the elderly, a household's local property taxes are not directly affected by its socio-economic characteristics. The lognormality assumption is not unduly restrictive, since similar qualitative results could be obtained with other positively skewed distributions. Furthermore, if the domain of the 2-parameter lognormal is felt to be excessive, it is possible to restrict the domain to strictly positive and finite incomes without excessively complicating the mathematics. Marginal valuation curves are troublesome in that they are assumed to depend on pretax income, i.e., the amount a voter is willing to pay for an additional unit of output is independent of his tax liability for previous units. Such an assumption requires a constant marginal utility of income over the range of budgetary outcomes under consideration.

VOTING EQUILIBRIUM WHEN ALL VOTERS ARE USERS

Let the price of the local government service be unity. Output per voter is $q = Q/N$, where Q is the size of the government budget and N the number of voters. Local taxes levied on a voter with income y when output per voter is q are

(1) $$t(q,y) = \tau(q)B(y) = \tau(q)ky^b,$$

where
$\tau(q)$ = nominal tax rate
$B(y)$ = tax base of a voter with income y
k = a constant
b = income elasticity of the tax base

We would expect k to be larger for real property taxes in rural communities, since real property is a larger fraction of total wealth for farmers.[1] The marginal valuation curve is assumed to be Cobb-Douglas in income and output.

(2) $$E(q,y) = Vy^{a/n} q^{-1/n},$$

where
E = marginal valuation of an additional unit of output per voter, as perceived by a voter with income y.
n = absolute value of the price elasticity of demand
a = income elasticity of demand

Let the natural logarithm of y, denoted $ln\ y$, be normally distributed with

1. For this reason equal assessment ratios may cause horizontal inequities in communities that are not exclusively agricultural or residential. Bucks County, a formerly agricultural area north of Philadelphia, is rapidly becoming suburban. New residents, typically wealthy commuters, are paying property taxes based upon current market value of land and residential structures; older residents, typically farmers, have not had their real property revalued for several years. New residents are pressing for a reassessment on the grounds that older residents are not paying their fair share. Equal assessment ratios, especially if farm land were valued at its price as residential land, would mean larger taxes relative to total wealth for farmers.

mean u and variance s^2. Let $\exp\{x\}$ denote e^x. As is well known,[2] the modal, mean, and median values of income are $\exp\{u-s^2\}$, $\exp\{u+\frac{1}{2}s^2\}$ and $\exp\{u\}$ respectively. The coefficient of variation of income equals $\exp\{s^2\}-1$.

If local taxes must cover all local expenditures,

$$(3)\quad Q = Nq = N\tau(q)k \int_0^\infty y^b f(y)dy,$$

where N is the number of voters and $f(y)$ the density of voters with income y. Since y is lognormally distributed,

$$\int_0^\infty y^b f(y)dy = \exp\{bu+\tfrac{1}{2}b^2 s^2\}$$

Therefore, the nominal tax rate, $\tau(q)$, equals $q\,[k\,\exp\{bu+\frac{1}{2}b^2 s^2\}]$. The gross tax price of an additional unit of output per voter for a voter with income y is

$$(4)\quad dt(q,y)/dq = y^b / \int_0^\infty y^b f(y)dy = y^b \exp\{-bu-\tfrac{1}{2}b^2 s^2\}$$

The marginal social cost of dq is Ndq, since the cost of supplying a unit of output to each of N voters is N times the market price of unity. Gross tax price equals unity for a voter with income $\exp\{u+\frac{1}{2}bs^2\}$, which is larger than the median income if $b>0$ and smaller than the mean income if $0<b<1$.

The most preferred budget for a voter with income y, $q^*(y)$, is one at which net tax price (gross tax price less reduction in federal income tax liability) equals marginal valuation, i.e.,

$$[1-j(y)]\,[dt(q,y)/dq] = E[q^*(y),y],$$

where $j(y)$ is the voter's marginal federal income tax rate. For practical purposes $1-j(y)$ can be approximated by the schedule

$$1-j(y) = \begin{cases} 1 & y < \underline{y} \\ my^{-r} & \underline{y} \le y \le \bar{y} \\ m\bar{y}^{-r} & y > \bar{y} \end{cases}$$

where $\underline{y}$ is the minimum income at which itemizing becomes worthwhile and $1 - m\bar{y}^{-r}$ is the maximum effective marginal tax rate. $\underline{y}$ is quite low for a homeowner, because he can deduct mortgage interest payments as well as state and local taxes.

Letting $\underline{y} < y = \exp\{u+\delta s^2\} < \bar{y}$ we see that net tax price equals $m \exp\{-ru+(b-r)\delta s^2-\frac{1}{2}b^2 s^2\}$ and

$$(5)\quad q^*(y) = (V/m)^n \exp\{(a+nr)u+[a-n(b-r)]\delta s^2+\tfrac{1}{2}nb^2 s^2\}$$

The function $q^*(y)$ jumps at $\underline{y}$ because net tax price is discontinuous at that

2. J. Aitchison and J. A. C. Brown, *The Lognormal Distribution* (Cambridge: Cambridge University Press, 1957).

point. Net tax price increases with income above the lower bound if $b > r$. Voters with incomes larger than $\underline{y}$ will have different preferred budgets unless $b = a/n + r$. Since a is unlikely to be much less than unity and n greater than unity for local public services, b would have to exceed unity for $q^*(y)$ to be independent of y. Local taxes are generally thought to be regressive and state taxes at best proportional with respect to income. Therefore, we assume that $b < a/n + r$, which implies (1) $q^*(y)$ is an increasing function of y; (2) the coefficient of variation of $q^*(y)$ is a decreasing function of b.

Voting equilibrium occurs at a budget per voter, $\hat{q}$, where $\hat{q}$ is the preferred budget for a voter with median income, $\exp\{u\}$. Since $\delta = 0$ for the median voter, making this substitution in equation (5) we find that

(6a) $\hat{q} = V^n \exp\{au + \frac{1}{2}nb^2 s^2\}$ if the median voter uses the standard deduction for his federal income tax

(6b) $\hat{q} = (V/m)^n \exp\{(a + nr)u + \frac{1}{2}nb^2 s^2\}$ if the median voter itemizes deductions for his federal income tax.

Median income is currently between \$10,000 and \$11,000 for the United States as a whole, which is below the level at which itemizing becomes widespread. The assumption underlying (6a) is probably realistic for urban areas, whereas (6b) is relevant for wealthy suburbs. Holding u constant, majority rule will select a larger budget per voter the more dispersed the income distribution, i.e., the larger is s^2. This is because net tax price of the median voter, $m \exp\{-ru - \frac{1}{2}b^2 s^2\}$, is a decreasing function of s^2. Although that particular expression for net tax price depends upon the assumption of lognormality, the result that dispersion lowers tax price for the median voter is quite robust for positively skewed distributions.

Equations (6a) and (6b) have implications for studies of local public expenditures in socialist versus capitalist countries and for estimates of the income elasticity of demand. There is no a priori reason to expect that expenditures on communal goods will be larger in (democratic) socialist countries than in (democratic) capitalist countries. Socialist countries are likely to have larger values for r and b^2, but smaller values for s^2 than capitalist countries. With regard to estimates of the income elasticity of demand, studies using cross-section data have not allowed for the effect of r and s^2. The true regression equation

$$\ln \hat{q} = n \ln(V/m) + (a + nr)u + \frac{1}{2}nb^2 s^2 + \text{error term}$$

requires nonlinear estimation of a and n. Even if r were small enough to be neglected, a biased estimate of a is obtained when s^2 is omitted from a linear regression of $\ln \hat{q}$ on u. Since u and s^2 are probably positively correlated, omitting s^2 imparts an upward bias to the estimate for a. Another specification error is to use mean, rather than median, income as the sole explanatory variable.

In that case the dependent variable is regressed on $u + \frac{1}{2}s^2$, which is a combination of the two correct explanatory variables with weights 1 and n/b^2 respectively. Simply knowing that u and s^2 are positively correlated does not suffice to predict the direction of bias.

The voting equilibrium, by constraining everyone to consume the same amount of the local government service, introduces allocative inefficiencies if an individual can purchase Q at the same price as the community. Voters with incomes above the median receive less government services than they would like given their tax prices, and poor voters receive more. Collective consumption can be justified on resource allocation grounds only if the group can purchase services at a significantly lower price than can individual voters.

Consider the case where individuals are able to purchase Q from private producers at a price of unity.[3] Define "fiscal surplus" to be the difference between consumer surplus achieved at the voting equilibrium and consumer surplus achieved at individual equilibrium. Fiscal surplus is negative for high income voters, since net tax price exceeds unity for $y > \exp\{u+(1/b-r)$ $(b^2/2 - rn/s^2)\}$ and $\hat{q} < q^*(y)$ for $y > \exp\{u\}$. The decrease in consumer surplus could be limited to

$$[my^{(b-r)}\exp\{-bu-\tfrac{1}{2}b^2 s^2\} - 1]\,\hat{q}$$

if a high-income voter could purchase from private producers $q^*(y) - \hat{q}$ units at an average price of unity. For elementary and secondary education, however, this is unlikely owing to the increasing opportunity cost of a student's time after the regular school day. The alternatives are probably to switch to a private school altogether or to move out of the tax district.

A low income voter can generally expect to receive a positive fiscal surplus despite the fact that $\hat{q} > q^*(y)$, since his net tax price is below unity. Fiscal surplus for a voter with income $y = \exp\{u- \gamma s^2\} < y$ is area $ABCD$ minus area CEF in Figure 19.1. Integrating under the marginal valuation curve we find that

$$(7) \quad \text{fiscal surplus}/y = [1 - \exp\{-bs^2(\gamma+\tfrac{1}{2}b)\}]\,V''\exp\{(a-1)$$
$$(n-\gamma s^2)\} + V''\exp\{(a-1)u+(n-1)\tfrac{1}{2}b^2 s^2\}\,[g(\gamma) - h(\gamma)]$$

$$\text{where} \quad g(\gamma) = \exp\{-(a/n-1)\gamma s^2\}\left[\exp\{-[(n-1)/n]a\gamma s^2\right.$$
$$\left. - (n-1)\tfrac{1}{2}b^2 s^2\} - 1\right]$$
$$h(\gamma) = \exp\{(1-b)\gamma s^2\}\,[1 - \exp\{-\gamma s^2(a-nb)\}].$$

3. While there are doubtless economies of scale in purchase of materials and monitoring program content in a standardized school district, proponents of private education claim that creativity and innovation are stifled by school board bureaucracy. On balance it is not clear a priori that private schools must cost more per dollar of educational value added. A recent study [Cohn, 1968], finds no evidence of substantial economies of scale as measured by costs per pupil across school districts.

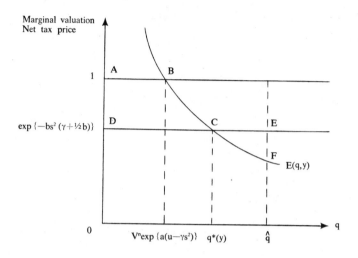

Figure 19.1. Fiscal surplus for low income voters.

If b is large enough this expression will be positive, although voters with incomes just above $\underline{y}$ will be better off than those just below $\underline{y}$. Fiscal surplus per dollar of income increases with income for reasonable parameter values, implying that middle income voters get the largest relative gain. A corollary is that, contrary to accepted doctrine, low-income voters may not experience a rise in fiscal surplus if high-income voters enter their tax district. Fiscal surplus will decrease if the reduction in tax price is more than offset by an increase in q.

Fiscal surplus should be capitalized into prices of real property, since a homeowner receives not only residential services, which depend upon the physical characteristics of his property, but also the vector of communal goods provided by his local government. Oates[4] has presented evidence from a cross-section of northern New Jersey communities that, *ceteris paribus,* median home value varies inversely with effective property tax rate and directly with public education expenditures per pupil. He also finds that, holding median family income constant, the regression coefficient for the variable "percentage of families in the community with income below $3000 per year" is positive. Oates explains this result by the fact that low-income families are more likely to reside in rented dwellings; consequently, median family income understates median family income of homeowners. An alternative explanation is that, for a given u, percentage of low-income families is a proxy for s^2. With

4. Wallace E. Oates, "The Effects of Property Taxes and Local Public Spending on Property Values: An Empirical Study of Tax Capitalization and the Tiebout Hypothesis," *Journal of Political Economy,* 77, no. 6 (November/December 1969), pp. 957–71.

a positively skewed income distribution net tax price of the median voter is smaller, and hence his fiscal surplus larger, the larger is s^2.

Our model suggests another test of the capitalization hypothesis. Modest homes in heterogeneous school districts should command a price above the value of their physical characteristics, as measured by the value of a similar home in a homogeneous school district, and vice versa for very expensive homes. Two other potentially verifiable hypotheses are that (1) social groups with particularly strong preferences for quality education spend a comparatively large fraction of their income on housing; (2) since fiscal surplus of the median voter is an increasing function of u, teachers in wealthy, homogeneous school districts have an especially strong incentive to form closed-shop unions. Collective bargaining in such a labor market provides teachers with a means by which they can appropriate some of the residents' fiscal surplus in the form of high wages.

A model in which voters choose the budget for a single good financed by a single tax source is an accurate description of most school districts. In some, however, only a fraction of the local property tax is earmarked for public schools, the remainder going to the city; furthermore, the public does vote for a vector of other communal goods, such as police, fire and sanitation services, when it approves the regular city budget. Let us therefore consider briefly a voting model where the budget consists of various communal goods in fixed proportions. Specifying in advance the shares of individual services adds another source of inefficiency, but imposing such a constraint may be less costly than incurring the time and information costs of voting for separate budgets.

Suppose that there are two communal goods, q_1 and q_2, which have budgetary shares θ and $1-\theta$ respectively. Voting for an additional \$1 in local taxes provides an additional θ units of q_1 and $1-\theta$ units of q_2. The preferred budget for a voter with income y occurs where a weighted average of marginal valuations equals his net tax price. If $\underline{y} < y = \exp\{u+\delta s^2\} < \bar{y}$,

$$\theta V_1 \exp\{(u+\delta s^2)a_1/n_1\} q_1^{-1/n_1} + (1-\theta) V_2 \exp\{(u+\delta s^2)a_2/n_2\}$$

$$\left[[(1-\theta)/\theta]q_1 \right]^{-1/n_2} = \exp\{-ru+(b-r)\delta s^2 - \tfrac{1}{2}b^2 s^2\}$$

Note that the voter would choose to consume services in the ratio

$$(q_2/q_1)^* = [V_1^{n_1}/V_2^{n_2}] y^{a_2-a_1}$$

and that, if $(1-\theta)/\theta = (q_2/q_1)^*$, the same budget is adopted with "composite" or separate voting.

Assume that q_1 and q_2 have the same price elasticity of demand, n. Substituting $\delta = 0$ for the median voter,

$$\hat{q}_1 = \exp\{n(ru+\tfrac{1}{2}b^2s^2\}\,[\theta\,V_1\exp\{ua_1/n\}$$
$$+ \theta^{1/n}(1-\theta)^{1-1/n}\,V_2\exp\{ua_2/n\}]^n.$$

The total budget, $\hat{B}$, is given by

$$\hat{B} = \hat{q}_1/\theta$$
$$= \exp\{n(ru+\tfrac{1}{2}b^2s^2\}\,[\theta^{1-1/n}\,V_1\exp\{ua_1/n\}$$
$$+ (1-\theta)^{1-1/n}\,V_2\exp\{ua_2/n\}]^n.$$

If politicians (or municipal workers) wished to maximize the size of the total budget, which value for θ would they select? It is easily seen that

$$d\hat{B}/d\theta \gtreqless 0, \text{ as } (1-\theta)/\theta \gtreqless (q_2/q_1)^*, \text{ if } n > 1$$

i.e., if the demand curve is elastic the budgetary shares should be fixed in the ratio preferred by voters. Since $d\hat{q}_2/d\theta$ is greater than or less than zero according as $-\hat{B}+(1-\theta)d\hat{B}/d\theta$ is greater than or less than zero, θ should be smaller (larger) than its optimal value as perceived by voters if the goal is to maximize $\hat{q}_2(\hat{q}_1)$. When n is everywhere less than unity, the total budget is maximized by setting θ arbitrarily close to 0 or 1. This is a consequence of the Cobb-Douglas marginal valuation curve, where $E(q,y)$ gets arbitrarily large as q_1 or q_2 approache zero. If the demand curve is inelastic in a neighborhood of $(q_2/q_1)^*$, the value for $(1-\theta)/\theta$ that maximizes the total budget will not equal the preferred ratio of government services.

Voting Equilibrium and Pareto Optimality When All Voters Are Users

Define a constrained Pareto optimal budget to be a level of services per voter, q^*, which is the socially efficient value for q given that all voters must consume an equal amount of the communal good. q^* is determined by the condition that the weighted sum of marginal valuations equals the social cost of an additional unit of output per voter, i.e.,

(8) $\int_0^\infty Vy^{a/n}\,q^{*\,-1/n}\,f(y)dy = 1$

Equation (8) implies that

(9) $q^* = V^n\exp\{au+\tfrac{1}{2}(a^2/n^2)s^2\}$

If the median voter uses the standard 10 percent deduction for his federal income tax, using (6a) we see that

(10a) $q*/\hat{q} \gtreqless 1$, as $a/n \gtreqless b$

Note that if $a/n = b$, not only do the voting equilibrium and constrained Pareto optimum coincide, but all voters using the standard deduction will have as their most preferred budget $q*$. Since it is likely that a/n exceeds b (cf. p. 282), communities which pay for all of their communal goods are likely to have budgets below $q*$ if their median incomes are less than \$13,000-\$15,000 (the income range in which itemizing becomes common). On the other hand, if the median voter itemizes,

(10b) $q*/\hat{q} \gtreqless 1$, as $m \, \exp\{-ru+\tfrac{1}{2}s^2[(a^2/n^2)-b^2]\} \gtreqless 1$

If s^2 is small enough and community median income high enough, majority rule will select a budget above the constrained Pareto optimal level.[5]

Given the likelihood that $\hat{q} \neq q*$, it might be thought that the way to achieve an unconstrained Pareto optimum would be to allow a continuum of homogeneous local communities to develop. Within each community of size $Nf(y)dy$, each voter would have the same tax price and $q*(y) = \hat{q}(y)$. Net tax price would be less than unity in communities with incomes above y, however. Therefore such localities would adopt budgets larger than the Pareto optimal level, since at $q*(y)$ marginal valuation equals $1-j(y)$, which is less than the marginal social cost of output, unity. Not only would there be excessive spending on ordinary communal goods, but wealthy communities would have an incentive to transfer private goods to the public sector. Expanding the range of local government activity is worthwhile when the loss due to joint purchase (higher gross purchase price, public choice of brand or quantity different from an individual's preferences) is offset by the difference between market price and net tax price.

Another implication is that removing the tax deductibility privilege would have a different impact on wealthy voters in heterogeneous communities than on wealthy voters in homogeneous communities. If the median voter does not itemize, disallowing itemizing has no direct effect on $\hat{q}$; consequently, the decrease in fiscal surplus to a wealthy voter in a heterogeneous community is simply $j(y)$ multiplied by his local taxes, $\hat{q}y^b \exp\{-bu-\tfrac{1}{2}b^2s^2\}$. Wealthy, homogeneous communities will decrease public spending, so the decrease in fiscal surplus is less than $j(y)$ multiplied by existing output per voter. Reasonable parameter values imply that the latter voter will suffer the greater absolute loss in fiscal surplus. Disallowing itemizing would therefore reduce

5. How likely is it that $\hat{q} > q*$? Nationally, $u \approx 9.3$ and $s^2 \approx 0.14$. u could easily be 10 (implying a median income around \$20,200) and $s^2 = 0.07$ in a wealthy, homogeneous suburb. Since the *effective* marginal federal income tax rate is about 0.13 at \$15,000 and reaches an upper bound of 0.35-0.40, r could be as small as 0.1 and $m \approx 2.2$. In that case $\hat{q}$ would exceed $q*$ if $5.5 > (a^2/n^2) - b^2$. This condition is satisfied if $a \approx 1$ and $n < 0.40$.

the difference between prices of a high quality home in exclusive versus mixed communities.[6]

Of course, if creating perfectly homogeneous communities significantly increased local expenditures, federal taxes would have to be raised to keep the same federal deficit. A federal tax increase should, *ceteris paribus,* shift down marginal valuation curves based on pretax income. This point is especially important with regard to federal and state matching grants, which are used to stimulate spending on communal goods in localities where $\hat{q}$ is felt to be too low. When each locality constitutes a small fraction of the grantor's tax base, voters will disregard the impact of their own budget on revenue needed to finance matching grants. If n is large enough, the divergence between average and marginal tax prices can create a voting equilibrium where a majority of voters would prefer to lower the matching rate.

Consider a heterogeneous community which is one of many in a federal union. Suppose that $a/n > b$, so $\hat{q} < q^*$. The voting equilibrium will be a constrained Pareto optimum if the price of output is decreased to $\gamma < 1$, i.e.,

$$-ln\ \gamma = \tfrac{1}{2}s^2(a^2 - n^2 b^2)$$

The higher level government agrees to match local expenditures at rate $(1-\gamma)/\gamma$, with the revenue coming from a tax base which has an income elasticity of unity. Let the new voting equilibrium have a union-wide average budget per voter $\tilde{q}$. Average federal taxes per voter in our community are

$$\tilde{\tau}\ _0\!\!\int^{\infty} yf(y)dy = (1-\gamma)\lambda\tilde{q}$$

where γ exceeds (is less than) unity according as the community's tax base is larger than (smaller than) the average community tax base.

Income after federal taxes, y_t, for a voter with gross income y is

$$y_t = [1 - (1-\gamma)\lambda\tilde{q}\ \exp\{-u-\tfrac{1}{2}s^2\}]y$$
$$= \psi(\gamma,\tilde{q})y$$

6. Let $\hat{q}_1$ be the voting equilibrium budget per voter with itemizing and $\hat{q}_2$ the voting equilibrium budget per voter when net tax price is unity. The loss experienced by a wealthy voter in a homogeneous community is

$$j(y)\hat{q}_2 + \ _{\hat{q}_2}\!\!\int^{\hat{q}_1} E(q,y)dq - [1-j(y)]\ (\hat{q}_1-\hat{q}_2)$$

This loss exceeds $j(y)\hat{q}_2 = j(y)V^n y^a$; the decrease in fiscal surplus will be larger for the wealthy voter in a homogeneous community if

$$j(y)V^n y^a > j(y)y^b \exp\ \{(a-b)u-\tfrac{1}{2}b^2s^2(1-n)\}$$

Letting $y = \exp\{u+\delta s^2\}$ the above inequality is satisfied if

y_t is lognormally distributed with mean $u_t = ln\ \psi\,(\gamma,\bar{q}) + u$ and variance $s_t^2 = s^2$. Assuming the median voter does not itemize, $\hat{q}_t$ is determined by

$$\hat{q}_t = (V/\gamma)^n \exp\{au_t + \tfrac{1}{2}nb^2 s_t^2\}$$

This voting equilibrium exceeds the one where sharing rate is zero provided $\psi(\gamma,\bar{q})^a > \gamma^n$. Average tax price of a voter with income $y = \exp\{u - \delta s^2\}$ is

$$(1-\gamma)(\tilde{q}/\hat{q}_t)\exp\{-\delta s^2 - \tfrac{1}{2}s^2\} + \gamma\,\exp\{-b\delta s^2 - \tfrac{1}{2}b^2 s^2\}$$

Since $b < 1$, average tax price is lower when $\gamma < 1$ provided $\bar{q}/\hat{q}_t$ is not much larger than unity.

Fiscal surplus for a given voter may be smaller than before matching, however, if the matching rate is large enough and b large enough. Figure 19.2 displays fiscal surplus for the median voter, which is area ABC before matching as compared with area LDF minus area DGH after matching.[7] The attempt to impose upper bounds on federal contributions to state programs, e.g., Medicaid and state social services, may be a response to decreases in fiscal surplus caused

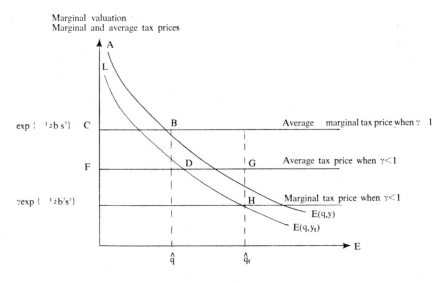

Figure 19.2. Fiscal surplus for the median voter before and after matching.

$$1 - n + (2\delta/b)\,[(a/b)-1] > 0,$$

which in turn is satisfied if price elasticity is no greater than unity and $a > b$.

7. $E(q,y_t)$ will be less than average tax price at the old voting equilibrium if

$$\psi(\gamma,\bar{q})^a < (1-\gamma)(\bar{q}/\hat{q}_t)\exp\{-\tfrac{1}{2}s^2(1-b^2)\} + \gamma$$

by overly generous matching rates. On the other hand, owners of factors used in the production of communal goods should favor larger sharing rates, since these reduce the elasticity of derived demand at the local level.

VOTING EQUILIBRIUM WHEN SOME VOTERS ARE NONUSERS

It becomes necessary to specify more precisely the nature of the marginal valuation function when the communal good is not consumed by all voters. $E(q,y)$ is the sum of marginal benefits a voter derives from having an additional unit of output per voter available for his own use, plus the marginal benefits he derives from knowing that users in his community are also receiving an additional unit. Call the former direct marginal benefits and the latter indirect marginal benefits. A voter has ownership rights in both, since q is supplied to all users and total benefits are included in fiscal surplus.

Because of tax benefit capitalization, a voter may favor a positive budget for a communal good which yields him neither direct nor indirect benefits. In fact, if a nonusing egoist were planning to move in the near future, he would vote for the most preferred budget of the typical customer for his home. The voting equilibrium gives a nonuser a wealth increment equal to the larger of (1) his own fiscal surplus; (2) the product of fiscal surplus for a user with similar income and the proportion of such users in the community, discounted to the expected date of sale of the nonuser's home. Nonusers will be worst off if they constitute a significant minority in the community. The voting equilibrium, which is determined by users' preferences, is likely to give a nonuser a negative fiscal surplus; and there is a good chance that, when a nonuser decides to move, he will be selling his home to another nonuser. Price supports have a similar impact on small, inefficient farmers. The lion's share of current benefits goes to large, efficient farmers, but the benefits from price supports are capitalized into the market value of farm land. The small farmer can realize a better return on his equity by selling the farm and investing the proceeds at the going rate of return.

Suppose that direct marginal valuation for a voter with income y is $Vy^{a/n}q^{-1/n}$ and indirect marginal valuation $G\pi Vy^{a/n}q^{-1/n}$. π is the proportion of voters who are users, and G a constant which measures one's concern for the welfare of others. Making G a constant means that voters place the same value on their neighbors' consumption regardless of their neighbors' incomes. The marginal valuation curve for a user with income y is $(1+G\pi)Vy^{a/n}q^{-1/n}$, and $G\pi Vy^{a/n}q^{-1/n}$ the marginal valuation curve for a nonuser.

Since there are only πN users, whereas all N voters are taxed, taxes paid by a voter with income y are $\pi qy^b \exp\{-bu-\tfrac{1}{2}b^2s^2\}$. Disregarding, for simplicity, the itemizing of local taxes, the most preferred budget for a user with income y is

(11) $q_u^*(y) = [(1+G\pi/\pi]^n V^n y^{a-nb} \exp\{nbu+\tfrac{1}{2}nb^2 s^2\}$

q_u^* is a decreasing function of π, because decreasing the proportion of users reduces tax price for an additional unit of q but reduces only the indirect part of marginal benefits. A nonuser with equal income will have a most preferred budget, $q_{nu}^*(y)$, where

(12) $q_{nu}^*(y) = G^n V^n y^{a-nb} \exp\{nbu+\tfrac{1}{2}nb^2 s^2\}$

$q_{nu}^*(y)$ is independent of π, since the tax price reduction from exploiting non-users is exactly offset by the reduction in indirect benefits. Consequently, $q_{nu}^*(y) = [G\pi/(1+G\pi)]^n q_u^*(y)$.

We take as our benchmark the preferred budgets of voters when $\pi = 1$, the situation of universal users. When $\pi < 1$, a user with income y will vote like a universal user with income

$$[(1+G\pi)/(1+G)\pi]^{n/a-nb} y > y$$

A nonuser with income y will vote like a universal user with income

$$[G/(1+G)]^{n/a-nb} y < y$$

Voting Equilibrium When Nonusers Are Wealthy Voters

If wealthy voters are unable to supplement public output with private pur-chases, it is worthwhile for them to become nonusers if the consumer surplus from $q^*(y) - \hat{q}$ exceeds private price times $\hat{q}$.[8] This condition is illustrated in Figure 19.3, where area ABC is larger than area $ODB\hat{q}$ when the unit cost of privately purchased output is p.

Let y_1^h be the income at which the voter is indifferent between being a user or nonuser. y_1^h is an increasing function of n and b and a decreasing function of a and s^2, because of the effect of these parameters on $\hat{q}$. A proportion of the community,

$$1 - \pi_1 = \int_{y_1^h}^{\infty} f(y)\,dy\,,$$

8. Noel M. Edelson, "Efficiency Aspects of Local School Finance," Symposium on Efficiency of Local School Finance, *Journal of Political Economy*, 81, no. 1 (January/February, 1973), pp. 158-73, and Yoram Barzel, "Private Schools and Public School Finance," ibid., pp. 174-86.

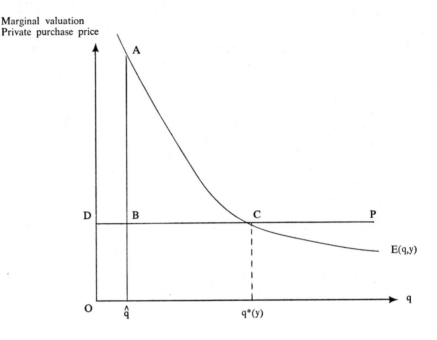

Figure 19.3. Private purchase preferable to communal consumption.

advocates budgets based on the marginal valuation functions of nonusers, while voters with incomes between zero and y_1^h advocate budgets $q_u^*(y)$. An interesting question is whether the new voting equilibrium has a larger or smaller budget per user. If $\hat{q}_1$ is larger than its initial value the lower bound for income of nonusers will be higher than y_1^h, and nonusers will be an even smaller fraction of the community than $1-\pi_1$. But if $\hat{q}_1$ is smaller than $\hat{q}$, there is a possibility that the voting process will unravel, i.e., that there will be a mutually reinforcing sequence of defections to private output and decreases in $\hat{q}_i$, until only a small group of low-income voters remain users.

What is a sufficient condition for $\hat{q}_1 \geq \hat{q}$? Nonusers with incomes larger than $\psi^{-1}\exp\{u\}$, where $\psi = [G/(1+G)]^{n/a-nb}$, have preferred budgets larger than $\hat{q}$, so only nonusers with incomes in the interval $(y_1^h, \psi^{-1}\exp\{u\})$ tend to lower the voting equilibrium. But, because of the price effect on users, voters with incomes in the interval $(\Phi^{-1}\exp\{u\}, \exp\{u\})$, where $\Phi = [(1+G\pi)/(1+G)\pi]^{n/a-nb}$, will have preferred budgets larger than $\hat{q}$. The new median income, $\hat{y}_1$, is determined by the condition

$$(13) \quad \int_{\hat{y}_1}^{y_1^h} f(y;u+ln\ \Phi,s^2)dy + \int_{y_1^h}^{\infty} f(y;u+ln\ \psi,s^2)dy = 0.5$$

The new voting equilibrium will be as large as $\hat{q}$ if

(14) $\int_{\Phi^{-1}\exp\{u\}}^{\exp\{u\}} f(y)dy > \int_{y_1^h}^{\psi^{-1}\exp\{u\}} f(y)dy$

Since the lognormal distribution is skewed to the right, a sufficient condition for (14) is that

(15) $\exp\{-u\}\, y_1^h > \Phi^{-1} + \psi^{-1} - 1$

Although the right-hand side of (15) decreases with n, so does $\exp\{-u\}y_1^h$. Therefore, a small enough price elasticity is not a sufficient condition for the budget to be at least as large as $\hat{q}$. What is apparently required is that G, the measure of one's concern for others, be large enough. A U-shaped income distribution significantly increases the likelihood that unravelling occurs. The characterization, "a community consisting of many low-income voters, some very wealthy voters, and virtually no middle class," accurately describes America's urban centers. If an equilibrium has not yet been reached in those communities, a voting model predicts downward pressure on urban center budgets for communal goods where private substitutes exist.

Voting Equilibrium When Nonusers Are Drawn Uniformly from All Income Groups

Voters may prefer to purchase services privately not only on efficiency grounds but also because of ideological or religious reasons. In the case of elementary and secondary education, for example, nearly all private school pupils are in religious schools. When nonuse of a communal good is dictated by one's conscience, it is more reasonable to assume that nonusers are drawn randomly from the community rather than concentrated in the upper tail of the income distribution.

Let the proportion of users be π and the proportion of nonusers $1-\pi$. Since users with income y vote like universal users with income Φy, where Φ is defined on the previous page, the income distribution of voter-users is lognormal with mean $u + \ln \Phi > u$ and variance s^2; for nonusers the distribution is lognormal with mean $u + \ln \psi < u$. Denote $\ln \Phi$ by $\epsilon_u s$ and $\ln \psi$ by $-\epsilon_{nu}s$. The income of the median voter, $\exp\{u - \rho s\}$, is defined by

(16) $\pi \int_{\exp\{u-\rho s\}}^{\infty} f(y; u+\epsilon_u s, s^2)dy$

$+ (1-\pi) \int_{\exp\{u-\rho s\}}^{\infty} f(y; u-\epsilon_{nu} s, s^2)dy = 0.5.$

The voting equilibrium will be less than, equal to, or greater than the voting equilibrium with universal users as ρ is positive, zero, or negative.[9] ρ is more likely to be positive the smaller n and G are.

Suppose that $\frac{2}{3}$ of the community are users and $\frac{1}{3}$ nonusers. The standard deviation of $\ln y$ is currently about 0.38 for the United States income distribution. Assuming that $\psi = 0.8$ and $\Phi = 1.08$, i.e., that G is relatively large and n relatively small, $\epsilon_u = 0.2$ and $\epsilon_{nu} = 0.60$. The fact that the quantiles of the lognormal distribution are $\xi_j = \exp\{u + w_j s\}$, where w_j is the quantile of order j for the unit normal distribution,[10] enables us to solve (16) for ρ.

The quantile for users is $-(\rho + \epsilon_u)$ and $(\epsilon_{nu} - \rho)$ for nonusers. ρ is found to be 0.06, implying that about 60 percent of users and 30 percent of nonusers have incomes larger than the new median income, $y = \exp\{u - 0.06s\}$. The majority rule budget per user with $\pi = \frac{2}{3}$ is $\exp\{-(a - nb)(0.16)s^2\}$ times as large as the majority rule budget when all voters are users. On the other hand, if $\pi = 0.8$, $\Phi = 1.16$ and $\psi = 0.77$, $\rho = -0.19$. About 58 percent of users and 20 percent of nonusers have incomes higher than the new median income, $y = \exp\{u + 0.19s\} = \exp\{u + \frac{1}{2}s^2\}$, the mean of the income distribution. The majority rule budget per user when $\pi = 0.8$ is $\exp\{(a - nb)(.5)s^2\}$ times as large as the majority rule budget when all voters are users.

It is possible to get an expression for $d\rho/d\pi$ by implicit differentiation of (16), but that effort provides only modest gains in understanding: signing all the terms of that derivative seems to yield nothing more than the result, obtainable from intuition alone, that increasing the proportion of nonusers will decrease output per user unless n is quite large. What is clear is that most nonusers will obtain more of the communal good than they desire. Nonusers can reduce the negative fiscal surplus by (1) moving to communities where median income and hence $\hat{q}$ is lower, (2) engaging in vote-trading with other voter blocs so as to reduce $\hat{q}$.

9. It is not clear whether, for a given proportion of nonusers, the majority rule budget when all nonusers are drawn randomly from a lognormal distribution will be larger or smaller than the majority rule budget when all nonusers have incomes larger than some lower bound. Manipulating (13) and (16) it can be seen that the two voting equilibria will have the same median income, $\hat{y}_1$, if

$$\frac{\pi}{1 - \pi} = \frac{\int_{\hat{y}_1}^{y_1^h} [f(y; u + \ln \Phi, s^2) + f(y; u + \ln \psi, s^2)] dy}{\int_{y_1^h}^{\infty} [f(y; u + \ln \Phi, s^2) + f(y; u + \ln \psi, s^2)] dy}$$

We conjecture that there are values for G and s^2 which permit this equation to hold. This result appears to be counterintuitive, since one might expect that defection of high-income voters should depress the voting equilibrium more than random defection. The reason this is not the case is because some high-income voters, even when they become nonusers, prefer budgets larger than the voting equilibrium with "universal users."

10. Aitchison and Brown, *Lognormal Distribution*.

Whether vote-trading is more effective at the local level or at the state and federal level depends on the proportion of nonusers at various governmental levels, the value of their votes on other issues, and the degree of assurance that agreements with others will be honored. If differences in median income between localities are large relative to variance within localities, and if state and federal budgets are large relative to local budgets, the value of nonusers' votes will be greater at state and federal levels. On the other hand, governmental decision-making bodies are likely to be smaller at the local level, making it easier to conclude and enforce vote-trading across issues.

SUMMARY OF CONCLUSIONS

1. Holding u, b, n, a, and π constant, $\hat{q}$ will be larger the larger is the variance of voter incomes.

2. Fiscal surplus is likely to be positive for low-income and negative for high-income voters in heterogeneous communities, with the largest relative gain going to middle income voters.

3. Eliminating the privilege of itemizing local taxes should decrease fiscal surplus of wealthy homeowners in heterogeneous communities by the product of their marginal federal income tax rate and their local taxes, but by less than that product for wealthy homeowners in homogeneous communities.

4. Social groups with especially strong preferences for a communal good should spend a relatively large fraction of their incomes on housing.

5. Owners of factors used to produce communal goods should attempt to appropriate some of the fiscal surplus of wealthy, homogeneous localities. They should also favor grants, especially matching grants, from higher governmental units.

6. The budget selected by majority voting is probably smaller than the constrained Pareto optimal budget in heterogeneous communities. Because of itemizing, however, the opposite may be true in wealthy, homogeneous communities and the range of governmental activities excessive.

7. Bloc grants may be more effective in eliminating the disparity between Pareto optimal and majority rule budgets than matching grants, because the latter may cause the sum of local communities' expenditures to be excessive.

8. Increasing the proportion of nonusers will reduce output per user unless n is quite large. In any case, most nonusers will receive more of the communal good than they want, encouraging them to live in lower income communities and/or to engage in vote-trading.

Conference Review Hour

Noel Edelson: I have a practical question. How does one separate the value of land and the ʳalue of structure for assessment purposes when they are sold as a packet? How do assessors, in fact, do it?

Ronald Grieson: They ask what it would cost to reproduce the building. If the building is worth $10,000 now and the market is $12,000, the land is worth $2,000. If there is a vacant piece of property near, they try to determine what it would sell for. Generally they can get a reasonable estimate.

Noel Edelson: I would have found that a very difficult question to answer in view of the fact that that land could be used for different purposes. Assessors have to estimate what the highest bidder would pay.

Daniel Holland: Most assessors will tell you that they can get quite a satisfactory approximation of what somebody would be willing to pay for the site if there were no building on the lot.

Ferdinand Schoettle: As far as I can tell from studying the literature and trying to teach it to lawyers, the assessors do say they can find comparable sales. In those jurisdictions that are doing the valuation by linear regression analysis through the use of computers, they can factor out the land values by understandable mathematical techniques. If you ask a good statistician if he can do it, he will say yes.

I want to ask a question, though, about Ronald Grieson's suggestion that large coefficients of dispersion and unequal assessment ratios may be a good thing from the economists' point of view because they are efficient in some way. Somehow they enable the assessor to operate in an economical way.

Lawyers who look at the system are concerned. I guess Jonathan Rowe of Ralph Nader's group would be the first to say that this sytem where the taxpayer goes in and bargains for his tax, where he pays an amount of tax which is not set by statute, but one determined by some private understanding is a bad system.

We have been rather anxious to improve conditions, and we see moving the property tax to a state level as a step in the proper direction. I would ask the economists whether they think the current system may be optimal in some way. Does this mean lawyers should not spend much time worrying about getting lower coefficients of dispersion?

William Vickrey: There are members of the Chicago school who will say that bribery, insofar as it represents a free contract between consenting parties, is necessarily a good thing.

James Green: If they do, they should be ashamed of themselves.

John Shannon: This question of whether the property tax is regressive or progressive, whether the wealthy pay more in the final analysis than the middle income group, may overlook an issue that is increasingly in the minds of public policymakers. Does the tax impose an extraordinary burden on especially low income and on elderly homeowners in relation to their total annual income?

You may not worry about whether the tax is progressive above $25,000. But if the average U.S. homeowner pays 3 or 4 percent of his total money income in residential property taxes, whereas the elderly are paying over 16 percent according to the most recent 1970 census (and 16 percent is the national average for 1,200,000 elderly homeowners with incomes below $2,000), this is an extraordinary burden.

The tax bears down very harshly on this group. We may argue from now to doomsday whether the tax is progressive or regressive, but some corrective action has to be taken.

It is removing this harsh character, or this extraordinary burden of the tax in relation to the norm, that I think is increasingly the concern of policymakers.

William Vickrey: My mother, who is 85 years of age, is probably one of those for whom these crocodile tears are shed. She pays according to my estimate something around 40 to 50 percent of her income in property taxes. Before you feel too sorry for her, she lives in a $50,000 home in Scarsdale with a live-in maid. I mean, this is the kind of statistic that enters into the data.

My mother is entered into the statistics as one of the impoverished people who are having a hard time. I do not support her financially. She is perfectly financially solvent in the sense that she has several savings accounts on which she is drawing; eventually she may have to mortgage her house in order to keep living at this scale, but there is no hardship involved.

William Oakland: I would like to support John Shannon's point that it is the horizontal equity of the property tax that we are concerned with more than regressivity. I think we give its regressivity far too much attention. It is just an unfair tax. The main charge against it is that people in unlike circumstances are treated alike.

However, the other point I want to raise is that if local governments are going to exist and have tax structures and if you don't have land taxes or property taxes, what are these governments to use?

It has been suggested that income taxes might be preferable to property taxes. However, there is no evidence that the elasticity of supply of people or the mobility of people would create any less dead weight loss than does the mobility of capital in response to different levels of income taxes in different localities.

Ronald Teeples: What conceptually is the experiment we would set up that could determine the incidence of the property tax? In the process of trying to define the design of the pure experiment, we would need to define what we mean by incidence. Perhaps we are all talking about incidence in a different way.

Incidence is a final outcome of some process, and it has to be observed in the world.

What would we do, given the world the way it is? If we could design some experiment for that world, what experiment would it be, and could we agree on what the controls of that experiment are going to be, and can we agree on what it is in the final outcome of that experiment that we would look at and call "incidence"? I am just asking a question.

I am willing to go out and work; however, I am a simple-minded person, and I don't have the creativity to set up the experiment. I am willing to work for you if you just tell me what that experiment is.

James Green: I have a question for John Shannon in regard to the 16 percent burden of the property tax on lowest income groups. How about the homestead exemption? Is that figured in? What effect does it have?

John Shannon: These statistics were based on the 1970 residential survey which used a total income base. It includes the social security, veterans benefits, etc. It is a much broader view of income than appears on the 1040 IRS form. The respondents were asked to give the amount that they actually pay in property taxes. Obviously in some of the Southern states where there are household type exemptions, the property tax burden is very low.

In fact, whereas the national average for all homeowners is running around 4 percent and for elderly around 16 percent, the regional variations are very dramatic. In the South, where there are household exemptions, the average burden on the elderly homeowners drops to 7 percent. In the Northeast section of the country, it is almost 30 percent.

Morris Beck: I have detailed results in my paper on the latest study, and one of the best, on the distribution of tax burdens. It was done for the New

Jersey Tax Policy Commission. I had nothing to do with it, so I can be perfectly frank.

The data for New Jersey show that for families earning less than $2,000 to $3,000, the ratio of property taxes to income is a bit over 14 percent. The burden is not just on the elderly but on all low income homeowners and the ratio declines monotonically to a little less than 3 percent for the income class over $25,000.

Mr. Vickrey's reference to his mother's situation may be perfectly valid. Whatever she pays constitutes a very high percentage of income as reported, but what is the income denominator? I agree that there may be a lot of elderly people with small reported incomes (i.e., social security plus some retirement income) who pay a high proportion of this reported income in property taxes directly or in their rent. These people may be fairly well off.

However if you take a large enough sample, as we did in the state of New Jersey study, you get a very significant reduction in the ratio of property taxes to income as you move up the income classes. There may be some flaws in the procedure; it may be impossible to get perfect estimates of either income or taxes paid.

The results are based on estimates, and they are not perfect. However, I cannot understand how anyone can argue that the property tax is progressive, especially in view of the fact that the proportion of income spent for housing also tends to decrease as income increases.

Ronald Grieson: In studying how much of old people's income goes to property taxes, did you include the owner-imputed rent on their owner-occupied homes as part of that income?

John Shannon: No. The base is total money income. It is much broader than the 1040 IRS concept, but obviously narrower than the ideal from the economist's standpoint.

Seymour Sacks: I would like to make a number of points since we are talking about factual matters. Many elderly people owning housing live in cities. The elderly have a much greater propensity to remain in the house where they presently live and not move.

Increasingly the cities are made up of the black minorities and old ladies. They are an exceptionally large portion of the elderly poor. If you attempt a solution solely in terms of school finance, you are not going to be able to help the older people.

The problem of the older people basically derives from taxes other than the school property tax. The high taxes for schools exist in suburbia. Steep nonschool property taxes are found in the cities. Except for some rural or suburban areas, the problem is not basically the school taxes. The very high burden figures for the impact of the property tax on the elderly, so that you get the 30 percent burdens, are in fact very much central city phenomena.

Charles Waldauer: One of the great conceptual problems is how to define economic well-being. This involves an element of wealth, imputed income, pension rights, etc. I would hope when future studies are done these concepts are taken into account.

However, I think the social problem of the burden of the property tax on the elderly and poor still remains. Perhaps it would be better treated by other economic measures.

Daniel Holland: Mr. Brazer, didn't you report to us that your study did include imputed income?

Harvey Brazer: We did estimate that, yes.

Daniel Holland: You got very different burden results from the usual pattern?

Morris Beck: Reduce the regressivity, but not convert it to progressive.

Harvey Brazer: It would reduce regressivity. Obviously, just using some figures from Mr. Vickrey's example: his mother's property tax was found to be 40 percent of her income; he doesn't tell us what the income is; however, we know that the value of her house is $50,000. Her imputed rental income, therefore, is approximately $4,000 a year. If her other income were $4,000 a year and the property tax $1,600 (which probably isn't too far from the truth) the inclusion of her imputed rental income immediately cuts her effective tax rate by half to 20 percent.

If this example is a fair sample, John Shannon's 16 percent burden figure is cut to eight percent, which, of course, is still high.

William Vickrey: Actually, I am fundamentally uneasy about the use of current annual income, on whatever sophistication you measure it, as a measure of ability to pay for the purpose of characterizing a given tax as regressive.

Back in 1944, I did some experiments with the schedules from the consumer survey. I looked at tax burdens when you classified people by income. Then I turned around and classified the same group according to their per capita expenditures. This is, I think, an equally good measure of standards of living. I found that on this basis what were regressive taxes, like sales taxes, turned out to be progressive, and what were progressive taxes, like income taxes, turned out to be regressive. To take an example: if a person has an income that fluctuates between $10,000 and $5,000 over the years, he may have an expenditure of $7,000. In this case, the sales tax looks regressive, and the income tax looks progressive. If you then turn around and classify the burden according to some measure of the base groups' long-run economic status, you find the reverse is true.

Eli Schwartz: My question is to Seymour Sacks. The problem of the property tax on the elderly exists whether it is a school property tax or a nonschool tax. Why differentiate?

However, I wonder about the cure. Sometimes the cure to one kind of social ill brings about another. There is an argument that the property tax, once set, should continue, no matter what the status of the individual whether he gets older or his income goes down. The property tax represents some payment for a share of the local services in the area. If the owning couple is now older and the family has moved on, although it sounds harsh, it may be reasonable for the older people to sell out, move to smaller quarters, allowing some newer, younger family to enjoy the house. To subsidize the elderly in their present quarters is to artificially decrease the available supply of housing.

Moreover the cost of governmental services continue whether the elderly stay or move, and there is a question who should pay for these. However, I do think the elderly poor are trapped, and so I am very sympathetic.

Seymour Sacks: No one has said anything here about the state assumption of the general property tax, just about a possible state assumption of the *school* property tax. In terms of the policy alternatives that is what we are talking about.

Eli Schwartz: However, since all the taxes in the city are high on an absolute basis (even though the percentage of school property tax relative to other taxes is not as it might be in other areas), abatement of the school tax would still have a significant effect.

Richard Rossmiller: I guess as the educator in residence, I should make some comments. In looking at the presentations, we had two extremes.

At one extreme we are talking about the basic value positions (although I guess the area of public finance has to deal with that), yet at the other extreme we are dealing with very narrow and somewhat esoteric economic ideas.

I feel some vague dissatisfaction that the two have not yet been wedded.

Daniel Holland: Does public finance strike you as a unique special discipline in this respect?

Morris Beck: Briefly, several people have argued that the figures with regard to the tax burden on the elderly overstate the case. Two factors lead me to believe that the opposite is true.

The data understate the weight of the burden on low income families generally—never mind the elderly. First consider the geographic dispersion of tax burdens: Dick Netzer's book contains a table which shows that the effective property tax rate is highest in the cities and decreases as we move outward to the inner and the outer ring. Combine this with Seymour Sack's information regarding the concentration of elderly and poor in the cities, despite the fact that there is also rural poverty, and perhaps what we have is not 16 percent but even some higher ratio of property taxes to total income.

Secondly, in the high property tax states, those that emphasize property taxation, the actual regressivity is worse, more severe than the numbers indicate. To approximate tax burdens, it is customary to use a statewide average of property taxes as the numerator for the income classes. If the poorer income classes and the elderly are concentrated in the cities where the taxes are higher, the distribution is more regressive than the figures indicate.

Terrie Gale: On the problem of older people, I think the usual situation is that the elderly person has low income and his or her wealth consists almost entirely of a house that he doesn't want to move out of. I think there are juris- dictions that allow the tax liability to be accrued every year; however, the tax payment can be delayed until the person dies. It is then taken as lump sum out of the estate. I don't see any problems with this plan. However, it is not very common, and I wonder why. Are there some economic objections to it that I don't perceive?

Richard Lindholm: I can tell Miss Gale that Oregon has a law allowing tax accrual for the elderly, but it is not very popular.

Terrie Gale: Why?

Richard Lindholm: It is hard to say why. Perhaps one reason it is not popu- lar is because the children are interested in maintaining their inheritance. They don't want the old folks to live it up.

William Vickrey: Of course, it is usually true you can postpone the tax for two or three years. It may take a little bit more doing to get a longer postpone- ment; I don't know the situation around the country.

I was just going to raise the question of the urban elderly poor. How many are renters, and how many are owner-occupants?

Seymour Sacks: A much higher number of owners than you would expect. They are really living off their capital, and they don't want to move. If you use an income/ownership ratio, the elderly are one group where ownership and income are not particularly well correlated. The correlation is way out of line.

Paul Downing: I would like to make the point again that in dealing with possible financial schemes to support education, we have to some extent ignored the distinction between nondirect and direct users.

We are somewhat concerned about the regressivity in the case of the elderly who may have current economic problems. They are indirect users. It seems to me that there are two classes of beneficiaries and there should be two different tax prices.

One for the user, that is the parent or the child himself, and one for the general receiver of externalities.

If you do not have two prices, how many years or what quality of school- ing are we going to get under a land value tax, for example, that everybody in the community, whether he uses the schools or not, would have to vote for?

Terrie Gale: I am in favor of a graded tax instead of a land tax, and it is the graded tax that is used by the California irrigation districts. The land tax only covers water costs. As far as other public services are concerned, I think they tax both land and improvements.

As far as the problem of agricultural assessments goes, under the present tax system there are places where there are arrangements for farmers to get a preferential taxation agreement. California has jurisdictions where farmers agree to keep the land in actual farm use for so many years; during that period of years, they are assessed at farm land rates. After that the regular rates apply according to the value of the property.

It seems that something like that could be worked out just as easily under the site value tax system.[1]

William Vickrey: I am just going to say something about the notion of user benefit charges. If one were to go in that direction, perhaps the thing to do is to allow the local government to borrow for its school expenditures. The borrowing would be repaid from the proceeds of an income tax levied on the future earnings of the students. This creates a picture of each individual school district trying to keep track of its alumni all over the United States—not a very practical proposition.

However, I just threw it out as I think that is what the logic of that particular argument leads to.

M. Mason Gaffney: I am very confused why in a meeting where concepts of equity and regressivity and progressivity, etc. have dominated the discussion, it should suddenly be considered moralistic to point out that the exemption of farm land from the tax base would constitute a very large loophole.

I think that it is inconsistent with the tenor of this meeting; moreover it overlooks the fact that there also are large efficiency effects if farm land were exempted.

Getting back to equity, the question of progressivity is extremely important. I left out of my earlier remarks the fact that if U.S. farms are classed by value, there is an extremely pronounced tendency for the higher value farms to have a much higher ratio of land value to building value.

If the concept of progressivity is employed, then to have a farm land value tax would be extremely progressive.

1. Editor's note: However, such a formula would miss the point of land value taxation, which is to encourage the landholder to put the land into its highest use.

Conference Summary and Synthesis

Richard W. Lindholm

Conference Summary and Synthesis

    In these concluding comments I have attempted to compact into a few hundred words the richness and variation of the papers and discussions of the conference. The aim of the Summary portion, which proceeds paper by paper in the order published, is largely to demonstrate the development of the theme of the conference and the rationale of the particular paper order used.

    The second, or Synthesis, portion is an effort to tie together a large number of ideas and concepts into three general areas of interest. Of course, my choice and approach is that of only one reader. It is hoped, however, that it will be found useful in uniting and relating the ideas developed to the requirements of an opportunity for a good education to all, the equal protection clause of our state constitutions, and a tax that encourages efficient use of resources.

SUMMARY

    The tieing of the property tax to the finance of a general and compulsory education is largely a unique American institutional relationship. Professor Lynn points out that the system evolved in Ohio and Illinois and took with various degrees of completeness in all the states. The American idea of general compulsory education has spread around the world, but the American method of finance has not.

    The greatly expanded education program initiated by the Soviet government has placed its top education priority on the quality of general education schools. This is largely in the American tradition; but the method of financing is European, and the state budget of the U.S.S.R. is the principal source of funds. Professor Noah reports the result is continued friction between school people and the representatives of the Ministries of Finance rather than between school people and the voters and school boards, as in the U.S.

    The voting of taxes to cover the costs of schools providing compulsory education is seen by Professor Bohm to be inferior to the payment of tuition. Perhaps America took the wrong turn when it combined compulsory education with a tax which at that time was most closely associated with ability to pay. Quality compulsory education and free education may be incompatible.

The *Rodriguez* v. *San Antonio* decision assumed public revenue financing of compulsory education, but the U.S. Supreme Court said this was not a federal government requirement. The Court in *Rodriguez* said, ". . . the selection may be made from a wide variety of financing plans so long as the program adopted does not make the quality of public education a function of wealth other than the wealth of the state as a whole." Wealth here refers to the wealth base used by the property tax. Because Professor Creswell sees large educational units as inefficient, he fears finance reform that leads to more centralization of revenue sources as a possible cause of more inefficiency in education.

In terms of the American education experience, compulsory education supported with financial sources that can be localized is most likely to develop the spirit of capitalism and the spirit of "everything is possible." Professor Green sees that in Latin America a tax on land would not only make the right kind of education available, but would also speed up economic pressures for full use of land resources.

The spirit of school finance reform is in the air. Because the property tax is to a considerable degree a special school tax, property tax reform is also under consideration. Professor Riew feels that much of the reform desired could be enjoyed if a statewide uniform rate land tax were introduced. Part of the rationale for this position arises from the large portion of the externalities of education that affect land values.

The successful use of a number of taxes by state and local governments provides a choice of revenue sources to finance education. In fact, Professor Thorson sees an advantage in using a tax such as the income and the retail sales taxes, which are generally levied on a statewide basis, if statewide uniformity in education standards is desired.

Hawaii is the only state that finances its compulsory education entirely with state funds. On the other hand, Oregon, Hawaii's neighboring state, is the state that makes least use of state funds to finance education. Both of these states have experimented with a property tax that emphasizes land values. Professor Lindholm demonstrates how a 2 percent statewide land tax could finance compulsory education K through 6th grade and reduce the portion of the costs of education arising from taxes imposed on residential property.

One of the problems of the use of the property tax in the finance of education in urban areas arises from the high costs of city governments and the financing of these costs from property tax collections. Professor Raymond sees this to be a problem of sufficient severity in urban states such as New York to justify abandoning the property tax as a source of education financing. It is the income tax to which he turns as the principal source of replacement revenues, but he needs help from higher retail sales taxes.

A uniform statewide property tax possesses many characteristics that are considered desirable. Professor Grieson points out that the use of a uniform statewide property tax also has undesirable impacts. For example, it reduces the possibility of individual communities using lump sum assessments and zoning as means of reducing the deadweight load of property taxes. He concludes that if a statewide property tax is to be used it should be limited to a tax on land only.

Although writers on school finance are often tempted to view the property tax as a tax dedicated to school finance, this assumption does serious violence to conditions of the real world. The term "municipal overburden" refers to the reliance of cities on property taxes to finance the large variety of services needed in an urban area. A result of the property tax's dual finance responsibility is competition between cities and school districts for the property tax dollar. However, a combination of legal requirements and political realities have not generally prevented cities or schools from prospering at the expense of each other. Professor Sacks and his associates point out that cities which have high school property taxes also have a high municipal overburden, and vice versa.

The legal bombshell of the *Serrano* v. *Priest* court decision in California and later decisions in other states have stimulated consideration of alternatives to the existing school finance systems. The proposals are practically limitless, but according to Professors Stubblebine and Teeples they fall into six categories, i.e., expansion of state role, redistricting, full state funding, power equalization, tuition grants, and coordinated tax base funding. Now that the 1973 legislative season is ended it is apparent that legislatures have largely moved only to expand somewhat the role of the state, while granting additional property tax relief to residential property. The decision of the U.S. Supreme Court on March 21, 1973, failed to uphold the dicta of the *San Antonio Independent School District et al.* v. *Rodriguez* as a federal requirement. This appears to mean that each state will have to determine if its constitution is violated by the method utilized in financing its schools. The opinion of the Court quotes with approval, "Education perhaps more than welfare assistance, presents a myriad of 'intractable economic, social and even philosophical problems.'"

The necessity for a very major shift in the tax system and school finance in New Jersey was touched off by a new court interpretation of the New Jersey constitution. Professor Beck reports that prospects existed for adoption of an income tax, a uniform statewide property tax, and other related tax measures; all of the tax reform activity was stimulated by the school finance problem. The legislative proposals of 1972 were not adopted but the position of the New Jersey courts remained, and the New Jersey tax crisis continues unresolved at the end of 1974.

The school finance system of Massachusetts works out in such a way that per pupil expenditures are twice as great in one district as in another. Reform is clearly needed. Professor Rubinfield works with the results to be expected from a uniform statewide property tax and a uniform rate of per pupil expenditures. Again the problem turns out to involve both a basic tax reform and a reconsideration of how public funds to finance education should be distributed.

Although state education finance problems gained considerable attention as a result of court decisions of the 1970s, it continues to be true that the cutting edge of the education finance crisis remains in the cities. Professor Oakland's case study of the Baltimore area is applicable to a degree to all large central cities. He wrestles manfully with the innumerable combinations of variables and the overriding pressure for change arising from inequality of per pupil expenditure for education from public funds. The efforts for improving the situation that are analyzed rest to a large extent on new distribution of assistance procedures, and the type of tax used is not an important element in the analysis.

The lack of information and the failure to use the data that is available in an imaginative manner have combined to make metropolitan area understandings inadequate for the development of public goods policies. Professor Schoeplein believes this is a particularly important shortcoming in efforts to understand the government facets of the suburbia process. He believes much more care must be taken in understanding residential choice and its relation to the demand for government services before one is justified in developing an urban model. Finally, education as a local service becomes an expenditure and tax element affecting choice of urban cluster by a shopper for a home. Research along these lines would give one confidence in predicting the impact on metropolitan development of a substantial change in education finance.

A number of the analyses have pointed to the desirability of states considering use of a uniform property tax that applied only to land. Ms Gale looks at how an expansion of the use of land as the base of the property tax would affect metropolitan areas as desirable places to work and live. Although she sees some school revenue shortage problems during the period of adjustment, the reduced cost of other metropolitan services have the potential of reducing the overall need for property tax collections.

Professor Waldauer examines the local impacts of alternative state and federal approaches to granting funds to finance education. He selects the states of New Jersey, New York, and Washington for comparison. He relates his findings to the problems the federal government would encounter in efforts to equalize education opportunity through a grants program. Again, the problems created by a shift look as formidable as the ones to be alleviated.

When one gets right down to the fundamentals of local control of education and the use of the property tax to finance education one is at the periodic school elections to approve the budget. Professor Edelson examines this process under several conditions. He is primarily concerned with the relative generosity of the budget decision in communities made up of voters with different demands for education and with different portions of the electorate within different income groups. His approach also permits him to make some comments on real estate values and teacher union activity as a result of the type of decisions expected.

In 1970 the Committee on Educational Finance of the National Education Association published the papers given at the Annual National Conference on School Finance under the title *A Time for Priorities: Financing the Schools for the 70's.* Many topics similar to those discussed in some depth in this publication are commented upon in this very informative NEA publication.

SYNTHESIS

There are several concepts that turn up again and again in the papers and the conference review hours. For purposes of this effort to draw together the analyses and the principal points of view expressed and the highlights of the various relationships that need to be considered when analyzing public policy in the area of education finance and secondary education, three major groupings or areas of controversy will be used to facilitate the organization of the materials considered.

First, there are the ways in which the carrying out of education as a productive activity affects the welfare of individuals directly participating, as well as the total society. The members of society are also anxious that education of their children be done "right" as they conceive right to be as previous participants in the education process. They want the education of their children to be suitable for the continuance of the kind of culture they are enjoying or aspire to experience.

Second, there are the considerations of fiscal justice and the rights guaranteed to citizens of our nation in basic constitutional provisions. In this area we have ideas of fairness in the distribution of taxes used to finance education and the allocation of education resources among the children of poor and rich neighborhoods. The incidence of various revenue sources and the relation of taxes paid to benefits enjoyed from education efforts are the central themes of the analyses.

Third, there are analyses of the manner in which the economic well-being is affected by the type of property tax used. Here the type of property tax used is related to the effectiveness of the education provided and the impact of the tax on wise resource use. Another consideration is the manner in which decisions are made to determine the type of education provided and the link between education priorities and the revenue sources used.

Efficiency of Education Provision

Education utilizes a considerable number of economic resources. The conference considered the efficiency of the use of these resources and became deeply involved in the distorting effect on education as an industry of its very large spillouts and spillovers. Papers demonstrated that education is a good that has always been collectively provided because noncurrent users benefit from the activity. The major question in the discussion of this aspect of the conference's efforts revolved around the problem of whether the price of education at the margin should not be changed because the spillouts are so significant that they ought to be collectivized. If a society wants uniform beliefs and attitudes to avoid the problem of spillouts, then it must assure itself of this result. One of the better ways to do this is to provide for centralized communally financed education.

The state is concerned with what the schools do to make its task easier. As the accepted services of the state have moved beyond maintaining law and order, the areas where the state would like the schools to be helpful have expanded. For example, the general assumption by the state of the responsibility for providing incomes to all has made it anxious that the education of young people be suitable for carrying out job responsibilities as adults. These are goals for education in which adult society is also generally interested, but they are much less those that exist in the minds of the schools' customers. The young customers enjoy freedom and playing around with ideas, experimenting with different life styles. Child-oriented schools encounter this conflict between students and voters, and they find themselves unable to arrive at an acceptable compromise. The closer the financing of the schools is to those directly concerned with this conflict, the less satisfactory schools are judged to be and the more difficulty is encountered in gathering in the resources required to carry out what the education professional considers to be necessary to perform the education function.

Professor Rossmiller was of the opinion that many of the judgments being made on the effectiveness of school expenditures were very simplistic. Be that as it may, there seems to be a relationship between ability to adjust to the requirements of life and the amount that is spent both at home and at school on the child as he is developing. Professor Schoeplein pointed out that although the California courts did not attempt to determine the relationship between expenditures and education benefits, wealth as defined in the property tax was identified as causing education problems because it was not distributed equally on a per student basis.

Both Professors Oakland and Schoettle thought that industrial property, if employed as a portion of the base of the property tax used to finance education, should be taxed on a national or state basis and not on a local level. Professors Becker and Grieson sharply disagreed and concluded that industrial property other than land should not be taxed.

The conference never really tackled the problem of industry's effect on the education offered when it is the direct source of much of the revenue used to carry out the education function. However, one way to neutralize the impact of industrial taxpayers on the kind of education offered would be to separate industry out of the tax base used locally. In addition, the very unequal distribution of industrial real and personal property allows competitive conditions to be affected by the educational responsibilities of the school district in which the plant is located. Whether industry has influenced the kind of education offered or whether it has just acted as a neutral source of funds, a problem still exists because of the unequal distribution of industrial real estate. Residential property very largely represents only the income distribution existing in the society, and therefore when used as a local tax base is not politically disruptive as industrial concentrations tend to be.

Needed Property Tax Adjustments

These discussions of the conference were carried out after several state courts had declared the property tax as it was being used in the state an illegal method of financing basic education. However, the U.S. Supreme Court had not yet acted on *Rodriguez* v. *San Antonio.* As a result, much of the attention of the conference was directed toward the injustice that resulted from the use of the property tax to finance education when the value of property available as the property tax base per student varied widely from school district to school district. As was brought out in the summary portion of this tie-up chapter, some papers favored remedying the injustice by adoption of a uniform statewide property or statewide land tax. Others thought that the elimination of school district financing of education removed the justification of the use of the property tax to finance education, and that financing should be done with the statewide income and retail sales taxes now being used by most states.

If the property tax were to be continued as a principal tax to finance basic education after financing had been largely shifted from the school district to the state, then the property tax must, as a tax at this level of government, be able to meet the competition of other taxes already being used at the state level. As a result, a considerable portion of the conference review hour discussions were devoted to consideration of the strengths and weaknesses of the general property tax and of the tax on land only, i.e., the site value tax.

It was the newspaper and television use of the term "the regressive property tax" that was being examined in the light of relatively new studies. Professor Brazer brought out that when imputed rent is included as a portion of income against which the property tax on residents is measured, the property tax, if applied to residences alone, is somewhat progressive and certainly at least proportional and definitely not regressive. As the discussion of the incidence of the property tax continued, it became clear that much that is accepted as fact regarding the economic burden of the property tax requires reexamination. For example, Professor Gaffney pointed out that rent paid in ghetto areas equals the capital value of the property in only two and one-half years while in high income suburban areas capital value relative to annual rent is much higher. Therefore, a property tax based on capital value and not on rent is automatically progressive.

When one starts considering the incidence of any single tax one is always drawn toward the conclusion that it is really the tax system that is important. This system can be a desirable one when it includes taxes that have the weakness of being regressive under certain individual combinations of conditions or when the economy is operating in a particular way, if these taxes also have good qualities, such as steadiness of revenue, attractiveness to capital, and ability to vary between jurisdictions; and finally if the system also includes taxes that are definitely progressive. It is when the tax system is looked at in this fashion that the taxation of land is seen to fill an important role.

It is also becoming more and more apparent, as Professor Stubblebine pointed out, that it is the incidence of the institution which uses tax revenues and performs certain services that is the correct center of focus. The education institution has for many years been considered an important element in the American Dream. Recently the services of the education institution have been subjected to new scrutiny, and the institution of compulsory education is seen not to be providing services that make the "less equal more equal." Under these conditions, justification for a regressive tax on the basis of the impact of services provided is substantially reduced in the institutional area of basic education.

When one is satisfied that the tax being used to finance education is the appropriate one when the financing is entirely or largely done by the state, he has only come half the distance needed to resolve the basic elements of the American school finance problem. The other half is that local control of education is a basic good and that local control is only possible when a significant portion of the cost of education is borne with local tax collections.

Two procedures were presented to bring forth an education finance approach that would meet the objections of the *Serrano* and *Rodriguez* decisions relative to the constitutionality of education finance procedures and still retain local option. A widely discussed plan called "power equalizing" was considered by Professor Edelson and criticized by Professor Vickrey because it requires a wealthy community to tax itself, say by $1.50 for each additional $1.00 it wants to spend. This difficulty is commonly met by providing sufficient state funds to meet school district costs so that a $1.50 voted by a rich district will make a total of education funds available that would be greater than the local tax.

Professors Stubblebine and Teeples considered an approach called "co-ordinated tax base sharing." Again the procedure is an effort to retain local option or control while meeting the test of equal contribution as a portion of wealth required by the court decisions in several states. Under this approach each district would vote its tax rate and would receive the funds this rate would provide on a per student basis if applied uniformly throughout the state. If per student wealth were higher than the state average, the taxes collected from the district would be greater than the amount available to finance education. The reverse would prevail if the per student wealth of the district were less than the state average.

Professor Rubinfeld rightly pointed out that these equalization plans are only efforts to equate the price of education as a percent of wealth across jurisdictions, and really does not reach down into the problem of local or state control of the schools. It is only if one assumes that local setting of expenditure levels—within given limits—means local control, that one can equate power equalization or coordinated tax base sharing with community establishment of education standards. And, of course, the Coleman report places per student expenditures low on the list of the determiners of the effectiveness of education.

Special Qualities of a Tax on Land

Professor Schwartz pointed up the basic difference in a property tax limited to land and one that also includes structures and other property in its base when he noted that the property tax levied on the structure is a portion of the cost and is shifted onto the renter by the owner in the long run by the availability of living space. New apartments are not built unless rents will cover costs of construction and maintenance.

A property tax limited to land does not affect the quantity of land in existence. Land is not produced by contractors and architects, and the quantity is not limited by the necessity of covering costs of construction. Therefore, the movement of the finance of education toward the taxation of land does not at the same time reduce the level of housing or increase the costs of producing and marketing goods.

Education is a major service provided by government. It, unlike highways and social security, evolved a procedure of financing that was originally based on the best measurement of general ability to pay that was available. Whether education should continue to be financed with the general property tax when other taxes, such as the overall-wealth taxes of Europe and an ideal income tax, are much better at reaching ability to pay was one of the underlying problems considered by the conference. The fact that the U.S. does not use a general-wealth tax and the income tax in effect is far from ideal and the retail sales tax has perhaps just about reached the rate limits it can sustain without serious evasion problems such as were encountered in Sweden, causes one to look at the property tax and its modern characteristics. When this is done the close relationship between the value of property and the quality of the people, which is determined to an important degree by the education enjoyed, becomes obvious.

Dr. Shannon, Professor Beck, and others pointed out that the property tax as administered takes a much larger percentage of the income of the elderly and those with incomes below $2,000 than it does of the average homeowner. This burden allocation has resulted in the passage of legislation by more and more states that provides for what is called a circuit breaker. It is also true that as our cities have grown, the duties of local government have expanded and this need for revenues has placed an additional burden on the property tax. This makes the property tax rate higher, as Professor Sacks pointed out, in the cities, where many of the residences occupied by the elderly and the poor are located. Finally, although shelter as a consumer good for middle and upper income persons enjoys important income tax advantages, as Professor Brazer mentions, it is also a necessity used by rich and poor that costs more because the value of the structure is a portion of the base used for the annual property tax.

These aspects of the property tax and the general character of the American tax system, plus the very complex relationship between the benefits of education, i.e., of the spillout, spillover, personal and local externality variations, and the relationship between the method of finance and degree of local control, caused a number of members of the conference to look at site value taxation for the finance of education. Terrie Gale pointed out that many of the benefits of government activity come to rest finally in higher land prices, and Professor Riew developed in some detail the manner in which a tax on land only to finance education would work out.

As sources for government revenues developed through the years, the general ad valorem property tax gradually evolved into largely a real estate tax used in rural, suburban, and small town areas to finance education, and in more urban areas to meet many of expanding local government services beneficial to this property. On the other hand, the value of land, which is now estimated to exceed $500 billion, is becoming a larger portion of the price of housing and the cost of producing food.

If the goal of local control of education continues to be as vital to a politically acceptable system of school financing as seems to be true in many areas, then the taxation of land to do the job becomes attractive. By using as the tax base land only, the problem of fugitive capital because of high tax rates is eliminated. Also, because the incidence of the land tax is in lower prices for land, the people of a community using this tax will in time find that what is being paid in land taxes to support their schools is being regained in lower prices on land, and therefore the price of education is no longer a portion of the cost of living consisting of housing. Professor Grieson argues that education would be most efficiently provided under a system of federal subsidies combined with local land taxes.

Index

Aaron, A., 131*n*
Abandonment rates, 141
Ability to pay: income and wealth, 298, 315; overall, 44; productivity decreases, 127
Accrual of property tax, 217
Achievement in education, 73
Administration of education in Russia, 16-20
Advisory Commission on Intergovernmental Relations, 92*n*, 120-23 passim, 159*n*, 187*n*
Agriculture land value in Oregon, 110
Aid formula in Milwaukee, 82
Aitchison, J., 281*n*, 294*n*
Aleksandrov, A. M., 23*n*
Alkin, Marvin C., 47*n*
Alonso, William, 247*n*
Alternative Programs for Financing Education, 271*n;* local impacts of, 247-58
American Dream, 314
Andrew, Ralph, 154*n*, 221*n*
Arden (Wilmington, Delaware), 257
Armstrong, Richard, 106*n*
Assessment level: bargaining for, 130; California, 164
Averch, Harvey A., 45*n*

Baltimore metropolitan area: finance of education, 229-44; fiscal setting, 213-229
Barlow, Robin, 27*n*, 48*n*, 60*n*, 297*n*
Barzel, Yoram, 279*n*, 296*n*, 297*n*
Bateman Act, 200*n*
Batyshchev, P., 25*n*
Beck, Morris, 63, 68, 299, 301, 302, 316
Becker, Arthur P., 99*n*, 208, 312
Benefit received, 68
Benefits internalized, 129*n*

Benson, Charles S., 7*n*, 10*n*, 168*n*
Benson, Robert S., 120*n*
Berke, Joel S., 113*n*
Blaug, M., 56*n*
Bohm, Peter J. G., 39*n*, 308
Bowles, Samuel S., 46*n*
Brazer, Harvey, 73, 135, 138, 300, 316
Brown, J. A. C., 281, 294*n*
Buchanan, J. M., 98*n*, 99*n*, 251*n*, 253, 254*n*
Budgetary outcomes in referendum setting, 279-95
Budget projection, 218-19
Buffalo school taxes, 152
Bureaucracy, xvi
Burke, Arvid J., 6*n*, 7*n*, 10*n*
Burkehead, Jesse, 47*n*
Business property, 74; progressivity of property tax, 98
Business taxes, New York, 116

California, 64, 93, 158, 284, 292; constitution, 50; education finance model, 171-76; elementary school costs, 164; school finance, 163-78; *Serrano* v. *Priest,* 164-65
California Joint Legislative Budget Committee, 166
Capital gains: on land, 119; tax loophole, 120
Capitalization rate, 141-43
Capitalism: basic requirements, 106
Carbert, Leslie, 103*n*
Chelliah, Raja J., xix, 57
Chicago, 66; ring application, 251-54
Child-oriented schools, 312
Cincinnati school taxes, 152
Circuit breaker, 316
City government: cost of services, 114-15;

COMPOSED BY HORNE ASSOCIATES, INC., HANOVER, NEW HAMPSHIRE
MANUFACTURED BY GEORGE BANTA COMPANY, INC., MENASHA, WISCONSIN
TEXT IS SET IN PRESS ROMAN, DISPLAY LINES IN TIMES ROMAN

Library of Congress Cataloging in Publication Data
Main entry under title:
Property taxation and the finance of education.
(Publications of the Committee on Taxation, Resources
and Economic Development, 7)
Proceedings of a symposium sponsored by the Committee
on Taxation, Resources and Economic Development at the
University of Wisconsin—Madison, 1972.
Includes bibliographical references.
1. Property tax—United States—Congresses.
2. Land value taxation—United States—Congresses.
3. Education—United States—Finance—Congresses.
I. Lindholm, Richard Wadsworth, 1914—   ed.
II. Committee on Taxation, Resources and Economic
Development. III. Series: Committee on Taxation,
Resources and Economic Development. Publications, 7.
HJ4120.P672   336.2'2'0973   73-2046
ISBN 0-299-06440-9